VARIORUM COLLECTED STUDIES SERIES

Studies in the Printing, Publishing and Performance of Music in the 16th Century

Stanley Boorman

Studies in the Printing, Publishing and
Performance of Music in the
16th Century

ASHGATE
VARIORUM

ML
112
B76
2005

This edition © 2005 by Stanley Boorman

Published in the Variorum Collected Studies Series by

Ashgate Publishing Limited
Gower House, Croft Road,
Aldershot, Hampshire
GU11 3HR
Great Britain

Ashgate Publishing Company
Suite 420
101 Cherry Street
Burlington, VT 05401–4405
USA

Ashgate website: http://www.ashgate.com

ISBN 0–86078–970–5

British Library Cataloguing in Publication Data
Boorman, S. C. (Stanley C.)
   Studies in the printing, publishing and performance of music in the 16th
   century. – (Variorum collected studies series)
   1. Music printing – History – 16th century 2. Music publishing – History –
   16th century 3. Music – Performance – History – 16th century
   I. Title
   780.9'031

Library of Congress Cataloging-in-Publication Data
Boorman, Stanley, 1939–
   Studies in the printing, publishing, and performance of music in the 16th century /
   Stanley Boorman.
         p. cm. – (Variorum collected studies series ; CS815)
   ISBN 0–86078–970–5 (alk. paper)
   1. Music printing – History – 16th century. 2. Music publishing – History – 16th
   century. 3. Performance practice (Music) – 16th century.
   I. Title. II. Collected Studies ; CS815.

   ML112.B76 2005
   781.4'3'09031–dc22   2005045303

VARIORUM COLLECTED STUDIES SERIES CS815

CONTENTS

This volume contains xii + 362 pages

INTRODUCTION

Much of my work over the last decades has centered on two groups of issues: the nature and history of sources, especially printed sources; and the relationships between the readings in those sources, and their implications for performance and presentation – extensions of the classically understood uses of stemmatics. The first of these has led from a strong interest in how and when sources were prepared (and why certain compositions were included in them) to an increasing concern with why they are as they are – in appearance, in organisation, and in content. The second, beginning with an interest in the ways readings differ from source to source, or (as in the case of Petrucci) from edition to edition and copy to copy, has turned increasingly towards what these readings can tell us about performance practice, about the status of the music, and particularly about the evidence for local traditions, of performing, of notation, and of repertoire. Taken together, these two interests have increasingly focussed on how the printed source reveals evidence to illumine unexpected questions, such as the adventurousness (in musical taste) of a cross-section of a market for musical editions, or the assumed abilities of a specific group of musicians.

It is a truism that the structure and arrangement of any source tells us much about the music it contains. Similarly, the source also tells us much, and often in relatively unobtrusive ways, about how the music was performed. Finally, it necessarily speaks to the status and market for that music – its standing as modern or old-fashioned, as popular or waning in its interest, as widely-known or a special interest.

While these facts have long been accepted for manuscripts, they are equally true for early printed sources, and particularly for sources of music. Indeed, while manuscripts often had to be very specific in the taste and performing activities that they reveal – reflecting the preferences of an individual musician or institution – printed books must necessarily have displayed a more generally-held position. Each edition was prepared, not for a single destination, but with the intent of being sold to as many as possible, and even to as diverse a cross-section of the market as possible. In theory, of course, for each edition there was a primary target – cathedral musicians, lute-players in southern Italy, amateur singers of villanelle, the members of laudesi companies, or the friends and patrons of a composer; and the publisher will have planned the contents of the book, his house-editor will have modified those contents, and the printer will have been instructed how to present them, in accordance with the interests and abilities of that primary target. But the publisher will only occasionally have known that he could make a profit merely by selling to the primary market: he also had to interest German or Netherlandish collectors with his Italian repertoire, the villanella singers with his easy madrigals, the socially aware with a book showcasing the music of Munich-based composers. To that end, the presentation (and not the contents) had to make clear statements about the social and musical significance represented by each title.

Here, I make a significant distinction between the contents – the musical and verbal text – and the presentation – the paratext. The former has been the continual subject of research, resulting in editions, analyses, biographical information on the composers, and so on: equally valuable have been the basic bibliographical studies of the printers and publishers themselves, drawing attention to their total output, to technical and repertorial issues of general import. But it is only recently that detailed study of early music printing has gone beyond the catalogue and the discussion of general technical issues, to look at individual technical matters, at anomalies of presentation, or at the criteria within which a publisher operated. There have been good reasons for this: the vast number of editions produced (in the sixteenth century alone) is daunting, the work involved in assessing even a small number of these editions in sufficient details is vast, and the interpretation of many details thus discovered is complicated. But it is only through such studies that we can begin to speculate about which aspects of a composition and an edition were of the greatest interest to the potential purchaser, which details of impagination mattered to the publisher, or whether publisher and patron cared about performance issues, or were able to deal with a conservative or an adventurous market.

The content of the studies which follow supports a contention that detailed bibliographical study will often reveal important (even unexpected) aspects of the music, of the reasons for its selection, of its performance practice, and of its status within society; and the two approaches outlined in the first paragraph above function hand-in-hand to reveal evidence for all these aspects of the source and its contents.

The first group of papers is concerned with details of printing-house procedure as revealed in the books themselves. Each takes an apparent anomaly in the appearance of the book or its contents to argue for some point about the history of printing or of the particular title. Each goes on, to show how the bibliographical conclusions affect our view of the music: in the first two, the impact is on the readings as preserved, and what they may have represented; in the third and fourth papers, it is on decisions about what to be included in an edition, or when to print it. The final paper in this group inverts the process: it shows how a specific need presented by the musical content imposed on the printer the need to discover a technical innovation.

A second group looks at the publishing end of the process. Each of the three papers is concerned with a different issue: the first making a series of statements of the problems faced by a publisher of music, as compared with publishers of verbal texts. The other two papers again start from the bibliographical analysis. In Chapter VII, the subject is anomalies in presentation, and the object is a view of the care with which publishers assigned works to composers, and how far we may trust their statements. Chapter VIII, in contrast, starts from large-scale descriptions of repertoires and presentation, to draw a picture of the extent to which a publisher could assume a market willing to explore new repertoires, or how far he had to persuade purchasers to buy his books.

A final group of three papers expands beyond printed sources, to include manuscripts of the same repertoires: each starts from details of notation, to find the implications for compositional and performing practice. The first employs differing patterns of notating the same or a similar passage to argue that there were specific groups of meanings for each. In the same manner, the last paper draws attention to the way in which differing patterns can reflect local practices, and even the extent to which a scribe could allow for differing preferences among his performers. The penultimate paper is concerned with a curious situation, in which it can be argued that a composer himself made certain decisions in order to ensure a specific musical result. Each of these three papers explores the limits of application of evidence; each speculates on a range of solutions, drawing on detailed evidence (although with a statistically small sample); and each attempts to open up new ways of looking at the source and its performance.

Of necessity, some of the conclusions remain speculative: it is certainly true that the Bologna copy of the *Odhecaton A* is sophisticated, or that the type required for a noted Salzburg missal was innovative. It is also clear that two type-setters working on the same book can have different patterns of behaviour, and that some books display a clear change of plan during their preparation. It is even evident that the publisher's view of the importance of an attribution changed during the early sixteenth century. But other papers deal with more difficult evidence. This is especially true of the last three papers in the collection: each examines patterns which have been seen as haphazard, or have been approached from a theoretical, rather than a practical, standpoint. Scribes used the notation of ligatures and coloration, and of *musica ficta* and false relations, in so many diverse ways, and apparently without sufficient regard to how we want to understand the theorists, that the results (as found in the sources) have seldom been studied in enough detail. However, it is my contention, in each of these three papers, that the scribe did know what he was doing, that he undertook extra labour (colouring notes, adding accidentals, even adding ornamentation to cadences) because he wanted the result that would ensue. While the notation of an accidental has a specific meaning, it may reflect different contexts, different interpretations of a musical situation, and (in particular) differing aural preferences. The notation of ligatures or the so-called "minor color" figure, while similarly specific in terms of duration, can be seen as indicating different potential problems in performance: both notations signify a class of issues, rather than one simple interpretative solution. How far my proposed interpretations can be stretched to other repertoires, to other times, even to other copyists, remains to be seen; but the effort does have to be made. The sources are at least as significant as the writings of the theorists.

A number of these papers were first presented at conferences focussed on specific themes. As a result, some make reference to other papers presented at the same conference. References to those papers can be found at the end of the relevant chapters, alongside other comments.

One or two more recent studies are relevant to several chapters: for more recent work on Gardano, see Mary S. Lewis, *Antonio Gardano, Venetian music printer 1538–1569: a descriptive bibliography and historical study* (New York: Garland, 1988–); for Petrucci, see my *Ottaviano Petrucci: catalogue raisoné* (New York: Oxford University Press, 2005); for Scotto, after 1538, see Jane A. Bernstein, *Music printing in Renaissance Venice: the Scotto press (1539–1572)* (New York: Oxford University Press, 1999).

STANLEY BOORMAN
New York, 2005

ACKNOWLEDGEMENTS

Grateful acknowledgement is made to the following persons, institutions and publishers for their kind permission to reproduce the papers included in this volume: The University of Chicago Press, Chicago, Illinois (I); Kraus-Thomson Organization GmbH, München and Herzog August Bibliothek, Wolfenbüttel (II); The Bibliographical Society, London (III); *Revista de Musicología* (IV); Cambridge University Press (V, VII); Associated University Presses (VI); Alamire Foundation, Leuven (VIII); Herzog August Bibliothek, Wolfenbüttel (IX); Frederick May Foundation for Italian Studies and The University of Sydney (X); Biblioteca Apostolica Vaticana (XI).

PUBLISHER'S NOTE

The articles in this volume, as in all others in the Variorum Collected Studies Series, have not been given a new, continuous pagination. In order to avoid confusion, and to facilitate their use where these same studies have been referred to elsewhere, the original pagination has been maintained wherever possible.

Each article has been given a Roman number in order of appearance, as listed in the Contents. This number is repeated on each page and is quoted in the index entries.

I

The "First" Edition of the *Odhecaton A* *

IN THE PROCESS of preparing a new analytical catalogue of the volumes, both musical and nonmusical, printed by Ottaviano dei Petrucci, I have had occasion to reexamine the various extant copies of the *Odhecaton A*. As is well known, these survive as follows (giving the commonly accepted dates): 1501 at Bologna; 1502/3 at Seville; 1504 at Madrid, New York, Paris, Treviso, and Washington.[1] From the early studies of library collections and the writings on Petrucci by Schmid and Vernarecci during the last century to and after the edition of Hewitt and the inventory of Sartori, many writers have discussed various aspects of this book.[2]

---

* This is an expanded version of a paper read at the annual meeting of the American Musicological Society, Washington, D.C., 1976.

[1] These are cited in RISM as 1501, 1503¹, and 1504².

[2] A number of early writers make reference to Petrucci's titles, among them Zacconi and bibliographers such as Gesner. Early nineteenth-century scholars had an erratic knowledge of Petrucci's *oeuvre*—Winterfeld, for example, seems only to have referred to sacred prints— though such knowledge increased rapidly. Among studies which discuss *Odhecaton A*, of which there is a vast number, some of the more significant are: Anton Schmid, *Ottaviano dei Petrucci da Fossombrone, erste Erfinder des Musiknotendruckes* ... (Vienna, 1845); Angelo Catelani, *Bibliografia di due stampe ignote di Ottaviano Petrucci* (Milan, 1856); François Fétis, "Note sur la découverte récente des plus anciens monuments de la typographie musicale," *Bulletin de l'Académie Royale des Sciences, des Lettres, et des Beaux-Arts de Belgique,* Ser. 2, XI (1861), 272; Fr. X. Haberl, "Drucke von Ottaviano Petrucci auf der Bibliothek des Liceo Filarmonico in Bologna," *Monatshefte für Musikgeschichte,* V (1873), 49–57, 92–99; Anton Vernarecci, *Ottaviano de' Petrucci da Fossombrone,* (Bologna, 1882); Carlo Castellani, "Ottaviano dei Petrucci da Fossombrone e la stampa della musica in Venezia," *La Stampa in Venezia della sua origina alla morte di Aldo Manuzio seniore* (Venice, 1889), pp. 61–68; Emil Vogel, "Der erste mit beweglichen Metalltypen hergestellte Notendruck für Figuralmusik," *Jahrbuch der Musikbibliothek Peters,* II (1895), 47–60; Maurice Cauchie, "L'Odhecaton, recueil de musique instrumentale," *Revue de musicologie,* VI (1925), 148–56; Jacques Tiersot, "Les Livres de Petrucci," *ibid.,* VII (1926), 18–27; *Ottaviano Petrucci: Odhecaton (Venice, 1501),* facsimile of the Treviso copy [recte 1504] (Milan, 1932); Gustave Reese, "The First Printed Collection of Part-music (the Odhecaton)," *The Musical Quarterly,* XX (1934), 39–76; Jean Marix, "Harmonice Musices Odhecaton A: Quelques précisions chronologiques," *Revue de musicologie,* XVI (1935), 236–41; *Annual Report of the Library of Congress* (Washington, D.C., 1944), pp. 191–93; Helen Hewitt, *Harmonice Musices Odhecaton A,* complete edition based on the third edition (Cambridge, Mass., 1946); Claudio Sartori, *Bibliografia delle opere musicali stampate da Ottaviano Petrucci,* Biblioteca di bibliografia italiana, 18 (Florence, 1948); Anne-Marie Bautier-Regnier, "L'Édition musicale italienne et les musiciens d'outremonts au XVIᵉ siècle (1501–1563)," *La Renaissance dans les provinces du Nord,* ed. François Lesure (Paris, 1956), pp. 27–49; Catherine Chapman, "Printed Collections of Polyphonic Music Owned by Ferdinand Columbus," this JOURNAL, XXI (1968), 34–84;

Most have freely accorded it place as the first printed book of polyphonic music, others qualifying the distinction by adding phrases such as "printed from movable type" or "printed at more than one impression." With the discovery of the Bologna copy, there was some discussion for a while as to whether this was indeed the earliest edition; the controversy was resolved by a general acceptance of the primacy of the Bologna copy—although this acceptance has never been based on any solid bibliographical study.[3] The present paper examines some of the evidence for the claim, and reaches some surprising conclusions, which themselves must lead to a new discussion of Petrucci's relationship to the other sources of this repertoire.

This is not the place to discuss the extent to which Petrucci was indeed the first printer to resolve the problems of printing polyphony, as he had claimed in his applicaton of May 25, 1498 to the Venetian Signoria,[4] although it is worth making two brief points. One is that other printers had had a movable music type;[5] the other is that the process of printing from two impressions was well known in Italy (including Venice), particularly in the printing of red sections of text in legal and liturgical works. The only area in which Petrucci would seem, in any real sense, to have been an innovator is that of the precise superimposition of completely different settings of type, as is required by his process. All two-color printing seems to have involved inking different areas of only one setting of type. Those earlier prints that do have both staves and notes from two impressions (some dating from the 1470s) tend to use larger type with more latitude for variation.[6]

Claudio Sartori, *Commemmorazione di Ottaviano de' Petrucci* ... (Fossombrone, 1968). This very selective list excludes all studies of the music and writings that do not touch on particular copies or on bibliographical questions.

[3] See, for example, the level of assertion made in 1935 by Marix, "Précisions chronologiques," an avowedly bibliographical study, and, at the same unselfconscious level, those by Hewitt regarding the Treviso copy (*Odhecaton*, p. 8).

[4] This has been printed or extracted in several places. Of the works cited in fn. 2, above, Schmid and Vernarecci contain the complete text, as does Sartori (1948). It is given, with English translation, by Reese and in David Gehrenbeck, "Motetti de la Corona: A Study of Ottaviano Petrucci's Four Last-known Motet Prints" (S.M.D. diss., Union Theological Seminary, 1970). The relevant sections, with those of other applications relating to Petrucci, are quoted in Raimondo Fulin, "Documenti per servire alla storia della tipografia veneziana"; and idem, "Nuove documenti . . .," *Archivio veneto*, XXIII (1882), 84–212, 390–405.

[5] Many of these are listed in Kathi Meyer-Baer, *Liturgical Music Incunabula: A Descriptive Catalogue* (London, 1962), although necessarily excluded is the use of mensural type in Niger's *Grammatica* (Venice: T. Francus, 1480), which seems to have been cast on very similar bodies to those used by Petrucci. Miss Meyer-Baer's work has the great advantage, in this context, of showing where the printer used double impression techniques.

[6] A brief survey of the state of knowledge twenty years ago on printing with two impressions and using red ink appears in Victor Scholderer, "Red Printing in Early Books," *Gutenberg-Jahrbuch, 1958*, pp. 105–7; and idem, "A Further Note on Red Printing in Early Books," *Gutenberg-Jahrbuch, 1959*, pp. 59–60—both reprinted in *Fifty Essays in Fifteenth and Sixteenth Century Bibliography*, ed. Denis Rhodes (Amsterdam, 1966), pp. 265–68. See also

A detailed listing of the contents of *Odhecaton A* is available in both the Hewitt edition and Sartori's catalogue[7] and need not be given here. Neither author, so far as I am aware however, remarks that two pieces were interchanged in order in the third edition—it can be shown that this was merely an error in press work. Further, neither of these volumes set out to give detailed bibliographical information (while much of that cited in RISM is inaccurate), and so some of these details need to be outlined here. A brief bibliographical description of the Bologna copy follows:

Bologna, Civico Museo Bibliografico Musicale, Q 51

Harmonice Musices / Odhecaton / A

Venice: Petrucci, ded. May 15, 1501.[8]

Oblong 4°-in-eights,[9] certainly A–M[8] and, by analogy with later editions, probably A–N[8]. Signed in two patterns using roman numerals, either capitals (BII) or lowercase (Aiii). Foliated in arabic numerals.

Defective copy, lacking in July 1975 the following folios: D2, D7, D8, G1, G2, G7, G8, H1, H8, M8, and all thereafter. (This does not conform to the entry in RISM, although it does agree with a collation made by Sig. Paganelli of the Bologna library.)[10]

Watermarks. (1): fols. A2–1, A5–6, E4–3, F1–2, F3–4, G4–3, K7–8; (2): fols. C2–1, C4–3, D6–5, E2–1, H2–[1], H3–4, J6–5, J8–7; (3): fols. B2, B3, L4, M3. The twins of each mark can be detected.[11] (These are shown in Table 1, below.)

the excellent chapter on "Red Print" in Sir Irvine Masson, *The Mainz Psalters and the Canon Missae, 1457–1459* (London, 1954), pp. 25–30. A study of the relevance of this to Petrucci can be found in my dissertation; see fn. 13, below.

[7] Cited in fn. 2, above.

[8] The evidence for the printer being Petrucci is such as to place attribution beyond reasonable doubt. All the typographical elements, as well as their layout on the page, conform to the patterns in later titles that Petrucci does sign.

[9] This terminology implies two sheets of paper for each gathering, each sheet folded into an oblong quarto format. One sheet is then placed inside the other, so that they can be bound together. Thus the inner sheet of a gathering comprises fols. 3–6 and the outer sheet fols. 1, 2, 7, and 8. This is the key to some of the anomalies in the present edition and is indicated in Table 1, below.

[10] I am grateful to Sig. Paganelli for his kindness when I was working on the Petrucci prints at the Civico Museo Bibliografico Musicale, Bologna. It might seem that several additional pages have disappeared since RISM was compiled. In fact, after allowance is made for the incorrect folio numbers cited there, and since the absence of the last gathering has long been known, it appears that only one folio may have been present when RISM was compiled, and it may have disappeared since—fol. D2 (= 26). I suspect that this was also missing then. Throughout this study, I have used folio signatures rather than numbers: this makes the bibliographical structure of the volume clearer.

[11] The basic design of each of these watermarks is as follows: (1) is one of a group of common marks within a circle, apparently representing a man drawing a bow. It cannot be defined absolutely, but it is similar to numbers 522 and 523 in A. and A. Zonghi, *Zonghi's Watermarks* (Hilversum, 1953). (2) is one of the many marks showing crossed arrows; it is closest to Zonghi 1212 and 1213, or to number 6281 in Charles Briquet, *Les Filigranes*

I

Type. Text: Roman, 20-line measure (= 83 mm.), used for prefatory matter, except contents page. Rotonda, for which a 20-line measurement cannot be made, used for contents page and text incipits. Rotonda, large format, used for title.[12] Greek letter: a few words on fol. A2^r. Staves: 5-line, on separate blocks, *ca.* 10 mm. high and *ca.* 175 mm. long—there is some variation here—usually six to the page, with a total height of *ca.* 111 mm. Music type: as normal for Petrucci.[13]

   Contents. The lists in Sartori and Hewitt are accurate, with minor exceptions, some of which are discussed below.

In the above very brief bibliographical description, one of the features most worthy of note is the distribution of papers. Although I do not give a

---

(Geneva, 1907). (3) is perhaps the mark that shows the twins most clearly; it appears in the countermark position at the lower outer edge of the page and is a simple form of the letter *A*. All three of these marks are reported as common in northern Italy in the first decades of the sixteenth century.

   There are no marks on some sheets as they now survive. In two cases, the outer sheets of D and M, we can deduce what the marks probably were. Two others, the inner of K and the outer of L, are still complete and never had a mark. The indication of the folios on which these marks appear follows a simple form of notation, which is a modification of that proposed by Alan Tyson in this JOURNAL, XXVIII (1975), 332–34. In oblong quarto format, the mark is regularly split, parts appearing on two folios. The two halves are to be found in the center of the top margin of the leaves concerned. In my notation, I indicate these two leaves, showing which carries the top of the mark first. Thus, A2–1 shows that the mark straddles these two folios and that the top of the mark is on fol. 2. H2–[1] shows that the lower part of the mark is missing from fol. H1 (in this case because of trimming of the folios after binding), but that the two leaves are conjugate. For the countermark position, as used by mark (3), only one folio is indicated. This is, in itself, sufficient in each case to indicate which side of the leaf is the felt and which the mold side. In many ways, for other titles, this range of information is of limited value; for the odds are low that the marks will appear on the same folios in other copies of the title. Even in the case of unique copies, such as the present one, the detailed location of marks is only of use to future scholars looking in the copy for an individual mark. It is, in some ways, sufficient to indicate on which sheets the marks appear. In this respect, the study of marks in early printed books is rather different from that in manuscripts.

   I do not wish to suggest that the study of the deterioration of marks, or of the pattern of twin marks, is not of value, merely that its value does not normally lie in determining patterns of work. As compared with a manuscript, the printed book involves the use of enormous quantities of paper. The pile at the press from which copies were printed would have been replenished many times and would have been subjected to many changes in the order of sheets, as compared to the order in which they came from the paper mill. Other leaves would have been inserted, accidentally or deliberately (or even fraudulently), some would have been wasted and others shuffled. Thus the pattern of deterioration and the identification of twins, while a necessary part of the study for anyone working on early printed books, will not normally provide any information other than that of crude or major changes. In the present case, these are already signaled by changes in paper and by other details.

   [12] There is at least a possibility that these titles were made in blocks. Certainly, the capital letter *A* was on a separate block. The evidence of the later editions suggests, though not conclusively, that the rest of the title may have been cut on three or four separate blocks.

   [13] Fuller details of these types and of how they are mounted on their bodies are given in my dissertation, "Petrucci at Fossombrone: A Study of Early Music Printing with Special Reference to the *Motetti de la Corona* (1514–1519)" (London University, 1976). See, in particular, Chap. 5 and App. 3.

detailed analysis covering the deterioration of marks or the pattern of twin marks, enough is stated to show that there are three basic papers distributed, apparently in blocks, throughout the volume. The pattern is more clear as laid out in Table 1, which also shows which sheets do not have any watermark.

TABLE 1

Folios	Mark	Signature	Staff inset?	Tenor text?	Longer staves?	Edition
A 1, 2, 7, 8	1	None	Yes	Yes	No	1
A 3–6	1	l.c. / 5	Yes	Yes	No	1
B 1, 2, 7, 8	3	Cap. / 6	No	Yes	Yes	2
B 3–6	3	Cap. / 6	No	Yes	Yes	2
C 1, 2, 7, 8	2	l.c. / 5	Yes	Yes	No	1
C 3–6	2	l.c. / 5	Yes	Yes	No	1
D 1	None	l.c. / 5	Yes	Yes	No	1
D 2, 7, 8	Lost					
D 3–6	2	l.c. / 5	Yes	Yes	No	1
E 1, 2, 7, 8	2	Cap. / 5	Yes*	Yes	No	1a
E 3–6	1	Cap. / 5	Yes	Yes	No	1a
F 1, 2, 7, 8	1	l.c. / 5	Yes*	Yes	No	1
F 3–6	1	l.c. / 5	Yes*	Yes	No	1
G 1, 2, 7, 8	Lost					
G 3–6	1	l.c. / 5	Yes	Yes	No	1
H 1, 8	Lost					
H 2, 7	2	l.c. / 5	Yes	Yes	No	1
H 3–6	2	l.c. / 5	Yes	Yes	No	1
J 1, 2, 7, 8	2	l.c. / 5	Yes	Yes	No	1
J 3–6	2	l.c. / 5	Yes	Yes	No	1
K 1, 2, 7, 8	1	l.c. / 5	Yes	Yes	No	1
K 3–6	None	Cap. / 6	No	No	No	1b
L 1, 2, 7, 8	None	Cap. / 6	No	No	No	1b
L 3–6	3	Cap. / 6	No	Yes	Yes	2
M 1, 2, 7	None	Cap. / 6	No	Yes	Yes	2
M 8	Lost					
M 3–6	3	Cap. / 6	No	Yes	Yes	2
N 1, 2, 7, 8	Lost					
N 3–6	Lost					

The presence of so many different papers in a volume is not, of itself, a matter for remark. Indeed, in a study of a manuscript it would almost be welcomed; in printed books of the period it is no less common. It might indicate the use of two different presses, a change in the size of the print run, details of the order of work, a hiatus in the process at some point, or even nothing at all. Other evidence is necessary before any more precise conclusions can be reached, and, in this case, other evidence can be summoned, principally typographical evidence.

Typographical evidence tends to fall into one of three basic categories:

there is first that which indicates the use of different type or blocks in different layers of the book, perhaps pointing to a division of labor or a break in time at some point. Secondly, there is evidence pointing to some change in house practice—details of layout, format, signature pattern, for example; this can also point to a division of labor or a break in the work. Thirdly, there is any available evidence of deterioration in the typographical material or damage to the blocks or type-sorts. This has to be interpreted with extreme care; although it does indicate an order of work, it does not necessarily point to a major gap in production. If more than one of these layers of evidence is available, then the ways in which they interrelate will help in deciding which of the two possible interpretations is the more likely—that is, whether two or more men were working on the source at the same time, or whether there actually was a break in the work.

Fortunately, all three layers of evidence can be seen in the Bologna *Odhecaton A,* in addition to the paper evidence. One of the most interesting involves house practice and concerns the two patterns of signature indicated in the outline bibliographical description. The two styles involve the use of two forms of roman numerals. That which uses lowercase numerals appears in the following gatherings and sheets: A (inner sheet—there are no signatures on the outer sheet, which carries the preliminary pages), C, D, F, G (only the inner sheet survives), H, J, and K (outer sheet only). The other style uses capital numerals and is found on B, E (with the anomaly that the fourth folio is signed EIIIi), K (inner), L, and M. (These are shown on Table 1.) It will be seen that, with the exception of gathering E, all the uses of papers (1) and (2) have lower case signatures.

Such variation in signature pattern within a volume is most unusual during the early sixteenth century. The majority of Italian printed books— and our discussion is not restricted here to music prints—uses one style of signature throughout, so that printer and binder could immediately identify the loose sheets as belonging together. It is for this reason that Petrucci adopted the common practice of distinguishing the signs used in different volumes, either by the use of multiple letters, as in the *Motetti de passione* (AA) or the second volume of Josquin's Masses (aAa), or else by the use of type signs, as in *Motetti C* (+A). Thus, the presence of two styles of signature in the present volume is, by itself, a warning sign suggesting that the volume may be what the bibliographer calls "sophisticated," made up from sheets of different editions or settings of type.

These signatures are also interesting for another detail, for they are not always set, as we would expect, below the lowest staff on the page. This is indicated in Table 1 by a number showing below which of the six staves the sign is printed. The pattern follows that of the numeral style, except that gathering E shows a placement which conforms to that of other sheets printed on papers (1) and (2).[14]

There are two other elements of house practice to which I wish to call brief attention. One is the use of a shorter staff at the top right of each verso to accommodate the attractive block capitals that grace the volume. This was a habit Petrucci soon abandoned—perhaps the shorter staves were not replaced as they became damaged—but, even in this volume, it is not followed consistently. As a result, some pages start with a full-length stave, over which the capital is printed. This pattern is shown in the fourth column of Table 1, and I shall return to the practice later. The second element of house practice is the failure of the craftsman to set any text incipit to the tenor voice on some folios. The presence or lack of text in the tenor is indicated in Column 5 of the table. The two patterns, taken together, match that of the watermarks: the sheets on papers (1) and (2) have both staff insets and text incipits; those on paper (3) have no staff inset but do have tenor text incipits, while both are lacking on the two complete sheets that have no watermark. This suggests strongly that the lost folio M8 must have had watermark (3) on it and, though less certainly, that sheet D outer probably had mark (2).

All this evidence works, as my second category of bibliographical evidence should, to distinguish sheets that were prepared either by different men or at different times, without indicating which is the more likely possibility. It is appropriate now, therefore, to turn to the other two layers of evidence to see whether the various sheets were perhaps not prepared at the same time.

The first layer, different typographical material, is unfortunately not very conclusive, despite the different patterns of paper. Most of the material is the same for all sheets: the music type is consistent, the pattern of text type follows that of the watermarks (although there is very little difference here), and the distribution of the blocks for the capitals shows only slight changes in patterns (which I mention below). The Greek text type might have been of use had it appeared on more than one folio, for the fonts used in later editions are quite different from that of the Bologna copy. However, there is a change in the staves.

Petrucci's staves apparently consisted of thin metal rules mounted in slots in woodblocks, and they are not of the same lengths. They do show patterns of approximate length, and there is a group of significantly longer staves on a few sheets: these are gatherings B, L (inner), and M. These have already formed a separate group—the presence of watermark (3) is enough to distinguish

---

[14] That the signature was not always printed below the lowest staff is a certain sign that it was not printed with the staves or with the music but in the layer that included the text incipits. Other evidence confirms that the first titles were indeed printed from three (rather than two) impressions, although I think that this practice did not last for long.

them—and by now we may surely conclude that it must have been on folio M8. Unfortunately, I do not know when these longer staves were introduced and cannot use them, therefore, to confirm a delay in the printing of these sheets.[15]

So far, then, there is no evidence to show that some sheets were printed materially later than others. When there are several copies of a title, such bibliographical analysis would often be redundant, for comparison of the suspect leaves in all copies would normally be sufficient. Thus, as Edgar Sparks has shown, there is a cancel sheet in some copies of *Motetti de la corona Libro quarto*, which is present in all but one of the extant copies, and which suggests that the print survives in two versions.[16] The process of detecting sheets that were printed later, however, is far from impossible, even when the copy is unique, or when all the copies have the same typesetting. I have argued elsewhere,[17] for example, that the unique copy of Petrucci's eleventh book of frottole is perhaps made up from two typesettings and that all the copies of Févin's Masses (except for one single partbook) must belong to an unknown second edition, carrying the date of the original edition. In each of these cases, the evidence is of all the ranges that I have outlined. But the critical proof came from study of the individual sorts (pieces of type or single blocks), particularly the identifiable capital letters that Petrucci had as unique wood blocks.

This analysis of individual sorts provides my third category of bibliographical evidence, and it is again conclusive in the case of *Odhecaton A*. There is convincing evidence of wear and damage to several of the capitals in this volume, while others appear to have seen little use. All letters in gathering A are still in pristine condition; some in gathering B already show signs of serious wear.

There are two weaknesses in using such evidence in unique copies:[18] one is

---

[15] At this time I have seen some titles only on microfilm. Apart from the obvious problems raised thereby, there are many more subtle aspects of bibliographical analysis that can only be prosecuted successfully on examination of the actual copy. To mention but one: in many cases Petrucci left the staves standing, though uninked, for the run through the press that included the title page or the last blank page. At the same time, he would use rows of uninked notes to prevent the paper from sagging when part of a page was to be left white. Both the staves and the notes often left indentations, which remain on the page after more than 450 years.

[16] Edgar Sparks, *The Music of Noel Bauldeweyn*, American Musicological Society Studies and Documents, 6 (New York, 1972), pp. 16–23. Sparks, in fact, arranges the two versions in the wrong order, as I have shown in my dissertation.

[17] Stanley Boorman, "Petrucci at Fossombrone: Some new Editions and Cancels," to be published in *Source Materials and the Interpretation of Music: A Memorial Volume to Thurston Dart*, ed. Ian Bent and Michael Tilmouth. Similar details can be found in Jeremy Noble's article on Josquin editions, to be published in the forthcoming Gilmore Festschrift. I am grateful to Mr. Noble for allowing me to consult his paper in advance of its publication.

[18] I have already discussed in some detail the problems inherent in using such evidence, in the article cited in fn. 17, above.

I

that the particular example may have been printed poorly (for one of several reasons), and the other is that it may merely have been printed late in an ordinary run. If the undamaged letter reappears elsewhere, however, the evidence will tend to point to a distinct order of work. Not surprisingly, the evidence of individual sorts in this volume supports the pattern of the other evidence. Thus, a badly damaged letter *J* appears on sheets B (outer) and M (outer), while the intact letter is on gathering A (inner and outer), sheets C (outer) and E (outer), and gathering F (both). Similar examination of other letters shows that the sheets of B (both), L (inner), and M (both) are not merely different from others in the volume, but that they definitely originated later in the order of work. The evidence for sheets K (inner) and L (outer) places them earlier than these, while both sheets of gathering E lie very little later than the other sheets on papers (1) and (2).

So, there is strong evidence in support of four distinct layers of printing in the copy as it survives. While no one strand of evidence is, by itself, sufficient to indicate a break in the work, the fact that all the strands show changes of pattern at the same points argues strongly against a continuous process with its own patterns of change. When as many changes occur at once as do between, say, the inner and outer sheets of gathering K, it is unlikely that they would represent the sort of haphazard changes that arise in any extended piece of work.

The first layer involves all the uses of papers (1) and (2), except gathering E. This gathering, by itself, comprises the second layer. The third is also made up of only two sheets, K (inner) and L (outer); these sheets are characterized by their lack of a watermark, their original staves (though without the short first staff), their lack of a text incipit for the tenor, and their lower placement of the signature. Finally, there are the last three extant sheets distinguished by long staves, different signatures, and the worst capital letters.

I have arranged these layers in order; ideally, it should be possible to go further and give them approximate dates. Indeed, this can be done. Part of the method involves applying the same techniques to the other early titles printed by Petrucci, placing between them the sheets of *Odhecaton A*. I do not propose to give the details of this analysis (for the process is fairly mechanical); I shall merely state the conclusions as they arise.

*   *   *

There are sound reasons for believing that the first group, totaling fifty-one folios, comprises the remains of the first edition. These reasons are partly bibliographical, for some of the capital letters had already begun to deteriorate by the time of Petrucci's next title, the *Canti B* of 1501/2, and are in their virgin state *only* in these folios of *Odhecaton A*. Also, nowhere in the other early titles does Petrucci use lowercase roman numerals in the signatures.

I

192

Other evidence may be seen in the way the music is laid out on the page. There are several places, for example, where the line end breaks into a semibreve beat, and at the end of the second staff on folio G6ᵛ or the first on folio H7ᵛ, it comes after an odd number of semiminims. At many of these points, Petrucci seems to have realized that the layout might cause problems for the singer or reader, and he altered it in the Seville edition. In other places, semibreve rests are hung below the staff: this, too, is gradually corrected for most occurrences in the later editions. At the same time, the direction of note tails has been adjusted in a number of places to make improvements (although it must be admitted that similar adjustments seem to make the situation worse in later editions). Occasionally, dots after notes are raised so as to touch the staff lines in the first edition, thus appearing to be minim rests: these are regularly adjusted in the later editions, and in the other folios of this copy. For some compositions, the last notes of the tenor voice had to be taken over from the verso to the facing recto. In one case in the Seville edition, this involved relatively few notes, and the whole part was rearranged so that it fits onto the verso alone.

This evidence (of layout) suggests two things: (1) that these particular fifty-one folios of the Bologna copy come from perhaps the first (or at least a very early) edition from Petrucci's press, for he was still grappling with problems of type and layout; (2) that they represent the first edition of this music in this format. Both these points are borne out by the evidence of the state of the letters. I am convinced, therefore, that these fifty-one folios (and only these) are of the first printing, published, presumably, somewhere near the date of the dedication, May 15, 1501.

We must come to grips, therefore, with another thirty-five extant folios in the Bologna copy—folios that are traditionally assigned to this edition but which do not belong to the same printing. I shall discuss them according to the groups outlined above. The first of these groups comprises the two sheets of gathering E. Although these are printed on papers of the first edition and conform to it in other ways, they are set apart by the signature pattern. This, except for the anomaly on folio E4, is the same as that used in *Canti B*. The papers seem to have limited uses: paper (1) is used again only in *Canti B* (first edition) and paper (2) not again for some years.[19] It is evident that the two sheets were printed before *Motetti A* of May 9, 1502 (for new papers were then in use) and perhaps even before *Canti B* of February 5, 1501/2, for the capital letters are still in good condition. There is, however, one small piece of evidence that does reinforce my belief that they were not printed with the other sheets from the first edition. The first folio of gathering E is numbered 23 (instead of 33), suggesting that it was not prepared immediately after the

[19] My first note of this paper after *Odhecaton A* is in Bossinensis's first volume of 1509, although I have yet to see the watermarks of the early volumes of frottole or the lute titles.

end of gathering D, foliated 32. It is my belief that gathering E, as it survives, is made up of two cancel sheets, printed soon after the first edition (and very probably during 1501) to replace defective sheets of that edition.[20] Since this is a unique copy, we have (of course) no way of telling what may have happened on the original sheets. There is some evidence elsewhere (to which I shall return) to show that Petrucci's men had problems in handling the unusual oblong format, and it may be that these pages were wrongly imposed on the bed of the press. Such an error might well not be noticed until the pages were all printed and were being arranged for binding. This is pure speculation, being advanced merely to provide a reason for what *is* indubitable—that these two sheets were printed later than the folios I have assigned to the first edition.

The remaining folios fall into two groups, distinguished from the rest of the volume by the papers they use. They do have slight patterns of a different use of capital letters as well, although that evidence is, by itself, insufficient. The capital C on folios B6^v and L1^v is clearly different from the letter on folio J2^v (which probably also appeared on the lost fol. D2^v). The first of these does not appear in any of the "early" folios of the Bologna *Odhecaton A*, although it is used in *Canti B*. Similarly, the letter A on folios B3^v and B8^v is distinct from that on folios A3^v, D1^v, E1^v, E3^v, G5^v, H6^v, and J6^v. The letter in gathering B is not found in any of Petrucci's titles before the sixth of them, Obrecht's Masses of March 24, 1503. Such limited patterns are no more than straws in the wind. Coupled with the state of the other letters, however, they do suggest that these sheets are later and that two of them (K [inner] and L [outer]) are earlier than the others. I think that these two are also cancels prepared for the first edition, although later than the two sheets of gathering E. The letters are in a worse state than in the earlier folios. In addition, those tenor parts that cross from the verso to the recto are marked by a sign (a small cross) that is found nowhere else in this copy. On the basis of the capital letters, these sheets would seem to have been printed at about the time of *Motetti A*, a volume that also uses the small cross to indicate changes of page.

Finally, nineteen folios must have been printed later still, partly on the evidence of the state of the letters, partly because the longer staves are used. As I reported above, I cannot tell yet when these staves were adopted by Petrucci; nor, of course, can I tell (from so few surviving copies) exactly when individual letters were damaged—except that the worst of the damage would place these sheets later than the Josquin Masses of September 27, 1502, and perhaps near the Obrecht volume. This would support the evidence of the use of the new pattern of capital letter A.

[20] This is by no means unusual in Petrucci's output. While I list the instances in Fossombrone titles in my dissertation (see fn. 13), both Jeremy Noble and I have found instances in the Venetian prints, too, and Martin Staehelin has kindly drawn my attention to what may be another case in the volume of Isaac Masses.

I

Fortunately, however, such detailed analysis is not needed: these leaves can be compared with those surviving in the Seville copy, and such comparison reveals that they are, in the bibliographical sense, identical. As far as I can tell, the Seville copy is consistent—all of one edition.[21] The remaining sheets of the Bologna copy, then, belong not to the first edition at all, but to the second, dated in its colophon January 14, 1502/3.

Of course, in calling this the second edition, I am making the assumption that something has survived from every edition of the *Odhecaton A* Petrucci printed. It is necessary to assume that there was a first edition—it has to be hypothesized when it does not exist—and in the present case it can be identified. It is not possible to hypothesize missing later editions. Therefore (except in those cases where the book itself states otherwise), we have to accept only those later editions that exist. If, however, sets of leaves or sheets survive that lie between surviving editions, as some of the Bologna sheets lie between the first and the Seville editions, they do raise the question of whether they are parts of otherwise lost editions.

It is, therefore, worth considering for a moment whether the sheets printed, as I believe, late in 1502 (K [inner] and L [outer]) might be the sole surviving remnants of a lost second edition, with the Seville copy (and nineteen folios of the Bologna copy) representative of the third. My view is that they are not—a view colored by the fact that all the last surviving sheets of the Bologna copy are from later printings. I suspect that Petrucci had originally printed rather fewer of these sheets (for whatever reason), that they ran out of stock, and that he had to replace them, perhaps also with reprintings of the rest of gathering L and of gatherings M and N. I am also influenced by the fact that notational and musical variants (as well as changes of layout) between the first and "second" editions are no fewer in number for these two sheets (K [inner] and L [outer]) than for earlier sheets. Both these points lead me to believe that they were printed separately, not revised (as was the second edition), and not part of a complete edition. The Seville copy, therefore, can be seen as the survivor of the true second edition, now increased by the nineteen folios present in the Bologna copy. Indeed, the presence of these folios at Bologna argues against there having been a complete intermediate edition. The results of this analysis appear in the final column of Table 1 (see above, p. 187).

I mentioned above, in passing, that Petrucci's men may have had some problems in adjusting to the layout involved in oblong quarto format. It was certainly still uncommon at this time, and I know of no examples of it in Italian nonmusical printing of the period. Within the sheets I believe to have

[21] Unfortunately, I have not yet visited the Colombina collection in Seville. I have examined a film of its copy of *Odhecaton A*, however, and there is no evidence therein to suggest any changes of the sort I discuss here.

been printed in 1501 (all from the first edition, with gathering E), Petrucci used a shorter staff at the top of each verso; as I show, he had already abandoned the practice by the time of the second layer of cancel sheets. Even in the earlier sheets, however, a full-length staff appears in three places: folios E7^v, F1^v, and F3^v. These are, significantly, balanced by three folios where a short staff appears at the bottom right of a recto, namely, folios E8^r, F6^r, and F8^r. This can most easily be explained by a brief account of the normal arrangement of the pages on a sheet in oblong format.[22]

Petrucci's technique of printing oblong 4°-in-eights involved four sets of material for each gathering, one for each side of each sheet of paper. I have been using the terms inner and outer sheet for those that comprise folios 3–6 and 1, 2, 7, 8 of each gathering, respectively. It is also customary to refer to inner and outer forms for the two sides of each sheet of paper, the outer being that which includes the first and last *pages* of the sheet. The arrangement of the folios, with page numbers in parentheses, for an ordinary gathering is abstracted in Figure 1 (showing the positions on the paper—in the bed of the press, a mirror arrangement prevails).

This produces a normal pattern of staves on the form (as in Fig. 2a) for the early sheets of *Odhecaton A*. The pattern of staves that was actually used for both sheets of gathering F (inner forms only) is as shown in Figure 2b, and the pattern for the inner form of gathering E (outer sheet) appears in Figure 2c.

It is apparent that one side of the whole number of sheets for all of gathering F was printed with staves at one time, and before the error was noticed. The pattern in gathering E implies a different arrangement of staves in the press and (as a result) pages that were printed at a different time, as I have already shown. It is clearly fortuitous, therefore, that the two gatherings are adjacent in the book as made up.

There is another piece of evidence that suggests that the printers had problems with imposition patterns. This concerns the order of pieces in gathering M, where the Bologna copy is of the second edition. In all three editions, the index (for here the Bologna copy *is* of the first) lists "Puisque de vous" as being on folio 90 (M1^v–2^r) and Agricola's "J'ay bien haver" on folio 96 (M7^v–8^r). In the second edition, they do appear on these folios, but in the third they have been interchanged. This was by no means difficult, for, as a glance at Figure 1 will show, the two pieces were arranged on the same form, merely inverted relative to each other. All that was necessary to produce this variant, therefore, was to reverse the music, that is, to fit the whole form into the press upside down. The change would not be noticed by the proofreader,

---

[22] What follows is related to the discussion in Donald Krummel, "Oblong Format in Early Music Books," *The Library*, Ser. 5, XXVI (1971), 312–24. His illustrations, however, show the arrangement of the type in the form and differ, therefore, from those printed here.

I

196

Figure 1.

sheet: outer   outer   inner   inner

form: outer   inner   outer   inner

| 8^v (13) 7^r (16) | 2^r (2) 1^v (3) | 6^v (12) 5^r (9) | 3^v (6) 4^r (7) |
| 1^r (1) 2^v (4) | 8^r (15) 7^v (14) | 3^r (5) 4^v (8) | 6^r (11) 5^v (10) |

Figure 2.

(a) Normal arrangement of staves

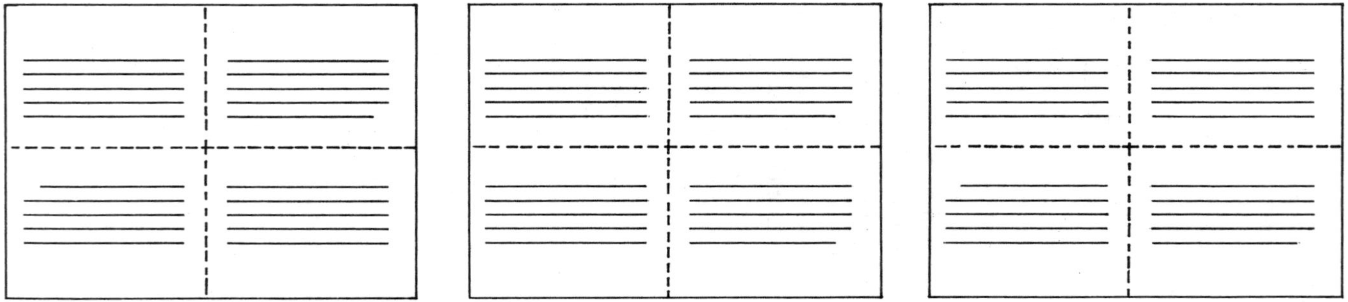

(b) Arrangement for both sheets of F, inner form

(c) Arrangement for the outer sheet of E, inner form

for all the music would be the right way up, both on the sheet and once it had been folded. No one would deem it necessary to check against the index. It is perhaps worth remarking here that there is some evidence in the various copies of the third edition that Petrucci was already indulging in all three methods of correcting copy that did not involve printing a cancel sheet. It was normal at this time for copy to be read as the first pages came off the press. In other words, there was no special pull of a proof copy, as is now customary. Thus, corrections could only be made by stopping the press in its run to alter the type in the form, or by correcting manually every copy after the completed press run. This latter involved one of two different processes: one required stamping the corrected reading into the copy (after erasure) using individual sorts of type, and the other the simpler expedient of manuscript correction. Such practices have been studied in the work of the principal nonmusical printer of the period in Venice, Aldus Manutius[23] and will probably be seen as widespread when more research is undertaken. All three of these processes were adopted by Petrucci in later volumes, according to the nature of the error, and can be seen in many of his Fossombrone volumes.[24]

The earliest title I have examined closely enough to be sure that all three methods were used by the printer is the third (1504) edition of *Odhecaton A*. Even here, I have not yet been able to see all copies in person and so cannot yet make any conclusive statement about how much was corrected. The changes in foliation in some copies of this edition are well known, however, and all appear to be stop-press corrections. Folio D7^r appears to start out with the folio number 25 (e.g., US–Wc), then to lack a folio number (I–TVcap), and finally to acquire the correct number 21 (US–NYp); other examples could be cited. However, both stamped-in corrections in type, and manuscript changes

[23] Curt Bühler has made a study of this practice in a number of editions printed by Aldus Manutius: see his articles, "Aldus Manutius and his First Edition of the Greek Musaeus," *La Bibliofilia*, LII (1950), 123–27; "Additional Note to 'Aldus Manutius and his First Edition of the Greek Musaeus,'" *Scritti sopra Aldo Manuzio* (Florence, 1955), pp. 106–7; "Aldus Manutius and the Printing of Athenaeus," *Gutenberg-Jahrbuch*, 1955, pp. 104–6 (all of which argue that the number of stop-press corrections in a volume is indicative of the point in the run at which individual sheets came off the press); "Stop-Press and Manuscript Corrections in the Aldine Edition of Benedetti's *Diario de bello carolino*," *Papers of the Bibliographical Society of America*, XLIII (1949), 365–73 (which suggests, although very tentatively, that the presence of house manuscript corrections may indicate at which point in the sale pattern of an edition a particular copy was sold); and "Manuscript Corrections in the Aldine Editions of Bembo's De Aetna," *Papers of the Bibliographical Society of America*, XLV (1951), 136–42, which, while supporting the earlier theory (rightly, in my view), goes on to argue that "The fact that the appearance of stop-press variants has absolutely no correlation to the occurrence of the manuscript emendations shows that the corrected sheets were scattered at random throughout the entire edition." I believe this to be an untenable position, leading to hypotheses of irrational complications in work patterns within the printing house.

[24] See above, fn. 13. All these variants will be discussed in the monographs in preparation to accompany the forthcoming reprint of Petrucci's titles, announced by *Les Éditions Renaissantes* of New York.

apparently made before the copies were sold exist for this edition. Further detailed study of all copies is needed before more can be said.

* * *

At this point, I wish to leave bibliographical questions, however much still remains unresolved, and turn to some of the differences that exist among the various editions. Such differences as I have already mentioned—line-ends and other matters of layout—have had no bearing on the musical readings. Many of the musical changes are, of course, minor; for example, the typesetters of the later editions were apparently less willing to use ligatures than were those employed on the first.[25] The pattern of notated accidentals is also made slightly more consistent, though it is marred by new variants. The nature of these changes and the patterns of their occurrence show convincingly that each edition was copied from the preceding, presumably from an annotated copy. The third incorporated changes made in the second, while adding more of its own. Thus, on folio B3[r] of the second edition, the mensuration sign was omitted; in the third, it had to be squeezed in, as an afterthought. (It is worth remarking that both later editions of *Motetti de la Corona I* appear to have been prepared from an annotated copy of the first edition.)

These changes (as much as the lesser musical ones) clearly have a bearing on our view of the filiation—the interrelationship of sources—as it relates to this volume. Most scholars appear to have based their work on the third edition. For many pieces this is quite satisfactory; however, only the first can show us just what Petrucci's craftsmen may have had before them, what they may have done with it, and perhaps something as to the nature of their exemplars. A particularly attractive case appears in Example 1. The most common manuscript reading of this section of Compère's "Vostre bargeronette" is shown on the third line, in the notation of Bologna, Civico Museo Bibliografico Musicale, MS Q 17.[26] The version printed in the later editions of *Odhecaton A* is immediately above it. The reason for this variant reading only becomes apparent when the first edition is examined. Here, Petrucci's version is a minim too long: the typesetter replaced the fifth note minim by a semibreve, a common error, though (I suspect) one more likely in manuscript copying than when working with Petrucci's particular font of type. The

[25] As I point out below, it is possible to distinguish, in some cases, which changes were probably the province of the editor, and which the result of the habits and taste of the typesetter. This is discussed in full in my dissertation, and a shorter discussion is to be printed as "Petrucci's Typesetters and the Process of Stemmatics" in the forthcoming report of the conference on *Formen und Probleme der Überlieferung mehrstimmiger Musik in Zeitalter Josquins Desprez* held at Wolfenbüttel, September 1976.

[26] There seems no reason to doubt the assertions that this manuscript is Florentine and dated from before 1500, made by Allan Atlas, *The Cappella Giulia Chansonnier (Rome, Biblioteca Apostolica Vaticana, C.G.XIII.27)* (New York, 1975), I, 236–37; and Martin Staehelin, "Pierre de la Rue in Italien," *Archiv für Musikwissenschaft*, XXVII (1970), 130.

I

Example 1

Compere, "Vostre bargeronette," Altus, mm. 51-54

Odhecaton (1), fol 47ʳ

Odhecaton (2 & 3), fol. 47ʳ

Bologna Q 17, fol. 66ʳ

annotator of the file copy, having discovered (or been told) that this phrase was too long, merely "corrected" the wrong note. Thus is a new musical tradition born.

Another, more important illustration appears in Example 2. Petrucci's is the only source to supply an added Altus part. This is different for a few bars in the different editions. At the same time, *Odhecaton A* has a unique variant in the Bassus—changing the usual reading of an *f* to an *e*. Only the first

Example 2

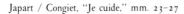

Japart / Congiet, "Je cuide," mm. 23-27

edition of the print *requires* this change. Whether because of the parallel octaves, or for some other (presumably stylistic) reason, the reading of the Altus was changed for the second edition. As a result, the pitch change in the Bassus loses its justification. As Atlas remarks in his study of the Cappella Giulia *chansonnier*,[27] Petrucci stands apart from the other sources in the Bassus reading, but it is only by studying the other editions of the print that one can see that this is not in fact a variant that places *Odhecaton A* in a different family of the tradition. Rather, it is something that was specifically engendered by the desire to have a four-voiced version, whether that wish was met by Petrus Castellanus or an earlier editor.

The variant here in Verona, Biblioteca capitolare, MS 757[28] is of some interest. Atlas suggests that the reading here is also an *e*, although I read it as a *d*. This manuscript has several additional measures at the end of the Bassus, preserving some form of decorative flourish. Otherwise, it is close to the accepted manuscript tradition of readings for this chanson, as evinced in other North Italian sources: Bologna, MS Q18; Rome, Biblioteca Casanatense, MS 2856; and Paris, Bibliothèque Nationale, Rés. MS Vm⁷ 676.[29] In many details, these stand apart from Petrucci. I am therefore inclined to believe that the Verona variant in the Bassus at measure 23 is a misreading for *f* rather than for *e*.

There is one respect, shown in Example 3, in which one of the Florentine sources (Biblioteca nazionale centrale, Banco Rari, MS 229)[30] might suggest that the scribe of the manuscript was working from a four-voiced version of this chanson. Without the Altus, as printed in Petrucci (or a similar part, as would have had to have been composed at this point), there seems to be no

[27] Atlas, *op. cit.*, pp. 130–31. The two references to P676 here should be corrected to Ver757. The rest of this passage is accepted in what follows in the present article without repetition.

[28] The contents of this manuscript are included in G. Turrini, *Il Patrimonio musicale della Biblioteca capitolare di Verona dal sec. XV al XIX* (Verona, 1952), pp. 4–16. Masakata Kanazawa remarks in "Two Vesper Repertories from Verona, ca. 1500," *Rivista italiana di musicologia*, X (1975), 159, that "there is no conclusive proof of the Veronese origin for any of these five manuscripts [including MS 757]. But the circumstantial evidence is too overwhelming to be mere coincidence," and this remark is soundly based. It is probable, moreover, that Verona 757 is also to be dated ca. 1500.

[29] An inventory, with discussion, of Casanatense 2856, is in José Llorens, "El Códice Casanatense 2.856 identificado como el Cancionero de Isabella d'Este (Ferrara), esposa de Francesco Gonzaga (Mantua)," *Anuario musical*, XX (1965), 161–78; one for Paris 676 is in Nanie Bridgman, "Un manuscrit italien du début du XVIᵉ siècle à la Bibliothèque nationale (Département de la musique, Rés Vm⁷ 676)," *Annales musicologiques*, I (1953), 177–267. The detailed dating of the former source is undertaken in Atlas, *The Cappella Giulia Chansonmier*, I, 239. Both sources are certainly from either Mantua or Ferrara. In the same study (p. 237), Atlas suggests that Bologna Q 18 is probably also from Ferrara. There is little in the readings to suggest otherwise.

[30] Howard Brown has kindly communicated to me his view that this manuscript was prepared in Florence, probably in 1491.

I

Example 3

Japart / Congiet, "Je cuide," mm. 15–17

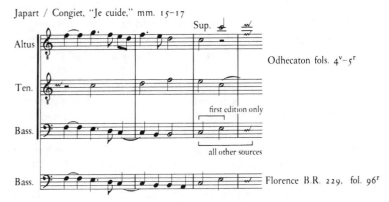

justification for seeing the movement of the Tenor and Bassus as cadential. The reading in Florence 229, however, is a specifically cadential ornamentation of the line. This is, of course, flimsy evidence and, even if taken to imply a four-voiced exemplar, certainly does not suggest that the fourth voice, as it survives in *Odhecaton A*, is identical to the original fourth voice. The matter is noteworthy, however, for its bearing on a possible stemma.

Neither of these two chansons adds anything to our knowledge of the relationship between *Odhecaton A* and other sources. Nonetheless, a study of these variants (and others like them) is clearly necessary if we are to use the print for stemmatic study.[31] It seems that the musicological application of filiation theories tends to divide into two patterns. Both of these are based on the fundamentals of filiation theory as propounded many years ago by Paul Maas, and both use the techniques so described to group the sources into families, as Atlas has done so successfully for Italian *chansonniers*.[32] But beyond this point a great dichotomy becomes apparent. On the one side are those scholars who believe that the process can be applied rigorously—that it will provide definite readings for earlier sources (now lost) and lead back

[31] The debt that any musicologist working in this area owes to the work of Allan Atlas will be great for some time to come. Though points I shall raise below run counter to details of his approach, both in principle and in practice, his work on stemmatics is still the most lucid statement of general principles as applied to music. There are, however, many developments in other fields that show other ways ahead. Of the great number of studies that discuss them in the context of literary, biblical, patristic or classical scholarship, some seem to utilize principles that may not be directly applicable to music. All of them, however, even those studies that have been successfully refuted in their own fields, present points of view without which no musicologist can construct a satisfactory theory for the study of Renaissance sources. I am presently working on the construction of such a theory, basing my work on specialized studies in these and other fields.

[32] Atlas, *The Cappella Giulia Chansonnier*.

through other sources, perhaps even to an *Urtext*.[33] Set against this view are those scholars (by far the great majority in disciplines outside music—even in such fields as biblical study in which extratextual reasons for finding an original reading are strong),[34] who state that we can never go very far in this process. The latter position has, I believe, a great deal of right on its side, for reasons vividly expressed in the following statement on a "text," that is, on a wide-ranging group of sources: "The known representatives of a 'text' . . . show such similarities that they may once have had a common archetype, but each of them has been so considerably modified by successive copying, or even revision, that this archetype can be only approximately reconstructed, with due allowance for alternative possibilities in almost every reading."[35] This view suggests that our attempts at reconstructing earlier versions can give us no more than a set of earlier readings—disjunct readings which cover a number of specific points in the composition. I believe this to be no less true in musical recension. (That is not to suggest, however, that this is the only value of such work, or that, by limiting it in this way, I feel the whole process to be too unwieldy for the results it produces. The grouping of sources into families also teaches us much about taste and performing habits, about the evolution of notation or the treatment of text, and perhaps even about local application of compositional patterns—all matters of the greatest importance.)

The latter approach, of course, led to the separation of "significant" and "insignificant" variants, in which a great many variants—often those the text critic calls "accidentals" (having no bearing on the meaning)—are assumed to be unimportant in the construction of a *stemma*. This attitude is, however, an oversimplification. Without going into full details here,[36] it should be apparent that such "accidentals" characterize the scribe and enable us to build up a picture of his habits and level of accuracy, fluency, and artistic license. These characteristics will, by themselves, resolve many of the problems in the readings which he preserved. Another distinguished biblical scholar has stated that "the knowledge gained from a study of . . . readings will lead to an understanding of scribal habits and practices without which the history of the manuscript tradition can not be written."[37] This is equally true of the habits of

---

[33] See, for example, the paper read by Thomas Noblitt at the Wolfenbüttel conference mentioned above in fn. 25 and at the annual meeting of the American Musicological Society, Washington, D.C., 1976. Although this paper does not take as extreme a position as I describe, the thinking behind it does seem to be based on such hypotheses.

[34] See the basic premises behind the work of Dom Henri Quentin, as stated in his *Mémoire sur l'établissement du texte de la Vulgate* (Paris, 1922).

[35] Silva Lake, *Family II and the Codex Alexandrinus: The Text according to Mark*, Studies and Documents, V (London, 1936), p. 5, fn. 12.

[36] Such details appear in my detailed study of the application of filiation theory (see above, fns. 25, 31).

[37] Ernest Colwell, "Hort Redivivus: A Plea and a Program," *Transitions in Biblical Scholarship*, ed. J. Coert Rylaarsdam (Chicago, 1968), p. 144.

I

Petrucci's typesetters and perhaps not least in *Odhecaton A*. The process will not, in most cases, aid us in the grouping of sources into families. That is best accomplished by the analytical processes discussed by Professor Atlas. But the details of relationships within the group, the "family" or the "text type," can only be deduced once we have characterized the work of each scribe.

In the light of this viewpoint, it is worth turning again to the *Odhecaton A* to see whether Petrucci could have supplied the material for any of the surviving concordances or they could have supplied the music for his versions. I include here the direct parent and descendant of each source, for I do not believe that sources that survive would have been used in the printing shop, and none of them appear to be directly related among themselves, with one minor exception. For that reason, we discuss Paris 676, for example: such a later source could be a literal copy of an earlier one and thus preserve readings among those from which Petrucci drew.

There is not space here to describe the detailed characteristics of Petrucci's craftsman or even to outline the analytical techniques used in discovering them. We cannot treat here the elements in a version that he favors, those he keeps, those he rejects, those he will insert or adapt. Nor shall I discuss how to determine whether the typesetter worked note by note or phrase by phrase, a factor that has at least as great an impact on the merit and character of the readings. Such analysis, however, is clearly essential. A scribe who is prone to decorate cadences, for example, could not have copied from an exemplar that had more decoration at such points than the version he produced. One who removed decoration, rather than added it, can be assumed to have had in his exemplar. some (at least) of the ornamental figures that he does copy. The same manner of analysis needs to be done for Petrucci's typesetters. It is possible to show, in some of the volumes, just which ranges of things were changed (though often not which particular examples within those ranges). Indeed, one can go further and show which would probably have been changed by the editor and which by the different typesetters.[38] In the case of the first edition of *Odhecaton A*, I cannot tell whether there was more than one typesetter: therefore, I have to assume that any changes are as likely to have been made by Petrucci's editor Castellanus as by the typesetter. This does not seem to matter, however, for there is a certain consistency when the readings are compared with those in other sources of the same family.

There is no reason to believe that Petrucci's versions need have been exemplars for any of the other North Italian sources. None have consistently the same patterns of detail that would suggest they could be direct copies—with one minor exception: the added Altus of "Je ne fay plus" (variously ascribed to Busnois, Compère, and Murieu) preserved in the Wolffheim *chansonnier* is, as noted by Atlas and Hewitt,[39] the same as that in *Odhecaton*

[38] See fn. 25, above.
[39] Atlas, *The Cappella Giulia Chansonnier*, I, 73; and Hewitt, *Odhecaton*, p. 131.

A. It is a later addition and is almost certainly copied directly from the print. Since, as Rifkin has shown,[40] this manuscript is probably Ferrarese, it is of interest that the Washington copy of *Odhecaton A* has a contemporary binding that is certainly North Italian (perhaps also Ferrarese). The presence of this one direct concordance, however, merely serves to underscore the point that other sources are not so copied. Furthermore, none of the other sources have, consistently, the same patterns of differences that would suggest they could represent a scribal pattern superimposed on the readings of *Odhecaton A*.

An extreme example of this lies in the versions of Hayne's "De tous biens plaine," of which a few details are shown in Example 4. The pattern of

Example 4

Hayne, "De tous biens plaine," Superius (mm. 13-15); Tenor (mm. 39-41)

Odhecaton, fols. 6ᵛ-7ʳ

Casanatense 2856, fols. 66ᵛ-67ʳ; Paris Vmᵗ 676, fols. 42ᵛ-43ʳ; Similar readings for superius in other sources

Mellon *chansonnier*

figuration shown for *Odhecaton A* (all editions) is followed consistently through the source for this piece, while both Casanatense 2856 and Paris 676 use a simpler form throughout. Thus far, the evidence is not of any value: either pattern of cadence might have been the habit of a scribe/typesetter preparing copy from a source with the other pattern: the typesetter of *Odhecaton A* might have been working from a simple source and decorating it as he prepared the print. Though Paris 676 has a number of small variant readings when compared with the print, they do not necessarily indicate that it could not have been copied from that source. The manuscript carries a three-voiced version, *Odhecaton A* one for four voices: both the changes of pitch are explicable on that basis. However, there is evidence elsewhere in the manuscript which suggests that the scribe was a fairly mechanical copyist (inconsistent treatment of color and ligatures in different pieces; consistent treatment of, for example, ornamentation within individual pieces, though differing from piece to piece); it would seem unlikely, therefore, that such a scribe could produce the simpler cadences present in his version of Hayne's chanson if he had been working from the print.

On the other hand, there is a large (and similar) body of evidence that

---

[40] Joshua Rifkin, "A 'New' Renaissance Manuscript," *Abstracts of Papers Read at the Thirty-seventh Annual Meeting of the American Musicological Society* (1971), p. 2. I am grateful to Mr. Rifkin for sending me a copy of the complete paper.

does suggest that the range of changes made by Castellanus to the text of
Odhecaton A included an increase in rhythmic interplay between voices and
in rhythmic activity in general.[41] A simple case is given in Example 5, and

Example 5

Agricola, *Si dedero,* Tenor and Contra, mm. 12–13, 60

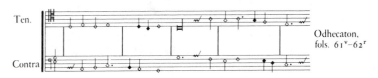

Odhecaton,
fols. 61ᵛ–62ʳ

Casanatense 2856,
fols. 101ᵛ–102ʳ;
Also in Bologna
Q 16, Q 17, Q 18;
Paris Vm⁷ 676, etc.

many similar illustrations could be provided. Given the general prevalence of
such readings in *Odhecaton A,* this would suggest that the editor might have
been adapting a source closer to the manuscript tradition, at least in this
respect. As it happens, in this particular case there is some evidence that points
Castelanus's version away from the surviving manuscripts, but the point
remains that this type of analysis will suggest which particular readings may
have been in the exemplars. It produces cases in which we can comment on
the specific readings that were in Petrucci's archetype, without being able to
reconstruct other details of that now-lost source. It conforms to the view of the
value of stemmatic analysis outlined above.

Some of these scribal (or typesetters') traits, if that is what they are, can be
seen in the Japart/Congiet chanson I have already mentioned, "Je cuide."
The scribe of Paris 676 again used simple cadential figures throughout: it is
the only source with consistently undecorated suspensions. By contrast, Bologna Q 18 has a wealth of *minor color.* While the latter is, I believe, a specific
scribal quirk, I have already suggested that the former is not. But one of the
most significant scribal habits demonstrated in the various sources of this piece
is that of combining repeated notes into one, and of redividing the time split
between them. If this is indeed a scribal trait, it will perhaps tell us a little
about the exemplars, though it is, of course, more clearly of value in helping to

---

[41] It is interesting to note that Edward Lowinsky makes similar points about the manuscript
Cambridge, Magdalene College, Pepys 1760: "The editor of the manuscript, who was
undoubtedly a Frenchman,...had a typically French interest in rhythm. He wished to
improve on the rhythm that comes to a stop without complementary motion in another voice"
(*The Medici Codex of 1518: A Choirbook of Motets Dedicated to Lorenzo de' Medici, Duke of
Urbino,* Monuments of Renaissance Music, III–V [Chicago, 1968], III, 133).

define the character of the copyists' work. When compared with *Odhecaton A*, however, the patterns assume a greater significance.

I must stress that no source will be entirely consistent in its treatment of such patterns. There are two reasons for this. One is that the scribe himself is never entirely consistent. At times he will be prone to copy exactly; at others he will be more willing to practice "artistic license"—it all depends on his assessment of his exemplars. In either case, his pattern will be superimposed upon that prevailing in his exemplar and will not be consistently revealed. The other reason is that surviving manuscripts and prints are almost certainly prepared from more than one exemplar. Since each of these exemplars will have its own patterns, each a similar mixture, and each showing through that of the new scribe to a greater or lesser extent, the new manuscript is certain to present a superficially confusing picture. When patterns recur across different layers or sections of an anthology, however, we may be justified in believing that these patterns reflect something to do with the editor or copyist (or, by stretching the impact of coincidence, with common elements of *all* his exemplars).

I believe that the way repeated notes and longer notes which appear in *Odhecaton A* compare with the readings in other sources does show something of such an over-all pattern consistent across many sections of the print. There are a number of pieces, of which "Je cuide" is one, in which the print is among the few sources with identical treatment of imitative points between voices, or with a satisfactory pattern of repeated notes when the text is considered. (I repeat, this does not—indeed cannot—apply to all the pieces, simply because no scribe is entirely consistent.) A number of instances are shown in Example 6. In the case of "Je cuide," we do not have text in any source. For this, as for the other pieces quoted, I have concentrated on sources from the North Italian orbit. In each, *Odhecaton A* is one of the sources that does provide a pattern of repeated notes suitable to the text, in the Tenor as well as the Superius. This pattern does not follow consistently right through the volume, but it does appear likely that many of the pieces in *Odhecaton A* were copied, either directly or at very few removes, from exemplars that had text underlaid. I cannot yet show that this was a matter that was of concern to

Example 6

Japart / Congiet, "Je cuide"

Sup.
Ten.

Bass.

Odhecaton, fols. 4ᵛ–5ʳ

Bologna Q 18
Casanatense 2856
(except the tenor)
Florence B.R. 229
Paris Vmᵃ 676
Verona 757

Hayne, "De tous biens plaine"

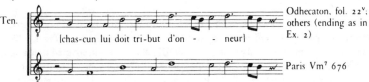

Ten. [chas-cun lui doit tri-but d'on - - neur]

Odhecaton, fol. 22ᵛ;
others (ending as in
Ex. 2)

Paris Vm⁷ 676

Ockeghem, "Ma bouche rit"

Sup. [Ma bou - che rit et ma pen - sée]

Ten.

Contra

Odhecaton,
fols. 59ᵛ-60ᵛ;
Dijon 517
Mellon *chansonnier*

Casanatense 2856

Brumel, *Mater patris*

Sup. [Ma-ter mi - se - ri -cor-di - e In hac val-le mi-se - ri -ae]

Odhecaton, fol. 67ᵛ
Florence Panc. 27

Bologna Q 18

Brumel, *Mater patris*

Sup.
Ten.
Contra

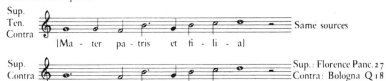

[Ma - ter pa - tris et fi - li - a]

Same sources

Sup.
Contra

Sup.: Florence Panc. 27
Contra: Bologna Q 18

Castellanus, despite the way in which patterns do distribute through the volume. Further detailed analysis of the habits both of the editor and of the typesetter(s) should help to establish more of the details.

In that case, we will have some evidence of what Petrus Castellanus may have changed and what he may have left, both in rhythmic treatment and in patterns of repeated notes related to texts. That will be a major step toward establishing some details of the now-lost earlier manuscript sources for the music of *Odhecaton A*, and thence details of its filiation.

I

POSTSCRIPT

The bibliographical aspects of this study are further discussed in my *Ottaviano Petrucci: catalogue raisonne* (New York: Oxford University Press, 2005), alongside a number of other issues. Bonnie Blackburn has discovered much about the role of Petrus Castellanus as a collector of music, and supplier to Petrucci: see her "Petrucci's Venetian editor: Petrus Castellanus and his musical garden". *Musica Disciplina*, xlix (1995), 15–45; reprinted in *Composition, Printing and Performance* (Aldershot: Ashgate, 2000), ch.VI: a further paper, "The sign of Petrucci's editor", was read at the conference "Venezia 1501: Petrucci e la stampa musicale" (held in Venice during October 2001). I have previously written on the notation which Blackburn uses as evidence, and produced an alternative explanation: see my "Notational spelling and scribal habit", *Datierung und Filiation von Musikhandschriften der Josquin Zeit*, edited by Ludwig Finscher (= Quellenstudien zur Musik der Renaissance, ii, = Wolfenbütteler Forschungen, xxvi) (Wiesbaden: Harrassowitz, 1983), pp. 65–109, reprinted here as Chapter IX.

II

Petrucci's Type-setters and the Process of Stemmatics

It grieves me that the final paper in a colloquium held in so fine a German library should have to be given in a foreign language, but, had I attempted to read it in German, I should have generated more mirth than thought.

My work in Petrucci can not be said to rival that of some of my colleagues here in producing the glory of a new source for us to enjoy: although I can say that I know of 19 copies of Petrucci titles that are not listed in RISM, as well as 5 errors of citation there (1). More importantly, the 14 editions listed by Sartori as having been printed at Fossombrone, coupled with three non-musical volumes, can now be increased to 27 separate printings, all of which can be arranged in order and approximately dated (2). There are some signs that a similar pattern may be emerging for the Venetian titles (3).

The existence of so many editions provides, of course, a treasure-trove for any scholar interested in how early sixteenth-century copyists worked from their exemplars. (Throughout this paper, I work on the assumption that, with few specific exceptions, there are close analogies between the processes adopted by a manuscript scribe and those of the type-setter: I have found no reason to question such an assumption.) This is particularly true here, for second and later editions are often copied from earlier editions (which do survive) rather than from the manuscript copy-texts (which do not).

One other preliminary thing needs to be remarked: in the study of filiation, we have to assume that there is some geographical restriction in the circulation, and upon the impact, of a given manuscript. Trade routes were important, and specific local contacts always significant, but the sphere of influence is presumed to have been limited, even in the

II

case of each of the Burgundian sources so clearly discussed here by Professor Kellman. Indeed, much of Allan Atlas' work on the chansonniers of the later fifteenth and earlier sixteenth centuries is based on just this probability of limited spheres of influence (4). For a print, however, this is hardly true. Copies of Petrucci's prints existed in the Colon, Fugger and Herwart collections, and this distribution has other support. One of the copies of Josquin's masses, at Harvard, has what has been described as an early sixteenth-century Spanish binding, and the library of John IV of Portugal owned copies of the *Motetti de la Corona* (although we do not know of which edition). Glareanus copied from *Motetti B*, while Gesner and later bibliographers knew of several other titles. In Italy, there were copies of some Petrucci prints in the Medici and (probably) Strozzi libraries, at San Luigi dei Francesi, Rome and, probably, elsewhere. Colon bought Bossinensis' second book in Rome only a year after it was published, and could still buy Frottole XI in Perugia in 1530, fourteen years after publication (5). Such a wide and long pattern of distribution of these sources must affect our view of the filiation in which they are involved.

An attempt at constructing a *stemma* (or, for that matter, at evaluating the sources if the editor prefers to follow the 'best-text' tradition of thought) is, or should be, the product of two concerns: one is the desire to trace a line of descent, and perhaps to come a little nearer to establishing the nature of the *Urtext*; the other is the wish to know what any particular source represents in the way of local repertoire or local readings, and the extent to which it is an adaptation of the wider pattern.

These two are often seen to be contradictory, or at least as being incapable of correlation. If there are differences in two sources, so the argument runs, then they must be on different branches of the family tree. If, conversely, the readings are the same, then one scribe made no changes and the sources have to be related. (This is, of course, a naive exaggeration of what is, nonetheless, a common position.) The point at which the changes are made, that at which the branches emerge from the trunk of the tree, is tacitly ignored.

Thus Professor Kirsch, in his earlier, most interesting, paper here, remarked that „*Petrucci 1519 ist unter-terz-freundlich*" and apparently implied that the type-setters were willing to alter such cadential patterns (6). But, in the same paper, he used the presence of these figures in varying numbers in different sources of some works as an aid to grouping the sources. In common with much musical filiation (though distinct from the view taken by patristic, New Testament, or literary scholars (7)), this approach ignores the possibility of deciding which changes are deliberate in any given source, and which represent earlier, now lost, sources. It is at this particular problem that my paper is directed: only when this is resolved can we say anything about local performance practice, about local taste in accidentals or underlay, or (eventually) about the spread of notational change or of new approaches to texts. And, once that is done, we may be able to evaluate the relationships of the readings in our various sources, and perhaps begin to look for the earlier.

My concern here, then, is not 'what did the copyist have in front of him?': it is rather what I see as an earlier question: 'what would the copyist be likely to do with what he had in front of him?' In other words, I want to discuss a method for finding his pattern for doing things, and also for finding details that might reveal local taste. From this, we should be able to show what he might (or, occasionally, must) have changed from his exemplar, and then explain gaps in our provisional *stemma* — or, at least, decide why some readings are not acceptable.

The deliberate musical change is analogous to the deliberate text change. There are, for example, four sources of Févin's *Nobilis progenie* known to me: in Bologna, San Petronio, A XXXVIII, the motet is, predictably, dedicated to S. Petronius; in Cambridge, Magdalene College, Pepys 1760, to S. Remigius; while in Padua, Duomo, A 17 and in *Motetti de la Corona I* (hereafter *Corona I*) it is addressed to S. Francis. (Clinkscale and Gehrenbeck, when discussing this work (8), both suggest that the subject was a local priest, though the Bolognese dedication clearly contradicts this hypothesis. I believe that S. Remigius was probably the original dedicatee of the motet. S. Francis was an international, if primarily Italian, saint; S. Remigius was local to northern France, and fulfilled the requirements of the opening words of the text rather better — he was the son of a Count of Laon.) The Bolognese scribe made this change for the benefit of his own church, that is, to suit a local need. We would not say, however, that such a change removes this source from the place on a branch of the *stemma* indicated by the musical and other readings. The same should be true for musical changes, if we can find plausible reasons for change in any specific source. (I do not believe, by the way, that the Cambridge source need present an earlier version of the music merely because it presents an earlier form of the dedication: the two need not be related, any more than the order of copying of diverse sources tells us anything about the relative order of the readings they preserve).

It should be beyond doubt that local styles in many details of music do exist. Local taste in the choice of repertoire has long been recognised and, although it is often partially over-ridden by the availability of music, it is a factor in the content of many manuscripts and prints. In the same way, groups of manuscripts copied at the same place should show patterns in the indication of accidentals or the treatment of text underlay. Certainly, some scribes are less sophisticated than others in their treatment of perfect mensurations, and I have the suspicion that Alamire was rather sparing in his use of *minor color*.

It might seem that we can only discover what a music copyist — scribe or type-setter — changed from his exemplar in those virtually non-existent cases where both exemplar and copy survive, allowing us to compare the details. It could be held that even restricted bodies of music, such as those circumscribed so brilliantly by Atlas or Kellman, are not sufficiently closely related to enable us to do such work. While I do not believe that a literary or biblical scholar would accept so simplistic an attitude (9), I do not need to summon the refinements of their art to my aid in the present context, for we have, in the series of re-printings by Petrucci, a ready-made series of exemplars and copies.

(Although these later volumes exist for all the sacred titles printed by Petrucci at Fossombrone, there is one case, the masses of Févin, where a single part-book is all that suvives of the official first edition (November 1515). All the other copies were printed much later, almost certainly in or after the summer of 1520. There are some such re-printings in the Venetian titles (10)).

Petrucci's prints are valuable for source-studies (as general demonstrations of method) in three ways: first is the group of limitations on what *could* be printed, which provide ready-made explanations of some changes in readings. Both Professor Noblitt and I have mentioned the limitations on ligatures, and that Petrucci probably owned no colored or half-colored ligatures (although later single-impression printers could make these by butting individual sorts together). Since all of Petrucci's type could be inverted, the list of individual sorts that were available is even smaller than Professor Noblitt's table might suggest.

Secondly, as a printer, Petrucci had to work in a different way to his market. Many of the Italian cathedral manuscripts that should perhaps lie closest to Petrucci's or Antico's sources must carry the repertoire, underlay, accidentals, text-spelling and other didactic marks that were needed at the sponsoring institution. I believe, for instance, that one of the scribes at Casale Monferrato made specific changes in the notation of some works in order to help unsure singers: I mention an example below. But Petrucci had to aim for, and reach, a wider market. His editorial decisions had to be simple and straightforward — his readings needed to be planned at the level of the highest common factor, and no higher. The probability that he measured this level fairly precisely can be seen in the number of later printings and in the closeness of their readings to those of the first editions.

The third particularly useful aspect of Petrucci's titles, and the one with which I propose to start, is derived from the fact that he used more than one type-setter at a time; two men set different part-books or different fascicles, copying differing versions of the same works, though presumably working from the same exemplar (11). These two men had slightly different, though detectable, patterns of work and of adapting what was in front of them: it is this that leads to the two differing versions.

Yesterday, Professor Brown said that the scribe of Florence 2442 was as consistent in his manner of working as in the repertoire he transcribed. He was talking about ligatures and underlay, though we should expect such a statement to be generally true, for every scribe acquired certain habitual manners of working. He learned manners of spelling unstandardised words, patterns of punctuation and abbreviation, standard arrangements for lay-out, and so on. The same is basically true of the performing musician; he also acquired patterns, of text declamation (and hence underlay), of adding accidentals, of ligature and color interpretation, of the meaning of mensuration and proportion signs, and of the decoration of cadences. Such things were products of his training and of his musical (rather than scribal) status. But if he were also a scribe, copying music, they would be no less a part of his approach to the written music from which he was to copy. There is no reason, therefore, why a music scribe should not show his own individuality in his copying of both music and text.

Scholars of early printing have recognised that the type-setter also had these habits and that they can be seen in the printed volume (12). However, it is accepted that such habits wil *not* show consistently in the newly copied source (13), for any copyist's work is a fusion of two layers of such habits. The first will be the collection of readings in the source (itself a similar fusion) while the other represents his own pattern — whatever he changed, consciously, unconsciously or carelessly. Thus a scribe who normally spells the word *alleluya* with a penultimate *y* will, if confronted with a source that consistently spells it with an *i*, himself occasionally spell it in the manner of his exemplar. (This, in fact, happens in *Corona I*, first edition.) I believe that an analysis of this sort of pattern in sources will enable us to distinguish the principal layers of change, one representing the scribe's conscious decisions — to change the saint's name, to transpose, to add accidentals or to change the notation of triple metre sections: the other is the truly habitual (which will show occasional lapses) — spelling and placing of texts, use of ligatures and *minor color*, and so on. I leave aside careless error, although it can not always be distinguished from the others. However, I would include among the habitual changes patterns of decorating cadential figures, in so far as they were probably, like spelling, within the range of adaptation that would arise through the scribe's normal use of memory in the copying process (14).

If we can trace both these layers, we can also distinguish between the copyist's own habits and local taste, even though the two are not entirely distinct. (The word 'local' is perhaps not the most apt in the context of Petrucci's prints, aimed as they were at a wide market: but it does carry the necessary connotations of change made deliberately for the benefit of the user of the source, and can perhaps be allowed to stand for the decisions made by whomever Petrucci employed at this stage as editor.)

This is particularly true if, as in Petrucci's *Corona I* (first editon), there are two type-setters, each with his own distinct habits, which can be contrasted with the local pattern common to both.

The spelling of latin, for example, shows certain patterns that can be used to distinguish the work of the two men. Among the variants are:
Type-setter 1: *michi, franchorum, iherusalem, alleluya,* etc.
Type-setter 2: *mihi, francorum, hierusalem, alleluia,* etc.

These patterns, coupled with similar patterns of type-usage and of other bibliographical detail, can be traced from page to page and part-book to part-book: as a result, a consistent image of each man's habits is built up, which demonstrates which pages were set by each (15).

The truly exciting aspect of the work is the extent to which certain details of musical notation follow exactly the same pattern. For example, *all but one* of the uses of *minor color* in this edition are on pages that are the work of the second man. Type setter one uses the proportion sign $\frac{0}{3}$ (often with the 0 added by hand: this does not weaken the argument for the 0 comes from a different fount than the 3, when printed), while the second man uses the simpler sign, 3. In many places, the first man uses a ligature where the second avoids one. Examples 1a and 1b show this clearly: in both, taken from Mouton's *Nos qui vivimus,* type-setter 1 prepared the superius and tenor, using ligatures for the imitative entry: the second man avoided the ligature in each case where it could have been used. In Févin's *Benedictus Dominus Deus,* the first type-setter was responsible only for the tenor voice: he used the only three ligatures that appear in this motet: two of them are shown in example 1c.

In the light of this kind of evidence, we might expect some general pattern to emerge as to the range of situations that calls forth a ligature in each man's work, for the second did not eschew them completely. The frequent use found in the folios set by the first man particularly includes those places that need specific help with underlay, help that is indeed supplied by the ligature — where it gives a direct single possible solution, brings forward the last syllable of a phrase, points up phrase structure and motivic elements, or encourages or prevents text repetition — indeed, help of the kind described by Professor Brown in his paper on Florence 2442. My second type-setter used ligatures less frequently and in manners which seldom do provide a single direct answer to problems of underlay, indeed which sometimes seem scarcely to help at all. He does not appear to have the clear understanding of the uses of a ligature that is apparent in the work of type-setter 1. It is tempting to suggest that a ligature in the second man's work may reflect the presence of one in the exemplar: it is much safer to say that the absence of one in certain circumstances in the work of the first man could well reflect the absence of one at that point in his source.

By contrast, the second man is much more clear-cut in his use of *minor color*. He employs it more frequently, and specifically as an aid either to the placing of text syllables or to an understanding of the rhythmic shape of a phrase.

This differentiation between the two men's work can also be extended to text placing and to patterns of triple metre notation, including the use of coloration. Particularly attractive here is the manner in which the second man appears to ignore the *similis ante similem* rule, while the first strives to follow it. Example 2a, from Brumel's *Laudate Dominum*, shows the second man, who set the altus and bassus, completely disregarding the rule; the first was responsible for the superius and tenor. The distinction between them is clear, even though the parts set by the first man have two different notations.

An interpretation of these patterns can be reached by determining a possible notation for an exemplar to this edition. On one hand, it is possible that the readings in the manuscript were as they are in Petrucci's print. If so, it has to be seen as a remarkable coincidence that the two voices which were, as it happened, to be set by type-setter 2 should be just those that so clearly ignore the *similis ante similem* rule. At the other extreme, it is possible that all voices had the same notation, and that it did take account of the rule. However, it then seems unlikely that the second man, though lacking in understanding (perhaps even because he was such), would have removed either coloration or a *punctus divisionis*. It seems to me much more probable that the manuscript exemplar was consistent in all voices, and that all ignored the rule: the second man would then have been content with it as it stood, while the first would have felt some need to correct the version. Such a hypothesis explains simply why he, working in two different part-books, might produce two different versions, for it is not unreasonable to suggest that the anomalous use of a *punctus divisionis* without color in the tenor book was a result of his not noticing the problem until the phrase was half set in type. This interpretation conforms to the other evidence concerning the two craftsmen, and suggests strongly that the notation of the exemplar was as in example 2b.

Indeed, the general situation is as if type-setter 1 were trained in a more old-fashioned, more rigorous school of notation, while the second was more up-to-date, as it were, technically younger. (It is perhaps worth adding, in the light of Professor Kirsch's paper, that the pattern of under-third cadences seems to show no correlation with that of the type-setters. Whatever may have happened elsewhere, Petrucci apparently did not allow his men any latitude in this respect.)

These differences in work patterns are, in themselves, important. They allow us to see the history of notation as it is being written. But their importance is greatly magnified in the present context by two other factors. One is the very real care that Petrucci took to present what he thought were satisfactory readings: though we recognise that there are many points where other sources appear to improve on his versions, we must not allow this to affect our understanding of his view of them. There is evidence of several levels of correction being made in the printing shop before the copies were sold: stop-press corrections, notes erased and new ones stamped in (with his type) after press-work was completed, cancel pages printed as replacements, even manuscript corrections (such as the proportion sign cited above) almost certainly made in the printing house (16). The presence of all these levels of correction makes the prints much more like manuscripts: each copy is unique in the range of alterations made in it, so that those marked in by Petrucci and by later users are analogous to scribal and later corrections in manuscripts. Later editions follow these corrections very carefully, showing that they were incorporated into the version that Petrucci wished to present. I am convinced that *nothing* can be said about such a version until all the surviving copies of the print concerned have been examined: and I am also convinced that this shows the care that Petrucci took over the version that he did present.

II

The second factor making this evidence of type-setter's patterns more important in the study of local taste and of stemmatic theory is the presence of the later editions. Three editions exist of *Corona I*, as hinted by Sartori, all dated 17 August 1514. The earliest is of that date: the other two were probably printed in July 1516 and January 1520. (I ignore the Roman edition of 1526, as being the work of a different printing house (17)). In the 119 pages of music, there are only 17 musical changes made in the second edition. Nine of them correspond to manuscript changes (made by Petrucci's men) in the unique surviving copy of the first edition (and if more copies had survived, more of the changes might have been seen to follow manuscript alteration). Only two of the variants appear to be faults in the second edition. The third edition has three new errors, that is, one for each forty pages of music. This suggests to me that Petrucci felt that he had, after all the corrections were made, a version that he wished to keep; it also suggests that the type-setters took considerable care to preserve that version.

In other words, we have here a source in which casual and habitual scribal changes can be distinguished from deliberate editorial changes, once the pattern of the individual craftsmen can be detected. Since this can be done for a print that was widely disseminated, and with compositions that survive in many other sources, the importance of such work both for filiation and for the study of patterns of underlay or proportional notation (or indeed any other element of early sixteenth-century notation) can hardly be over-estimated.

If two different type-setters found different things important, and if they had different patterns ingrained into their work habits, then the same can, of course, be said for manuscript copyists. Paseto, the scribe of Padua, Duomo, A 17 (18), copied very carefully, changing little, even errors. But he *was* concerned to clarify the treatment of the text, expanding it or adding the standard symbol, *ij*, to indicate repetition. One of the scribes in the complex at Casale Monferrato added much *minor color* (as did the copyist of the Cortona and Paris set of partbooks, though here perhaps for visual pleasure only). Another, at the same cathedral, felt it necessary to break up dotted semibreves. The opening of the anonymous *Vulnerasti cor meum* (ascribed in Regensburg, A. R. 940–1 to Conradus Rein, and offered to Mouton by Anglés (19)) is an extreme case. As preserved in Casale L (*olim* B) and shown here in example 3, it changes the possible solutions to text placing. I suspect that this change, like the uses of *minor color* in other Casale sources, is part of a pattern of change designed to help unsteady singers.

I suggest that analysis of these patterns of change, while beneficial to our view of stylistic development, will also produce much evidence to bolster the palaeographical evidence used in constructing *stemmate*. If a pair of sources of similar date and provenance carry the same basic readings, palaeographical study can aid the scholar. It may show that details of lay-out or of readings of one source were influenced by format, gathering structure, line-ends or other similar elements; that source then becomes a likely antecedent of the other. But a study of scribal taste may well work in a similar way, demonstrating that one scribe would not have produced the version he did if he had been working from the readings preserved in the other. Occasionally, too, the situation arises where notation and palaeography, or an analysis of scribal patterns and taste can suggest that two sources are not on the same branch of a family tree, despite the pattern of readings. I propose to offer examples of both these sitations, using the first edition of *Corona I* (I—Bc, Q 70).

The manuscript Vatican City, Palatini latini, 1980—1, is a pair of part-books bearing the Medici arms. Lowinsky has suggested that they were written for Giuliano de'Medici between 1513 and 1521, preferring the later end of the period (20). They contain two voices of Mouton's *Gaude Barbara beata*, also surviving as the first work of *Corona I* (and in six other sources). Plate 1 shows part of the tenor voice in both sources: there are no corrections of any sort on this page of the print. The two sources are identical here, both in readings and in notation.

The scribe of the Roman manuscript was apparently very careful over text placing, writing in the words after the music. Significant here is the placing of the word *proprio* in the fifth line of the manuscript, where the gap in the word appears to be simply to accommodate the up-tails of the *fusae* of the line below. Also, in the penultimate line, the *st* of *meruisti* is written as a ligature (as is normal) while in the word *petisti* (on the same line) it is divided, to allow for the musical ligature of the line below. Although the spacing of the text does not provide ready-made answers to underlay problems, it is clear that the words have been most carefully placed relative to the music, for otherwise these slight adaptations of writing style would not have been necessary.

With this in mind, I believe that there is enough evidence here to suggest that the Petrucci version lies later in a filiation than does that of the manuscript: less certainly, that it may be a copy of a copy of the Roman source (that is, in a straight line of descent). There are three points of evidence: one relates to the fact that the third line of this folio of the manuscript ends at the same point as the second of the print. In the manuscript, the line ends with the words *deo grata*, with the second word repeated early in the next line. The print lacks the first *grata*. I suspect that a scribe who placed his text as scrupulously as did this one would have been less likely to add text not in his exemplar than would Petrucci's type-setter to omit some, especially since comparison with the other voices suggests that the extra word is not essential. This is not strong evidence in either direction, of course, although there is a certain appearance of a cavalier attitude to text in other places in *Corona I*.

Second: the printer's men regularly arranged the text in groups of three or four words, followed by a space, a pattern that they doubtless had grown accustomed to from earlier sources. This was, in any case, slightly easier technically than was placing each syllable or word separately. Although (as I believe) they did often follow the text in an exemplar, it would appear that the type-setters grouped words together fairly frequently, possibly whenever they could see no justification for a particular spacing: the pattern does seem to vary slightly from piece to piece. The placing of the word *meruisti* may be significant, for it matches that of the manuscript precisely. However, part of the reason for this placing in the Roman source may well be that the word appears at the start of a line: there is no such palaeographical reason in the print. In the same way, the spacing of the phrase *gaude namque elevata es in celo* is exactly the same in both sources. This produces a series of small spaces between words in the print, as if the typesetter had decided that the underlay of his exemplar was meaningful at this point and should be followed. In the manuscript, however, the phrase is written out in the scribe's normal hand: in proportion to the music, the text hand is larger than is Petrucci's text fount, and thus no spaces appear. To argue that the scribe's spacing happened to fit the size of his text hand when he copied the exact spacing of his exemplar (or of the print) seems, again, to be relying too heavily on the coincidental. Since the resultant underlay is, arguably, weaker (in both sources) than that suggested by the concordant Florence and Cortona manuscripts, this evidence strongly suggests that the Petrucci version should be seen as later in the same filiation than the Roman source.

The third point concerns the same line in the print. The words *gaude* and *impetrare* both start phrases of text and music: the words are both placed slightly to the right of the notes they concern. It is common to find such displacements of up to 2—3 mm sideways in Petrucci's editions, although very rare to find vertical displacement (where pitches could be affected). Not surprisingly, in the manuscript, both these words are placed directly beneath the notes they concern. It is therefore interesting to note the rest of the text of this section, to see how the placing in the print relates to that of the manuscript. If the same relative positions were retained, then the scribe might well have been working from a copy of the print where the text was not so displaced to the right, for he was clearly a careful copyist. Alternatively, it would be possible for all the words except these two to have a consistent, though different relationship: then we would be able to suggest that the scribe, in working from the print, merely adjusted those words that he could see started a phrase. In either of these situations, there would be no valid argument for the priority of either source. However, this does not arise. Every other word is also displaced to the left in the manuscript *vis-a-vis* the print (like the opening words) except the last, *petisti* which is moved to the right. This is the particular word that we have already noted as written to allow for a musical ligature tail, and its placing can hardly be fortuitous. We have to accept, therefore, that the text placing in the manuscript does not reflect an attempt at following that in a copy of the print. Indeed, we are left with the only possibility that the manuscript appears at an earlier stage in the *stemma* than does the print.

There is no other evidence that I know of, in any of Petrucci's Fossombrone volumes (except perhaps that of Pisano, which is a problem in other ways) for exemplars coming from either Rome or Florence. While I believe that Petrucci's men would not have been allowed to work

257

from sources such as the present manuscript (but only from working copies made from these more important sources), yet I still suspect that the printing-house copy of this motet must have been related to this particular manuscript. It is, of course, possible in theory that Petrucci's exemplar and the surviving manuscript were themselves copied from one or more intermediaries; but this presupposes an ever-increasing number of equally scrupulous scribes, all presenting exactly the same readings, all managing to keep under control their own personal and local characteristics, with the intention of producing identical readings — and this is a postulate that I find very hard to accept.

If, indeed, Petrucci's type-setters worked from some descendant of the Roman manuscript, that would bring forward the date of the copying of this motet to early 1514, at the latest.

Fortunately, such cases, involving only details of lay-out, are, and will probably remain, rare.

Example 4 and plate 2 illustrate the second situation, in which, I suggested, notation and palaeography might over-ride the presence of musical variants to suggest a close relationship between sources. This motet, Févin's *Egregie Christi confessor*, happens to be another where the name of the saint was changed in some sources. It is S. Martin in *Corona I*; S. Christopher in two Alamire manuscripts, London, BL, Roy. 8. G. VII and Vienna, 15941; S. Evasius in Casale Monferrato P (*olim* E); and S. Petronius in Bologna, San Petronio, A XXXVIII. This time, I suspect that Petrucci does give the original name, though my reason for mentioning the change is that it again raises a situation where the scribes (or editors) made deliberate alterations without thereby removing their sources from the family branch. Indeed, I believe that both the Bologna and Casale Monferrato scribes were working from copies of Petrucci.

Example 4a shows the patterns of ligatures in the sources at the start of each voice. Here, as before, the two type-setters employed by Petrucci follow their routine pattern, and it is difficult to believe other than that the distribution of the ligatures is a direct reflection of their habits. It is the sort of pattern that I have suggested may have 'palaeographical' significance. The same pattern is followed in the two manuscripts, where there seems to be no sound reason for its adoption. This is, in itself, enough to suggest a close connection with Petrucci. In the Casale Monferrato source, the scribe continues to copy Petrucci exactly, except for the addition of six examples of *minor color*, apparently to cope with strong cross-rhythms. Crawford has stated (21) that the Casale scribes certainly copied from Antico: this is one of the relatively few cases where Petrucci seems to have provided the exemplar.

The question of the relationship with the Bolognese source is more complicated. For one thing, the central folio for this motet is badly torn, leaving extant only a few notes of the *prima pars* of the bassus and of the *secunda* for the tenor. In the rest of the music, there are three musical variants between Bologna A XXXVIII and *Corona I*. One, not shown here, is a simple decoration in Bologna. The second, example 4b, may perhaps be explained by the lack of text in the print at this point. It is probable that Spataro, in deciding which words to set under this phrase, joined together Petrucci's repeated notes. The third variant is shown in plate 2. Petrucci's version produces a bare fifth at the last note of the fourth line (see example 4c), when only two voices are singing. The Bologna version avoids this, and employs parallel thirds by the simple expedient of altering the order of notes: the result is more in keeping with the style of the composer. It might seem that this could be an argument for the priority of the manuscript: however, it is just this sort of effect that would be noticed by the singer, and the sort of change that is most likely to be effected empirically; the result is well within the bounds of what might have been done by Spataro, who seems to have been particularly willing to change readings.

I suspect, as a result, that the type-setters' influence on ligature patterns is stronger evidence than that of the readings, none of which can be put down to anything stronger than Spataro's inventiveness. It is clear that the two sources are related: it might be argued that the case has yet to be proven, despite the light it throws on the importance of copyists' practices (either in the printing house or in the scriptorium). I am personally satisfied that it does indicate that Petrucci's first edition provided the material for the manuscript.

Finally, as a bonus (as it were), I wish to use the different editions of *Corona I* to show that the study of individual copies and editions of printed texts is as important, in the present context at least, as is that of individual manuscripts.

II

In a number of cases, it can be shown that the scribe of Padua A 17 copied from *Corona I*. In a sense, it may not matter which edition was used for this, for the manuscript was not started before all three had been printed. But, in examining the versions of Mouton's *Ecce genuit nobis*, the method can be seen *in vacuo*, without it appearing to be influenced by possible datings for the manuscript. The musical readings are identical in all three versions of the print, and are followed in Padua A 17, except for one minor variant, almost certainly a copying error, shown in example 5. There are three other manuscript sources of this work known to me, Cambridge, Magdalene College, Pepys 1760; London, BL, Roy. 8. G. VII; and Florence, BNC, II.1.232. Of the four, Padua is the only one that follows Petrucci's treatment of the final triple metre section, and it also has the same series of text placings. In the several places where Petrucci's men omitted a phrase of text, Paseto followed suit, although he twice added the repetition symbol *ij*, as elsewhere in this source.

All these points are treated identically in the three editions of *Corona I*. However, there are several trivial details which serve to distinguish the editions, and which indicate which of them was available to Paseto. The copyist seems, apart from his desire to clarify text-setting, to have been peculiarly mechanical in his approach: musical errors are present that he should have corrected, and there are other indications that suggest that he did not make many changes even in details. In the present work, even the vast majority of note-tails follow the pattern laid down by Petrucci. As a result, the exceptions appear to take on some significance. In example 5, Paseto follows the details of the second edition. So does he at the start of plate 3 – see, for example the second line of the manuscript. I think it may even be significant that he spells *iohañes* as does the second edition (more than the agreement in abbreviating *vidēs* and *dicēs*), for this is again a case where my two type-setters are involved in their own personal spelling patterns, and follow them (with different results) in the two editions. However, the scribe of Padua A 17 did have a freer approach to text than to music – and seems to have thought more about it. Thus, it is not surprising that his approach to minor detail differs for the altus and tenor voices, for these were set up by two different men in the second edition of *Corona I*, as a result reflect their differing habits, and would prompt the scribe differently. As a result, I do not believe these minor anomalies weaken — indeed, I think that, if anything, they strengthen — the view that Paseto was copying from the second edition of *Corona I.*

It can be shown in the same way that the version of Divitis' *O desolatorum consolator* in the second layer of Bologna Q27 (where it is preserved without the initial *O*) was copied from the last edition of *Corona I*, not printed before January 1520. There is only one musical variant between any edition and the manuscript, which is to be found only in a type alteration in one edition. However, the wording of the text, as well as its placing, in the manuscript always follows that of the third edition, which is slightly different from that of the earlier two. The layer of the manuscript containing this motet has been dated c1520 (22). On this evidence it can not have been copied earlier than that year.

Thus, I believe, every edition of these early prints must be regarded as a separate source. Indeed, in the case of Petrucci, every copy must be so treated, since many corrections were made in the printing shop. Each copy has therefore to be examined separately, regarded as an individual manuscript would be, in the development of any *stemma.*

I have, of course, ended by discussing filiation, even though I stated that the object of this paper was to show that other things were equally important. It will be apparent that I feel that much musicological work on *stemmate* has been of little value in evaluating readings, for it has not taken account of all the necessary elements. I hope to have shown that any attempt at creating a *stemma* will remain unsatisfactory until we have studied exactly what a scribe or type-setter intended, what he perhaps preferred, and until we have found out what he felt free to adapt. After that, we can ascertain some of the reasons for the variants that are preserved in our various sources. As Charlton Hinman said in his monumental study of Shakespeare's First Folio edition: *Bibliographical analysis ... can frequently demonstrate exactly how a given corruption in the text came about* (23). Only when we have demonstrated this, can we begin to look for exemplars and find a more correct pattern. Indeed, it is perhaps because this has not been done, that many scholars start by looking at filiations, but end by accepting the 'best-text' standpoint for their editions.

II

Once we have done as much as we can of this analysis, we can turn to the manner in which changes in notation, in triple mensuration patterns, in ligature usage or in underlay spread from one centre to the next — exactly the sort of measurement of the history of music or of notation in its change that Petrucci has fortunately provided us. Then, perhaps, we can go further and find patterns for the spread of the humanistic approach to text setting or for modern patterns of tonality. Perhaps, after all that, it will be time for the *stemma*: we will certainly be in a better position to argue about whether we could recover an *Urfassung*, and also in a better position to realise its limited merits.

Notes

1   The two principal sets of parts not listed in the International Inventory of Musical Sources (RISM) are those at Güssing in Austria (described in Hellmut Federhofer: Musikdrucke von Ottaviano Petrucci in der Bibliothek des Franziskanerklosters Güssing (Burgenland). — In: Die Musikforschung 16 (1963), p. 157—158, and those at Chatsworth in England, cited in my dissertation: Petrucci at Fossombrone: a study of early music printing, with special reference to the Motetti de la Corona (1514—1519). — London University 1976. The latter set comprises altus part-books of the following: Josquin masses I (the Fossombrone edition), Févin masses, La Rue masses and Agricola masses. In addition, not all the part-books formerly owned by Professor Erwin Jacobi (and now in the Zentralbibliothek, Zürich) are cited in RISM. Missing are the Bassus parts of 'Motetti de la Corona' I—IV and of Févin's masses.
     Further details are as follows. Several folios of Odhecaton A (RISM 1501), the first edition at Bologna, are in fact from the second edition (see my The 'first' edition of Odhecaton A. — In: Journal of the American Musicological Society 30 (1977), p. 183—207: the copy of Josquin I (1502) at US—R, is in fact of the Fossombrone editions, and there is also a second superius part-book at the same library: the additional copy of Odhecaton A, third edition, RISM 1504^3, mentioned in Gustave Reese: The first printed collection of part-music (the Odhecaton). — In: Musical Quarterly 20 (1934), is now at the New York Public Library: a copy of Dalza's fourth volume of intabulations exists at the Newberry Library in Chicago, lacking the last gathering: for the Fossombrone copies of Josquin's first and third volumes of masses, at both Rochester and Vienna, RISM suggests different publication

dates: in each case, the colophon pages have been exchanged, and the volumes are of the same date as the others (Jeremy Noble reports the Viennese case in his Ottaviano Petrucci: his Josquin editions ... (bibliographical reference given above, p. 224, note 7), while I date these and the Rochester parts in my dissertation, and in my Petrucci at Fossombrone: some new editions and cancels, to appear in the memorial volume for Thurston Dart): the copies of Motetti de la Corona I—IV listed for Vienna are in fact from the later Pasoti and Dorico reprints of these titles: the copy of the reprint of volume I at Bologna, is, in fact, of the 1514 Petrucci edition: there is a second copy of the Fossombrone edition of Josquin's second volume at Vienna: among the numerous faulty collations in RISM is the implication that the unique copy of Pisano's Musica at Seville is intact: in fact, some folios are lacking from the Altus part.

2   See Claudio Sartori: Bibliografia delle opere musicali stampate da Ottaviano Petrucci. — Firenze 1948 (Biblioteca di bibliografia italiana. 18) as supplemented by his Nuove conclusive aggiunte alla Bibliografia del Petrucci. — In: Collectanea historiae musicae 1 (1953), p. 175—210. Many of the details of the new editions and of their order will be found in my article for the Dart volume (s. note 1) and, in more detail, in my dissertation, chapter 6.

3   Apart from the problems with the first edition of Odhecaton, there are several other cases: Jeremy Noble has reported on some in his article cited in note 1: Martin Staehelin has kindly informed me that the Isaac copies have some variants: and I.report on others in my dissertation.

4   Professor Kellman's paper will be published elsewhere. Atlas' study has now been printed as The Capella Giulia Chansonnier (Rome, Biblioteca Apostolica Vaticana, C. G. XIII. 27), New York 1975 and 1977.

5   References to these details can be found as follows: Lawrence F. Bernstein: The bibliography of music in Conrad Gesner's Pandectae (1548). — In: Acta musicologica 45 (1973), p. 119—163; Catherine Chapman: Printed collections of polyphonic music owned by Ferdinand Columbus. — In: Journal of the American Musicological Society 21 (1968), p. 34—84; Frank d'Accone: Transitional text forms and settings in an early 16th century Florentine manuscript. — In: Words and music: the Scholar's view. A medley of problems and solutions compiled in honor of A. Tillman Merritt, edited by Laurence Berman. — Cambridge, Mass. 1972, p. 29—58; Donald Krummel: Bibliotheca Bolduaniana: a renaissance music bibliography. Detroit 1972 (Detroit studies in music bibliography, vol. 22); Marie Louise Martinez-Göllner, Die Augsburger Bibliothek Herwart und ihre Lautentabulaturen. — In: Fontes artis musicae 16 (1969), p. 29—48; Leeman Perkins: Notes bibliographiques au sujet de l'ancien fond musical de l'église de Saint Louis des Français à Rome. — In: Fontes Artis musicae 16 (1969), p. 255—269 (although Perkins does not draw the conclusion, it seems to me very likely that some of the items he lists were Petrucci prints: he also obscures the close connection between the 1516 manuscript

II

and the Antico prints of 1520 and 1521); Richard Schaal: Die Musikbibliothek von Raimund Fugger: ein Beitrag zur Musiküberlieferung des 16. Jahrhunderts. – in: Acta musicologica 29 (1957), p. 126–137; and Joaquin de Vasconcelles: Index da Livraria de Musica do muyto alto, e poderoso rey dom Ioão o IV. Nosso Senhor. – Craesbach 1649 (reprinted Porto 1874). There is one concordance in Glareanus' Dodekachordon with both Motetti B and the Motetti de la Corona: the details of ligature patterns and other notational devices show that Glareanus was copying from the earlier print. The copy of the Fossombrone edition of Josquin masses I now at Rochester, N. Y. has a binding with the Medici crest and the inscription "MED. PALAT. BIBL. CAES." The Petrucci part-books at Harvard are in a binding with a pasted-in sale catalogue entry which calls it "Spanische Arbeit, ca. 1510".

6   Printed in the present volume.

7   The literature in each of these fields is large and growing rapidly. In many ways, the standard work, Paul Maas' Textual criticism (3rd ed. – Oxford 1958) will not be superseded, although it is sadly behind current thinking. Particularly useful studies and case histories are Maurice Bévenot: The tradition of manuscripts: a study in the transmission of St. Cyprian's treatises. – Oxford 1961; Ernest Colwell: Studies in methodology in textual criticism of the New Testament. – Leiden 1969 (New Testament tools and studies, vol. 9); Vinton Dearing: Principles and practice of textual analysis. – Berkeley 1974; James Thorpe: Principles of textual criticism. – San Marino, California 1972; and Martin West: Textual criticism and editorial technique. – Stuttgart 1973. Each of these writers takes up his own position on the three basic approaches to textual criticism – the 'best-text' tradition, the stemmatic approach and the statistical view – but each is able to stand back and examine the others as well. Except for the last, they have useful bibliographies. I am at present engaged on a detailed study of the implications of modern thinking on textual study for musical editing.

8   Edward Clinkscale: The complete works of Antoine de Févin. – Diss. New York 1965, p. 145; David Gehrenbeck: Motetti de la Corona: a study of Ottaviano Petrucci's four last-known motet prints. – Diss. Union Theological Seminary 1970, p. 251.

9   A very interesting demonstration of what can be achieved is given in Silva Lake: Family Π and the Codex Alexandrinus: the text according to Mark. – London 1937 (Studies and Documents, vol. 5). See also the work by Bévenot, in note 7 above.

10   See note 3 above.

11   It is reasonable to suggest that the editor worked at all the parts of each piece before any were set in type, if only because Petrucci probably did not receive all the music for any volume from one source. (We can not, of course, go further to assume that the editor was consistent, beyond the extent to which

any editor has normal preferences for any situation.) Indeed, from this point in the argument, it might seem possible to replace my comments on the two type-setters with similar remarks on two editors (whenever I mentioned editorial decisions), if it were not that the patterns of differences are consistent for editorial and spelling details.

12   Charlton Hinman: The printing and proof-reading of the First Folio of Shakespeare. — Oxford 1963; T. Hill: Spelling and the bibliographer. — In: The Library, 5th ser., 18 (1963), p. 1—20. The paper read by W. and L. Helllinga at the recent London Caxton conference would appear to be a classic example of this form of analysis.

13   This is a critical point, and is discussed regularly in Shakespeare studies: see also Hill (note 12). This process is not to be confused with that called 'contamination', which represents the deliberate absorption of readings from one source into a copy made from another.

14   The standard descriptions of the scribal process include the habit of memorising, from the exemplar, the section to be copied next: see A. Dain: Les manuscrits. — Paris 1949, p. 40—46. There is no reason to assume that music scribes worked differently, though I am, as yet, not so sure of the habits of Petrucci's type-setters. It seems to me at least possible that they memorised only one symbol at a time. An excellent analysis of the results of the use of memory in copying can be found implicit in the conclusions in Ernest Colwell: Scribal habits in early papyri: a study in the corruption of the text. — In: The Bible in modern scholarship, ed. J. Philip Hyatt. — Nashville 1965, p. 370—389.

15   Full details can be found in my dissertation (see note 1). The evidence suggests that Petrucci regularly employed two men to set type, at least at Fossombrone.

16   The evidence for cancel pages and stop-press corrections comes in part from detailed comparison of individual copies of each title, as well as from bibliographical study (watermarks, etc.). Such study also makes apparent many of the other corrections, as well as showing their inter-relationship in different copies. The use of stamped-in notes after erasure is confirmed by the measurements of the type employed, which do correspond to those of Petrucci's type. Manuscript corrections of the same errors, with the same ink and apparently the same pen, and plausibly in the same hand occur in different copies of the same titles. Further details are in my dissertation. Curt Bühler has shown similar changes (except for the practice of stamping-in, for which I know no other cases) in the work of Aldus Manutius: see, for example, his Stop-press and manuscript corrections in the Aldine edition of Benedetti's Diario de bello carolino. — In: Papers of the Bibliographical Society of America 43 (1949), p. 265—272, reprinted in his Early Books and manuscripts: forty years of research. — New York 1973, p. 138—144.

17   It is important to realise that the processes of analysis that produce these dates

II

are purely bibliographical not depending in any way on the musical readings or the visual appearance of the page. It is a reliance on the latter that has led some scholars astray. The details are discussed in full in my dissertation, chapters 5 and 6, and outlined in my article for the Dart memorial volume, see note 1.

18   This has been discussed by Lewis Lockwood in Josquin at Ferrara: new documents and letters. — In: Josquin des Prez, ed. Edward Lowinsky. — London 1976, p. 103—137. See also John Constant: Renaissance manuscripts of polyphony at the cathedral of Padua. — Diss. University of Michigan 1975, p. 42 and 51, and also the explicit of the manuscript.

19   Morales: Opera Omnia, vol. 3, preliminary p. 41. The motet is also preserved in Bologna, Q19, Casale Monferrato, L (olim B), and Madrid, Medinaceli, 607.

20   Edward Lowinsky: The Medici codex of 1518: a choirbook of motets dedicated to Lorenzo de'Medici, Duke of Urbino. — Chicago 1968, S. iii, p. 62—65.

21   David Crawford, Sixteenth century choirbooks in the Archivio Capitolare at Casale Monferrato (1976), p. 67—68. I believe that the Antico prints were probably more frequently used for copying manuscripts in other centres than were those of Petrucci.

22   Lowinsky: The Medici codex, iii, 114—115.

23   Hinman: The printing (see note 12), preface.

POSTSCRIPT

Filiation studies have historically been concerned with the inter-relationship of readings, and the possibility of recovering some parts of an Urtext. A valuable statement of the current position for music can be found in James Grier, *The Critical Editing of Music* (Cambridge: Cambridge University Press, 1996), and an important discussion of the distinction between variant and error in his "Scribal Practices in the Aquitanian Versaria of the Twelfth Century: towards a Typology of Error and Variant", *Journal of the American Musicological Society*, xlv (1992), 373–427. Once one steps beyond the conventional boundaries of the methodology, that distinction becomes significant for its ability to reveal evidence of local practices and taste, spelling and etymology. This is particularly important for music, where every element of the notation was somehow to be reflected or transformed during performance. It is for this reason that I see the present paper as merely a starting-point for more detailed investigation, of the sort presented in later chapters of this book.

II

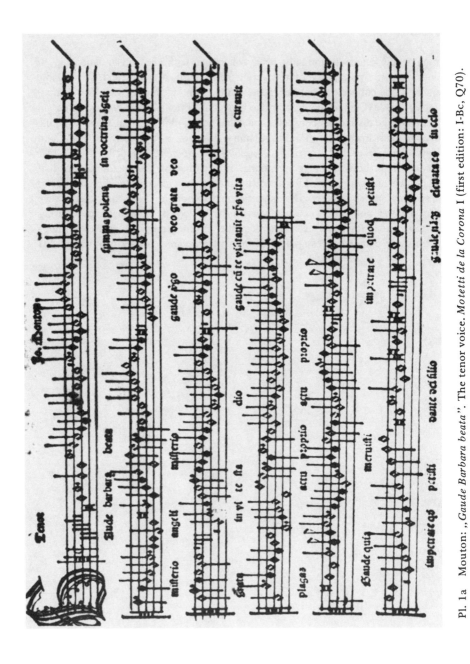

Pl. 1a   Mouton: „Gaude Barbara beata". The tenor voice. *Motetti de la Corona I* (first edition: I-Bc, Q70).

268

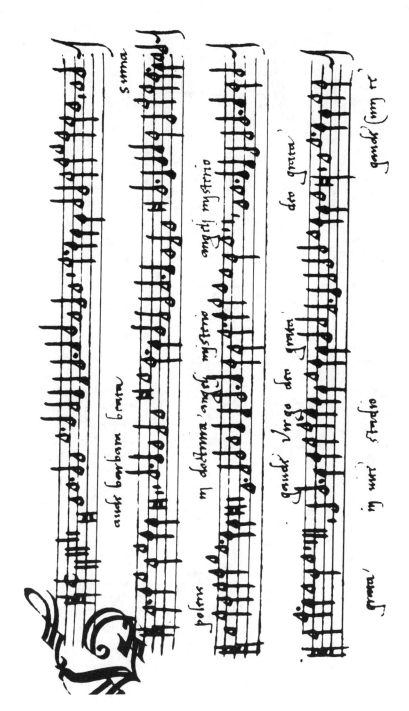

Pl. 1b   Mouton: „Gaude Barbara beata". The tenor voice. I-Rvat, Ms. Pal. lat. 1980-1.

II

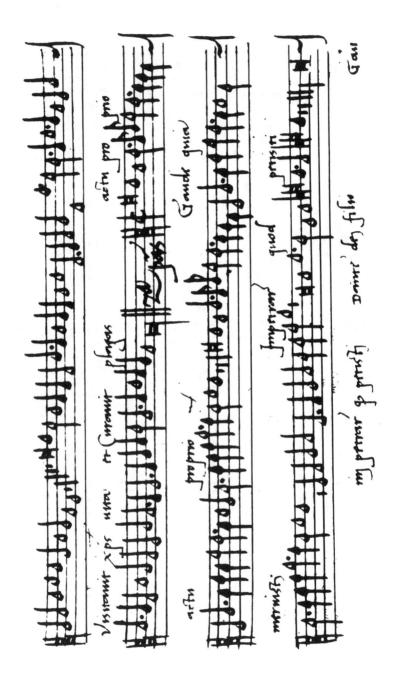

Pl. 1c Mouton: „Gaude Barbara beata".

II

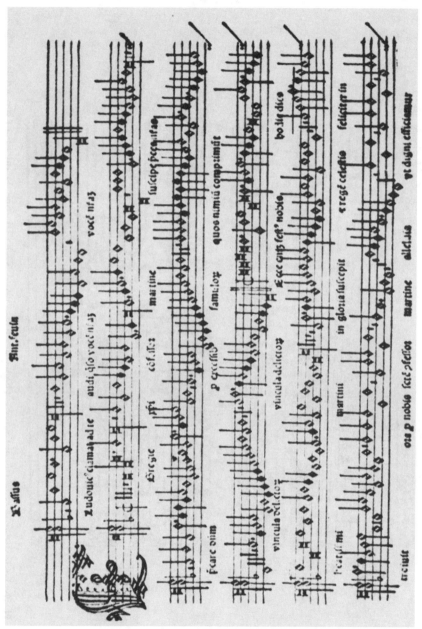

Pl. 2a Fevin: „*Egregie Christi confessor*". The bassus. *Motetti de la Corona* I (first edition: I-Bc, Q70).

271

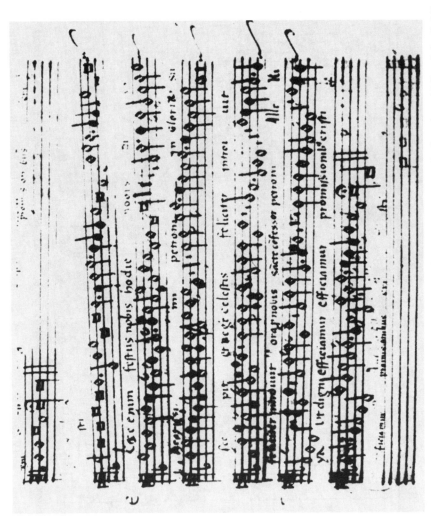

Pl. 2b Fevin: „*Egregie Christi confessor*". The bassus. I-Bsp, ms. A XXXVIII. See the middle of the 3rd line.

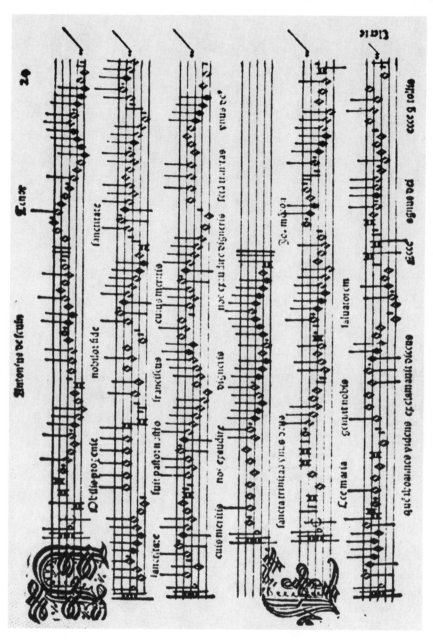

Pl. 3a Fevin: „*Nobilis progenie*". The tenor. *Motetti de la Corona I* (first edition: I-Bc, Q70).

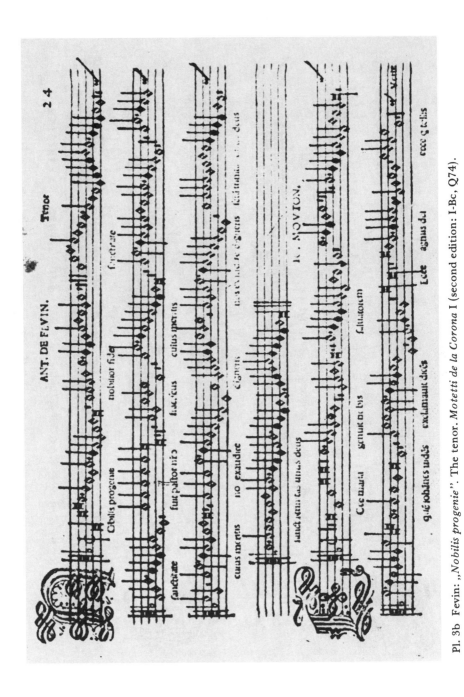

Pl. 3b Fevin: „Nobilis progenie". The tenor. *Motetti de la Corona* I (second edition: I-Bc, Q74).

274

Example 1a

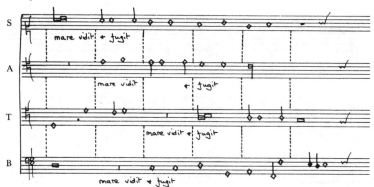

Example 1b

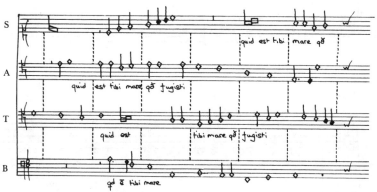

Example 1c

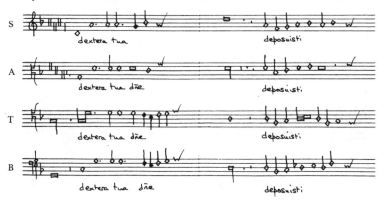

Example 2a

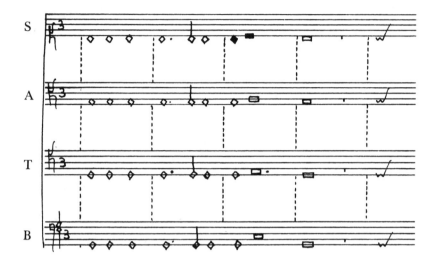

Example 2b

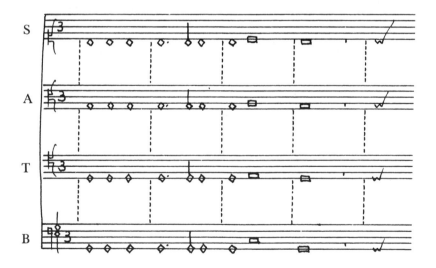

Example 3

Corona I: *et al.*

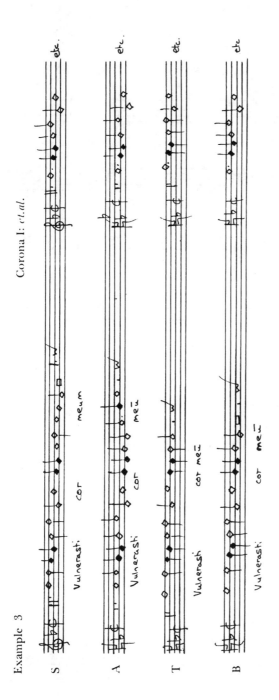

Example 4a

Corona 1   I-Bsp. A XXXVIII

Example 4b

Corona 1

I-Bsp. A XXXVIII

Example 4c [halved note values]

Corona 1

I-Bsp. A XXXXVIII

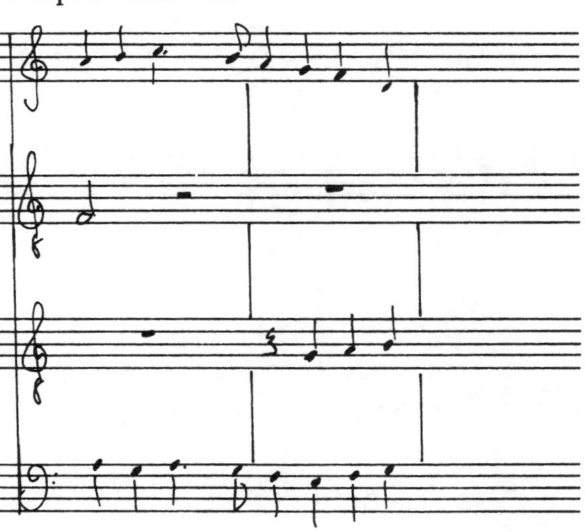

Example 5

I-Pc A 17

Corona 1, First Edition

Corona 1, Second Edition

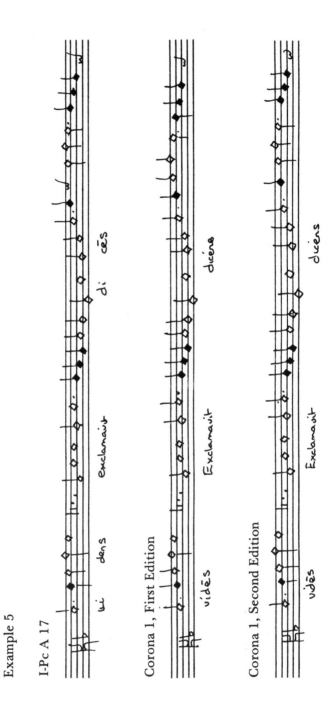

III

A Case of Work and Turn
Half-Sheet Imposition in the
Early Sixteenth Century

ONVINCING EVIDENCE OF THE TECHNIQUE used for half-sheet imposition in early books has always been hard to obtain, especially in
those cases — the majority faced by the student of early printing —
where relatively few copies survive. It might seem logical that the normal
procedure would be work and turn, in which two half-formes were
imposed in the same forme, printed together, and then the sheet turned for
perfection. The obvious advantages of this procedure over those of its
principal alternative (in which the two half-formes were imposed in different formes, completed either by furniture or by material from elsewhere in
the volume) as well as the evidence for its use in later periods, would tend to
suggest that the idea of work and turn must have occurred to printers early
in the history of the craft. However, as remarked by Gaskell, 'It is seldom
possible to tell which method [work and turn or worked together] has been
used in printing particular half-sheets in quarto or octavo'.[1] The present
paper offers convincing evidence of the use of work and turn as a way of
handling half-sheets of text for a small sample of books printed early in the
sixteenth century, and (incidentally) draws attention to a related aspect of
the printing of music.

The survival rate of books from this period is so low and relatively
haphazard that many of the most obvious ways of detecting work and turn
— ways which work for later periods — are virtually useless. Thus the
suggestion, first made by McKerrow and followed up by Povey, that
patterns of paper use should indicate the manner of half-sheet imposition, is
of almost no value unless one has a relatively large sample of the original

---

[1] P. Gaskell, *A New Introduction to Bibliography* (London, 1974), p. 83.

print-run.[2] The presence of two slightly different states of a half-sheet is much more likely to indicate the existence of a replacement or cancel leaf, or of stop-press correction: the possibility of it indicating that each half-forme had been set up twice to make a pair of formes, unlikely enough in itself, cannot be confirmed unless more than half the print-run has survived, an equally unlikely possibility. Thirdly, it is true that the careful identification of individual sorts on both half-formes should normally eliminate the possibility of work and turn procedures: but, even in the rare cases where it is possible to make such an analysis, the absence of any such sorts on both faces of the sheet is of no value as evidence. Finally, it should be possible to determine the process used on the basis of an analysis, for each copy, of which forme for the half-sheet was first through the press. It would probably be sufficient to find just one copy that differed from the rest — if identical in other respects (such as the treatment of stop-press corrections, etc.) — to be able to postulate that the two half-formes had been imposed together.[3]

Ideally, we need a form of evidence which could be adduced from one copy, and which would confirm beyond doubt that work and turn had to be the process employed: the obvious place to look for such evidence is in the skeleton forme. The pattern, for example, of running heads as retained from gathering to gathering will necessarily show whether a half-sheet was imposed in one forme or not. The retention of running heads can certainly be shown for Italian books of the early sixteenth century:[4] however, the nature of the books being set, as much as that of the captions themselves, often makes such evidence of only occasional value when addressing the present question. First, for many volumes, those features of the skeleton forme that leave evidence on the printed page are either very simple and (at least at first sight) consistent — width of lines on the page, placing of signatures, or placing and patterns of pagination, for example; or else subject to frequent change — the number of lines to the page, or changes in

<hr/>

[2] R. B. McKerrow, *An Introduction to Bibliography for Literary Students* (Oxford, 1927), p. 68; and K. Povey, 'On the diagnosis of half-sheet imposition', *The Library*, v, 11 (1956), 269–72. However, the suggestion, especially as Povey formulates it, takes no account of the effect of 'twin' marks on the patterns of use, nor of the virtual impossibility that all the sheets in a batch will reach the press in the same alignment after several handlings.

[3] Povey does make additional suggestions, including one regarding untrimmed copies: however, when he suggests that one can normally determine how a half-sheet was printed by examining two or three copies (p. 272), he ignores the problems inherent in sampling: any two extant copies have exactly a 50% probability of showing no useful evidence, with the sole exception of the identification of single sorts on both formes — evidence also obtainable, if at all, from a single copy. It needs to be stressed that so low, relatively speaking, is the number of surviving copies of any early book, that the absence of *any* piece of evidence in *every* surviving copy is of no value in determining many details of printing history.

[4] S. Boorman, 'Upon the use of running titles in the Aldus house of 1518', *The Library*, v, 27 (1972), 126–31. Similar evidence exists for earlier volumes.

the wording of the running heads themselves.[5] Secondly, the majority of early books will only show anything other than complete sheets in two places — in the preliminary matter or at the end of the volume (often an Index) — both places which are unlikely to employ the running heads to be found in longer runs in the body of the volume.[6]

However, music as printed from type by Ottaviano dei Petrucci has a much greater amount of material retained in the skeleton forme from gathering to gathering, sufficient to show that, for one printer at least, half-sheets were regularly imposed with both half-formes in the same forme, to be printed by the work and turn procedure.

Ottaviano dei Petrucci has been hailed as the first music printer or as the inventor of music printing. Neither claim is strictly true: music had occasionally been printed by wood-block before his first volume appeared, in 1501; and liturgical chant had already been printed from type for some decades, and particularly in Venice, the first city of his activity. However, Petrucci certainly was the first regularly to print choral and secular music from type. Since his productions are also among the most elegant of early printed music books, it is hardly surprising that he has attracted praise and extravagant claims.[7] But all the techniques he employed were largely available to earlier printers, especially in liturgical printing, and it seems likely that, at least initially, he merely adapted these techniques to his own special repertoire. During the first few years of his work, he seems to have

[5] Indeed, in a number of cases it is difficult to be sure that the headlines were truly part of a skeleton forme, rather than being lifted and replaced intact.

[6] I have not so far found evidence from this period of two half sheets, one at the end of the preliminary matter and the other at the end of the volume, certainly having been imposed in the same forme.

[7] The basic inventory of Petrucci's output is C. Sartori, *Bibliografia delle opere musicali stampate de Ottaviano Petrucci*, Biblioteca di bibliografia italiana, 18 (Florence, 1948), as amended and supplemented by his 'Nuove conclusive aggiunte alla "Bibliografia dal Petrucci"', *Collectanea Historiae Musicae*, I [= Biblioteca historiae musicae cultores, II], pp. 175–210. In almost every bibliographical respect, this work has now become outdated, apart from not including the non-musical works that Petrucci printed (see below, note 15). The list of Petrucci's editions, states and cancels is beginning to approach accuracy as a result of two recent and partially-overlapping studies: J. Noble, 'Ottaviano Petrucci: his Josquin editions and some others', *Essays Presented to Myron P. Gilmore* (edited by S. Bertelli and G. Ramakus), 2 vols (Florence, 1978), II, 433–45; and S. Boorman, 'Petrucci at Fossombrone: some new editions and cancels', *Source Materials and the Interpretation of Music: a Memorial Volume to Thurston Dart* (edited by I. Bent) (London, 1981), pp. 319–46. Detailed study of Petrucci's printing techniques and editorial methods is progressing: see S. Boorman, 'The "first" edition of the *Odhecaton A*', *Journal of the American Musicological Society*, 30 (1977), 183–207; and *id.*, 'Petrucci's type-setters and the process of stemmatics', *Formen und Probleme der Überlieferung mehrstimmiger Musik im Zeitalter Josquins Desprez* (edited by L. Finshcer), Quellenstudien zur Musik der Renaissance, I [= Wolfenbütteler Forschungen, 6] (Munich, 1981), pp. 245–80. See also C. Gallico, 'Dal laboratorio di Ottaviano Petrucci: immagine, trasmissione e cultura della musica', *Rivista italiana di musicologia*, 18 (1982), 187–206.

The present paper is part of a larger study of early music printing and printers (Petrucci, Antico, and Gerolamo Scotto), seeking to provide fuller bibliographical control over editions and contents, and to trace patterns of printing technique and editorial behaviour.

rapidly increased the rate at which he undertook to print volumes, and this may have something to do with the various changes in his technique that can be detected by 1509, some of which form the subject of this paper. During the second decade of the century, while he worked in his home town of Fossombrone from 1511 to 1519, he seems not only not to have advanced his technical procedures, but to have allowed the standards of his craftsmen to slip, at least as far as the visual impact of his books is concerned.

It is a feature of music printed from type that it requires the superimposition of one symbol (the note) upon another (the stave), either on the individual sort or (as in the case of virtually all music printed from type before the late 1520s) by a double-impression technique. In most volumes of liturgical music, where the stave is printed in red, the two separate impressions correspond with the two colours — staves and rubrication in red, text and musical notation in black — and this practice continued long after the introduction of single-impression type for polyphony.[8] However, the staves in most liturgical books do not appear consistently throughout a volume: they are used only when a text is to be provided with music, and are frequently interrupted for rubrics or for texts without music, and can hardly be considered as parts of a regular skeleton forme.[9] For the same reason, the headlines in liturgical books are continually changing, following the liturgical year, and so provide little scope for the analysis of their retention in any skeleton forme.

Petrucci was able to follow a more regular pattern. While running heads, when they appear at all, may last for only a few pages, there is a consistent and consistently laid-out sequence of musical staves (appearing on all pages with music).[10] Since Petrucci continued with the practice of printing the musical notation separately, to be superimposed upon the staves, the alignment of these latter elements had to be precisely controlled, so that the musical notation might be at the correct pitches. The actual tolerance is of

---

[8] I can see no ground for the commonly-held assumption that the red impression was always the first: indeed, it is demonstrable in a number of cases that it must have followed the black, for some sheets at least. Among other examples, there are the Hamman editions of the *Missale Romanum* of 15 October 1488 and 1 December 1493 (Weale 904 and 926), or his *Missale Sarum* of 1 December 1494 (Weale 1391) or the famous Emerich (Giunta) *Graduale Romanum* of 1499–1500 (Hain-Copinger 7844).

[9] The practice of setting red and black in the same forme, and then printing with friskets and patches, though well documented, cannot have been used for any forme with music and staves, since these two occupy the same space.

[10] Petrucci's staves consisted of blocks, probably of wood, into which were mounted five thin metal rules: the staves vary in length (at different times in his output) from 173 to 180 mm, and are usually just over 10 mm high on the page. Many liturgical printers used short segments of staves, which could be butted together to form a line; those for Hamman's *Missale Sarum* of 1 September 1494 (Weale 1390) for example, were in sections of about 16 mm or about 23 mm long, making up lines which at full were 87 mm. In later volumes he used single rules the length of the whole page. For further details, see M. K. Duggan, 'Italian music incunabula: printers and typefonts' (Ph.D. dissertation, University of California at Berkeley, 1981), pp. 163–219.

the order of 1 mm in a page of oblong quarto, the height of which was about 150 mm. The font of music itself had markedly different proportions from those employed for liturgical music, in particular having longer tails to many of the sorts, some of which I believe to have been kerned. Since these frequently impinged upon the area reserved for the text, between the staves, Petrucci seems to have been unable to follow the procedure of liturgical printers, that of printing the music and the text at one impression.[11] The evidence suggests that he printed his earliest volumes in three impressions — staves; musical notation and initial letters; text — not necessarily in that order.[12]

There are thus two levels of sets of formes, and two levels of passing the sheet through the press, for all works of Petrucci, and both need to be kept distinct in following this discussion. First is the set of formes (here, three), one for each impression of one face of the sheet of paper, comprising staves, notation, etc., and text, and each corresponding to one pass through the press. Then there is a different, second set of formes (and of passes through the press), all needed to perfect the sheet. In these early volumes, each sheet would thus have gone through the press six times: at least five formes were needed, for the forme of staves could be the same for each face of the sheet. However, sometime during 1503, Petrucci seems to have realized that staves and text could be printed at the same impression, and to have moved to a double-impression process[13] — albeit one that was different in its components from that followed by his colleagues printing liturgical music.[14]

Petrucci had now settled to the procedure that he was to retain throughout his career as a music printer. The books are all oblong in format, quarto in

[11] For details of his founts, with an examination of the evidence for the sizes of bodies and for kerning, see my 'Petrucci at Fossombrone: a study of early music printing, with special reference to the *Motetti de la Corona*, 1514–1519' (Ph.D. dissertation, University of London, 1976), chapter 5 and appendix 3.

[12] The evidence for this is not very strong: its essentials are that all three elements sometimes overlap each other — see, for example, the *Misse Josquin* of 27 April 1502 (sigs C4ᵛ, d5ᵛ and d7ʳ); some evidence of different depths of impressions for the three layers in the Harvard University copy of the same volume (Mus.786.2.501 (2)) — see sig. D1ᵛ in particular; and perhaps the fact that Petrucci seems at this stage to have had only one set of staves.

[13] The evidence from both *Misse Obreht* (24 March 1503) and *Motetti de passione . . . B* (10 May 1503) argues that Petrucci was using only one set of staves and was probably printing from three impressions: the next two volumes. which form the core of the present study, suggest that he had already made the change.

[14] Even the sheets containing pages without music, in so far as they never comprise a complete forme, went through the press twice. Apart from the technical necessity for this, evidence survives in the blind impressions of staves and of spare sorts used as furniture. Examples of both can be found in Petrucci's second book, *Canti B* (5 February 1501/2). In the only surviving copy (at Bologna, Civico Museo Bibliografico Musicale, Q52), uninked staves can be seen to have been used on the last recto, G8ʳ, and the blind impression of a row of musical sorts appears on the title-page, A1ʳ, as well as on D4ʳ and F7ʳ. Thereafter, this became normal procedure for Petrucci.

306   *A Case of Work and Turn*

eights, using two sheets to a gathering.[15] Each sheet now went through the press twice for each side — one impression with staves, usually six to a page, and the verbal texts; the other with the preliminary matter and colophon, as well as the music, the decorative capital letters, and, probably, such headlines as were used. Petrucci used both foliation and signatures, so that one sequence could be set with each impression. After the earliest volumes, he printed the individual voice-parts of sacred music in separate fascicles of one to three signatures. Since the contents of the four books of a set were often of different lengths (corresponding to the density of music for the different voices), Petrucci often had a single sheet or half-sheet at the end of one or more of the part-books. Thus the collation of the four parts of his *Misse Petri de la Rue* (31 October 1503) reads [Superius] A–B^8; [Tenor] C^{10}; [Altus] D–E^8; [Bassus] F^{8}G^6, and that for the *Misse henrici Jzac* [= Isaac] (20 October 1506), A^{8}B^{10}; C^{6}D^4; E–F^8; G^{8}H^6.

The music and the staves had to be precisely aligned in the two impressions, and, as a result, the habit of placing the staves in exactly the same places in the forme must have come early to Petrucci. It is a small step from that, albeit a crucial one for my argument, to the habit of *keeping* the staves in the same positions in the forme, merely altering the text for each sheet.[16] Evidence that Petrucci did just that, leaving the staves permanently in the forme, even from one volume to the next, can be gleaned from the damage done to some of the rules, damage which reappears in the same places on different sheets. This evidence marks many of the staves precisely, and can therefore be used to identify individual staves, and thus specific formes, for as long as the sets of staves are kept intact and in the same relative positions. The actual patterns of recurrence are, of course, conditioned by the special format of Petrucci's volumes, oblong quarto-in-eights, as much as by the number of formes in use. The following paragraphs give an example of the patterns that may normally be expected to result, given a simple collation.

[15] Three non-musical works printed by Petrucci survive. The most common today is by Paulus de Middelburgo: a folio edition of *De recta Paschae observatione* (8 July 1513); the other two are both quartos in the normal upright format: Castiglione, *Epistole de vita et gestibus Guidubaldi Urbini ducis* (29 July 1513) and Paulus de Middelburgo's *Parabola Christi* (20 November 1516). Two other titles are linked to Petrucci's name, but there is no evidence that they were actually printed by him. One, M. Fabio Calvo's translation of Hippocrates, survives in manuscript at the Vatican (Vat. Lat. 4416) with a colophon stating that it was printed by Petrucci on 1 January 1519 at the expense of Leontini Manente. The volume caused Petrucci some troubles and involved a visit to the papal court during 1519, but seems not to have been printed. The other is another work by Paulus de Middelburgo, a *Prognosticon*. There is no reason to believe that Petrucci might have printed this volume, for he had ceased printing over two years before the date that appears in the final sentence of the text. This is clearly a statement by the author and carries the date 1523 and the place Fossombrone. Among the various editions that have been noticed in the literature is one at the British Library (1609/754), which Dennis Rhodes has in a private communication tentatively assigned to Tacuino; a different one in Sander, No. 4573; and one cited by Manzoni as printed by Soncino.
[16] I doubt that the staves were strictly part of a permanent skeleton forme, if only because on occasion some of them are replaced. Further, there is one instance of the component staves appearing in different positions in the forme, as if easily removable; and there is also the situation to be found in the *Misse Brumel*, discussed below. However, the staves were clearly more permanent than most other elements of the forme, for they preserve the same positions, as the evidence here will show, while the text was necessarily reset.

A Case of Work and Turn

The third edition of the *Harmonice Musices Odhecaton A*, dated 25 May 1504, is a collection of (actually only 96) secular pieces, laid out with all the voices present in a single volume. The book collates A–N⁸, the musical staves begin on sig. A3ʳ, and the last leaf carries no music, bearing the colophon on the recto and a blank verso. Each page with music has six staves, when all are inked, of which three or four can normally easily be identified, as a result of curves in the rules or bends at one or the other end. These staves recur regularly in the same sequences on different pages, so that even the undamaged ones gain some identity by virtue of their juxtaposition with easily-recognizable examples. In addition, as a result of using the new staves which Petrucci had acquired (probably in early 1503, as I shall show), he was now working with sets that were slightly different in length, one series being about 173–175 mm long and the other about 178–180 mm: each page, in fact each forme, contains short or long staves only, without mixing the two lengths. The following table (Table 1) shows how the different sets of staves reappear throughout the volume: individual sets of staves are identified by italic numerals (merely as a means of keeping their notation distinct from all the other sets needed in a bibliographical analysis):[17]

TABLE 1. Pattern of identifiable recurrences of staves in *Harmonice Musices Odhecaton A* (third edition, Venice: Petrucci, 25 October 1504), copy at the Biblioteca Capitolare, Treviso

FOLIO	GATHERING												
	A	B	C	D	E	F	G	H	J	K	L	M	N
1ʳ	–	3	1	3	1	1	1?	1	1?	1?	1	3	1
1ᵛ	–	4	2	4	2	2	2	2	2	2	2?	4	2
2ʳ	–	1	3	1	3	3	3?	3	3	3	3	1	3
2ᵛ	–	2	4	2	4	4	4	4	4	4	4	2	4
3ʳ	1	1	1	3	1	1	1	1	1	1	1	3	1
3ᵛ	2	2	2	4	2	2	2	2	2	2	2	4	2
4ʳ	3	3	3	1	3	3	3?	3	3	3	3	1	3
4ᵛ	4	4	4	2	4	4	4	4	4	4	4	2	4
5ʳ	5	5	5	7	5	5	5	5	5	5	5	7	5
5ᵛ	6	6	6	8	6	6	6	6	6	6	6	8	6
6ʳ	7	7	7	5	7	7	7	7	7	7	7	5	7
6ᵛ	8	8	8	6	8	8	8	8	8	8	8	6	8
7ʳ	5	7	5	7	5	5	5	5	5	5	5?	7	5
7ᵛ	6	8	6	8	6	6	6	6	6	6	6	8	6
8ʳ	7	5	7	5	7	7	7	7	7	7	7	5	–
8ᵛ	8	6	8	6	8	8	8	8	8	8	8	6	–

[17] For convenience, the pattern presented here is taken from the copy now at the Biblioteca Capitolare, Treviso, since that is available in a reliable facsimile, published by the Bollettino Bibliografico Musicale in 1934. However, the patterns correspond in the copies at the New York Public Library (Mus. Res.*MN/P497), at the Bibliothèque de la Conservatoire in Paris (Rés. 538) and at the Library of Congress in Washington (M1490.P4. Case). I am grateful to Edward Jarvis of New York University for confirming many of the details that lie behind this general statement.

Since Petrucci is printing in quarto-in-eights, each gathering comprises two sheets of paper and four sets of formes, one for each layer of content, for each run through the press. These sets of formes, with the notation that I shall use to distinguish them in this paper, are as follows:

Outer sheet, outer forme (Io): 1^r, 2^v, 7^r, 8^v
Outer sheet, inner forme (Ii): 1^v, 2^r, 7^v, 8^r
Inner sheet, outer forme (IIo): 3^r, 4^v, 5^r, 6^v
Inner sheet, inner forme (IIi): 3^v, 4^r, 5^v, 6^r

It will be apparent at once that the four sets for each gathering use only two formes of staves, one containing the sets *1*, *4*, *5* and *8* (*I*) and the other made up of *2*, *3*, *6* and *7* (*II*). These staves had to be interlined with very little text; the regularity of the pattern and the consistency of most gatherings, as much as any other detailed measurement or analysis, show that they were kept in position throughout the printing of this volume. Indeed, gatherings A, C, E–L and N are identical — if one allows for a steady progression of slow modification as a result of the continuing use of the staves — while B and D can be seen to be the simplest of variations on this pattern, created solely by reversing inner and outer stave formes for one or both sheets of the gathering. The case of gathering M, apparently similar, is actually slightly different, although it has no bearing on the present discussion.[18] The evident result is that one of the two sets of skeleton formes used for printing this

---

[18] It might be argued from all this evidence that Petrucci was still using three impressions, and that all the staves were printed first, from a pair of standing formes containing nothing but the staves. However, there are several points which argue against this: one is the very presence of two formes of staves. If Petrucci were to run off all the staves first, there would be no need for a second forme of staves to perfect the sheet — a need that only arises when there is different content on the two formes. A second argument involves those sheets where the two formes appear in reversed positions: if this happened only in single copies, one would have no doubt that the staves were printed separately. However, it occurs in all extant copies, and the reason for it therefore should be sought in the process of type-setting, rather than in the presswork. Finally, there is some evidence on the printed pages which suggests that text and staves were printed together. There are cases where both have printed poorly, although the music is in good impressions: *Motetti de passione . . . B* (10 May 1503), copy at the Civico Museo Bibliografico Musicale, Bologna, sig. F7^r; *Canti C* (10 February 1503 [n.s. 1504]). copy at the Bibliothèque de la Conservatoire, Paris (Rés. 540), sigs K4^v and K7^r; *Motetti A* (second edition, 13 February 1504/5), copy at the Orszagos Szechenyi Könyvtar, Budapest (ZR523/coll. 1), several leaves (the existence of this unique copy has been signalled by Robert Muranyi, who has promised an article in a future issue of *Studia Musicologica*). There is a small number of cases where both text and staves are smudged: *Motetti libro quarto* (4 June 1505), copy at the Herzog–August–Bibliothek, Wolftenbüttel (2.8–11. Musica (4)), sig. N3^r (cf. sig. Q2^r, where the music and signature are smudged) is an example. Finally, comparison of two copies sometimes shows a slight lateral displacement of both text and staves in relation to the music.

The case of gathering M in the present volume is interesting. In B and D, the sequence of staves had been altered, so that inner and outer formes were exchanged. This does not affect the textual content of the volume, for both text and music formes were correctly imposed. However, in M, not only are the staves in the wrong sequence, but the text and music are both wrongly imposed in the outer sheet — the inner forme inverted in all copies. This is a case of presenting the sheet to the press with the foot in the place of the top. It seems to me likely that this was noticed after one impression, and retained for the second, although it was probably not noticed until the second was at least in part set up. As it happened, because of the layout of this volume, the rearrangement does not make nonsense, and could only be detected by a reader through comparison of contents with the index.

edition of *Odhecaton A* (that set which did not carry the music) comprised only two formes each of which had, as an integral part of its make-up, six staves for each page (Table 2).

TABLE 2. Pattern of recurrence of the formes containing staves in *Harmonice Musices Odhecaton A* (third edition) based on the evidence in Table 1

FORME	GATHERING												
	A	B	C	D	E	F	G	H	J	K	L	M	N
Io	*I*	*II*	*I*	*II*	*I*	*I*	*I*	*I*	*I*	*I*	*I*	*II*	*I*
Ii	*II*	*I*	*II*	*I*	*II*	*II*	*II*	*II*	*II*	*II*	*II*	*I*	*II*
IIo	*I*	*I*	*I*	*II*	*I*	*I*	*I*	*I*	*I*	*I*	*I*	*II*	*I*
IIi	*II*	*II*	*II*	*I*	*II*	*II*	*II*	*II*	*II*	*II*	*II*	*I*	*II*

The value of such evidence for detecting many details of Petrucci's sequence of work will immediately be apparent: not least, it provides a sure method for detecting the presence of work and turn procedures when handling half-sheets of matter.

I have already remarked that most of the volumes of sacred music divide the separate voices into separate part-books, and, as a result, have more complex collations. [19] Both the examples cited above, of music by LaRue and by Isaac, have half-sheets in their make-up, and both yield the crucial evidence to demonstrate that Petrucci did employ the work and turn pattern of half-sheet imposition, when necessary. The following Table 3 displays an analysis of stave distribution for the *Misse henrici Jzac*. (Note that the actual leaves represented on the inner and outer sheets will vary according to whether the gathering is of 6, 8 or 10 leaves; and that I have added to the notations Io, Ili, etc., that of III to indicate a half-sheet at the centre of a gathering, whenever it appears.)

It is again clear from this that all full sheets (with the exception of one in gathering F) were printed from only two formes of staves, and that these staves again follow a regular and logical pattern throughout the volume. Each of the half-sheets, however, only uses the staves from one forme, even though printed on both sides of the paper, and must therefore have been printed with all four pages of text imposed in one skeleton forme. The following collational diagrams (p. 311) show that the sequence of stave-sets presented in Table 3b is in fact the necessary one:

---

[19] Of the forty-nine different musical titles (both sacred and secular) that Petrucci printed, some of them in several editions, impressions or states, twenty-three were published in separate part-books — two of these in later editions with different collations. Of these twenty-five sets of part-books, twenty-two have at least one half-sheet in their make-up, while one other has survived as a fragment too incomplete for us to establish a collation.

A Case of Work and Turn

TABLE 3. Pattern of identifiable recurrences of staves (Table 3a) and of formes (Table 3b) in *Misse henrici Jzac* (20 October 1506), copy at the Civico Museo Bibliografico Musicale, Bologna

TABLE 3A

FOLIO	GATHERING							
	A⁸	B¹⁰	C⁶	D⁴	E⁸	F⁸	G⁸	H⁶
1ʳ	−	1	−	1	−	x	−	1
1ᵛ	2	2	4	2	2	x	2	2
2ʳ	3	3	1	3	3	3	3	3
2ᵛ	4	4	2	4	4	4	4	4
3ʳ	1	1	3	5	1	1	1	1
3ᵛ	2	2	2	6	2	2	2	4
4ʳ	3	3	7	7	3	3	3	5
4ᵛ	4	4	6	−	4	4	4	8
5ʳ	5	1	7		5	5	5	5
5ᵛ	6	4	8		6	6	6	6
6ʳ	7	5	5		7	7	7	7
6ᵛ	8	8	6		8	8	8	−
7ʳ	5	5			5	5	5	
7ᵛ	6	6			6	6	6	
8ʳ	7	7			7	x	7	
8ᵛ	8	8			8	x	8	
9ʳ		5						
9ᵛ		6						
10ʳ		7						
10ᵛ		−						

TABLE 3B

FORME	GATHERING							
	A	B	C	D	E	F	G	H
Io	I	I	II	I	I	I	I	I
Ii	II	II	I	II	II	II	II	II
IIo	I	I			I	I	I	
IIi	II	II			II	II	II	
III		I	II					I

TABLE 4. Collational diagrams showing the distribution of pages by formes in oblong quarto, for ten- and six-leaf gatherings, if the half-sheet is printed by work and turn

(a) Ten-leaf

Io
2^v	9^r
1^r	10^v

Ii
1^v	10^r
2^r	9^v

IIo
4^v	7^r
3^r	8^v

IIi
3^v	8^r
4^r	7^v

III
5^v	6^r
5^r	6^v

(b) Six-leaf

Io
2^v	5^r
1^r	6^v

Ii
1^v	6^r
2^r	5^v

III
3^v	4^r
3^r	4^v

In this diagram, if the four sets of staves that have appeared as 1^r, 2^v, 7^r and 8^v in most gatherings (or their equivalents in abnormal gatherings; that is, what I have called Io) are to appear as the only staves on both sides of a half-sheet, they will appear consecutively, as they in fact do in the centres of gatherings B and H. This is in itself sufficient to prove that, for the copy at Bologna, these gatherings include a half-sheet prepared separately and imposed for work and turn presswork.[20]

In the case of this volume, the only instance where the pattern of stave formes is inverted (the outer becoming temporarily the inner) is that of gathering C, which makes up one complete part-book, the Tenor. This evidence suggests, and the deterioration of the staves confirms, that the compositor was able to alternate the two stave-bearing formes throughout the title, and that this part-book presents its reversed arrangement merely because it follows on from the single half-sheet at the centre of gathering B. The half-sheet at the centre of gathering C returns the sequence to its normal appearance for the rest of the volume.[21] Finally, there is in gathering F an apparent anomaly, in so far as the outer bifolium seems not to use any of the fixed staves found elsewhere in the volume (although individual staves are found in other gatherings in different contexts): the probable explanation of this can be found by further analysis. In the copy at Bologna, and in the copies at the British Library in London (K.1.d.7) and the Österreichisches Nationalbibliothek in Vienna (S.A.77.C.4), this one bifolium is on a

[20] Strictly speaking, this evidence demonstrates only that one of the two impressions (that containing the staves) was printed using the work and turn technique. However, apart from the probability of such an easy solution to lay-out being applied consistently at both impressions, there is also the point that elements of the two formes involved — staves in one, music in the other — had to be very precisely aligned one with the other. The necessity for doing this must almost have ensured that formes would be selected which complemented each other, whether imposing a full or a half sheet.

[21] This evidence is, at first sight, rather strange, and suggests setting by formes rather than continuous setting: however, I believe that such a practice for the staves makes sense. There is good reason to believe that the formes containing the music were printed before those containing staves and text. The spacing is much more critical for the music, which is continuous, whereas the text is often interrupted by white space. (This is both because the text sorts take up relatively less linear space, and because the style of the music often involves a series of notes to be sung to the same syllable.) It would be reasonable therefore to set the music first and to align the text with it afterwards. Logically, the best manner of spacing the text correctly would be that of working directly either with the formes of music already set, or with a printed sheet from those formes. In either case , accurate spacing of the text, after the music has been prepared, would almost certainly presuppose setting by formes.

These conclusions also suggest (and they will be supported by other evidence, below) that the compositor set one book entirely, before beginning the next (i.e. the Cantus before the Tenor, then the Altus, etc.). However, this is far from true for all music printers. In the case of Petrucci's later volumes, I have been able to show the existence of two compositors, apparently working simultaneously (see the reference in footnote 11, above). Mary Lewis has demonstrated the existence of what she calls 'vertical setting' in some volumes from the press of Antonio Gardane. In this, all the voices for each separate gathering in an anthology were set up in sequence, before proceeding to the next. (M. S. Lewis, 'Antonio Gardane and his publications of sacred music, 1538–1550' (Ph.D. dissertation, Brandeis University, 1979), pp. 123–25.) Such a procedure, feasible only when each piece begins a new page, does have advantages if there are problems in the supply of copy for a volume, and perhaps, also, as Lewis suggests, benefit from retaining in the forme headlines and composers' names.

distinctive paper (one to be found in other, later Petrucci volumes), uses different individual sorts and initials in a different state, and suggests that a different compositor was involved. This all tends to argue that the bifolium is a replacement for the original leaves 1 and 8: so far I have not found a copy of the original form of the bifolium.

Thus, the examination of a sufficiently complicated skeleton forme can demonstrate, even in the case of a single copy, whether or not the printer used work and turn when faced with a half-sheet. In the case of Petrucci, it is perhaps worthwhile to try to discover when he began to use this technique.

Petrucci appears to have obtained a new set of staves sometime during the first half of 1503. *Motetti de passione . . . B* (10 May 1503) uses only one set of staves throughout, and one stave-forme appears also to have been used for two volumes which might otherwise have yielded evidence of half-sheet imposition — the first edition of *Misse Josquin* (27 September 1502; the four part-books collate A–C^8; D^{8}E^6; F–G^{8}H^4; J^{8}K^{10}) and the *Misse Obreht* [= Obrecht] (24 March 1503; A–B^{8}C^4; D^{8}E^6; F–G^{8}H^6; J–K^{8}L^4). The first volumes to show clear evidence of the new staves, also showing two different skeleton formes of staves, and therefore also yielding certain evidence of the imposition of half-sheets, are the *Misse Brumel* (17 June 1503; A–B^{8}C^4; D^{10}; E–F^{8}G^4; H–J^8) and the *Misse Ghiselin* (15 July 1503; A^{8}B^{10}; C^{10}; D–E^{8}F^4; G^{8}H^{10}), volumes that are of interest to bibliographers for other reasons as well. There are four half-sheets distributed between the two volumes, and for each the staves were printed by the work and turn procedure. The following Table 5 (p. 314) presents the information on sets of staves, and hence on skeleton formes, for both volumes (— the sets of numbers used here to denote each set do not correspond to the numbers used in the earlier tables, although they are consistent within these two volumes).

The evidence for half-sheet imposition is again clear in all the cases in *Misse Ghiselin*, while the identification of the individual formes of staves used for these gatherings confirms that none of the half-sheets was imposed with any other.[22]

The probability is that the half-sheet of sig. D5–6 of the Brumel volume was set in the same manner, although here one cannot be certain. With only one forme of staves in use, there can be no way of telling whether Petrucci actually removed one half of that forme and installed it, carefully aligned, in another forme; nor whether he set the two half-formes separately, and then ran the sheet only half-way into the press for each side, happening to choose the two different half-formes for the two sides of the sheet. However, he had

---

[22] In fact, the evidence that I have discovered so far seems to indicate that Petrucci did not set type for each piece or group of pieces in each book simultaneously: he seems rather to have worked through each part-book, one at a time. The only exception that I have found involves *Motetti C* (15 September 1504), where a second paper appears in the last gathering of each part-book, presenting a picture similar to that found in a number of volumes published by Antonio Gardane. See the reference to M. Lewis in the previous footnote.

A Case of Work and Turn

TABLE 5. Pattern of identifiable recurrences of staves and formes in *Misse Brumel* (17 June 1503), copy at the Österreichisches Nationalbibliothek, Vienna, and *Misse Ghiselin* (15 July 1503), copy at the Biblioteca Comunale, Assisi. (Note that the folio numbers are those of the forme, not of the gathering.)

TABLE 5A

FOLIO		Brumel A	B	C	D	E	F	G	H	J	Ghiselin A	B	C	D	E	F	G	H
Io	1^r	–	1	1	–	–	–	1	–	1	–	6	–	–	1	6'	–	6'
	2^v	2	2	2	2	5	5	5	5	5	7	7	5	5	5	7'	7'	7'
	3^r	3	3	3	3	3	3	3	3	3	8	8	3	3	3	8'	8'	8'
	4^v	4	4	–	–	4	4	–	4	–	9	–	–	4	4	–	9'	–
Ii	2^r	1	1	1	1	6	6	6	6	6	1	1	6	6	6	1'	1'	1'
	1^v	2	2	2	2	7?	7?	7	7	7	5	5	7	7	7	5'	5'	5'
	4^r	3	3	3	–	8	8	–	8	–	3	3	8	8	8	–	3'	–
	3^v	4	4	4	–	9	9	–	9	9	4	4	9	9	9?	4'	4'	–
IIo	1^r	1	1		1	1	1		1	1	1	6	1	1	6'		6'	6'
	2^v	2	2		2	5	5		5	5	5	7	5	5	7'		7'	7'
	3^r	3	3		3	3	3		3	3	3	8	3	3	8'		8'	8'
	4^v	4	4		4	4	4		4	4	4	9	4	4	9'		9'	9'
IIi	2^r	1	1		1	6	6		6	6	6	1	6	6	1'		1'	1'
	1^v	2	2		2	7?	7?		7	7	7	5	7	7	5'		5'	5'
	4^r	3	3		3	8	8		8	8	8	3	8	8	3'		3'	3'
	3^v	4	4		4	9	9		9	9	9	4	9	9	4'		4'	4'
III	1^r				1						6	6						6'
	1^v				2						7	7						7'
	2^r				3						8	8						8'
	2^v				4						9	9						9'

TABLE 5B

FORME	Brumel A	B	C	D	E	F	G	H	J	Ghiselin A	B	C	D	E	F	G	H
Io	I	I	I	I	II	II	II	II	II	III	III	II	II	II	III'	III'	III'
Ii	I	I	I	I	III	III	III	III	III	II	II	III	III	III	II'	II'	II'
IIo	I	I		I	II	II		II	II	II	III	II	II	III'		III'	III'
IIi	I	I		I	III	III		III	III	III	II	III	III	II'		II'	II'
III				I						III	III						III'

been using this particular forme with its staves in place for some time (it can easily be traced in the *Motetti de passione . . . B*) and there can have been little advantage in breaking it up and going through the process of aligning not merely the newly-created half-forme, but a new half-forme for the musical notation as well.[23]

Further, if the half-forme, sets *1 + 2* or *3 + 4*, had been removed, we could reasonably have expected it to remain in its newly-created forme when the new sets of staves were introduced. In fact, three of the sets of staves, *1*, *3* and *4*, are still to be found in the same forme, even though the fourth, *2*, disappears from the scene. Some of the staves from *2* do re-surface, but within the same forme, the third and fifth of the set of six becoming the third and second of the new set, *5*. As a result, when two sets of staves were finally introduced, one of them (the set *1 + 5 + 3 + 4*) was as nearly one of the the original sets as possible. It seems evident that some accident befell the set *2* at this point: but the retention of the others in the same forme does not argue against the possibility that sig. D5–6 was set with both faces in the same forme.

It is a coincidence — or at least looks like one — that the set of staves *2* should be broken up at exactly the same moment that the new forme of staves *6 + 7 + 8 + 9* first comes into use. Indeed, the whole situation at this point is of some interest for the light it throws on Petrucci's manner of organizing work in his shop, for there is other evidence of changes in the order of printing at this point. In order to illumine the sequence of events, and thus to throw light on when and where Petrucci began to use half-sheet imposition, I want to consider briefly his apparent rate of production, and then to introduce some new (and potentially contradictory) evidence. All this will bear on the probability that the two volumes, music by Brumel and Ghiselin, overlapped in their production.

When Petrucci was printing music at his fastest, in 1503 and the two following years, he produced about one hundred and twenty sheets in the year. This figure actually represents twice as much work for the pressman, and about one and a half times as much for the compositor, since all the sheets were involved in the two impressions. Furthermore, it does not take into account the number of cancel bifolia and replacement sheets that Petrucci prepared over the years.[24] However, even allowing for them, and

<hr/>

[23] The existence of only one forme of staves does not necessarily imply that Petrucci also worked with only one for the music. There is considerably less text on a forme than there is music on the corresponding forme, and the text was almost certainly much quicker to set: the compositor would almost certainly also work from one of the pair of formes when aligning the matter in the other (see above). It seems to me, therefore, that one can easily accept the use of two formes for the music and only one for the staves and text as an efficient manner of working.
[24] These seem to have represented a not inconsiderable proportion of his output. For some guide to this in his first title and in the late editions, see the references in footnote 7 above: a similar pattern is beginning to emerge for the volumes that Petrucci printed in Venice, although the details are still to be published.

for the inevitable holidays for the craftsmen, it seems unlikely that Petrucci's shop was able to set, print and perfect more than a maximum of about three sheets per week. The record for these years is the principal evidence for this, and suggests that there must have been times when the shop was working at full stretch. The publication dates and sizes of the extant volumes produced during part of 1503 make this clear (Table 6):

TABLE 6.   Production from Petrucci's press during part of 1503

TITLE	SHEETS AND HALF-SHEETS	DATE	ELAPSED TIME
Misse Obreht	18 + 2	24 March 1503	
Motetti de passione	18	10 May 1503	47 days
Misse Brumel	16 + 1	17 June 1503	37 days
Misse Ghiselin	15 + 3	15 August 1503	28 days
Canti B (2nd edition)	14	4 August 1503	20 days
Misse Petri de la rue	13 + 2	31 October 1503	88 days
Canti C	42	10 February 1504	102 days

(Easter fell within the period of preparation for *Motetti de passione . . . B*, and Christmas within that for *Canti C*; it may be relevant to note that *Misse Obreht* is dated the day before the Feast of the Annunciation, and *Misse Petri de la rue* the day before All Saints'.)

Any attempt at making precise calculations is, of course, fruitless — not least because of volumes that have been lost. It is unlikely, however, that additional titles were printed during the early part of 1503. This was in any case the time when he appears to have been most prolific, and the time of preparation of *Motetti de passione . . . B* with *Misse Brumel* and *Misse Ghiselin* or that of *Canti C* suggests that the shop was taking at least two days per sheet. The second edition of *Canti B* (demonstrably prepared from the first) would certainly have been quicker to prepare, apart from the possibility suggested by the paper pattern of the uniquely surviving copy (at the Bibliothèque nationale in Paris) that not all the volume was newly prepared at this stage: but, if all of it were newly set, then it was prepared at the rate of almost five sheets per week.[25] Surprisingly, *Misse Ghiselin*, taken by itself,

[25] In fact four different papers appear in this volume, of which three might reasonably have been expected to be there. The fourth, employed for four sheets, plausibly represents a different event, standing for leaves printed at a different time. If this is so (and I cannot yet prove it), the rate of work drops to little over three sheets per week.

also seems to represent over four sheets per week: fortunately, there is concrete evidence to suggest that this volume was started before *Misse Brumel* had been completed — evidence which helps to suggest that Petrucci's rate of work at this time did not normally exceed about three sheets per week.

The principal evidence suggesting an overlap in production is that of the patterns of paper used in the two volumes, which is not as straightforward as is normally the case in Petrucci's volumes. Of the surviving copies of the two volumes, I present here information on the papers for two of each.[26] Throughout, only two papers are used, with one small exception. They are:

(i) an anchor within a circle, surmounted by a star (49.5 mm wide, and very close to Briquet 493) with a countermark of the letters 'A B' (similar in style to the countermark shown under Briquet 497):

(ii) a countermark consisting of a small flower and a fleur-de-lis, the flower nearer the edge of the paper: they are 13 and 18 mm wide, respectively, and the stems are 39 mm apart:

(iii) a smaller anchor, without any circle (like Briquet 437, but 36 mm wide).

The patterns of use of these papers are shown in Table 7. It is notable that paper (i) is used for all the material in *Misse Brumel* which is printed with only one forme of staves ($1 + 2 + 3 + 4$) — with the exception of the half-sheet at

TABLE 7.   Distribution of papers in copies of *Misse Brumel* and *Misse Ghiselin*

	PAPER 1	PAPER 2	PAPER 3
Forme *I*	*Brumel*: A–C, DI–II	*Brumel*: DIII	
Formes *II/III*	*Ghiselin* (Assisi): AII	*Brumel*: E–J	*Ghiselin* (Assisi): AI
	Ghiselin (Bologna): A, BI	*Ghiselin* (Assisi): B–EI	
		Ghiselin (Bologna): BII, C–D, EI	
Formes *II/III* modified		*Ghiselin*: EII, F–H	

[26] The surviving copies of each are as follows:

Misse Brumel: Bologna, Civico Museo Bibliografico Musicale, Q57, lacking the last leaf of D, which contains no text, but has blank staves on the recto; Brussels, Bibliothèque royale, lacks the part-book for the Bassus, gatherings H and J; Milan, Biblioteca del Conservatorio G. Verdi, S.B.178/8, gatherings D, H and J only; Vienna, Österreichisches Nationalbibliothek, SA.78.C.10, complete.

Misse Ghiselin: Assisi, Biblioteca Comunale, Stamp.N.189 (2), complete; Bologna, Civico Museo Bibliografico Musicale, Q58, lacks the Tenor, gathering C; Florence, Biblioteca Marucelliana, R.u.115⁴, Bassus only, gatherings G and H, imperfect; Güssing, Franziskanerkloster, gathering C only, imperfect; Vatican City, Biblioteca Apostolica Vaticana, Sist. 235–8, complete. The copy of this title at Vienna, Österreichisches Nationalbibliothek, SA.77.C.15 is of a later edition.

the centre of gathering D. On the other hand, those sheets of the *Misse Ghiselin* printed on paper (i) do use the new sets of staves, even though gathering B of this volume preserved them in a different order. (Note that both the copies cited, as well as that at the Vatican Library, use the same staves in the same positions, even though some sheets are on different papers.)

A related element of evidence lies in the deterioration of these staves through continuing use. In some cases, particularly the set numbered *1*, gatherings A and B of the second volume show a better state than do E–J of the *Misse Brumel*. The change in order of these formes at the centre of gathering E of the Ghiselin volume coincides with an overhaul of the staves in both sets. While both can still be identified, clearly they were in part dismantled and reassembled in a better condition.

The conclusion seems inescapable that none of the sheets of the Ghiselin volume can have been perfected before the staves were printed for the half-sheet D5–6 of Brumel, still using *1* + *2* + *3* + *4*, since they use the modified version, *1* + *5* + *3* + *4*. On the other hand, the Ghiselin formes that use the stave-set *6* + *7* + *8* + *9* could have been printed at any time: this includes one forme for each sheet on paper (i). There seems to be no reason in the musical text why these sheets should not have been immediately perfected using the same staves, *6* + *7* + *8* + *9* (following the tradition then prevailing, as seen in the earlier gatherings of the Brumel volume): therefore, presumably, the use of the other set of staves was a part of a new house procedure.

The two transitions, that from paper (i) to paper (ii), and that from one forme to alternating formes, do not take place strictly at the same place in the two volumes, nor do they appear to follow a logical and convenient pattern. However, I believe that the evidence allows for a simple and instructive solution.

Despite some evidence suggesting that the musical text of these volumes was set by formes, I believe that it was probably set seriatim, at least for the second volume, the music of Ghiselin.[27] The pattern of paper distribution for both books is consistent with this, and with the situation where one

---

[27] Three places, shown in Table 7, imply that the musical text was cast off before being set, for each suggests that the inner forme might have passed through the press after the outer. (I am here assuming that the musical formes preceded those bearing the staves and text.) Two involve the transition from one paper to another: the innermost forme of gathering D of the Brumel is on a new paper, and the change from paper (i) to paper (ii) in the two Ghiselin copies follows a similar pattern. Perhaps more significant is the first appearance of the modified states of formes *II* and *III* of staves, on the inner sheet of gathering E of the Ghiselin.

Yet none of this is conclusive: the evidence of papers is open to the alternative interpretation that I offer here; while that of the formes relates only to the staves. There is some evidence that Petrucci's compositors were not yet setting music so carefully that they took account of the two different formes of staves — in their different lengths, for example: and, as I have shown above (note 21), the impression containing the staves (and the text) was probably set by formes. This, however, makes no assumptions about how the music was set.

paper is running out and is being replaced by a new one. (I believe we should ignore the unexpected appearance of paper (iii) in Ghiselin.)[28] If so, the Ghiselin book was started during the preparation of gathering D of Brumel's volume; the first and part of the second gatherings were printed largely using paper (i), although that began to run out during the printing of gathering B. Sometime during this process, the tenor part (gathering D) of the Brumel book was also nearly finished, but was exhausting the stock of paper (i) at that press.[29] I suggest, therefore, that the irregular appearance presented by Table 7 is no more than the evidence of two presses, working simultaneously, and running out of paper independently.

There is certainly no need to suggest that gatherings A and B of Ghiselin could not have been started before the end of D of Brumel: the only restraint is that they could not have been perfected before it was finished — for they show the modified staves $1 + 5 + 3 + 4$. Indeed, one of the two impressions of the second side could have been printed, even on the formes using this modified group of staves, for the music could have been prepared quite independently.

It seems to me likely that Petrucci decided to test his new set of formes on a new title, rather than introducing them in the middle of one part-book of the book of Brumel. He therefore would have had part of Ghiselin's first gatherings prepared and printed, both musical and stave formes, to see that all was well. At least some of this probably happened while the remainder of gathering D of the Brumel was going through the press. However, it would make sense to finish gatherings A and B of the new book, for that completed one part-book — the Cantus, forming a discrete unit in the finished volume. After that, as the deterioration in the typographical material suggests, Petrucci logically went back and finished the volume of Brumel, before continuing with that of Ghiselin.

The plan, apparently developed by Petrucci sometime during the early months of 1503, to run two sets of staves, can only make sense if he were also

---

[28] The presence of paper (iii) for one sheet of the Assisi copy is almost certainly accidental, and to be attributed to an anomaly in the paper supply. This paper is not to be found in any other volume printed by Petrucci in these years, and yet the Assisi copy is clearly of the same setting of type as that found in the copy at Bologna. Further, the inner forme of this sheet is not even one of the first through the press, for it contains a stop-press correction to the signature of sig. A2^r — a correction found, stamped in by hand, only in the Bologna copy.

[29] I am assuming here that Petrucci had two presses in operation by this time. I think it is possible to present a case for his having the use of only one press for as long as he was using only one skeleton forme of staves. As I have suggested above (footnote 23), the relative time taken to set the text in these formes, as well as what was probably a very slow process setting Petrucci's particular form of music type, suggest that he needed only one text forme, and was able to distribute and compose for it twice in less time than it took to set a music forme once. However, the adoption of two stave-and-text formes does argue for a change in house practice; coupled with the noticeable increase in productivity, it suggests a greater capacity in both composition and press-work. It is also true that the presence of two presses would make the distribution of papers that are found in the two volumes here discussed much more of a commonplace.

planning to adopt a process involving only two impressions. For, as long as he was working from three impressions, the staves were printed separately and could, at least from the start of 1502, have been prepared in bulk for the whole volume — or even for more than one, if his plans were well enough formulated.[30] Under such circumstances, there was no real need to have a second set of staves. Indeed, there were advantages to having only one set. There could then be no danger of printing a forme of music over the impression of the 'wrong' forme of staves, and of consequent misalignment of notes on the stave. However, as soon as Petrucci went to two impressions, the staves became part of a forme whose content changed, for it contained the verbal texts and certain other incidental matter. At this point there must have been real advantages to having more than one skeleton of staves. Even though the setting of the text would have taken a fraction of the time required to set the music, the presence of only one forme would have slowed the process. With more than one, the only restraint would have been in ensuring that the forme used for the musical notation matched that used for the text and staves.

(It is possible that Petrucci had experimented a little with two impressions before he put into train the preparation of the second set of staves. Several leaves of *Motetti de passione . . . B* show (in more than one copy) very poor inking of both text and staves — in places where the music has a fine impression — suggesting that both were inked at the same time, and therefore perhaps in the same forme. However, the distance between staves and text is very inconsistent from leaf to leaf, ranging from 6 mm to 9 mm (measured from the foot of an 'x' to the foot of the staves): further, the staves appear in the same sequence from forme to forme. If Petrucci were exploring the possibilities of two impressions, he must have been working with staves that were already part of a skeleton forme, and fitting the text between them.)

One result of this change to two formes of staves is that Petrucci now had to decide how to print half-sheets, for the lay-out offered by the two formes would be slightly different. Earlier half-sheets — there are two in *Misse Josquin* (27 September 1502) and two in *Misse Obreht* (29 March 1503) — appear in volumes printed from only one forme of staves. Indeed, in the first case, it is not entirely clear that these staves had acquired a consistent position within the forme, retained in place either rigidly or merely by practice. For the second title, there is one set only, a permanent feature of each sheet, but there is no evidence from the state or use of this forme as to whether the two half-sheets were prepared by work and turn procedures.

---

[30] It is possible that Petrucci printed the staves separately and in bulk for his first title, the first edition of *Harmonice Musices Odhecaton A* of 1501, even though each leaf shows one inset stave, to leave space for an initial capital letter. This practice did not last into 1502: see S. Boorman, 'The "first" edition of the *Odhecaton A*', passim.

However, by the time of the half-sheets in the Brumel and Ghiselin volumes, Petrucci had clearly realized that the staves should be a permanent part of one skeleton forme in a two-impression process, and had decided how to handle the half-sheets. As the evidence above has shown, the half-sheet at the centre of gathering B of the *Misse Ghiselin*, planned at much the same time as that at the centre of gathering D of the *Misse Brumel*, was probably printed after it, since the stocks of paper (i) seem finally to have run out. In that case, Petrucci's first attempt at half-sheet imposition by work and turn can be assumed to have been the bifolium D5–6 of his *Misse Brumel*, printed some time before its publication on 17 June 1503, probably towards the end of the previous month.[31]

[31] I wish to express my thanks to the curators of all the libraries owning copies mentioned here, who have allowed me free access to their collections and supplied me with microfilm. I also acknowledge with gratitude the kindness and the facilities afforded me by the Harvard Centre for Italian Renaissance Studies at Villa I Tatti, Florence, and by the Music Librarian there, Kathryn Bosi.

III

POSTSCRIPT

This paper was written for a bibliographical journal, and the conclusion stops at the point where technical issues no longer come into play. However, it is important to speculate about why Petrucci should have had to print the Ghiselin volume in such a hurry. The evidence that Ghiselin had been hired by Ferrara, and was on his way there when this book went to press (even though he did not take up the position), is presented in Lewis Lockwood, *Music in Renaissance Ferrara, 1400–1505: the creation of a musical center in the fifteenth century* (Cambridge, MA: Harvard University Press, 1984). A similar pattern of dates concerns the first book of Josquin's masses (with the luxurious spacing present in the first edition) and the hiring of Josquin, also at Ferrara, and the details are given in Lewis Lockwood, "Josquin at Ferrara: new documents and letters". *Josquin des Pres: Proceedings of the International Josquin Festival-Conference held at the Julliard School at Lincoln Center in New York City, 21–25 June 1971*, ed. Edward E. Lowinsky, with Bonnie J. Blackburn (London: Oxford University Press, 1976), 103–136. I draw the conclusion that some faction at the Ferrarese court had promoted the publishing of these two books, in my "The 500th anniversary of the first music printing: a history of patronage and taste in the early years / 500. obletnica prvega glasbenega tiska: k zgodnji zgodovini mecenstva in okusa", *Musikoloski Zbornik*, xxxvii (2001), 33–49.

IV

PRINTED MUSIC BOOKS OF THE ITALIAN RENAISSANCE FROM THE POINT OF VIEW OF MANUSCRIPT STUDY

THE tradition of manuscript study, in musicology, seems to have grown from a concentration on the single source: we have long asked how the individual manuscript was copied, and how that might relate to its content and function. It is only more recently that we have turned to the larger study of individual scribes and scriptoria, building up pictures of their whole output, their policies on presentation and repertoire, and the taste they represented.

By contrast, the tradition of study of printed sources, again within musicology, has proceeded in exactly the opposite direction. We began with catalogues of the whole output of a printer, and studies of his general techniques and repertoires. Only more recently have we begun to study the individual source: only more recently have we started to treat the individual edition or copy as a curious phenomenon, worthy of examination at the same level as that accorded the individual manuscript.

It is this last approach that I wish to discuss today: I believe that the printed book went through almost all the processes that were also involved in preparing a manuscript. As did scribes, printers cared about their patrons, they changed their minds, deciding to expand a book or to replace some folios; they sometimes acquired their music from diverse sources; they divided the work among different people; and, not infrequently, they miscalculated.

The evidence for these actions and events lies in the sources: it is what has elsewhere been called «scientific». While this is not an unfair term to use, yet we must realise that the interpretation of this evidence is necessarily subjective. I am reminded of the Rembrandt project, which has tried to define the painter's *oeuvre* on the basis of technical features and processes, while eventually having to fall back on connoisseurship for final decisions.

In the same way, the technical evidence found in printed books, presented, indeed, obvious, in almost all copies, needs interpretation, after which it reveals histories as complex as those of many manuscripts. I propose, today, rather than building up a grand theory for handling these types of evidence, and for their interpretation, to offer a few simple case-studies.

*   *   *

Among the most interesting of these forms of evidence are those which indicate some sort of a hiatus in the preparation of the book, a hiatus which often can be related to the musical content.

An interesting case concerns the *Frottole libro sexto* published by Petrucci in early 1506.[1] As Example 1 shows, the paper pattern in both extant copies is enough to alert the scholar to one of a number of possibilities: perhaps the two odd sheets were replacement sheets, of four folios each, because of some technical problem: perhaps they come from a different edition entirely; perhaps they represent some problem in the preparation of the content.

In fact, the Tavola gives the key to the problem. This was printed at the front of the volume following the title, on folio A1v, and was almost certainly prepared last. In addition, however, the pieces in gathering A are entered in the Tavola out of sequence, as my Example 1 also shows. It seems reasonable to argue that parts of gathering A, at least, had to be re-done, at a late stage in preparing the volume. The presence of works by Honophrius Antenoreus and Philippus de Lurano mark off this layer, neither re-appearing until the end of the book, except for one piece on folio B8v. This first gathering is also remarkable among Petrucci's frottole volumes in containing the only three-voiced works, the *giustiniane* which represent an earlier tradition, and which are otherwise unknown in Petrucci's volumes.

There must be some significance to the fact that it is the *first* gathering which is changed, to include pieces by two minor composers, and these *giustiniane* settings. I am convinced that, at a late stage in the production of Petrucci's book, some-one wanted to change this important

---

[1]   *Frottole libro sexto*, Venice, Petrucci, 5.ii.1506 (n.s.). RISM 1506³: copies at A-Wn and D-Mbs. See Sartori, *Bibliografia delle opere musicali stampate di Ottaviano Petrucci*, Biblioteca di bibliografia italiana, 18, Florence, 1948, n.° 25. This will be entry number 30 in my forthcoming *Ottaviano Petrucci: catalogue raisonné*. Throughout this paper, I cite the particular copies consulted. Printed editions survive in copies almost as unique as are sequences of manuscripts.

Watermark pattern

gathering and sheet	watermark
A outer	initials A and B
E inner	initials A and B
all others	hill and cross

Tavola

Sequence of pieces entered for certain initial letters, giving the page number found in the Tavola (and the folio for gathering A):

initial letter	pages listed	
	first sequence	later additions
A	12-45,	6 (A5v), 5 (A4v)
C	13-43,	3 (A2v)
M		4 (A3v), 8 (7v)
N	25-51,	2 (A2r)
Q	42,	9 (A8v)
S	11-50,	7 (A6v)

Content

Gathering A	works by Philippus de Lurano Honophrius Patavinus Anon. à 3
B to the end	Cara, Tromboncino, Nicolo Pifaro

(The gathering joins have single-page pieces: B8v has a single-page piece by de Lurano)

Example 1. *Frottole libro sexto*, Venice, Petrucci, 5.ii.1506.

first part of the content, and that Petrucci acceded to this plan. When we note that Petrucci's early music editor, Petrus Castellanus, was away from Venice, in Recanati, for part of 1505,[2] it seems clear that this

---

[2]   Boer, *Chansonvormen voor het einde van de XVde eeuw*, Amsterdam, 1938, p. 51, fn., quoting from the *Monumenta Ordinis Praedicatorum Historia*, ix, p. 48. Blackburn, in *Petrucci's Venetian editor*, a paper read at King's College, London, in 1991, develops this point. I am grateful to Professor Blackburn for giving me a copy of this paper.

collection of music was overseen by some other editor, who had his own agenda to meet.

In other cases, there is evidence of a change not only of paper, but also of the printing type. Several copies of Petrucci's editions from the second decade of the century, the mass volumes of Josquin among them,[3] contain two different type faces, appearing on different pages. The clearest evidence comes from the text type, which is in a rotonda face on some pages, and in roman on others. While it might be that two different craftsmen prepared the text for printing, in this instance the pages actually come from two different printings, prepared some years apart and sold and bound up together.

Similar evidence has also recently surfaced, though as yet unpublished, from music printers of the other end of the century. Indeed, I have also heard recently of a case where parts of editions from different printers and cities were bound up together, probably some time after purchase, to make a single composite volume.[4]

In most such copies, although both layers were printed in the same shop, we are effectively dealing with a document which has been made up from two different sources prepared at different times. These cases should be treated like any *konvolut* manuscript, that is as combinations of different sources. Such documents have something to tell us about the popularity of the music they contain.

There *are* other cases, where similar changes reflect a delay in production, rather than the blending of two impressions. The earliest such that I have found so far again concerns Petrucci: his edition of Brumel's masses was halted after production of the Cantus and Tenor books, which already use two papers (see Example 2).[5] An important technical innovation, the use of two rather than three impressions, can be seen in the later part-books. It might seem that the delay was merely so that Petrucci could perfect his new and simpler process. But, more significantly, work on an edition of Ghiselin's masses began at exactly this time, before the Brumel book was finished. Once the Ghiselin was well under way, work

---

    [3] Jeremy Noble, «Ottaviano Petrucci: his Josquin editions and some others», *Essays presented to Myron Gilmore,* edited by Sergio Bertelli and Gloria Ramakus, Florence, 1978, ii, p. 433-445; Stanley Boorman, «Petrucci at Fossombrone: some new editions and cancels», *Source Materials and the Interpretation of Music: a memorial volume to Thurston Dart,* edited by Ian Bent, London, 1981, p. 129-153..

    [4] See the forthcoming paper by Anne Gross on the many editions of the *Septiesme livre des chansons,* to be published in *Fontes artis musicae.*

    [5] Brumel: RISM B4643; Sartori, *Bibliografia,* n.° 8: copies at A-Wn, I-Bc, I-Mc and PL-Kj. Ghiselin: RISM G1780; Sartori, *Bibliografia,* n.° 9: copies at A-GÜ, I-Ac, I-Bc, I-Fm, I-Rvat and PL-Kj. The paper patterns are basically the same for all copies.

Edition and sheets		Paper	Impressions
Brumel:	Cantus and Tenor	1	3
	Tenor (centre sheet)	2	3
Ghiselin:	Cantus	2 and 3	2
Brumel:	Altus and Bassus	3	2
Ghiselin:	other parts	3	2

Example 2. Brumel: *Misse*, Venice, Petrucci, 17.vi.1503.
Ghiselin: *Misse*, Venice, Petrucci, 15.vii.1503.

seems to have progressed on both volumes simultaneously.[6] There must have been some incentive for Petrucci to turn to the Ghiselin material and produce it at short notice, delaying work on the Brumel. Perhaps the same incentive encouraged him to develop the more rapid technique.

It can hardly be a coincidence that Ghiselin was re-hired by the Ferrara court at the turn of 1502-03, and apparently arrived there some time during the summer of 1503. Given the Ferrarese bias of other Petrucci volumes, the implication seems to be that Ferrara, which certainly had been consistently favourable to Ghiselin and his music, commissioned this particular volume, and caused Petrucci to delay work on that of Brumel's music.

Each of these cases has employed an apparent disruption in the preparation of a book to argue for a musical or historical point. Each has been based on evidence drawn from the materials used to prepare the edition. Each has concerned paper or typographical material of some sort, and has led to questions about the circumstances in which a book was prepared.

* * *

The next group of examples is concerned with the manner in which a book was put together, with the number of compilers or with evidence for how the music was collected, including apparent changes of plan.

In these, there may be no apparent anomalies—the paper, the type, the format, all the technical elements will probably be consistent throughout.

---

[6] The details of the bibliographical analysis are presented in Stanley Boorman, «A case of work and turn half-sheet imposition in the early 16th century», *The Library*, ser. 6, viii (1986), p. 301-321.

Here, though, I am turning to another aspect of bibliographical study, with its own parallel in codicology: this concerns the patterns whereby printers laid out material, and the routine manner in which they went about their work.

One of the harder elements to detect, but one of great importance, is the presence of two type-setters working on the same edition. The analogous position, that of two scribes in the same manuscript has a self-evident importance for study. It is often made more evident in manuscripts, in the different character of their two hands: but in printed sources, the music and text types will usually be visually the same. We can often only identify the presence of two craftsmen from some aspect of their normal working habits.

Some years ago I pointed out evidence for Petrucci's division of work between two craftsmen, in the form of different ways of spelling certain words and of handling proportional signs.[7] Often, though, the most obvious evidence is not in the text, but in the peripheral matter. It is only recently that I have noticed some other instances:

Two men seem to have been involved, for example, in Scotto's 1603 edition of Metallo's *Magnificat a quattro & a cinque*.[8] This first becomes evident because Scotto miscalculated the size of the volume being set, and each part-book took one more gathering than expected. This problem was apparently not detected until after the gathering signatures had been allocated to each part-book, and sections of each had been set in type. As Example 3 shows, the original plan was for three letters to be assigned to

Signature patterns			
Cantus	Tenor	Altus	Bassus
A-D^4	D-F^{4}ff^4	G-K^4	K-M^{4}mm^4

Example 3. Metallo: *Magnificat à 4 & à 5*, Venice, eredi G. Scotto, 1603.

---

[7] Stanley Boorman, «Petrucci's type-setters and the process of stemmatics», *Formen und Probleme der Überlieferung mehrstimmiger Musik im Zeitalter Josquins Desprez*, edited Ludwig Finscher (= *Quellenstudien zur Musik der Renaissance*, I, = *Wolfenbütteler Forschungen*, VI), Munich, 1981, p. 245-280; and Stanley Boorman, «Notational spelling and scribal habit», *Datierung und Filiation von Musikhandschriften der Josquin Zeit*, edited Ludwig Finscher (= *Quellenstudien zur Musik der Renaissance*, II, = *Wolfenbütteler Forschungen*, XXVI), Wiesbaden, 1983, p. 65-109.

[8] RISM M2435, copy at GB-Lbl.

each part-book. With a fourth gathering becoming necessary, the two type-setters seem to have taken different ways of coping with the problem of adding a signature. One merely inserted the next letter, ignoring any complications this might raise for the binder: the other followed a more common pattern, repeating a letter, though with distinguishing symbols.

Evidence for two workers also exists in the second edition of the *Odhecaton A,* of 1503,[9] though here involving the part-names chosen for the fourth voice—*Contra* and *Altus.* Example 4 shows the pattern, spread out across the 13 gatherings of the book: with only one exception, this voice part, whatever we call it, is found on *rectos* only. It is surely significant that the first 6 gatherings, A-F, follow one pattern, while the next 6, G-M, follow the other. I presume that two type-setters divided the work up evenly. When they came to the last gathering, they did the same, each taking two openings, usually one composition, at a time.

I think that two craftsmen were also involved in Gardano's second edition of *Flos Florum Primus liber cum quatuor vocibus,* of 1545,[10] on the basis of similar changes of pattern at the mid-point of each part, at the beginning of the fourth of six gatherings.

Part names (all called *Contra* in the first edition)

    Altus: A4r-F8r, N1r-N2r, N5r-N6r

    Contra: G1r-M8r, N3r-N4r, N7r, N7v

Compositions in gathering N

M8v-N2r	Obrecht	*Tsaat een meskin*
N2v-N4r	Hayne	*Ala audienche*
N4v-N6r	Anon.	*La turatu*
N6v-N7r	Josquin	*De tous bien plaine*
N7v	Anon.	*Meskin es tu*
N8r	[Colophon; Register; Device]	

Example 4. *Odhecaton A* (2nd edn.), Venice, Petrucci, 14.i.1503.

---

    [9]   RISM 1503²; Sartori, *Bibliografia,* n.° 5. In addition to the copy cited in RISM as at E-Sc, parts of this edition also survive in the copies at I-Bc (otherwise of the first edition) and US-NYp (otherwise of the third).

    [10] RISM 1545⁴. The book is described in Mary Lewis, *Antonio Gardano, Venetian music printer, 1538-1569: a descriptive bibliography and historical study,* i, New York, 1988, p. 501-502.

2594

Once again, I want to insist that these represent situations in which two scribes were at work on the same source, each with his own inclinations and habits: in some instances, one seems to have been more up-to-date or advanced in his approach to part names or to signatures. In *all* such cases, however, we are justified in regarding the two typesetters' work as representing two different sources, ones which, as so often with manuscript sets, do not survive as complete volumes. The details of evidence which produce such a situation seldom change our view of the musical contents, though they always affect a history of dissemination.

Similar details, however, *can* be used to show evident changes in the planned content, made during the production of a printed edition. Perhaps one of the best late Renaissance examples concerns a volume of motets by Massaino, his Opus 31, published in 1606 by Gardano.[11] This book begins with eight-voiced pieces, and contains an index of them, before beginning on the larger works. The folios allocated for the index are indicated on Example 5. It might be thought that this index was seen as a mere convenience for the users, although I find the idea of an index in the middle of a volume more than a little disconcerting. *Prima facie,* it is more likely that the larger-scale works were a later addition to the book.

Signature pattern			Index for à 8	Blank page
Cantus	A-B^{4}C^6	AA^{4}BB^6	C6r	C6v
Tenor	D-E^{4}F^6	DD^{4}EE^6	F6r	F6v
Alto	G-H^{4}I^6	GG^{4}HH^6	I6r	I6v
Bassus	K-L^{4}M^6	KK^{4}LL^6	M6r	M6v
Cantus 2	N-O^{4}P^6	NN^{4}OO^6	P6r	P6v
Tenor 2	Q-R^{4}S^6	QQ^{4}RR^6	S6r	S6v
Alto 2	T-V^{4}X^6	TT^{4}VV^6	X6r	X6v
Bassus 2	Y-Z^{4}Aa^6	YY^{4}ZZ^6	Aa6r	Aa6v
Nonus	Bb-Dd^4			
Decimus	Ee-Ff^4			
Undecimus	Gg^6			
Duodecimus	Hh^6			

Example 5. Massaino: *Sacri modulorum Concentus... Opus 31*, Venice, Angelo Gardano, 1606.

---

[11] RISM M1285, copy at I-Rsc.

In fact, the bibliographical evidence confirms that the book was conceived originally as containing only eight-voiced works: the signature pattern for this book used the single letter sequence, A-Z, followed by Aa to complete the second Bassus book. Not coincidentally, the internal index lies on the last recto of each single signature: C6r, F6r, and so on, to Aa6r, while the last verso of each is blank. Finally, Aa1r has a typical addition to the signature, the word «finis», used by Gardano and others to indicate the last gathering of a book.

At this point, someone decided to add the pieces for larger ensembles, which required the addition of extra gatherings to the extant part-books, as well as new part-books for voices 9-12. These all had to be signed in a distinctive manner: Aa had already been used in the second Bassus, so that such an alphabet could not be used for additions to the existing parts—although, as you can see, there was no problem in using it for new partbooks. Thus, the first eight books have a third pattern of signature present on their additional gatherings, one which uses doubled capital letters as its signature.

Here bibliographical evidence—the patterns of signing gatherings, coupled with the placing of an intermediate index—makes it clear that the larger pieces were a later addition to the planned volume. Massaino, or Gardano himself, decided that these works would add to its popularity.

Another curious example is in Gardano's edition of Willaert's first book of 6-voiced motets (see Example 6).[12] The signature pattern is

Signature pattern					
Cantus	Tenor	Altus	Bassus	Quintus	Sextus
A-E^4 + ^{4}	F-K^4 + ^{4}	L-P^4 + ^{4}	Q-V^4 + ^{4}	X-Z,AA-BB^4 + ^{4}	CC-GG^4 + ^{4}

Contents	Composers
gatherings 1-5 (except last folio)	Willaert (18, one rightly Mouton); Berchem (2: n.ºs 3 and 18)
gatherings 5 (f. 4) and 6	Pieton; Willaert; Berchem; Verdelot; Jachet; Anon.; Maistre Jan

Example 6. Willaert: *Musicorum sex vocum... Liber primus*, Venice, Antonio Gardano, 1542.

---

[12]   RISM 1542^{10} and W1112; the details are taken from Mary Lewis, *Antonio Gardano*, i, p. 343-347. The volume is edited in Adrian Willaert, *Opera Omnia*, edited by Hermann Zenck and Walter Gerstenberg, Corpus mensurabilis musicae, iii, vol. 4.

enough to alarm the scholar: it is unlikely that a printer such as Gardano would miscalculate by some 17%. The signatures would rather suggest that the last gathering of music was an afterthought, especially when we consider the pattern of attributions for this last gathering. Mary Lewis has already suggested that Willaert probably had little to do with this edition:[13] the addition of such a group of pieces, perhaps to help in sales, would confirm that suspicion.

Similarly instructive, I believe, are the 1558 Scotto edition of *Madrigali a notte negre,* the first book of Casulana's madrigals à 4 (printed by de Sabbio of Brescia in 1583), and the 1626 Vincenti edition of Buonamente's fourth book of instrumental music.[14] The patterns of signatures suggest that the printers were faced with last-minute additions. This appears to be confirmed from the arrangement of the contents, in both the Buonamente edition and that of *Madrigali a notte negre.* Then, too, we should examine the Vincenti and Amadino edition of *Musica de diversi autori, libro primo* of 1584,[15] in which the signature problems account for almost 40% of the content.

Such supplementary additions seem to have occurred quite often: indeed both Scotto and Gardano published a supplement to their editions of Rore's settings of Petrarch, containing the last five stanzas of his setting of *Vergine bella.*[16] However, the examples I am discussing here emerge through a study of the bibliographical structure of the sources.

Sometimes the evidence for an expansion of a volume lies more in the layout and repertoire than it does in the bibliography. Certainly, in manuscript study, the appearance of new pieces on the last versos or first rectos of internal gatherings of a volume in choirbook-format is enough to alert the scholar. So should it in a printed source. As an example, I mention the edition of *Fioretti di frottole II* of 1519.[17] (See Example 7) The first six gatherings concentrate on the music of de Maio, with a few

---

[13] Lewis, *Antonio Gardano,* i, p. 347.

[14] These are recorded in RISM as, respectively, 1558[11], C1517 and B4941. The third is published in facsimile as *Archivum musicum, Strumentalismo italiano,* xlvii.

[15] RISM 1584[4]. A description and study, by Beth Lee Miller, of this and other editions produced by Vincenti and Amadino is forthcoming.

[16] The original editions are cited in RISM at 1548[9] and 1548[10]. The second of these editions is described in Lewis, *Antonio Gardano,* i, p. 610-616. See also Alvin Johnson, «The 1548 editions of Cipriano de Rore's third book of madrigals», in *Studies in musicology in honor of Otto E. Albrecht,* edited by John Hill, Kassel, 1980; and Mary Lewis, «Rore's setting of Petrarch's 'Vergine Bella': a history of its composition and early transmission», *The Journal of Musicology,* iv (1985-1986), p. 365-409.

[17] RIMS 1519[4], copy at I-Fm. The book is inventoried in Knud Jeppesen, *La Frottola,* i, Copenhagen, 1968.

Contents	
gatherings A-F:	Anon. (2): de Maio (10): Bernardo (1): Cara (1): Carpentras (1)
gatherings G-M:	Cara (2): Tromboncino (10): L.M. (1): Ranieri (1): Anon. (4)

The change of content at the end of gathering F	
F2v	I.T. de Maio
F4v	I.T. de Maio
G1r	L.M.
G1v	[Anon.]
G3v	B.T.

Example 7. *Fioretti di frottole I*, s.l., s.n., 9.x.1519.

other pieces, one of which suggests a Roman origin for the group. However, on arriving at gathering seven, signed G, the repertoire changes radically: it is now totally north Italian, Cara, Tromboncino, Ludovico Milanese and Ranier comprising all the named composers. It seems likely that we have here something more than merely a change in repertoire.

In such cases, the evidence is sometimes indicative of a late addition, especially when the printer normally prints his *Tavola* or his colophon at the end of a book and a new group of pieces begins just before the end of a gathering. An example would be that of Petrucci's first book of frottole (Example 8).[18] The burst of pieces by Michele (Pesenti) begins just where one might expect an addition, on a last verso of a gathering (D8v), and itself imposes the need for a miscellany to fill out the last gathering.

I can not be certain, of course, whether these changes represent an actual and unexpected change in plan, or whether the intention to produce a volume of a decent size necessitated using music from different sources. However, the suddenness of the changes, coupled with the coincidence of their placing, suggests that they were not merely the fortuitous result of the need to build up a larger volume.

If the coincidence of repertoire and composer in these two examples argues that the additional music was acquired while the volume was in production, in many other cases such evidence says more about how the

---

[18]   RISM 1504⁴; Sartori, *Bibliografia*, n.° 16, copies at A-Wn and D-Mbs. The music has been edited by Rudolf Schwarz, *Publikationen älterer Musik*, Jahrgang viii, Leipzig, 1935; and in Gaetano Cesare and Raffaelle Monterosso, in *Instituta et Monumenta*, vol. 1, Cremona, 1954.

Folios	Space occupied	Works	Composers
A2r	1 folio	1 piece	Brocco
A2v-B7v	$13\frac{1}{2}$ openings	16 pieces	Cara
B8r	1 folio	1 piece	Brocco
B8v-D3r	11 openings	11 pieces	Tromboncino
D3v-4r	1 opening	1 piece	Michele
D4v-5r	1 opening	1 piece	Tromboncino
D5v-6r	1 opening	1 piece	Michele
D6v-8r	2 openings	2 pieces	Tromboncino
D8v-G1r	17 openings	21 pieces	Michele
G1v-G7v	$6\frac{1}{2}$ openings	a miscellany, seven pieces by seven composers.	

Example 8. *Frottole libro primo*, Venice, Petrucci, 28.xi.1504.

editor or collector had acquired the music for himself, music which later was arranged for printing. As an example, I cite Petrucci's *Frottole IV*.[19] A very synoptic pattern of the distribution of pieces can be seen in the handout (Example 9). It tends to suggest that someone built up the collection of music from a group of diverse sources, probably over a period of time.

Folios	N.º of pieces	Composers
A1r-1v	[Title and Tavola]	
A2r-8v	10 pieces	Cara (1); Capreolus (5); Anon. (3); B.T. (1)
B1r-8v	14 pieces	Lurano (1); Tromboncino (3); Cara (3); d'Ana (1); Anon. (6)
C1r-C8v	16 pieces	Patavino (4); Anon. (3); d'Ana (7); B.T. (1); M (1)
D1r-D8v	16 pieces	Anon. (9); B.T. (5); M.C. (1); F.V. (1)
E1r-E8v	11 pieces	Anon. (2); Philippus de Lurano (3); Capreolus (6)
F1r-F8v	15 pieces	Anon. (13); Compère (2)
G1r-G7v	9 pieces	Philippus de Lurano (9)

Example 9. *Frottole libro quarto*, Venice, Petrucci, [1505].

---

[19] RISM 1505[5]; Sartori, *Bibliografia*, n.º 21: copy at D-Mbs. The music was edited by Rudolf Schwarz, *op. cit.*

Unfortunately, we can not aver that the printed collection was acquired in such a manner: it is just as likely that the edition represents an earlier slow gathering together of manuscript collections on the part of the editor.

This sort of evidence arguing for the manner in which the music was gathered, is particularly effective for volumes of frottole and madrigals, where each opening often contains a single piece.

There is more evidence, in fact, more concrete evidence for additions at press-time, however, in the sort of problems of planning that I mentioned when discussing the editions of Metallo or of Willaert.[20] However, it is not always easy to tell whether such evidence truly indicates the addition of one or two pieces, or whether it merely implies a lack of foresight.

In some instances, it seems that the printer did actually miscalculate: such would include Animuccia's first book of madrigals, printed by Gardano in 1547, the edition of Falcidio's masses, printed by Gardano's sons in 1570, or their edition of Asola's first book of three-voiced masses, of the same year.[21] And yet, we forget at our peril that the printer's craftsmen were just that, craftsmen, and experienced in music. For that reason, I incline to accept errors of calculation more willingly when only one or two part-books are involved, and to look more confidently for evidence of changes in plan when all the books of a set show the same strange structure.

These points are laid out in the various instances presented in Example 10. A printer who can plan to produce model 1 should not normally produce model two. There is the same amount of music in each,

	Cantus	Tenor	Altus	Bassus	
1.	A-C^{4}D^6;	E-G^{4}H^6;	I-L^{4}M^6;	N-P^{4}Q^6	planed accurately in advance and signatures set to plan.
2.	A-D^{4}D^2;	E-H^{4}H^2;	I-M^{4}M^2;	N-Q^{4}Q^2	not planned accurately. More probably a late addition.
3.	A-D^4 + ^{2};	E-H^4 + ^{2};	I-M^4 + ^{2};	N-Q^4 + ^{2}	either possibility, although an addition is more likely.
4.	A-D^4 + ^{2};	E-H^4;	I-M^4 + ^{2};	N-Q^4	planned from the Tenor book.

Example 10. Music and ancillary matter for 18 folios in the Cantus.

---

[20] See examples 3 and 6 above.

[21] These are cited in RISM at, respectively, A1421 (also in Lewis, *Antonio Gardano*, i, p. 552-554), F68, and A2505.

and he could have produced model one at any point before working on the last four folios. Model three is, of course, the same as model 2, although it is marginally more possible that model 3 would have been intended from the start. Model four is, I think, self-explanatory as a result of a plan made by the printer, but using the wrong data.

A miscalculation is typified by the edition of Corfini's second book of motets, printed by Alessandro Gardano in 1581.[22] (See Example 11.) There are extra gatherings at the end of several books. Gardano probably based his calculations on the amount of music in the Tenor book. The other books did not fit so satisfactorily into the same space. Similar patterns can be found in many 16th-century and early 17th-century Italian editions. The Tenor seems to have been the controlling element for music printers, however much we, as historians, may say that the Cantus had taken over, in stylistic terms.

*   *   *

There were other problems, not always satisfactorily resolved by the printer. Gardano's type-setter seems to have missed out a large section of music in Massaino's *concentus* of 1576.[23] A single leaf is tipped into the

Signature pattern					
Cantus	Tenor	Altus	Bassus	Quintus	Sextus
A-D^{4}D[2]^2	E-H^4	I-M^{4}M[2]^2	N-Q^{4}Q[2]^2	R-V^{4}V[2]^2	X-Z,AA-BB^4.

Actual gathering structure of the Cantus						
A1-2:	A3-4:	B1-2:	B3-4:	C1-2:	C3-4:	etc.

Imposition of the Cantus		
Correct	As imposed	
3r 2v	3r 4v	and similarly imposed
4v 1r	2v 1r	for the other forme.

Example 11. Corfini: *Il Motetti à 5-12*, Venice, Alessandro Gardano, 1581.

---

[22] RISM C3932: copy at I-Bc.
[23] RISM M1266.

Cantus part, with the annotation «Questa carta va posta drieto il numero 22 in Cantus».

Another technical problem involved the manner in which pages were to be arranged in the press. The differences in order found in the third edition of Petrucci's *Odhecaton A* (1504)[24] are merely the result of laying out the pages incorrectly in the forme, of faulty imposition. Much the same seems to have happened in the Cantus part of the edition of Corfini's motets which I have just discussed: (see again Example 11).

A very similar problem also beset Giacomo Vincenti, when printing music by Stella in 1618, also involving the Cantus voice.[25] (See Example 12) As surviving, the order of folios, and therefore of music, makes a nonsense of three page joins, between folio 4v and 7r for example. As the example makes clear, the problem is not at all a musical one, but a simple case of placing the type in the wrong place in the press. While the outer sheet (the top line in the example) is imposed correctly, the second sheet

---

Existing order of folios in the first Cantus

1-4;   7-8;   5-6;   9-10.

Actual impositions

9r	2v		2r	9v			
10v	1r		1v	10r			

5r	4v		4r	5v		8r	7v
6v	3r		3v	6r		8v	7r

Correct:	7r	4v	4r	7v	6r	5v
	8v	3r	3v	8r	6v	5r

Example 12. Stella: *Ad Completorium*, Venice, G. Vincenti, 1618.

---

[24] RISM 1504³; Sartori, *Bibliografia,* n° 14: all surviving copies. This evidence and the conclusion are outlined in S. Boorman, «The 'First' edition of the *Odhecaton A*», *Journal of the American Musicological Society,* XXX (1977), p. 183-207.

[25] Stella, *Ad Completorium,* RISM S5730: copy at I-Bc.

2602

was imposed as if the gathering had only eight folios, rather than ten. This resulted in imposing the remaining folios on the separate half-sheet. There is no way that these folios could be bound together in one simple gathering and make musical sense.

These and similar situations do not *raise* new or interesting questions about the content of a musical edition, its provenance or authenticity, or the homogeneity or inconsistencies of its readings. Instead, they *resolve* such questions, making sense of anomalies which might otherwise cause us considerable concern. In this way, the bibliographer, in his or her study of the printed source can not only raise questions, but also resolve others raised by the content. Surely this is a direct parallel to the activities of the codicologist.

However, I want to end by pointing out that there is one area wherein printed sources can actually outperform manuscripts. We can often tell, for the printed source, which corrections, manuscript or other, were actually made in the printing shop. In other words, we have real evidence of proof-reading, evidence that the student of the manuscript often has to assess from a much more conservative standpoint. As a corollary, we can similarly suggest more securely which changes are necessarily later, the product of attention on the part of the user.

There were several ways in which the printer could correct copies before he sold them: they have been found in the work of Petrucci and Antico; by Mary Lewis in that of Gardano; and by Beth Miller in that of Vincenti and Amadino. Gardano cared about, and corrected simple things, even indications of *prima* and *secunda pars*; he and the other printers corrected notes and text, ascriptions, clefs and accidentals. Every printer whose work I have examined corrected his copy before he sold it. We may therefore have, once enough printers have been studied, a much clearer view of what, for the sixteenth century musician, had to be correct, and what did not matter: certainly, such a view can only come with any confidence from study of the printed sources, rather than from that of manuscripts. In this way, the printer and his edition can be considered at least the equal, if not the superior, of the scribe and his manuscript.

V

The Salzburg liturgy and single-impression
music printing*

The relationship between the musical source and the performing habits of its users
is of course a complex one. We can rarely say whether, or how far, the source reflects
performing habits ingrained in the thinking of the editor or the copyist; nor can we
regularly say how little the users of the book will have adhered to the readings it
contained, or in which ways they will have deviated from it. This is no less true in
the performance of liturgical music, although, from the nature of the sources, we
have considerably less evidence. It often seems as though such sources were edited,
prepared, and published with little regard to changes in performing habits, and as
though the only significant evidence lies in those manuscripts or editions which
announce their editorial principles. However, in some missals prepared for the archdiocese of Salzburg, there is some unusual evidence, reinforced in its significance
by the fact that its inclusion imposed on the printers a search for the solution to
serious technical problems.

I

Given the flood of liturgical books which went to print in the later fifteenth and
early sixteenth centuries, some dioceses are notable for the number of volumes they
produced, and others for the virtual absence of any printed editions at all. This is
particularly apparent for those editions which contain music.

Among those for which we have a number of sources, Salzburg is one of
value. The early editions seem to have been commissioned from the Nuremberg
printer, Stuchs, who also printed noted books for Hildesheim, Olomouc, and
Regensburg. Three elegantly produced books, dated 1492, 1498, and 1505, survive
from this press. However, soon after the last of these editions, new printers in
different cities were commissioned to print missals: the change may have been the
product of the archbishop's desire to include more information in the books.[1]

As is to be expected, the archdiocese of Salzburg commemorated a number of
local saints, including several specifically associated with the city, in particular Sts.

*   I am grateful to Professor Mary Lewis, and to Jeannie Im, Edward Jarvis, and Karl Kügle, for assistance
    in preparing this essay.
1   The four editions concerned are from the Venetian press of Liechtenstein (1507 and 1515), the Viennese
    house of Winterburg (1510), and the Basle house of Wolff (printed by Pforzheim, 1510). While these
    editions are remarkably consistent in the readings they preserve, I have nevertheless indicated from which
    edition I have taken any citation.

Rudpert and Virgilius.[2] The translations of these two saints were celebrated on 24 and 26 September; the juxtaposition of these celebrations and that of the dedication of the Church of St. Rudpert, on 25 September, closely followed by the feast of St. Michael Archangel on 29 September, within the octaves of the other feasts, must have made this a time of special celebration in Salzburg.

Several other saints with regional associations, venerated throughout the area, are listed in Salzburg calendars. The Emperor Henry II, his widow Cunegunde, and his tutor Bishop Wolfgang had all been strongly supportive of the Benedictines who had founded the abbey; the first of these was given a feast of the highest rank, alongside those of the two Salzburg saints. Other such feasts were mostly the traditional ones, here including St. Augustine and St. Anne.

Duplex feasts were accorded to St. Afra of Salzburg, St. Elizabeth of Hungary, St. Cunegunde, St. Sigismund, and the Quatuor Corona, as well as to apostles (St. James the Great, St. Luke, St. Mark, etc.), the Fathers of the Church or of monasticism (St. Ambrose, St. Augustine, St. Gregory, St. Jerome) and the most popular of saints (St. Barbara, St. Catherine, St. Margaret, St. Thomas à Becket, and St. Vincent).

The same pattern can be seen at each lower level – of nine lessons, three lessons, or merely with a Proper antiphon.

In this respect, the Salzburg liturgy is not unusual: it reflects the normal pattern – of a blend of international, monastic, and local saints at each level. The calendar indicates a traditional view, in which local saints are accorded different status according to their importance for the institution or their regional prestige.

The clearest evidence of special texts or music for these feasts lies of course in the Propers of the Sanctorale. However, an additional series of Proper texts can be found in the Prefaces, the group of versicles and prayer that precedes the Sanctus of the Mass, and that is therefore copied in the Canon.

The Preface is conventionally presented in liturgical sources in a section of texts beginning with the final phrase of the Secret – *Per omnia secula seculorum Amen*. This is followed by the three versicles which are common to all celebrations: *Dominus vobiscum*, *Sursum corda*, and *Gratias agamus*. After these is presented the Preface itself, which is Proper (either to specific feasts or, more commonly, to groups of feasts), to be said on the relevant feast-day and during the following octave. Each Preface opens with a standard phrase (beginning with the words *Vere dignum*) and ends with the word *dicentes*, leading directly into the Sanctus. The center of each Preface is different. In several cases, the first twenty-one words are the same; in others, the text diverges after eight words; yet others are common for twenty-five words, before following them with a more specific group of phrases. As a result, the text of the whole Preface was not presented each time, since the first phrases are constant. A clue to the point at which the text diverges is in practice sufficient.

Thus, in the 1515 Salzburg missal, the Preface *Ad summum festum generalis* reads *Vere dignum et justum est: equum et salutare. Nos tibi et ubique gratias agere: domine sancte pater . . . supplici confessione dicentes*. The text for the Preface *De apostolis festivaliter* diverges after the words *equum et salutare*: therefore a missal does not present

---

[2]   The former was Bishop of Salzburg, and died in 710: he was venerated in particular for founding the cathedral church, building the monastery and a nunnery within the city. St. Virgilius was another local saint, first abbot and later bishop, who died in 784.

any text or music for the first words, but begins *Equum et salutare. Te domine sup-pliciter* . . . . The earlier shared text is indicated merely by a conventional sign ⊕. The various Prefaces were not arranged in the order of other texts in a missal, following the calendar. Instead, each was presented once, with a rubric indicating all the feasts for which it was appropriate.

This example comes from the liturgy for Salisbury:[3]

> Sequens Praefatio dicitur in omnibus festis apostolorum et evangelistarum, et per octavas apostolorum Petri et Pauli atque Andreae quando de octavis dicitur missa; praeterquam in festo sancti Johannis apostoli et evangelistae in hebdomada Nativitatis Domini. In octavis vero ejusdem dicetur, et in festo ejus in tempore Paschali.

A diverse level of feasts is subsumed under this rubric: for example, the feast of St. Mark (25 April) is described in the calendar as *iij lectionum inferius duplex*, while that of St. John in the week of Christmas (27 December) is *Minus duplex ix. lectionum*; the octave of the feast of St. Andrew (3 January), is apparently a simplex feast, with a triple invitatorium and three lessons.[4] However, these different feasts do not appear to need different levels of musical complexity. The Preface text is accompanied by one setting. Nor do the different days (and levels of celebration) within each octave stimulate any difference to the setting.

While the Salzburg liturgy also has a series of Proper Prefaces, the musical approach is markedly different, and the distinctions work at two levels. Firstly, each of the various Preface texts is presented with three distinct, though closely related, musical settings. Each setting is to be sung on different days within an octave.

For example, the same group of feasts, for apostles and Peter and Paul, is treated in the following manner in the books for Salzburg:

(i) *De Apostolis festivaliter et minus festivaliter more solito*, with a musical setting;
(ii) *Ad binos et ad novem lectiones more solito*, with a variant setting;
(iii) *Eadem ferialiter: ut in apostolorum vigiliis*, with the simplest setting.[5]

Thus, on the feast-day of an apostle, and on other high feasts within the octave, the first setting, often labelled *solenniter*, was to be sung; during the octave, duplex feasts and those with nine lections, the second setting was used; while for the vigil of each feast and any lesser days within the octave singers followed the third, simplest setting.

This division reflects more carefully the hierarchy of the different celebrations which are grouped together in other liturgies. While these other sources group feasts according to the character of the person being commemorated, they do not (as I have shown for the Use of Salisbury) make clear distinctions between triplex, duplex, or simplex feasts.[6]

There is one strange feature in the example of Salzburg rubrics, presented above, for the feasts of evangelists and apostles. That is the use of the phrase *more solito* – "according to usual custom" – which is to be found in the first two rubrics.

---

3   This rubric is taken from Francis Dickinson, *Missale ad usum insignis et praeclarae ecclesiae Sarum* (Burntisland 1861–83/R Farnborough, 1969), col. 605.
4   See the Kalendar in Dickinson, *Missale*.
5   The 1515 Liechtenstein edition, fols. 186v–7v.
6   Liturgies do, of course, have hierarchic levels of musical settings for some other texts, among them both troped and untroped Kyries and Glorias, and different levels of Psalm settings.

The phrase might seem to suggest that there was some unusual (though customary at Salzburg) practice about defining the level of feasts. The correct explanation, however, emerges upon examining rubrics for other Prefaces.

These include rubrics such as the following:

> Ad summum festum generalis prefatio. notis rubeis coassumptis. que tamen ad minus festum omittuntur.[7]

or, for the Nativity:

> Ad minus autem festum notas rubeas abijce. ut prefetur in prima prefatione. Sed ad binos eandem prefationem sic intonabis cum notis rubeis. quas ad novem lectiones relinques.[8]

These rubrics appear in sets, each tied to the same Proper Preface, in its various settings. For example, one set, where the text begins *Aeterne Deus. Per Christum Dominum nostrum*, reads:

(i)   De Ascensione domini festivaliter. et minus festivaliter. solita differentia servata cum notis rubeis.
(ii)   Eadem ad binos et novem lectiones solita differentia.
(iii)   Eadem ferialiter.[9]

Another contains the following three rubrics:

(i)   De resurrectione solenniter. sed minus festivaliter note rubee non cantentur.
(ii)   Ad binos et .ix. lectiones differentialiter. ut prenotatum est.
(iii)   Ferialiter.[10]

The reference to *more solito* seems to be to the practices outlined in these rubrics. It appears that the hierarchy of musical settings for a Preface is in fact divided, not into three, but rather into five groups, as shown here in Example 13.1. The first pair of these five are musically very close throughout, with the higher of the two including a number of additional notes, excluded from the lower. They could be, and were, presented together, with the additional notes *printed in red*. The same coupling can be used for the third and fourth levels, again with red notes in the edition. Only the lowest is presented alone, and the musical reason for that will become evident.[11]

The five levels seem to work as follows: the first pair were divided between the actual feast being commemorated and other festive Masses during the octave; the second was intended for double feasts, and days with nine lections; the third was sung at those with three lections and on lesser occasions.

What is remarkable about this multiple division is not only its existence, and the implications of floridity and hierarchy that it conveys, but also, and perhaps more interestingly for the present purpose, the use of red notation to indicate the differences, even in printed books.

---

7   1507 edition: fol. 178v; 1515 edition: fol. 176v.
8   1507: fol. 181v; 1515: fol. 179v.
9   1515: fols. 182v–3r.
10   1515: fols. 181v–2v; the first is on fol. 183v of the 1507 edition.
11   Red notes are indicated in a manner commensurate with their treatment in polyphonic sources, with half-brackets above the stave. The one red word in the text, *die*, is indicated in the same manner.

The Salzburg liturgy and music printing

Example 13.1 De resurrectione

[A:] ¶ De resurrectione solemniter. sed minus festivaliter note rubee non cantentur.
[B:] Ad binos et .ix. lectiones differentialiter. ut prenotatum est.
[C:] Ferialiter.

From the 1515 edition, fols. 181v–2v.
In the Pforzheim edition of 1510, at fol. 157v, the two red notes in the middle voice
below *omni* are replaced by one red and one black note.

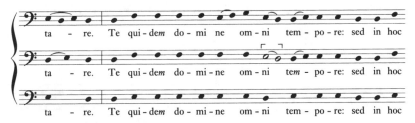

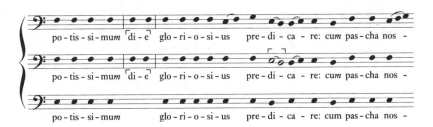

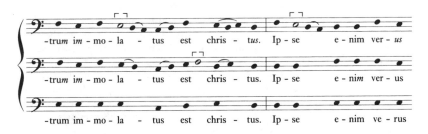

239

est ag - nus: qui ab - stu - lit pec - ca - ta mun - di.

est ag - nus: qui ab - stu - lit pec - ca - ta mun - di.

est ag - nus: qui ab - stu - lit pec - ca - ta mun - di.

Qui mor - tem nos - tram mo - ri - en - do de - stru - xit: et vi - tam re-sur-

Qui mor - tem nos - tram mo - ri - en - do de - stru - xit: et vi - tam re-sur-

Qui mor - tem nos - tram mo - ri - en - do de - stru - xit: et vi - tam re-sur-

gen - do re - pa - ra - vit. Et i - de - o.

gen - do re - pa - ra - vit. Et

gen - do re - pa - ra - vit. Et i - de - o cum an - ge.

II

The use of red ink for printed liturgical books was, of course, a normal part of the procedure for their production. Not only the rubrics, but also the staves carrying music, were normally printed in red. This required at least a double-impression process, in which the red and black content were distinguished, inked separately, and passed through the press at different times.

It is evident that, for many printers, the red verbal text was most satisfactorily set at the same time as the black. Both then lay in the same forme, and were printed from the same setting. All that was required was that the black sections be masked, by the use of a specially cut frisket, when the red were being inked for printing, and that the red were similarly masked for the black impression. This did require some extra work on the part of the press-man, cutting the friskets, and making sure that no stray ink crept onto the printed area. Yet the advantages to the type-setter, in ensuring that the two groups of material were well arranged with regard to each other, apparently outweighed any such problems.

There is ample evidence that this was the procedure normally followed during the fifteenth and early sixteenth centuries. For example, there are often "smudges" of ink of one color against the edges of letters printed in the other, and these can be seen to be from the edges of the same letters. Sometimes, though more rarely, individual letters or words are printed in the wrong colors.

However, the music could not be set up in the formes containing the staves, for the two occupy the same space. Therefore, in those instances where musical notation was to be included, the two impressions (for red staves and for black notation) needed two settings, perhaps in two distinct formes. In such cases, it appears, three impressions could have been used. Two would suffice for the single set of formes with both black and red text, with the staves or the music mounted in those formes; a third impression printed the other notational element, music or staves, in a separate set of formes.[12]

Much circumstantial evidence suggests that, in practice, two impressions were sufficient and that only one set of formes was used. This set contained the texts, in both colors, and the staves. From this set, the red impression would be taken, printing rubrics, many initial letters, and the staves. Then the staves could be removed, and the musical notation set up, in the same spaces in the forme. The black impression (text and music) could then be taken, a new frisket having been cut to mask the red sections of the page. Alternatively, of course, the black impression could have been set up with notes, and the red staves inserted after this first impression and therefore printed second.[13]

Whichever mode of operation was followed, the music itself was printed from a multiple impression process, from two distinct impressions, one involving the staves, and one containing the notes.

This was also the procedure used by Petrucci and other early printers of polyphony. Others (such as Antico), in using woodcuts, avoided the labor-intensive need for two impressions, but did not solve the equally important issue of using, and being able to reuse, type. The first printer to resolve both problems, by developing a single-impression music type, has long been thought to have been John Rastell, who briefly preceded Attaingnant, the printer who made this faster and simpler process commercially successful.[14]

In liturgical music, for as long as all the notes were black and the staves were red, there was no incentive to explore the technical possibilities of a single-impression approach to music printing: the two colors made it irrelevant, requiring different impressions for the two elements. However, the presence of red notes in a liturgical book not only made a solution worth seeking: it actively raised the technical problem. With the staves already in red, the addition of red notes, occupying the same space, seemed to require a third impression.

There was a number of potential solutions. The red notes could, after all, be printed alone, in an additional, third, impression, considerably increasing the labor involved for what was in fact a relatively small series of additions. Alternatively, they could be printed at the same time as the staves and rubrics, if some way could be found to insert them in the same forme as the staves.

---

12   There is little evidence for the use of three sets of formes. Very rarely, poor alignment of one of the musical elements *vis-à-vis* both red and black text does suggest the possibility. It would be logical to suppose that this was the earliest approach. However, the evidence suggests that two sets of formes were the norm: early noted missals regularly omit either the staves or the music from the printing process, suggesting that only one set of formes was used – containing both red and black text and the one musical element. This would then lead to the practice of using only two sets of formes, with the second containing the missing element of the musical content.

13   Many liturgical books bear evidence that the red was printed first, while others equally clearly show the red ink of stave-lines over the black of the music.

14   For Rastell, see A. Hyatt King, "Rastell, John," *Grove6*, vol. 15, 595, and the literature cited there.

V

Much of the problem stemmed from the manners in which the staves were printed. Most printers saw them as single units. For some, each four-line stave could be printed from a single block which spanned the whole width of the column. Others also regarded the column width as the critical measurement, although each stave was made up of four separate single rules. This was a feasible approach for many printers, for the rules making up the staves could also be used as separate units wherever single rules were needed. For both these solutions, shorter sections of stave were also prepared. They were needed for those occasions when the printed music was interrupted by a rubric or spoken text, or had to be inset a little to allow for a decorative initial letter.

The third procedure was to use a series of smaller blocks, each with one or four lines on it, and to build up the full length of the stave from several of these butted together. This approach was most convenient for sections of liturgical books where the musical text was very short, or where it was frequently interrupted by rubrics: in missals, this included the series of Gloria settings early in the Ordinary. The Venetian printer Liechtenstein used stave segments that were about 13.5 mm or about 7.5 mm long, butting them together to make lines of various lengths.[15]

In each of these approaches, the staves were still seen as units. Even when they were made up of segments, these were used as a matter of necessity, and each was longer than the space occupied by several notes. If the staves had been designed from the beginning as made up of very small segments, each of a length similar to the space occupied by a single notational symbol, the single-impression solution might have been found quickly. But, so long as printers saw a stave as a single unit, the insertion of red notes was apparently regarded as a problem requiring *ad hoc* solutions, rather than as an opportunity for solving a larger and more general problem.

In fact, the different printers of Salzburg missals in the early years of the sixteenth century adopted different solutions. The editions in which I have found these red notes, and their printers, are as follows:

Missale Salzburgensis. Venice: Liechtenstein, 27.xii.1507.
    Copies: Berlin, Staatsbibliothek Preussischer Kulturbesitz, 4⁰.Dq.12108.
    London, British Library, L.18.a.10.
Missale Saltzburgensis. Vienna: Winterburg, 27.iv.1510.
    Copies: Cambridge, University Library, F.151.c.7.1.
    London, British Library, C.111.c.15.
    Vienna, Österreichisches Nationalbibliothek, *48.s.38.
Missale Salzburgensis. Basle: Wolf, Pforzheim, 6.xii.1510.[16]
    Copy: London, British Library, C.41.g.4.
Missale Salzburgensis. Venice: Liechtenstein, 15.x.1515.
    Copies: Salzburg, Museum Carolino Augusteum, 40166.[17]
    Harvard University Library, Typ.525.15.262.F.

---

[15] There has been some discussion of these techniques in studies of incunable liturgical music printing. Kathi Meyer-Baer, in her *Liturgical Music Incunabula: a Descriptive Catalogue*, Publication of the Bibliographical Society for the year 1954 (London, 1962), includes a field for the stave character in many of her bibliographical entires. Mary Kay Duggan's *Italian Music Incunabula: Printers and Typefonts* (Berkeley, 1992), discusses the manner in which Italian printers printed their staves, on pages 49–64.

[16] There are no red notes in the *Agenda Saltzburgensis*, printed by Pforzheim on 20 December 1515.

[17] I am grateful to Professor Cliff Eisen, who examined this copy for me, and procured photographs of the relevant folios.

The Pforzheim edition shows the simplest approach to solving the problems raised by red notation. In this edition, each stave (measuring up to 154 mm in length) is made up of single rules. The rules were thin and tended to bend slightly under the pressure of the press, producing a characteristic irregularity in individual lines. The staves do not have to be interrupted for many of the large initial letters within texts, for the initials are printed in black, and the red staves continue through them. When the pattern of color required a red initial, or when the opening of a Preface was indicated in red with the customary symbol ⊕, shorter rules were used, providing a space at the beginning of the system.

The individual red notes, however, can appear anywhere in a system. They are identical to the black notation, and were evidently cast from the same matrices. All are small, and do not take up the space of more than two stave-lines. Indeed, the *punctum* can be fitted between two adjacent lines. This argues for something that is evident from other evidence: that the neumes were mounted on type-bodies that were as small as possible. Inserting a *punctum* therefore did not result in breaks in the stave-lines. A *clivis* crossed the space of one stave-line, and a *virga* overlapped the space normally occupied by two lines: both therefore result in breaks in the lines. The metal rules were broken, with shorter sections on either side of the red notation.[18]

Much more important for the history of music printing were the processes adopted by Liechtenstein and Winterburg.

Liechtenstein, in his editions of 1507 and 1515, developed an innovative solution. He cast a series of red staves, on each of which a single note was mounted, making single-impression sorts. Each of the staves is made from the longer of his two matrices – 13.5 mm in length. There are only four notational symbols used: a *punctum* on the top space; the same note on the middle space; a *virga* on the second line down; and a *clivis* on the middle space. Each of these notes is placed in one of two places on the sort, either exactly in the center or at the extreme right end. There are therefore eight musical sorts which include a portion of stave.

Liechtenstein was able to print all the red notes required in a Salzburg missal using only these eight different characters, for each of which he had a number of different copies, or sorts. This is not yet a single-impression music font, even in terms of liturgical printing. Liechtenstein did not have a set of all symbols at every pitch; nor did he have the ability to print red notes in sequence, for the sorts are much longer than the space occupied by a single sort. His method represents more of an *ad hoc* solution to a particular problem, of limited value in his other work, and not extensible to polyphony.

The type used by Winterburg of Vienna for his red notes is already more advanced. It is likely that he had seen copies of Liechtenstein's 1507 edition, and it would have required only a simple analysis to deduce the Venetian's procedure.

Winterburg's normal staves are again built up in sections, each containing all four lines. His pieces tend to be about 8.5 mm long, with some sorts which are

---

[18]   For the printer, this was not a particularly wasteful process. The rules that were used for stave-lines by printers such as Pforzheim were thin, flexible under the pressure of the press, easily and frequently damaged, and easily replaceable. Thus, to break a few and make short segments was not as extravagant as it might seem.

   In addition, since there are no situations in which all four stave-lines have to be interrupted, the stability of the whole stave could be retained, under the guidance of the uninterrupted stave-lines.

longer, at about 14 mm. The full stave is about 118 mm long, made from a number of such sections. Winterburg's notation contains a wider range of sorts than are found in other editions; but again only the *punctum*, the *virga*, and the *clivis* appear in red notation.

Again, the red notes were printed with a short section of stave; again, the dimensions of note and stave are constant for each character; and, again, both stave and note were mounted on the same body. Figure 13.1 shows an enlargement of a red *clivis* from fol. 130v. The outline of the edge of the sort can be seen quite clearly. The sharp edge of each stave-line shows through the ink, which has spread slightly beyond the edge, as it should. This edge merges with the edge of the musical character, so that the two present a continuous outline. Given the size of the sort, in which the stave does not extend beyond the sides of the note, this is evidently a true single-impression music sort.

Winterburg also had a wider range of these sorts. The *punctum*, for example, can be found in each of the three spaces on the stave, and each is on a sort of slightly different width.

It seems that Winterburg had taken the innovation of Liechtenstein, and made it more practicable – by mounting the sorts on smaller pieces of staves – and also more truly a different kind of font. His segments of staves were not the same lengths as those without red notes (as Liechtenstein's had been), but were separately and individually prepared.

Intentionally or not, between them, Liechtenstein and Winterburg solved the problems of single-impression music printing some fifteen years before Rastell, and even longer before Attaingnant adopted the process. In so doing, they had special sorts cast, for the same symbol at different pitches, and they learned how to incorporate these into the rest of the notation.

The cost of doing this must have been fairly high. A count shows that Winterburg probably needed no more than ten sorts of any single symbol at any given pitch. However, each had to be inserted into a forme which otherwise contained simple red staves, and each involved a slower setting of its system. For each such stave, the type-setter will have had to leave a space for the red note when setting the black, and will have had to ensure that the red was at the right point in the line, when setting it with otherwise blank staves.[19]

There must therefore have been a greater expenditure of labor, particularly for the formes which otherwise would have had nothing but red staves.

Indeed, this is true for all the editions of the Salzburg missal being discussed here. Even the work of Pforzheim involved extra labor in setting the red notes. The archbishop, or his agent in commissioning these editions, must have been quite insistent in demanding the red notes, and must also have been willing to pay for the labor involved. We are justified in wondering why it was so important to present the music in this way.

---

[19] Liechtenstein, on one occasion, mounted the red note at the wrong place on the stave. In the 1507 edition, on fol. 186v, one red *clivis* is entered two syllables too soon. After the press-work, a replacement *clivis* is stamped in at the correct place.

Interestingly, the same error can be found in his 1515 edition. The relevant folio, 185r, is not retained from the earlier edition, for everything is reset. The implication seems to be that the printer kept an uncorrected copy in his house file, and that this was used for setting up the later edition.

The Salzburg liturgy and music printing

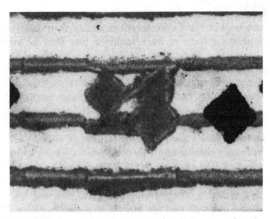

Figure 13.1 A single-impression music sort of a *clivis* mounted on its own short piece of stave. (*Missale Salzburgensis* [Vienna: Winterburg, 27. IV. 1510], fol. 130v.)

III

This red notation is only one possible solution for providing a series of optional versions of the same setting of a text.

For most texts in the liturgy, of course, there was only one setting; when the same text was used for different feasts, then different settings were supplied (or the same was repeated), at the relevant places in the Temporale or Sanctorale, if the missal were fully noted. The principal exceptions to this are well known: they involve the different musical settings of the movements of the Ordinary of the Mass, sometimes troped, sometimes in different modes; the similar settings of the *Ite missa est*; and the tones for the psalms and the *Magnificat*. The various settings of each of these are musically so diverse that they could not have been combined in the manner I have been describing here. Most missals have little other music – settings for the first Christmas Mass "in gallicantu," for Palm Sunday, and for Holy Saturday – leaving the rest for the Gradual. Thus, there was no need for red notation elsewhere in a missal.

The patterns of the texts of the Prefaces and of their settings, in Salzburg at least, did encourage some such solution as red variants. While the texts were themselves Proper, and the levels of performance rendered their settings even more specific, these texts and settings had conventionally appeared in the Ordo, in that part of the missal which was "Common." Secondly, since the different divisions of the same Preface text did not correspond to the conventional divisions of common texts – for the Common of Martyrs, of Virgins, of a Doctor, and so on – there was no chance of moving the settings elsewhere, to the start of the Sanctorale, where such texts appeared. Finally, of course, it would be plainly uneconomical to move the texts to the many places in the Sanctorale to which they belonged, repeating them on each occasion, for that would involve setting music in many more places in the book, increasing radically the costs of production, and also moving the texts away from their accustomed location.

While, therefore, the common usage of missals ensured that these texts and their settings remained in the Ordo, the demands of their traditional layout and of the Salzburg practice seem to have required that they be presented in this novel manner. The three "basic" versions of each setting could not have been printed simultaneously. The ferial setting consists of a reciting tone with its simple inflections; both the other two settings raise the reciting tone one pitch, from *e* to *f* as in Example 13.1. This is itself a form of decoration, and also permits the addition of extra decorative notes at all inflections, even while it prevents either version being printed with the ferial form. Each of these settings is also different enough that the two are not mutually compatible. The middle-level setting – the one commonly addressed to services of nine readings or for *minus festivaliter* – tends to concentrate on the new reciting pitch, with a series of fairly simple inflections. The most festive version is built on this setting, rather than on the ferial one, and has more decorative additions, including a few that take the melody in different directions. In addition, there are the red notes, added to each of the two more festal settings, and making each into a pair of slightly different versions, fulfilling local demands for diversity of richness to correspond with diverse levels of feast.

And yet these local demands were relatively slight. For several of the settings, there are few red notes, and these merely decorate the fundamental line. They have limited functions and appear in specific places, so that the easiest solution was indeed to print them within the "black" versions.

In practice, all the variants on the ferial tone (at each of the upper levels) are members of a limited group. In addition to the raised reciting tone, there seem to be three basic modifications of the simple structure.

The clearest is the treatment of the *terminatio*. In the ferial setting, each cadence falls into the same pattern, shown in Example 13.2*a*. The upper, more festive versions prepare the cadence in a consistent manner: each begins by inflecting the reciting *f* with an *e*. At the cadence, both add notes for the same syllables, and also extend the simple range one note at the top. This note, an *f*, while obligatory in the uppermost version, is only used in the middle version on the more festive occasions: hence it is printed in red.

Occasionally, after a long recitation, an additional preparatory embellishment appears in the most festive version, as at the word *unius* in Example 13.2*b*, or for the words *pascha nostrum* of Example 13.1. (This figure has a small life of its own, for it can sometimes be found five or six syllables before the beginning of the cadential figure. However, the two do seem to be solidly connected, even in these cases.)

At the mid-point of the chant phrase, different decorative additions to the mediation are customary. The syllables in the upper versions that correspond to a lower inflection in the simplest version have a pair of ligatures. These are approached, in the most festive version, by an upward extension. These two features are shown in Example 13.3*a*. The details of the treatment vary slightly, depending on the number of syllables between the highest pitch, *g*, and the cadence itself. (See Example 13.3*b*, and also the treatment of the words *gloriosius predicare* and *enim verus est agnus* in Example 13.1.)

In these instances the middle voice seems to raise a curious situation in the placing of the red notes. It appears that one syllable can only be sung when the red

(a)

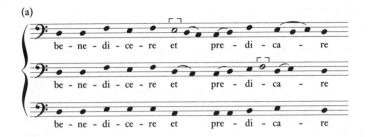

(b)

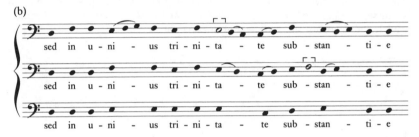

Example 13.2 (a) From *De beata virgine*, 1515 edition, fols. 185v–6v.
(b) From *De sanctam trinitatem*, 1515 edition, fols. 184v–5v.

(a)

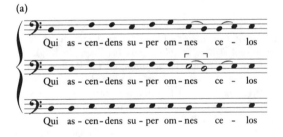

(b)

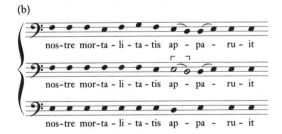

Example 13.3 (a) From *De sancto spiritu*, 1507 edition, fols. 185v–6v.
(b) *De epiphania*, 1507 edition, fol. 182r–v.

247

notes are sung; in Example 13.3*a*, for example, the syllable "nes" is assigned a pair of red notes in ligature. When singing the "black version," the singer would probably have chosen the upper of these two notes, even though it is not the note given in the simplest version, on the third stave. There are two strands of evidence for this: the first is that, if the singer had been required to sing the lower, the printer could have printed the upper (*e*) in red and the lower in black. However, he did not have a red *punctum* for the lower note, so that he could only print it in red as part of a ligature. The second lies in the treatment of the phrase *Gratias agamus* shown in Example 13.5, to be discussed below.

Two examples that are musically more interesting can be found in the Prefaces for Christmas, where some melismatic writing appears (see Example 13.4). In both of these, the most festive version adds longer melismas, and clearly amplifies not merely the range but also the effect of a whole phrase.

Example 13.4 From *De nativitatem domini*, 1507 edition, fols. 181r–2r.

The impact of these instances, simple and few as they are, is reinforced by the various readings found in the first chant, that of the General Preface, with its precedent Responses. This is presented here in its entirety (as Example 13.5), for there is more than one point of interest. From the beginning of the Preface, at the words *Vere dignum et iustum est*, three musical versions are printed, with red notes in the upper two – as in other Prefaces. The ferial setting is as restrained as others, as also is the middle-level setting: the formulas and the use of red notes follow the practice I have described above.

The most festive version, however, shows a greater sense of imagination: the opening phrase, *Vere dignum*, has a completely different musical contour, which is reflected at *Per quem maiestatem*. A different pattern is also found above some of the simplest flexes in the ferial tone: at *gratias agere* and *et nostras voces*, for example, the interval of a third, with its following line, is new. In other places, too, such as at *angeli adorant*, a more melismatic and freely shaped line is adopted in the setting *Ad summum festum*.[20]

At least as interesting is the treatment of the initial Versicles: the festive version (line [A]) is clearly related to the Preface which follows on from it, with similar musical formulas. The middle version, however, is here divided into three levels, of which the first (line [B]) follows the pattern to be found elsewhere in other second-

---

[20] The same effects are only to be found in one other Preface setting, that headed *De sancto spiritu festivaliter*.

level settings. The next two lines ([C] and [D]) provide modifications to this pattern, and reduce some of the decoration. One place is at *Gratias agamus*, which I have mentioned above. The other principal change lies in the sequential reduction of the notes in the melisma at the beginning of phrases such as *Sursum corda*. These changes only apply to the responses; since these, in both the [A] and [B] settings, are more florid than the decoration to be found in the Prefaces, this is reasonable.

These changes, in lines [C] and [D], show how line [B] represents a conservative approach to melisma, in which changes often comprise little more than a slight extension of range. Such changes are to be seen as in distinction to other ornaments, such as are found, in particular, in the most festal setting.

This raises again the question with which this essay opened. There seems little reason to doubt that decorations such as that at the festal treatment of *Gratias agamus* in the *Prefatio General* must have been conceived and copied as deliberate acts of decoration – and whether this happened by extemporization or in the scriptorium is not relevant.

Many other ornaments, and particularly those printed in red, seem to have a different role: they represent no more than a momentary reaction to the black notation, as can be seen in all the red notes of Example 13.2 or Example 13.4. They fill in the interval of a third, add a single higher note at the end of a rising line, or reinforce that highest note. This pattern is followed throughout the Prefaces.

I believe that we have here evidence of some performing practices found in the Salzburg archdiocese, probably in the cathedral itself, at the very beginning of the sixteenth century.

We do presume that a number of the various readings of the same musical text in chant sources is the direct result of performing experience. It might seem possible that this is true of the other variants in these settings – those that I have just described as "deliberate acts." However, such changes can normally not be characterized as either "compositional," or "empirical" and resulting from performance. For one thing, we do not have the necessary evidence; for another, they seem to be carried through too consistently to reflect no more than a fortuitous performance discovery, involving, as they do, changes in phrase-shaping and in other parts of a composition.

The red notes in these Preface settings, however, do seem to argue for evidence of performance inventions. Although they have also been treated consistently in this small group of pieces, that reflects no more than the activity of the archbishop's editor. Each change, however, is so slight, so much a product of simple singing procedures, that it seems to have been discovered solely during performance. If that is so, then we have one simple explanation for the complexity of presentation. The editor of the volume, having encountered these ornamental patterns, and knowing that singers would not easily abandon their use, decided to codify them, to restrict them to certain classes of feast – thus in effect allowing the singer to continue to embellish the chant with such simple decoration.

The editor cannot have known that, while he was thereby making his missals more expensive to produce, he was also encouraging printers to explore the invention of a type-font that would make music printing cheap enough to reach a much wider market.

V

Example 13.5 General Preface

[A:] ¶Ad summum festum generalis prefatio. Notis rubeis coassumptis, que tamen ad minus festum omittuntur.

[B:] ¶In festivitatibus *vero* minoribus, ut ioannis baptiste. heinrici. feria tertia pasche. penthecostes et similibus. notas rubricas omittere oportebit. ¶Ad binos aute*m* sequens melodia serva*tur* cum notis rubeis.

[C:] ¶Ad novem lectiones sic variabis ut sequitur. [and at end:] Cetera cantabis ut in precedenti prefatio*ne*. notis omissis rubeis.

[D:] ¶Dominicaliter parum mutatur. ut infra. [and at end:] Cetera ut ad nove*m* lectiones prefiguratu*m* est cantabis.

[E:] ¶Ferialiter *vero* et *pro* defunctis seque*ns* melodia officia*ndo* servabitur.

From the 1515 edition: fols. 176v–9r.

A is printed with a clef on the top line. It reverts to a normal clef on the third line at *Gratias agamus*.

C has a clef on the third line throughout. However, the first phrase is pitched a third too high, as if copied from an exemplar with the higher clef. (The 1507 edition from the same press does have this higher clef.)

D has a clef on the top line, only for the first phrase.

250

Example 13.5 (continued)

V

Example 13.5 (continued)

252

The Salzburg liturgy and music printing

Example 13.5 (continued)

POSTSCRIPT

An interesting parallel case, involving polyphony, is discussed in Mary S. Lewis, "Composer and printer in the sixteenth century: Gardane, Rore, and Zarlino". Paper read at the annual meeting of the American Musicological Society, Minneapolis, 19–22 October 1978.

VI

Early Music Printing:
Working for a Specialized Market

As a subject for the present volume, music has one advantage over almost all other Renaissance printed matter: its intended market can be defined with some precision. As a result, the interaction between print and reader, between printer and market, comes into a sharper focus.

I do not mean by this, sadly, that we know *who* bought printed music. The number of named, specific purchasers is much smaller than one could wish. It does include the obvious bibliophiles, Fernando Colón, for instance; it includes the most important musical institutions—the Accademia Filarmonica in Verona, the chapel of the Elector of Bavaria, and, almost certainly, that of the Pope in the Vatican are examples; it certainly includes individual composers and theorists of music; and it also includes some musical amateurs who have left their names on surviving books. But all these together account for relatively few copies.[1]

However, even when we do not know the names of most of the purchasers of music, we do know a few specific things about them. With the probable exception of the Colóns of the world, virtually every purchaser would have been able to read music. However cheap musical books became during the sixteenth century,[2] they were not pocket reading: not only were they difficult for the nonmusical reader, but they were also not usually easy for musicians to read. The evidence that I shall be describing argues very clearly that the only real purpose for publishing music was to foster its performance aloud, rather than for silent reading or consultation. Thus, to a very great extent, the purchasers of any volume must have been either performers or promoters of performances—patrons or those responsible for cathedral music, for instance. This is a situation, the connection between content and specific users, that is not to be found elsewhere in the domain of printed matter, even allowing for the probability that many readers read aloud what they saw. That this had a direct impact on what was printed, how it was printed, and which version and reading was to be preserved will be immediately apparent, and forms the subject of this paper.

In describing this market for musical publication, I have already made one tacit restriction on my discussion, one that must be made explicit. Strictly speaking, musical material appeared in printed books in three, almost entirely distinct guises. The first consists of texts on the theory of music, on its notation, and on its performance.[3] To a large extent, we can ignore this body of material in the present discussion: a major portion of it consists of studies of music as a part of the *quadrivium*, as a theoretical subject treated in similar manner to any other, written for audiences of philosophers and, perhaps, gentlemen-scholars.[4] Much of the remainder of theoretical printing, especially in Germany, involves "how-to" books, training manuals for students in gymnasia, for Lutheran proselytes and proselytizers, or for professionals seeking "career advancement."[5] As such, these publications do reveal something of the size and abilities of the market for music books, although many of them present a clearer picture of the spread of elementary instruction.

A second genre is that of church song, plainchant or for the reformed churches, among which the Huguenot psalter of Marot and de Bèze has been the subject of some study.[6] As a whole, this makes up a further self-contained repertoire, one which runs parallel with other, nonmusical liturgical genres. The pattern of publishing is quite different from that for other musical matter, involving different printers, different techniques (even apparently of printing on occasion), and different approaches to reaching the market, which had itself been defined in a different manner.[7] Many of the issues raised by these details concern ecclesiastical usage rather than musical questions; however, as in the case of theoretical publications, they presumably also reflect the extent to which the users of these books could read simple notation, often chant notation.

Finally, and at the core of this study, is the repertoire that musicians call polyphony, labeled variously as "art music," "classical music," or "serious music." It comprises deliberately composed works, without an overt history of oral transmission or of tranformation, and appears to exclude anything more than occasional references to popular music.[8]

This repertoire first appeared in print in its own right, rather than as an adjunct to something else, in 1501, some twenty-five years after the first printed editions of chant or of theoretical writings.[9] It remained a very minor part of the output, and the responsibility of few printers until the late 1520s, when a technical innovation opened the field to many more printers—partly by cutting radically the time involved in setting and printing music, and partly by allowing the use of typesetters less highly skilled in music. Although music continued to be most successfully exploited by specialist printers, general printers were now more easily able to respond to calls for a few, often simpler, volumes.[10]

This discussion falls into three sections: in the first, I point to some of the special peculiarities of music prints, those that set them apart from other printed volumes. The second concerns the extent to which the special nature of the purchaser of the music print can be defined more closely, and leads, in the third, to a discussion of some specific ways in which these interact, in particular to a suggestion that one can detect evidence of changes in market size and composition in Italy during the first half of the sixteenth century, evidence that is preserved in the volumes themselves.

It must be emphasized that early music volumes had a relatively small amount of material appearing in them. A volume may have sixty-four folios, but each page will often effectively contain a maximum of five or six lines. Further, since each voice part has, of course, to be written or printed separately and with its text, the total number of lines of music and text can be divided by the number of voices involved, to find out the actual amount of music being published. Therefore, sixty-four folios, with six lines to a page, may well reduce to settings of less than one hundred and fifty lines of poetry. Even large volumes contain little more than the equivalent of thirty short poems. This is indeed the average number of madrigals that may be found in many printed collections from the middle and later part of the sixteenth century, and represents an increase from earlier prints. Petrucci regularly printed five settings of the ordinary of the mass in one volume; Attaingnant published a series with only three in each; and the same printer also produced a series of volumes of short chanson settings with over thirty on sixty-four folios, and thirteen volumes each with less than thirty motets.[11]

These rather random comments cannot provide a balanced picture of the scale of music printing. They merely demonstrate the small amount of material in many volumes, a fact which has particular relevance when we examine the extent to which printed volumes are unified.

A number of early volumes of music do show some level of unity, being organized around music in one genre or by one composer. Even in those cases where only one composer's music is printed, however, one cannot leap to the obvious conclusion regarding a connection between the publisher and the suppliers of the material to be printed, the *Stichvorlage*. Most volumes (even when restricted to one genre) are anthologies, twenty works by twenty composers, none of whom need know that they were being printed, need live within hundreds of miles of the printer, nor need even be alive. Music by the star of the time, Josquin, was being printed and reprinted (and added to) for well over forty years after his death—particularly in Germany, which he never visited—and there are more extreme examples.[12] While a number of early volumes do contain only the work of one composer, they can probably all be tied to the power of a patron of the printer, and, in any case, do not become general until well into the 1530s.[13] These later, more frequent, examples are part of the vast increase in the number of musical prints, and are, I believe, a reflection of the composers' awareness of the viability of the printed book as a means of circulation.

Even once volumes became frequently devoted to the works of a single composer, truly unified collections remain rare: while Verdelot or Marenzio may be the sole composer of the music in a volume, that music is usually unified only on the basis of genre—madrigals, masses or motets. Volumes such as Palestrina's cycle of settings of the Song of Songs, or Isaac's music for the rite of Constance, or the music performed during the festivities for a specific wedding remain very much in the minority.[14] In some cases, such as the last, this is clearly a reflection of the small size of the market for a volume of music performed at the wedding of a Florentine or Mantuan or French ruler: in others, such as liturgically ordered volumes (which might seem to have a wide market), other factors are important, involving the different habits of churches and dioceses.[15] However, it needs to be stressed that the unity implicit in a volume of text, a treatise, or history, for example, is almost nonexistent in musical sources, even in liturgical volumes.[16]

Another highly relevant aspect of music printing lies in the nature of music notation itself; it involves the continual superimposition of one set of symbols, notes, on another, stave-lines. It also requires some knowledge of a new language, with its own alphabet of musical symbols, as abstruse to the layman as those for Greek or Hebrew; and presumably also one as little-known to the average Renaissance typesetter.[17] I admit that anyone, whether he could read or not, could be taught to set type in any of these three alphabets, although his work would be both very slow and very unstylish. However, the best logical arrangement of music on a line, the most lucid and attractive, is not as easily codified as is that for text, with its long-established rules of word-division, line ends, and punctuation. If it is to be done well, music must be set attractively and, above all, at a reasonable speed, by someone literate in music. Further, the setting involves at least a double process: setting the music, and then setting the text correctly aligned with the music.[18] For each line of content there is, therefore, at least twice as much labor involved as for a nonmusical volume. Indeed, in the early stages, three times as much was involved, since early fonts for music do not include the staves with the notes.

This threefold division of the typographical material held good for almost all liturgical volumes of the fifteenth century; in many such books only the staves and text were printed, for the printer seems not to have had access to either a font for music or a musician to use it. The music would have been added later in manuscript, although, on the basis of the surviving evidence, not usually at the printing house or by the publisher. Later, music fonts appear, but they involve a double-impression process, staves printed at one impression and the notes at another. This, or the use of woodblocks, was the norm until late in the 1520s, when the idea of casting type with both stave and note on it revolutionized music printing.[19] Then, for the first time, music could be set in a straight line, as was text, even though this involved a three- or fourfold increase in the number of sorts in any case. However, musical typesetting would still have taken a disproportionate amount of time. While it was certainly not the most expensive part of the printing process, this may to some extent help to explain why musical volumes contain as little as they do; although I believe that equally important was the pattern of use of early printed volumes (those appearing while the publishing patterns were still being set). Lewis has suggested that Gardane could produce two titles a month when pressed: Petrucci seems to have worked perhaps three times as slowly.[20] In either case, a printer had to be sure of his market if he were to make a secure living: he hardly had the opportunity, facing an Aldus or a Plantin, of recovering from a poor sale with an immediate winner.

It is perhaps not surprising, then, that very few musical volumes are really "coffee-table" books. There are few lavishly designed titles or outstanding sets of woodblock capital letters. One well-known example is that of the title page for Antico's *Liber Quindecim Missarum*, the design for which was closely copied by Dorico for later volumes. Dorico also seems to have taken over some of Antico's initials, while other printers reused blocks until they decayed, replacing them with close imitations.[21] By and large, music volumes were not the lavish luxury productions that some of them have been claimed to be; while expensive, they were made so more by the limitations of the market and by their size than by any sense of luxury or lavishness.[22] It is perhaps significant, too, that very few early music books have dedications or other marks of affluent destination; although I wonder how far this is merely a reflection of the primacy of Venice at a time when the printing of polyphony was starting.

A key element in this discussion of the nature of music printing concerns the manner in which musical volumes were laid out. We are accustomed to seeing music presented so that everything that happens at the same time can be read on the same page—that is, in score. This is almost unknown throughout the majority of the sixteenth century, particularly in printed volumes. The only exceptions consist in those books designed for lute or keyboard or in those containing songs accompanied by solo lute—that is, the few intended for *one* performer.[23] All other volumes separate the individual voice parts, usually into separate and separately bound partbooks. For performers, this is a natural convenience: each has his own music in a small volume, and each can read it without having to share with a different type of voice. However, this arrangement means that the titles were useless to anyone except a complete set of performers. The act of silently studying the music from such books was, if not impossible, very tedious. Other volumes, usually when printed in folio size, placed all the parts on one opening, but in different corners, so that simultaneous sounds are still not visually related.[24] The first printed scores of such music specifically state that they are for keyboard instruments or for study.[25]

This makes explicit what is implied by format, that the sort of use-for-reference that characterizes, say, legal printing, is an impossibility for almost all printed music. Thus, until the appearance of these volumes in score, one cannot say that there was a *reading* public for musical printing, but only a *using* public. This is the primary reason for believing that virtually all musical volumes were destined (in the printer's mind) for groups of performers, and that this was a central factor in his decisions.[26]

There is a question, the centrality of which is not immediately apparent, as to whether or not the printed version of a piece of music actually is that piece of music. I do not wish to enter the discussion as to what music is, or whether it only exists at the moment at which it is sounded, or whether the musical score is really music or only a series of instructions for recreating music. I do not believe they were questions that concerned the Renaissance musician.[27] He had no

VI

occasion to consider them, for he always saw the printed version of a
piece of music as a basis for his own version, which involved a series
of performing decisions—about where to sing individual syllables of
text, whether to add accidentals, what sort of scoring, speed, or pitch
to employ, and how much ornamentation to add; indeed, in some
cases, whether to add more voice-parts, to change the text, or to
recompose sections of the original. All these were, still in 1500, part
of the normal responsibility of the performer or choir-director, and
willingly ceded to him by the composer. As a result, no printed or
manuscript version of a piece of music, delivered to a new performing
ensemble, would be seen as binding in its reading; it was rather a
series of restraints to the imagination.[28]
    The effect of this on the printer is not easy to see. Music had to be
transmitted in some version or other, for without it there was no
skeleton for the performer to build on for his own version. It might
appear that the music printer was thereby released from much responsibility for the details of what he printed, but I shall suggest that this
was not always so, partly because of his own concerns, but partly
because of what he knew of the needs and wishes of his probable
purchasers; some of these we can deduce.
    I have already stated that the one thing we can assume about almost
all the purchasers is that they were musically literate—and, for most
of the remaining, probably buying for musical institutions—as in the
case of the Elector of Bavaria or most of the cathedral chapters that are
recorded as buying music books. Indeed, one can go further to assert
that the market that the printer had in mind, during the first thirty to
forty years of music printing, was that of the regular, contracted
performing institution and its members.[29]
    Two questions arise from this statement, related and both difficult.
One concerns the extent to which early printed music looks as though
it has never been used; the other, the spread of amateur musical skill.
Both of these have been raised by Krummel, in suggesting that
musical editions were not necessarily very large, a contention that I
would support.[30] Certainly, early in the sixteenth century at least,
there is little evidence to support a claim of a widespread ability to
read and perform music, perhaps even in court circles. Such an
interpretation of Castiglione, for example, would represent a confusion of a material distinction for the Italian Renaissance, that between solo song (accompanied or not) and true polyphony, motets,
masses, chansons, and (later) madrigals. There is very little in Castiglione or, indeed, in other contemporary references, to suggest that
nonprofessionals could regularly read complex music from notation.

Many references are, as so often, vague; but the majority of those that are specific speak of solos or of essentially simple and relatively popular art forms such as the *frottola*.[31]

In the course of this paper, I am asserting that the situation did change rapidly after 1540: however, I believe, we have still to speak of relatively small groups of amateur musicians, principally arising in the Accademie, which increasingly regarded musical ability as an important cultural attribute.[32] It is almost certainly this development that leads to the enormous expansion in madrigal prints during the middle of the century. The evidence for the small size of this group of amateur musicians lies partly in the treatises: these still cater primarily to professionals—the emergence of volumes giving instructions for skilled ornamentation, for instance, or (particularly in Germany) of volumes consisting of elementary instruction in singing chant and simple music.[33]

I should also add that there is another reason for believing amateur performers did not reach a high standing, or a very great proficiency, in Italian court circles. Later in the sixteenth century, a number of the more important musical centers gained their prestige, not from the general musical level of court and courtiers, but from the presence and excellence of virtuoso professionals.[34] Significantly too, when Monteverdi was attacked at the end of the century for stylistic modernisms in his madrigals, the replies that he and his brother wrote in his defense are couched in terms that would be explicable to the theorist and perhaps to the professional musician, but would be of little use to any amateur without a theoretical basis of understanding.[35] Such evidence argues against the existence of a large body of skilled and knowledgeable amateurs, able to work at the highest levels of performance, even though there is clear evidence for a number of groups of competent *dilettanti* emerging during the course of the second two-thirds of the century, capable of reading and performing polyphonic music and also able to understand and even write for the best professionals.

I wish to suggest, as a result, that the music printer of at least the first third of the sixteenth century had a fairly clear idea, not only of the nature, but also of the size of his market: he could not generally expect any significant part of this to come from casual buyers; indeed, many of his probable purchasers might be known to him and his agents by virtue of their professional obligations. Bearing in mind the small size of this market, a good music printer would be bound to take some account of its requirements. This could range from the simple matter of trying to ride with the popularity of some composers or of attempting to "cash in" on some new craze, through to ensuring that the readings presented did not conflict with the types of decisions that the performers wanted to preserve as their prerogative.

It is worth stressing that these performers' decisions really differed to a significant degree from one center to the next. To some extent, they are preserved in manuscripts copied at these various centers, for the act of copying included that of making some decisions: such were made partly on the basis of conscious editorial decision, partly in the manner of spelling changes made by textual scribes and typesetters: and, for reasons familiar to the literary scholar, these manuscripts also necessarily contain layers representing similar decisions in earlier exemplars. Since these changes involve the actual sound of the music, they cannot be called spelling variants. On the other hand, however, since the music as written was, as I have said, only a guide to the performer, it is questionable whether they can be called substantive variants. Thankfully, however, a discussion of the ways in which one describes these changes lies well outside the scope of this paper.[36]

Thus, the idea of a homogeneous and consistently controlled collection of versions of music is not a fifteenth- or early-sixteenth-century concept: the earliest printers of music received copy that demonstrates this fact. In this respect, perhaps, the transmission of music remains medieval throughout the fifteenth century and is not dragged into the Renaissance for some decades after the start of musical printing.

There is a truism that printing led rapidly to a certain level of consistency or homogeneity in many of the more popular texts, a truism that has been attacked on philosophical grounds by Eisenstein.[37] In music, it holds true, though only partly: clearly, the printing of liturgical books allowed for consistency within the diocese or order concerned: the vast numbers of such volumes printed before 1500, and the large proportion of them destined for a specific diocese (that is, not just for the Roman Use) confirms this function: while the inclusion of volumes for minor dioceses and for centers in Denmark, Sweden, or Portugal, prepared by printers with little or no other experience of music, shows how widespread such a concern was on the part of the ecclesiastical authorities.[38] It is possible to make too much of this: Haebler reported a missal originally printed in 1485 for the archdiocese of Zaragossa, which apparently did not sell, and was rebound three years later, where only the staves were printed with the text and the music had to be added later by hand.[39] But there is a fair number of liturgical volumes that have early manuscript ownership marks from outside the relevant diocese.

However, there are cases where a real concern for accuracy, or for the preservation of specific readings, can be demonstrated, contemporary with the spurt of concern for the reading of scripture, which led to the first great scholarly printed editions. Mary Berry, of Cambridge, England, has drawn my attention to the three different type-settings involved in copies of the Hopyl edition of the Sarum antiphoner of 1519–20, parts of which are specifically stated to have been edited by Sampson of King's College, Cambridge.[40] The different settings involve a number of notational changes, almost all of which can be put down to changes in the habits of the typesetters. Dr. Berry has suggested that the patterns of change between *virga* and *punctus* are significant, and indicate a general change in patterns of notation for isolated notes in chant. However, it seems to me to be equally probable that they may merely signal the state of the typesetter's case: more research needs to be done before either suggestion can be supported. What is clear, however, is the care taken to avoid changes in the musical content, alongside a number of minor, though significant and apparently deliberate changes in text-music alignment. The evidence suggests that this need for careful and precise placing of text syllables under specific notes must have slowed the production process to a significant extent, surely a strong indicator of its importance to the patron. This pattern of breaking up words into constituent syllables becomes more widespread during the first half of the sixteenth century, I believe, as a direct response to closer ecclesiastical control.

Other evidence of the concern for accurate detail is widespread: I have found small pasted-in printed words used as corrections in some liturgical incunables; Johann Winterburger, in a Salzburg missal of 1513, experimented with printing his musical notes in two colors (casting special sorts and anticipating the invention of single-impression music type), as a result of which two versions of the same chant could be superimposed, one for greater and one for lesser feasts.

When such patterns of extra labor for typesetters are put beside the increasing number of pocket instruction manuals for singing chant and the emerging habit of placing such manuals at the front of small liturgical books (that is, those not destined for the lectern), one is tempted to see a pattern of growing concern for the careful singing of the chant. Any historian of sixteenth-century religious politics will not be surprised by this and, indeed, will be able to advance many well-known reasons for it.

Certainly, the mere massive dissemination of printed liturgical music can tell us nothing; any authority would seize on the "power of

the press," and the reformed and Catholic churches, though preemi-
nent, were by no means alone in that. What is significant, though, is
the extent to which printers were taking extra pains to provide clear
and simple versions, the manner in which they clarified points of
doubt in later reprintings, and the extent to which many dioceses still
preserved their own forms of liturgy into the first half of the sixteenth
century.

If we should expect homogeneity and consistent readings as a
natural outgrowth of (as well as stimulus for) the urge for liturgical
printing, the same cannot be said for polyphony. The extent to which
local performing practices differed, the manner by which a single
piece was transmitted from one end of Europe to another, the absence
of any allegedly divine claims for an authorial version; all these argue
for freedom. I have already stated that these freedoms produced
different results in different centers, and I would like to cite a couple
of examples that are relevant to the problems faced by the printer of
music. The scribe employed in Padua cathedral in the 1520s took
excessive care with text placing, writing out in full customarily abbre-
viated text repetitions, while making his alignment of syllables and
notes very explicit. At about the same time, scribes preparing the first
collection of polyphony for the cathedral at Casale Monferrato took
time and energy in ironing out difficulties of complex rhythms and
syncopation. These scribes in two centers were copying from the
same printed books, the work of Petrucci and Antico. Similarly, the
compiler of a chanson manuscript from northern Italy added two
measures of ornamental cadence to a piece he copied from a print of
Petrucci.[41]

These examples of scribal freedom highlight the dilemma faced, or
ignored, by the printer of music. Was he to act as another scribe,
producing a version containing his own range of decisions, knowing
that they would be ignored by many purchasers? Or was he to try to
produce a version that was generally useful as a skeleton, appealing to
as many buyers as possible? The situation is complicated by the fact
that there was a surge in the increasing number of courts and churches
employing professional musicians for polyphony, by no means all of
whom appear to have been competent in the extempore interpretative
skills that had been traditional. It is further complicated by our
almost complete lack of knowledge of the immediate sources, the
provenance of the press-copies, for early printed music.

There is a little evidence: the preface to one volume indicates that
Peter Schöffer, the younger, had music sent to him from the Maestro
(Werrecore) at Milan cathedral: Egenolff appears to have copied a
large part of the contents of one of his polyphonic volumes from an

earlier print by Petrucci, and Gardane admitted to copying from Moderne.[42] In other cases, the name of an editor is attached to a specific volume, as in that of the first polyphonic volume of all.[43] For most other volumes, we are reduced to speculation: it seems a plausible assumption that almost all early music printing was the result of a request or commission from an unnamed patron, although this assumption is made on the basis of an argument involving the repertoire chosen for the print, the readings, and their possible provenance, an argument that is partly circular.

To return to the partial dilemma faced by the printer, I believe that most music printers before 1535–40 did not even consider the extent to which they should, or could, differ from musical scribes: they did not see as part of their responsibility the provision of a basic version that could be as widely used as possible. In this, I have changed my views recently: I have suggested elsewhere that Petrucci did try to provide such a basic version,[44] but I now think that this was an oversimplification of two elements of evidence.

On one hand, there is evidence of considerable care in the preparation of his version—extending to cancel sheets, to stop-press corrections, and to manuscript corrections made in-house—along with an equal care in its preservation and "improvement" from one edition to the next. Such concern is not surprising for a printer learning his craft and working in a Venice where his most successful colleague was Aldus Manutius. On the other hand, there is strong evidence that Petrucci's typesetters were allowed to follow their own inclinations in significant aspects of notational and musical detail. This would argue that Petrucci permitted his men to act as if they were independent scribes working on separate manuscripts. One may be, indeed, one was, a musician of a different generation from another: as a result, differences in approach, changes in notational style, have become fossilized in adjacent layers.[45] It seems to me logical to infer from this that Petrucci regarded his duties as being exactly those of any preparer of a musical manuscript, creating a version of the music that embraced his own inclinations (or those of his craftsmen). The idea of a reliable or generally authentic version went no further than ensuring that later editions faithfully reflected the first. As a result, it is not surprising that scribes in Padua, Casale Monferrato, or elsewhere, when copying from Petrucci's prints, made their own adjustments to his versions: indeed, Petrucci, well aware of the normal conduct of his professional colleagues, presumably would have expected such behavior and felt it to be inconceivable that he should claim any special authority for his version.

This pattern changed, and had changed before the end of the 1540s:

where and when the change took place we do not know. It must have been, in any case, a general process. But little evidence exists for the crucial years, for there were very few printers of polyphonic music in Italy before the late 1530s, and many of those printed but little. Antico, and Pasoti and Dorico, the first successors of Petrucci, followed in his footsteps, as far as content and editorial style were concerned.[46]

The major breakthrough presumably occurred late in the 1530s as a result of the confluence of two or three factors: first is the appearance of two major new printers of music in Venice—Scotto, closely followed by Gardane;[47] second is the development, which I have mentioned, of a new technique for setting music, which was more amenable to accurate use by musical laymen; third is apparently a rapidly expanding market which had to be satisfied, during the late 1520s and the 1530s, by manuscript copies, in particular of the new madrigals; and finally, composers seem to be establishing their own relationship with printing and printers.

I believe these last two are closely related. The surviving records of patrons and other amateurs seeking to acquire copies of music by the leading composers—and apparently experiencing some difficulties—not only speak to a growing demand for the music, but also speak equally eloquently of the composers' reluctance to release these copies freely.[49] This desire on the part of the professional composer to retain control over his music, perhaps allowing him to influence performances, may be seen partly as a reflection of a growing pride in creation, in the novelty or uniqueness of the work. It must equally be seen as a fear of bad copies and editions, or of inept and amateur performances, both ignoring the conventions of performance favored by the composer. In either situation, what looks like a desire for secrecy is really a new phenomenon, the composer's belief in the primacy of his own versions—perhaps as the only acceptable versions.

While some composers were trying to keep their work from circulating in manuscript, others were working with publishers. Carpentras oversaw the publication of a large part of his works at Avignon during the 1530s: he may have been a little ahead of his time, for it is recorded that he found the version of his lamentations, performed at the Vatican in 1524, to be so corrupt that he commissioned a new manuscript to be presented to the pope, Clement VII, for future use.[50]

Certainly, during the following years, printers do not seem to have been subjected to the pressure of the composers' demands. The biggest collections of music printed in Italy catered to the new enthu-

siasm for madrigals, principally by Festa and Verdelot, both composers who came to maturity in the older atmosphere of *laissez-faire*. The
existence of these collections seems to suggest that the growth in the
market for printed music preceded most composers' interest in controlling the versions printed. Certainly, it preceded any such concern
on the part of the printers themselves. When Gardane printed the
Motetti del Fiore in 1539 (editions of motets from volumes published
in Lyons and elsewhere) he made notational and other changes, many
of which would have affected details of performance. True, most of
the composers were not within reach, but it is significant that Gardane felt free to make such changes. [51]

If Gardane and Scotto, working side by side in Venice, with other
printers elsewhere in Italy, signal by their productivity a large growth
in the market, that growth is very unbalanced. Of some thirty volumes produced by Gardane in his first four years of printing, only a
quarter were of sacred music addressed to the traditional 1520s market of church musicians at their employment. The rest were all aimed
at secular performance, either by the same or other professionals in
social situations, or by the growing ranks of amateurs. I accept that
this imbalance is in part because many ecclesiastical institutions still
relied on printed church music only as a source from which to copy
into manuscripts for their own use; secular music, on the other hand,
seems to have been copied from print into manuscript with much less
frequency—perhaps because the same amateurs that encouraged its
printing did not waste their energies in copying it out, and perhaps
because they did not have any tradition of making independent
performing decisions that would be clarified by making their own
copies.

It is in these circumstances that composers began to be protective.
In 1543 Morales entered into a contract with the publisher Dorico, by
which the composer undertook to supply all the music to be
printed. [52] Soon after, as Mary Lewis has shown, other composers
went even further: Rore and Zarlino stipulated that Gardane should
follow instructions exactly: both wanted precise spacing of syllables
according to their own ideas: in the former's case, this apparently
involved a re-edition of works that had been inadequately presented
earlier. Rore also demanded that Gardane acquire additional type to
cover certain special musical symbols. [53]

This last point is of additional interest. In sixteenth-century musical notation, there are certain symbols that, on the surface, duplicate
each other, serving the same immediate function. I have shown
elsewhere that they still had subsidiary, hidden functions presenting
performing guidance. [54] During the 1520s and 1530s, some of these

VI

236

signs declined markedly in frequency: since they were operative in just that realm where the performer felt free to make changes, and since they required the casting of additional complex sorts of type, it is easy to see why they fell partly out of use, especially in printed volumes. That Rore was able to demand of Gardane that he should reinstate them in the composer's music is a reflection of Rore's concern for the representation of his wishes, as well as of Gardane's recognition as a working printer of the composer's right to make such demands.

I have tried, by following a number of diverse threads through this paper, to illustrate a series of correspondences. These include the shift from an emphasis on mixed anthologies to one on volumes for a single composer; the increasing demands made by the composer on the printer; an apparent change in the size and composition of the buying public for music, from professional to mixed professional and secular; the invention of an easier manner of printing music; a change, on the part of the printer, from activities typical of a musical scribe towards those typical of the humanist printer. I have suggested that all these changes probably took real effect in the 1530s and 1540s and that they follow, by only a few decades, what appears to have been (from the limited evidence of which I know) similar changes designed to make consistent and keep precise the singing of the clergy—a group perhaps only slightly less jealous of their professional skills than were the singers.

The significance of these changes, taken as a whole, can only be understood in the light of the nature of printed music. Both the format and the notation of music books preclude casual "browsing," and the volumes themselves would not have attracted any but the most avid of book collectors (because of appearance as much as content): purchasers can therefore be assumed to be readers and, in the case of musical volumes, performers, responsive to a greater or lesser degree to the guidance offered by printer and composer.

In the three hundred years before the early sixteenth century, despite enormous changes in notation and musical style, the performer had always been at least the equal of the composer in skill and esteem. He had added, by virtue of his gifts, almost everything that made first impact on the listener. The first major step in the erosion of this position (a process that was to continue for another three hundred years) is the one that I have described. It is the product of a new audience able to *use* printed music, and of composers seeking to impose *their* versions of the music on this group, basically unsophisticated in the traditions of performance. It is only because copies of music embodying these new attitudes and requirements could be printed cheaply and easily that the revolution in the role of the composer was successful.

Notes

1. The majority of indications of ownership come from isolated references—the presence of a name on the title page, for example. However, in a number of cases, inventories and library catalogues do survive, though not usually of specifically musical collections. The most distinguished exception is probably the collection at the Accademia Filarmonica in Verona, which is discussed in G. Turrini's "L'Accademia Filarmonica di Verona dalla fondazione (maggio 1543) al 1600 e il suo patrimonio musicale antico," *Atti dell'Accademia di Verona*, 5th ser., 18 (1941): 3–346. The majority of musical institutions were merely part of a larger organization (as was the chapel of a royal household, for example) and, in these cases, the musical books (except for theoretical writings) were kept apart from the library: any inventory of the whole institution tended to make only cursory mention of the existence of a number of volumes of music. (This is, of course, in distinction to the famous inventories of the French royal library at the end of the Middle Ages.) A notable exception comprises the series of indices to the remarkable collection of Ferdinand Colón: the printed music in these is discussed by C. Chapman in "Printed Collections of Polyphonic Music Owned by Ferdinand Columbus," *Journal of the American Musicological Society* 21 (1968): 34–84, and the analyses are extended to other musical material in D. Plamenac, "Excerpta Colombina: Items of Musical Interest in Fernando Colón's 'Regestrum,'" *Miscelanea en homenaje a Monsenor Higinio Angles* (Barcelona: Consejo Superior de investigaciones científicas, 1958–61), 2:663–87. Among collections owned by other individuals could be included that of Johann Herwart in Augsburg (see M. Göllner, "Die Augsburger Bibliothek Herwart und ihren Lautentabulaturen," *Fontes artis musicae* 16 [1969]: 29) or that part of the collection of the Earl of Arundel that found its way into the Lumley Library, and thence to the British Library (see S. Jayne and F. Johnson, *The Lumley Library: The Catalogue of 1609* [London: British Museum, 1956]).

The purchases of many institutional collections of music can best be reconstructed from ownership and library marks. The music surviving in the collections of the Cappella Sistina and the Cappella Guilia in the Vatican has been inventoried by J. Llorens in the series *Studi e testi:* both collections included early printed editions of music, as did that of S. Luigi dei Francesi (see L. Perkins, "Notes bibliographiques au sujet de l'ancien fond musical de l'Eglise de Saint Louis des Français à Rome," *Fontes artis musicae* 16 [1969]: 57–71, and M. Staehelin, "Zur Schicksal des alten Musikalien-Fonds von San Luigi dei Francesi in Rom," *Fontes artis musicae* 17 [1970]: 120–27). The music acquired by the chapel of the Electors of Bavaria is almost all in the Bayerisches Staatsbibliothek in Munich, while that for the chapel of the Fugger family of Augsburg is in the library there. (This collection includes much more than merely chapel music; see R. Schaal, "Die Musikbibliothek von Raimund Fugger d.j.: ein Beitrag zur Musiküberlieferung des 16. Jahrhunderts," *Acta Musicologica* 29 [1957]: 126.)

Among the ownership inscriptions of composers and theorists there is that of Gregor Aichinger (see M. Lewis, "Antonio Gardane and His Publications of Sacred Music, 1538–55" [Ph.D. diss., Brandeis University, 1979], 2:553–54: this section of the dissertation includes references to other collections of early printed music, bound as sets, some of which have ownership inscriptions) and what may be signatures of Willaert and Lassus on surviving books.

Finally, references in theoretical writings as well as the variant versions of copied music show further details of the wide dissemination of printed music: this point is touched on below.

2. It is clear, despite the paucity of the information, that prices for music books dropped fairly consistently throughout the first half of the century. Data in Colón's catalogues (see n. 1) show that Antico's printing of the 1520s was cheaper than the luxury volumes of Petrucci from the previous two decades. D. Heartz, *Pierre Attaingnant, Royal Printer of Music* (Berkeley and Los Angeles: University of California Press, 1969), 105–20, offers some details for the following years, and the early records of the Accademia Filarmonica of Verona [see n. 1] include lists of prices paid. These are discussed further in Lewis, "Antonio Gardarne," 23–28. Much important information on the sale of music books in northern Europe is in A. Göhler, *Verzeichnis der in den internationalen Frankfurter und Leipziger Messkatalogen der Jahre 1564 bis 1759 angezeigten Musikalien* (Leipzig: Kahnt, 1902; reprinted Hilversun: Olms, 1965).

3. The only general inventory of these theoretical printed volumes is in the series *Répertoire International des Sources Musicales*, which is attempting to provide a catalogue of all printed and manuscript music and writings on music datable before 1800. (The volumes are in two series, A—which covers printed volumes of music by one composer, and B—which comprises all the other categories of material. I shall refer to the volumes hereafter with the abbreviation *RISM*.) These texts are listed in series B, volume VI, parts 1 and 2, *Ecrits imprimés concernant la musique*, ed. F. Lesure (Munich: Henle, 1971): although many additions need to be made to this list, it does give a representative view of the field.

4. One should perhaps refer here to the continuing distinction, still found after 1500, between the *musicus*—the scholar expert in the theory of music—and the *cantor*—the performer, more lowly in rank. The distinction is becoming blurred during the fifteenth century, with some of the leading theorists (among them Tinctoris at Naples, Gafori in Milan and Spataro in Bologna) also holding leading musical positions.

5. There are very few examples of this during the early years of the sixteenth century, and the principal case involves the frequent printing of elementary instruction in singing plainchant.

6. There is no general catalogue of all this repertoire, which is vast. *RISM*, B, VIII, *Das Deutschen Kirchenlied* (Kassel: Bärenreiter, 1975–80) is an inventory of publications of the reformed genre. K. Meyer-Baer, *Liturgical Music Incunabula* (London: Bibliographical Society, 1962) is a desperately outdated list of titles with comments on the amount and style of music printed in each: there is no comparable work on liturgical music printed after 1500, although I am in the process of trying to compile a similar list for the period before c. 1540. English reformed liturgical printing hardly enters into the field under discussion: the best general study is in D. Krummel, *English Music Printing, 1553–1700* (London: Bibliographical Society, 1975). The best study of the Huguenot psalter from a musical point of view is P. Pidoux, *Le Psautier Huguenot du XVIe siècle* (three volumes: Basle: Bärenreiter, 1962–69): see also R. Kingdon, "Patronage, Piety and Printing in Sixteenth-Century Europe," *A Festschrift for Frederick Artz*, ed. D. Pinkney and T. Ropp (Durham, N.C.: Duke University Press, 1964), 19–36.

7. This is particularly true in the fifteenth century and the early years of the next, perhaps with the sole exception of those printers who also printed introductions to singing chant. But the early printers of composed music, Petrucci, Antico, Dorico

VI

Early Music Printing: Working for a Specialized Market   239

and Pasoti, and others, printed almost no liturgical books between them. At the same time, many of the greater liturgical printers, while printing many such volumes, also printed other material: examples would include Ratdolt, Sensenschmidt, and Spira of the fifteenth century, Giunta, Petit, or Winterburger of the early sixteenth.

8. The bulk of this material, especially after c. 1550, comprises printed volumes devoted to one composer (on which, see below). These are inventoried in *RISM*, A, *Einzeldrucke vor 1800*, in nine volumes with two of supplement to appear. Anthologies for the period before 1700 are listed in *RISM*, B, I, *Recueils imprimés, XVIe–XVIIe siècles* (of which the first volume appeared in 1960, edited by F. Lesure, and a very necessary revision and completion by H. M. Brown is in progress).

The easiest definition of polyphony is perhaps that adopted in *The New Grove Dictionary of Music and Musicians* (1980), s.v. "polyphony": "A term used . . . to designate various important categories of European music: music in more than one part, music in many parts, and the style in which all or several of the musical parts move to some extent independently." The word "part" here means an individual musical line that is to be performed concurrently with other lines, and has nothing to do with the number of sections into which a piece of music may fall.

9. The first printer of such music was Ottaviano dei Petrucci, working in Venice and, later, Fossombrone. The first volume was his *Harmonice Musices Odhecaton A* [1501]: see S. Boorman, "The 'First' Edition of the *Odhecaton A*," *Journal of the American Musicological Society* 30 (1977): 183–207. More detail on this and other volumes printed by Petrucci can be found in S. Boorman, "Petrucci at Fossombrone: A Study of Early Music Printing with Special Reference to the *Motetti de la Corona* (1514–19)," (Ph.D. diss., London University, 1976), which is a study of the printing techniques and the musical versions printed.

The first volume of liturgical music in which the music was printed (rather than added by hand) is a Gradual for Constance, printed apparently c. 1473 (see A. H. King, "The 500th Anniversary of Music Printing," *The Musical Times* 114 [1973]: 1220), followed by a Roman missal printed by Han in Rome, 1476. From 1481 the techniques of printing liturgical music spread rapidly through the principal centers of printing.

10. Famous examples of this pattern would include John Day, Granjon, Haultin, and Plantin. Because of the high rate of loss of early printed polyphony (exemplified, for example, in the numbers of entries in Colón's catalogues for which no copies survive), it is difficult to tell how music printing was viewed by such men as Nikolaus Faber, Marcolini, or the younger Peter Schöffer, from whom very little music printing survives.

11. Examples of five masses per volume in the work of Petrucci would include many of the most important composers of the turn of the century—Josquin, Isaac, Agricola, La Rue, Obrecht, Ghiselin, and, of the next generation, Mouton and Févin. (Brief details can be found in C. Sartori, *Bibliografia delle opere musicali stampate da Ottaviano Petrucci*, Biblioteca di bibliografia italiana, vol. 18 [Florence: Olschki, 1948], supplemented by his "Nuove conclusive aggiunte alla 'Bibliografia del Petrucci'," *Collectanea historiae musicae* [Florence: Olschki, 1953], 175–210). Details of Attaignant's volumes can be found in D. Heartz, *Pierre Attaignant: the* series of seven mass volumes appeared in 1532, were each anthologies, and had from thirty-six to forty folios; the chanson volumes were a continual mainstay of his output and the thirteen volumes of motets appeared in 1534–35: both sets tended to be printed in separate part-books of sixteen folios each. The most useful inventory of the music in madrigal prints is E. Vogel, *Bibliothek der gedruckten weltlichen Vocalmusik Italiens aus den Jahren 1500–1700* (Berlin, 1892: this has been revised,

with the incorporation of additions by A. Einstein, C. Sartori, and F. Lesure to the alphabetical series. The chronological list of anthologies still awaits revision.)

There are two principal exceptions to the ranges of figures cited here. One concerns the frottola repertoire: the eleven volumes of frottole printed by Petrucci regularly contain about sixty pieces, but these are so short and so repetitive that all four parts can be fitted onto some fifty-six to sixty-four folios. The second exception is German and apparently a direct reflection of the need felt by Reformed congregations for music to perform and hear. A number of large volumes was printed, containing pre-Reformation motets by Franco-Flemish composers of the international circuit, alongside more recent compositions by Germans. The earliest such volumes are the work of Andraeae (usually referred to as Formschneider or Graphaeus in musical citations), two volumes printed in Nuremberg in 1537 and 1538: *Novum et insigne opus musicum* has 48 motets on 430 folios (in six part-books) and the *Secundus tomus* has 43 pieces on 368 folios. The other principal printers were Petreius (also of Nuremberg), Kriesstein in Augsburg, and Rhau in Wittenberg (in 1543; the title of his volume of hymns records 134 items for four to six voices, which are printed in four volumes of over 130 pages each, and his volume of vesper music of 1540 is similarly large). The practice of producing such large volumes eases during the 1540s, presumably because the most urgent demands for music had been met. But, during the 1550s, Berg and Neuber (again in Nuremberg) produced two large multivolume sets, one in 1553 of three volumes of psalms (with a somewhat smaller fourth in 1554), and one of motets in 1558–59—224 pieces on nearly 1,500 folios. The implied number of folios for each piece must be divided by the number of separate part-books, each carrying its own voice, so that (in the last example) the 224 pieces only occupy some 300 folios for the top voice: but even this figure gives some idea of how much more space is required to lay out a text when it is with its musical setting.

12. The most famous example is probably that of the first book of madrigals for four voices by Arcadelt: the first surviving edition is dated 1539 (although it implies an earlier, now lost, edition) and at least fifty-four others are still extant, printed over a period of 115 years. The case of Josquin is rather more interesting, for the pieces that are first ascribed to him after his death in 1521 include several that are very unlike anything surely by him. A work by Févin was ascribed to Josquin in a printed edition of 1578, works by Bauldeweyn, Mouton, and (probably) Gombert in an edition of 1564, and others appear in earlier editions. Other motets, which are almost surely by Josquin, also appear in German sources, with additional voices supplied to enrich the texture, which (incidentally) destroy the clarity and balance that were recognized as hallmarks of the composer.

13. The mass volumes that Petrucci devoted to single composers are not really relevant here, since they contained only five works. More significant is the fact that motet, frottola, and other secular volumes that he published were always anthologies, showing no sign of plan in the choice of composer, text, or style. The earliest secular volumes devoted to the work of one composer are that for Bernardo Pisano in 1520 (and claiming to have been printed by Petrucci), one for both Tromboncino and Cara in 1520 (although this has two composers' works, it is relevant in that both are carefully named on the title page), and then a rapidly increasing number of volumes of madrigals by Festa and Verdelot and others during the 1530s, even though a number of these quietly include works by other composers.

14. There are very few examples of this last type of anthology; the two most important are both for Florentine weddings, that of Cosimo de' Medici and Eleonora of Toledo in 1539 and that of Ferdinando de' Medici and Christine of Lorraine in 1589, although others survive, notably several for minor events in German cities such

as Coburg. While some other such events may be commemorated in volumes without being specified, many composers merely incorporated their special compositions into a miscellaneous volume of motets or madrigals. Wert is a particular example, for he preserved several celebratory madrigals in this manner.

15. Recent arguments by Lewis ("Antonio Gardane," 185ff.) and Powers (in "Tonal Types and Modal Categories in Renaissance Polyphony," *Journal of the American Musicological Society* 34 [1981]: 428–70) do not really bear on this question. In very few of the cases that they cite can it be shown that the composers intended the modal arrangement while composing or arranging the order of the pieces. In the majority of their examples, the arrangement is one that clearly postdates the composition of all the works in the anthologies cited, not infrequently because the contents of the volumes involve several composers. In other words, a conscious modal ordering of a sequence of pieces, and its preservation in their subsequent editions, is as rare as any other unifying device, and most of its early occurrences are the work of a printer or editor, and not a composer.

16. The unity of a liturgical volume, of course, resides not in its content, but solely in its function: in this respect, it is analogous to the limited unity displayed by a volume of hymns or madrigals, namely one of the occasions when it might be used.

17. There is the amusing and well-known instance in the work of Petrucci, involving one of the few nonmusical books. Hieronymus Posthumus, the corrector of Paulus de Middelburgh's *De recta Paschae celebratione* (1513) explains that the errors in the volume are a result of the ignorance of the printer (presumably the typesetter), Joannes Baptista. If this volume, printed in Latin (though with Greek and other complexities), could stimulate such a result, how much more was it likely with more obscure alphabets.

18. It is true that, at least until the early work of Gardane, the exact alignment of each syllable of the text with its own note was not normally considered necessary. However, many syllables are so placed, and the opening of each phrase of text was carefully aligned in most cases. There is a considerable body of evidence to show that, when manuscripts were being copied, the text was sometimes written in before the music, and that, in certain situations, a scribe might change the order of copying, according to the style of the text-setting. Some evidence has emerged to suggest that the order of setting and printing the type for music and text could also be varied when convenient.

19. This revolution first appeared in the two surviving musical fragments printed by Rastell in London, perhaps in 1526 (see A. H. King, "The Significance of John Rastell in Early Music Printing," *The Library*, 5th series, 26 [1971]: 197–214). However, its first real user was Pierre Attaingnant in Paris, beginning in 1528. D. Heartz has suggested (in *The New Grove*, 675) that Rastell may have had the idea from knowledge of Attaingnant's experiments.

There is one minute exception that concerns the use of a few sorts of type with both stave and note in some printings of a missal for Salzburg, principally by Winterburger in 1513, but also on other occasions. These are unique in that they still involve two runs through the press: only certain notes are set in this way, to indicate that they should only be sung on festal occasions. The rest of the music is still printed in black, with the slave lines in red. I have yet to determine whether this occurrence (which is mentioned below) is a direct response to some special notation in the tradition of manuscripts for Salzburg.

20. See Lewis, "Antonio Gardane," 158–60. In the case of Petrucci, there is one very indicative instance: the masses of Brumel and of Ghiselin were printed almost exactly one month apart. However, they both show a change from one paper to

VI

another, in the case of the earlier volume almost halfway through, and in the case of the later, near the beginning of the work. The implication of this and other typographical evidence has to be that they were being prepared simultaneously: therefore, they can not be taken as an indication of how fast Petrucci's shop could work. See my forthcoming article, "A Case of "Work-and-Turn" Half-Sheet Imposition in the Early Sixteenth Century."

21. The Antico volume was printed in 1516, and dedicated to the Pope, who is seen on the title page receiving a copy of the volume. (On this, see my "Renaissance Music Printing: An Indirect Connection with the Raphael Circle," to appear.) Dorico copied this title closely in his volume of Morales masses, book 2 of 1544, and in the first volume of Palestrina's masses, dated 1554. S. Cusick, "Valerio Dorico, Music Printer in Sixteenth-Century Rome" (Ph.D. diss., University of North Carolina, 1975), 108–16, discusses the possibility that Dorico may have acquired some initial letters from Antico, the only previous significant publisher of polyphonic music in the Roman area. Petrucci used his woodblock initial letters until some of them were nearly unrecognizable from damage and general wear: see S. Boorman, "Petrucci at Fossombrone: Some New Editions and Cancels," *Source Materials and the Interpretation of Music: A Memorial Volume to Thurston Dart*, ed. Ian Bent (London: Stainer & Bell, 1981), 129–53. I believe it can be shown that several of Petrucci's materials later surfaced in Rome, while I suspect that Scotto may have acquired certain letters from Dorico during the 1530s. Certainly Gardane continued to use some initials for several years: see Lewis, "Antonio Gardane," 68–77 (which shows the extent to which some early letters were modeled on the contemporary Scotto styles) and 142–55. Dorico seems to have been unusual among early printers of polyphony in that he apparently designed some letters to have a relation to the content of the page—thus, at least theoretically, limiting their reuse.

22. Cusick, "Valerio Dorico," 152–54, shows that Dorico was required to buy special paper for at least one of the large-format luxury volumes, as a result of a contract with the composer, Morales. While no such evidence survives for Petrucci or other printers, the ordinary volumes are often printed on rather poor paper.

23. There are examples of lute music and of song *(frottola)* with lute accompaniment printed by Petrucci before 1510, whereas the first volume of keyboard music is not until 1517. This is partly because of the difficulty of printing chords for organ: indeed, the first volume is printed from woodblocks.

24. From his first volume, Petrucci established the practice of printing partbooks in oblong format, a custom that prevailed for most of the century. Unusually, he also printed in the other arrangement, with all parts on one page, but still in the small oblong format. All his volumes, as a result, are in oblong quarto, with two sheets to the gathering. Folio size was often used for the more special volumes of music.

25. Although there are theoretical references stating that scores were being used for the process of composition during the first half of the century, and even an illustration of a score in one treatise (Lampadius, *Compendium musices*, 1537), the first publications of scores as a means of circulating music are not until 1577. These make clear in the titles that they have a specific function: *Musica di diversi autori* (Venice: Gardane, 1577) states "partite in caselle per sonar d'instromento perfetto" (put into score with bar-lines for playing on a keyboard instrument), and *Tutti i madrigali di Cipriano di Rore* (idem) reads "spartiti et accomodati per sonar d'ogni sorte d'istrumento perfetto, et per qualcunque studioso di contrapunti" (put into score and arranged for playing on any sort of keyboard instrument and for any student of counterpoint).

26. It is perhaps worth mentioning a slight reservation: while the intended public,

and also the actual public, is almost entirely a using (performing) public, there were other users. Theorists of music must necessarily have worked from the printed editions, reconstructing the score if they needed: it can be shown that the great Swiss scholar Glareanus certainly worked from some printed editions in preparing his own works.

27. It is true, as I have suggested above, that the theorists of the late fifteenth and sixteenth centuries turned more towards a distinction between the abstract (the theoretical structures of music and of composition, and statements about intervals and harmonic series) and the practical (not only in beginning to write instruction for the performer, but also in a recognition that the ear—that is, the response to actual music—must play a greater part in explanations of theory).

28. This is apparent, although only to a limited extent, in the range of variant readings preserved in many sources of the same pieces, especially in those few cases where one can still demonstrate the existence of an exemplar for a surviving version. On this point see S. Boorman, "Petrucci's Type-setters and the Process of Stem-matics," *Formen und Probleme der uberlieferung mehrstimmiger Musik in Zeitalter Josquins Desprez*, ed. L. Finscher, Wolfenbütteler Forschungen, 6:245–80. The manner in which one can trace the changes made by the printers and the extent to which one can demonstrate editing procedures are both discussed below.

29. It is necessary, again, to except that repertoire that was available to the single performer, in particular the *frottola*, as a genre. Petrucci's eleven volumes of this music speak to an interest on the part of at least some public, one which, as I suggest in the next section, is probably specifically related to court circles. The books also raise the question of who might have encouraged Petrucci to print such a repertoire, a question to which there is at present no answer.

30. D. Krummel, "Musical Functions and Bibliographical Forms," *The Library*, 5th ser., 32 (1976): 317.

31. A famous section dealing with music in the *Book of the Courtier* makes this clear: Federico Fregoso states, early in the Second Book, that the most beautiful singing, in his opinion, is that of recitative to the viol, which forms a good description of one manner of singing *frottole*. He continues to describe the beauty of four-stringed instruments and of keyboard music, while adding that it is enough for the courtier to be acquainted with such music. Certainly, courtiers were able to hold their parts in singing simple music together: W. Rubsamen, in *Literary Sources of Secular Music in Italy (ca. 1500)* (Berkeley and Los Angeles: University of California Press, 1943), 5, quotes from a letter written by Galeazzo Visconti to Isabella d'Este, in which he describes a pleasure trip he took with the Duchess Beatrice Sforza and her jester: "I was required to join the duchess and Dioda in her carriage, where we sang more than 25 songs, well harmonised for three voices. . . ." On the other hand, there were courtiers who were versed in musical theory, as Castiglione implies held for Giuliano de' Medici.

32. See, for example, the details about the statutes of the Accademia Filarmonica of Verona, dated 1543, as given in E. Lowinsky, "Music in the Culture of the Renaissance," *Journal of the History of Ideas* 15 (1954), reprinted in *Renaissance Essays*, P. Kristeller and P. Wiener (New York: Harper and Row, 1968), 337–81. The relevant extracts are on page 343 and do not make it entirely explicit that the members, as opposed to the hired professional musicians, were to be fluent in (or taught) polyphony, although this seems to be the implication. It is certainly true for some later academies.

33. It is apparent that many German cities witnessed a growth of lay musical ability during the century, almost certainly as a direct result of the effect of religious

VI

244

reform on education. One may question whether the amount of music published in Germany is a true reflection of this growth, or whether it is at least in part that of the protestant movements' general awareness of the power of the press, coupled with a real need for editions of polyphony approved by the religious leaders.

34. For details of the two most significant examples of this trend, see A. Newcomb, *The Madrigal at Ferrara, 1579–1597* (Princeton, N.J.: Princeton University Press, 1980), with its useful references to other cities, and I. Fenlon, *Music and Patronage in Sixteenth-Century Mantua* (Cambridge: At the University Press, 1980).

35. The whole controversy is discussed in detail by C. Palisca, in "The Artusi-Monteverdi Controversy," *The Monteverdi Companion*, ed. D. Arnold and N. Fortune (London: Faber & Faber, 1968), 133–66. In the first attack, Artusi does put the discussion into the mouths of a theorist and a learned amateur: however, half of his volume is concerned specifically with theories of tuning, a classic subject for theoretical argument late in the century. In any case, a number of the Accademie made provision for amateur study of music theory, and, indeed, the famous changes that led to opera and the new styles of the seventeenth century themselves stem in part from a theoretical discussion of classical Greek music.

36. For a discussion of the extent of such variants in a principal repertoire of the late fifteenth century, see A. Atlas, *The Cappella Giulia Chansonnier (Rome, Biblioteca Apostolica Vaticana, C.G.XIII.27)*, Musicological Studies, Vol. 27 (Brooklyn: Institute of Medieval Music, 1975): for a study of the function of these changes, and of the application to them of stemmatic theory, see S. Boorman, "The Uses of Filiation in Early Music," *Text* 1 (1981): 167–84; and for detailed studies of aspects of the problem, see the papers by A. Atlas, M. Bent, and S. Boorman, in *Music in Medieval and Early Modern Europe*, ed. I. Fenlon (Cambridge: At the University Press, 1981).

37. See E. Eisenstein, *The Printing Press as an Agent of Change* (Cambridge: At the University Press, 1979), the sections starting on p. 80 and p. 88.

38. Meyer-Baer, *Liturgical Music Incunabula*, n. 6.

39. K. Haebler, *Bibliografía ibérica del siglo XV* (The Hague and Leipzig, 1903–17), as reported in *Liturgical Music Incunabula*, catalogue entry no. 52.

40. In an unpublished paper, "English Editing of Gregorian Chant between 1519 and 1520: The Two Editions of Part III of the Sarum Antiphonals, Printed by Wolfgang Hopyl of Paris in 1519 and 1520."

41. For details, see Atlas, *The Cappella Giulia Chansonnier*, 130–31.

42. The dedication to Schöffer's edition (of 1539) of *Cantiones quinque vocum selectissimae . . . Mutetarum liber primus* states that he had received the music from Werrecore: the connection between Egenolff and Petrucci's versions of music can be shown on grounds of the readings preserved: in 1539, Gardane published two volumes of motets that he had taken from the work of Moderne: on this last, see S. Pogue, "A Sixteenth-Century Editor at Work: Gardane and Moderne," *The Journal of Musicology* 1(1982): 217–38.

43. One of the two dedicatory letters in Petrucci's *Harmonice Musices Odhecaton A* [1501] refers to the editorial work of an otherwise unknown Petrus Castellanus. Editors' names are attached to several of the German post-Reformation collections of church music.

44. See note 28: my argument here hinged on largely on the extent to which Petrucci showed concern for what he was printing.

45. For many examples of this, see my dissertation, "Petrucci at Fossombrone."

46. The early volumes of Pasoti and Dorico actually include a number of new editions of Petrucci's titles, in which the layout and format, while not identical, clearly reflect the earlier editions. Antico's titles of 1520 and 1521 include basically the

same repertoire as that put out by Petrucci, although he does then extend it towards the work of younger composers in the same genres. In the previous decade, while at Rome, he had attempted to rival Petrucci: he published mostly secular music (as far as we can now tell) with the notable exception of the large folio *Liber quindecim missarum* already mentioned. His expansion into sets of volumes of sacred music follows the end of Petrucci's output.

47. Girolamo Scotto was a member of the printing family of Venice. His uncle and his brother, both Ottaviano, published considerable numbers of liturgical volumes, and the second also financed some of the work of Antico. Girolamo seems to have had some contacts with the printers of the 1520s, and his early volumes dating from the mid 1530s show considerable similarities with theirs. He has not been adequately studied recently, although Jane Bernstein is compiling an inventory of his output.

Antonio Gardane has been thought to have been trained in Lyons at the house of Moderne. There is considerable evidence that he and Scotto worked either as rivals or as close allies on a number of volumes. In some cases, both produced a title, while apparently working from different exemplars: in others, the versions suggest that one copied directly from the other. However, they lived and worked, apparently without severe strain, in the same city for many years. The most recent study of Gardane that discusses these issues is Lewis, "Antonio Gardane." Also, Lewis, "Antonio Gardane's Early Connections with the Willaert Circle," *Music in Medieval and Early Modern Europe*, ed. I. Fenlon (Cambridge: At the University Press, 1981), 209–26, discusses the evidence for how Gardane obtained copy for some of his volumes. For an extension of this into later music, see below, note 53.

48. For a survey of the manuscript sources for this genre during the 1520s and 1530s, see I. Fenlon and J. Haar, "Fonti e cronologia dei madrigali di Costanzo Festa," *Rivista italiana di musicologia* 13 (1978): 212–42; and J. Haar, "The Early Madrigal: A Re-appraisal of Its Sources and Its Character," *Music in Medieval and Early Modern Europe*, ed. I. Fenlon (Cambridge: At the University Press, 1981), 163–92.

49. See Lewis, "Antonio Gardane's Early Connections," 209–10.

50. On the Avignon contract, see D. Heartz, *Pierre Attaingnant*, 110–17. The manuscript is Vatican, Cappella Sistina, Ms. 163.

51. These editorial changes are discussed in Pogue, "A Sixteenth-Century Editor at Work." Significantly, too, printers seem not to have been very concerned to assign works to the correct composers, either when first printing a volume or in subsequent editions: see my forthcoming "Some Nonconflicting Attributions, and Some Newly Anonymous Compositions, from the Early Sixteenth Century."

52. This is discussed in Cusick, "Valerio Dorico," 152–55.

53. Mary Lewis, "Composer and Printer in the Sixteenth Century: Gardane, Rore, and Zarlino," paper read to the 44th annual meeting of the American Musicological Society, Minneapolis, Minnesota, 1978.

54. "Notational Spelling and Scribal Habit," *Quellenstudien zur Musik der Renaissance, ii, Datierung und Filiation von Musikhandschriften der Josquin-Zeit*, ed. L. Finscher, Wolfenbütteler Forschungen, 26:66–109.

SOME NON-CONFLICTING ATTRIBUTIONS, AND SOME NEWLY ANONYMOUS COMPOSITIONS, FROM THE EARLY SIXTEENTH CENTURY*

A surprisingly large number of early madrigals carry conflicting attributions in the printed sources of the 1530s and early 1540s. For example, twenty-four of the ninety-five settings listed in Hans Musch's recent book on Festa appear in various sources under at least two composers' names;[1] among other pieces in the same position are some ascribed to Arcadelt or Verdelot – or at least appearing in volumes dedicated to those composers and carrying no other names at the head of the page.

In a number of cases, these conflicting 'attributions' cause little concern for the present-day scholar. The presence of a madrigal in the early editions of Arcadelt's first book, published without ascriptions,[2] does not mean that the printers believed it to have been by

* I wish to express my gratitude to the Harvard University Center for Italian Renaissance Studies for awarding me a fellowship during the year 1983–4, and to the Director and Staff at Villa I Tatti for facilitating my research and making my stay so congenial.

[1] H. Musch, *Costanzo Festa als Madrigalkomponist*, Sammlung musikwissenschaftlicher Abhandlungen 61 (Baden-Baden, 1977), pp. 157–69. Additional pieces and some new concordances are cited in I. Fenlon and J. Haar, 'Fonti e cronologia dei madrigali di Costanzo Festa', *Rivista Italiana di Musicologia*, 13 (1978), on pp. 159–69.

[2] For a study of this volume and its multitudinous editions, see T. W. Bridges, 'The Publishing of Arcadelt's First Book of Madrigals' (Ph.D. dissertation, Harvard University, 1982). A modern transcription, with comments on the earlier editions, appears in *Jacobi Arcadelt opera omnia*, ed. A. Seay, Corpus Mensurabilis Musicae 31/ii (n.p., 1970). This edition will be cited hereinafter as *Arcadelt*.

For many of the printed volumes mentioned or discussed in this paper, the references and descriptions in RISM (K. Schlager, ed., *Einzeldrücke vor 1800*, Répertoire International des Sources Musicales A/1, Kassel, 1971–81 [designated by letter and number]; F. Lesure, ed., *Recueils imprimés, XVIe–XVIIe siècles*, ibid. B/iv/1, Munich and Duisburg, 1960 [designated by date with superscript number]) or the New Vogel (F. Lesure and C. Sartori, eds., *Bibliografia della musica italiana vocale profane pubblicata dal 1500 al 1700*, Pomezia, 1977; rev. edn of E. Vogel, *Bibliothek der gedruckten weltlichen Vocalmusik Italiens, aus den Jahren*

Arcadelt, as is made clear by the consistency of an attribution to, say, Corteccia, once names became normal. The situation is a little more complex with Verdelot's early books, during the period when Scotto was printing and publishing material from wood-blocks cut by Andrea Antico,[3] and was apparently following rather different principles for supplying composers' names.

It is the purpose of this paper to show that a number of these 'conflicting' attributions are really irrelevant, that one of the names involved is, in each case, the product of one of a limited range of printing-house procedures or errors, traceable through bibliographical analysis. Some of these variant attributions have not been seriously accepted by any modern scholar: however, the process of demonstration in those cases will also throw light on others that are more in need of resolution.

I

During the 1530s and the very early 1540s the processes of Italian music printing underwent changes far more drastic than those involved merely in the introduction of single-impression music type. No doubt this innovation was in some measure responsible for other changes; but they involve, as a whole, the conversion of music printing from a craft (which it clearly had been for both Petrucci and Antico) into a business, streamlined, relatively efficient and (eventually) systematic in its procedures.

One of the places where this is most immediately apparent is in the layout on the page, including the methods for handling head-lines, composer ascriptions and so on. The transition is quite marked, as

---

1500 bis 1700, Berlin, 1892) are not satisfactory or sufficient to enable the reader to distinguish editions or single copies. Therefore, at the first reference of substance to a new volume, I give below a transcription of the title-page, together with such notes as are necessary to supplement these reference works. In my transcriptions and notes, which are not intended to be comprehensive, the word 'flower' refers to a printer's flower, which need not represent a flower as such; the collation, when given, arranges the partbooks in the standard order of Cantus, Tenor, Altus, Bassus, Quintus, etc. Thereafter the volume is cited by its reference siglum in RISM (whenever possible) in order to save excessive duplication of bibliographical detail.

References to composers' names appearing in the early editions are here given in italics if they are direct quotations of the original form. In such cases, a final point may well appear (if part of the original), and this should not be confused with the end of a sentence in the present text.

[3] These are discussed by C. W. Chapman in her doctoral dissertation, 'Andrea Antico' (Harvard University, 1964).

Non-conflicting attributions and newly anonymous compositions

can be seen from a comparison of any early Scotto edition (from the mid 1530s) with almost any madrigal volume from the presses of Gardane or Scotto of the later 1540s. The most obvious change is in layout, in the placing of the start of each piece. The various Scotto editions from Antico's blocks always start a new piece at the beginning of a new line,[4] although this could be any line on the page, including the last. Thus the twenty-one pieces in the Bassus part of the first surviving (and probably actually the first) edition of Verdelot's first book of five-voice madrigals[5] start variously on any of the five staves which occupy each page: only four madrigals actually open a page, while six begin on the last stave. By contrast, Gardane's edition,[6] which appeared in 1541, has already gone a long way towards arranging the pieces in a manner to which we are more

[4] This is something that is not always found once single-impression type takes over from blocks. With wood-blocks, there was a strong incentive for starting new pieces at the beginnings of new lines, for this gave the printer the flexibility to alter the order of items in subsequent editions, in exactly the manner permitted by blocks prepared for a volume of drawings or of maps. There is no reason to suppose that the Antico–Scotto partnership did not anticipate the possibility of later editions: the history of earlier music printers – Petrucci, Antico himself, or the Dorico brothers – suggests that this was seen as a normal practice, while some of the first Scotto editions were themselves taken from Antico blocks previously printed by other men.

[5] RISM V1223; New Vogel 2887. Both suggest the date *ca*[1535].
The Altus and Bassus partbooks survive, labelled
Madrigali a cinque Libro primo. / A [B].
Oblong quarto-in-eights: EF⁸; GH⁸.
The *Tavola*, on the first verso, is in one column, in order of the compositions in the book, and is of the same setting of type for both parts. This setting was probably used for all four parts, for it lists the nineteenth piece *Deh non gionger tormenti*; these words are the second phrase of the madrigal *Purtroppo donn'in van'*, and the first words sung by the Cantus, Altus and Quintus parts. This piece is misnumbered *20* in the Bassus, fol. H6ʳ; *Altro non e'l mio amor*, the twelfth piece, is misnumbered *11* in the Altus.
The copies consulted for this study were, Altus: Paris, Bibliothèque Nationale, Rés. Vmd. 30; Bassus: Bologna, Civico Museo Bibliografico Musicale, R 140(2); both complete.
For the actual date of this volume see below, note 62. *Pace* the New Vogel, these partbooks contain sixteen folios (i.e. thirty-two pages) each, as probably did the other partbooks; the last folio of the Bassus is completely blank.

[6] RISM 1541¹⁷; New Vogel 2885.
[flower] CANTVS [flower] / LE DOTTE, ET ECCELLENTE COMPOSITIONI DE I MA=/drigali di VERDELOT, A cinque Voci, & da diversi perfettissimi Musici fat=/te. Novamente ristampate, & con ogni diligentia correte. / M.D. [Gardane's mark] XXXXI. / Excudebat Venetiis, apud Antonium Gardane.
The title-page also carries the signature line:
Primi, Verdelot a cinque. A
The other voice parts carry the same title-page (with changed part-name) and signature line (with changed letter).
Oblong quarto, 48 pages per part: A–F⁴; G–M⁴; N–S⁴; T–Z,AA⁴; BB–GG⁴.
The copy consulted is at Washington, D.C., Library of Congress. The Cantus partbook at Paris, Bibliothèque Nationale, Rés. 1169 is of the same press-run.

accustomed from later in the century. Of the forty-three pieces, the Bassus starts all but six at the top of the page. The sequence of pieces is almost certainly partly conditioned by the arrangement of the Cantus partbook, for here only three pieces start anywhere other than at the beginning of the page, while rather more have to do so in both the Tenor and Altus books.[7] It so happens that, in this volume, there is no opening carrying three pieces. Thus there is no reason to doubt that (other things being equal) the ascription at the head of the verso refers to the first composition on the opening, and that on the recto to the second.

However, in many volumes, both Gardane and Scotto contrived to fit three pieces onto an opening. The decision to do this seems again most often to have been made with the Cantus book in mind, for the spacing is often more tidy here than in the other partbooks. Occasionally, for example, the second or third piece will have to open in the middle of a stave for the Altus or Bassus part. This is normally not a problem for the reader, in so far as he can easily see the ornate blocks used for the initial letters. In one or two cases, however, the music is so cramped that even these are done away with, for only a type capital can be fitted into the available space.[8]

This point is worth mentioning, for it also affects the manner in which composers' names became attached to compositions. The common practice (when there were only two pieces on an opening) was for the composer's name, when present at all, to appear in the head-line to the page, set in type with the running head (comprising the part-name for that book) and with a numeral representing page or folio number or number of the composition in the volume. This name would then refer to the work which appeared below it, even if that piece did not start until the second or third stave on the page. Although this is what we as modern readers might expect, it has to be confirmed by comparing those partbooks where pieces start well down a page with the other books where the same pieces start at the beginning of the first stave.

[7] This is one volume where the pieces do not always open at the start of a line: the need to fit Barre's *Come potro fidarmi* and Baldassare d'Imola's *Non vi gloriate* onto a single opening, as well as that of squeezing Verdelot's *Donne se fiera stella* after Barre's *I sospiri amorosi*, led to the start of each second piece appearing part-way along a line in one or two of the partbooks.

[8] Examples would include fol. Y3ʳ (p. 45) of the Altus of RISM 1541[18], or K1ᵛ (p. 26) of the Tenor of 1541[11].

Non-conflicting attributions and newly anonymous compositions

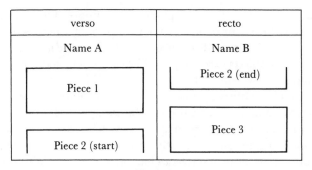

Figure 1

The implications of this for an opening with three compositions are clear (see Figure 1): name *A* was meant to refer to the first piece on the opening, and name *B* to the third. (This is apparently the normal situation, although I shall mention some exceptions below.) In theory (and, as will be shown, sometimes in practice) neither of these ascriptions need refer to the second piece on the opening: the printer's view of the composer of this piece has to be determined as much by bibliographical as by any other method. There are often two or three such situations in madrigal volumes of the early 1540s.

Printers were not unaware of the situation, with its potential for confusion, and they did sometimes supply an additional composer's name, immediately above the second piece. In many cases, however, they could not easily do this, for the text at the end of the previous piece occupied the relevant space in the forme; in other cases, they seem not to have bothered. On these occasions, the name of the composer of the second piece cannot necessarily be assumed to have been either *A* or *B*. We need to examine the manner in which the typesetter behaved throughout the volume, and also to determine the place of the volume in what appears to have been a gradual change in printer's habits.

RISM 1541[18], a collected edition of Verdelot's first two books,[9]

9 RISM 1541[18] = V1229; New Vogel 2872.
   [flower] CANTVS [flower] / DI VERDELOT TVTTI LI MADRIGALI DEL PRIMO ET SE=/condo Libro, a Quatro Voci: Novamente ristampati, & da molti errori emen=/dati. Con la gionta de i Madrigali del medesmo Autore. / AGGIONTOVI ANCHORA ALTRI MADRIGALI / novamente Composti da Messer Adriano, & da Altri Eccellentissimi Musici. / M D [Gardane's mark] xxxxi / Excudebat Venetiis, apud Antonium Gardane.
   The lower voices have the same title (with the part-name changed) and with the addition of a signature line:

113

provides examples of all the points made above. On the opening K4ᵛ–L1ʳ of the Tenor book (the relevant pages are numbered 16–17 in all books), there are three pieces: *Lasso che se creduto havesse, Vostre dolce parole* and *Con lagrim'et sospir.*[10] The composer's name at the head of both pages is *Verdelot*, which, as I have said (and as other evidence in this volume confirms), means only that the first and third of these pieces were thought to have been by that composer. If only the Tenor book had survived, there might be some reason for believing Verdelot to be the composer of the second piece also. However, in all three other parts, the name *Iachet* has been fitted carefully above the opening stave of this second composition, low on the verso of the opening. The ascription is missing from the Tenor only because the previous piece has text (as well as music) that runs to the end of the last line, and therefore leaves no room for a composer's name. This pattern suggests that Gardane recognised the normal situation to be as I have described, with the name at the head of the following recto belonging to the work beginning on the page, and not to the second of the three madrigals.

In the same book, the Tenor also behaves differently on pp. 6–7 (fols. 13ᵛ–4ʳ). The three pieces involved are *Ogn'hor per voi sospiro, Non vi fidat'o simplicett'amanti* and *Quanto lagrime lasso*. Cantus, Altus and Bassus all carry the composer's names *Verdelot*, on the verso, and *Iachet Berchem*, on the recto. The Tenor alone moves the name of Berchem down, to the space above the start of the third piece. This confirms that, for the other three voices, the ascription on the recto applies to the piece that begins on that page, and not to the one that hangs over from the previous verso, even though that is what actually appears on the first stave.

Verdelot primi, & secundi. [with the appropriate signature letter]
Oblong quarto, 64 pages per volume: A–H⁴; I–Q⁴; R–Z,AA⁴; BB–II⁴.
The copy consulted is at Vienna, Österreichische Nationalbibliothek, sa.77.d.53.
Typically, the composer listings in the entry in New Vogel are far from consistent. Of the pieces which straddle an opening, and which have no ascription of their own, *Non vi fidat'o simplicett'amanti* (pp. 6–7) is assigned to the composer on the verso (almost certainly incorrectly, as I am about to argue), while *Io son tal volta* (pp. 50–1) is left anonymous. *Igno soave* lies across two pages that both carry the name of Verdelot, and should perhaps be assigned to him in any account of this edition, while *Vostre dolce parole* (pp. 16–17) has the name *Iachet* fitted above its first stave in three of the four partbooks.
10 These three have survived elsewhere, without conflicting attributions, as the work of Verdelot, Jachet and Verdelot, respectively. The present discussion does not throw any doubt on this pattern, but is offered solely to draw attention to the procedure adopted by the printer.

Non-conflicting attributions and newly anonymous compositions

In neither of these cases is there any problem in deciding on the intended ascription; both have at least one partbook making clear where the composer's name belongs, and, in both cases, this accords with the general pattern of ascriptions for the piece.[11]

RISM 1541[11] is the second edition of Arcadelt's third book of four-voice madrigals[12] and contains a large number of such problems of

[11] It has to be admitted that there is no firm bibliographical evidence here for the authorship of the second piece on pp. 6–7. My contention, supported by the concordance pattern and by other evidence (to be advanced), is that a piece in this position is normally, by this time, to be assigned to the composer named at the head of the verso, although by no means consistently following that pattern. Indeed, such a view raises questions about the opinion which Gardane held of the authorship of *Io son tal volta* (G1ᵛ–2ʳ): however, as I shall show, this kind of ambiguous situation is just that which led to changes of ascription as printer's habits became more settled and consistent. I shall return to this, and some other problems of ascription in the present edition, in connection with a different range of evidence.

[12] RISM 1541[11] = A1376; New Vogel 158.
[flower] CANTVS [flower] / IL TERZO LIBRO DE I MADRIGALI NOVISSIMI / di archadelt a quattro voci insieme con alchuni di constantio festa & altri dieci bellissimi / a voci mudate novamente ristampati con nova gionta & nova corretione. / M.D. [Gardane's mark] L.XI. / Venetiis apud antonium gardane
The other partbooks have the same title (with changed voice-name), plus a signature line: Terzo Libro d'archadelt. [plus signature letter]
Oblong quarto, 48 pages per volume: A–F⁴; G–M⁴; N–S⁴; T–Z,+⁴.
The copy consulted is at London, British Library, K.2.h.5. The second part of the date, L.XI., is changed in manuscript to XLI.
Again, New Vogel is in error, or misleading, in its ascriptions for this volume: *E morta la speranza*, spread between pp. 12 and 13, is strictly anonymous – the caption *Archadelt*. heads p. 12, while *Con. festa*. appears on p. 13 (this might be another case for arguing that the piece starting at the foot of the verso was thought to be by the composer named at the head of that page, for this madrigal is ascribed to Arcadelt in 1539²³); *Se i sguardi di costei* is only attributed to *Con. festa* in the Cantus and Tenor books; *Lasso che pur hormai*, on pp. 26–7, is anonymous; *Madonna s'io credessi* (p. 29) is clearly attributed to *Archadelt*.; *Languir non mi fa amore* is only ascribed to *Corteccia*. in the lower three voices, while the Cantus reads *Archadelt*. (see below); and *S'altrui d'amor* is clearly ascribed to *Archadelt*. in all voices. (Some of these works will be discussed below. One must deplore the haphazard procedure adopted in New Vogel (for this and other volumes) whereby the name of the composer to whom the whole volume is dedicated is not repeated against individual madrigals: it does not allow the reader to distinguish between anonymous works and those that appear below the name of the composer given on the title-page, in this case, Arcadelt.)
In stating that 1541[11] is the second edition of this title, I am making the following observations: (1) that RISM [c1556]²³, copy at Venice, Biblioteca Nazionale Marciana, Mus. 365–7 (Tenor, Altus and Bassus) is of the same edition as 1539²³ = A1374 (Tenor, Altus and Bassus of the copy at Munich, Bayerische Staatsbibliothek, 4⁰. Mus.pr.95/2), as has been noted by other scholars (see *Arcadelt*, IV, p. ix, or New Vogel, no. 156), and that this is probably the first edition; (2) that the Cantus of the copy at Munich represents part of the same edition, although cited separately in New Vogel as no. 157; (3) that the remaining editions are as cited in RISM: 1541[11] = A1376; 1543²⁰ = A1377; 1556²² = A1378.
The bibliographical evidence for asserting that the Cantus book at Munich is part of the same edition as the other partbooks is far from clear. The most difficult problem is a direct result of the Cantus carrying a dedication, on fol. A1ᵛ: although the music follows the same sequence as that found in the other partbooks, it cannot be arranged in the same manner, for it starts on a recto, rather than on a verso. Where the Cantus places three pieces on an

ascription: there are eleven pieces which carry, or appear to carry, a
different composer's name in other sources, plus one more where the
evidence of ascription is not as strong as we might like. So muddled

opening, it cannot reflect exactly the layout of the other three parts, for there these pieces
would occupy a recto followed by its own verso, and would involve a page-turn in the
middle of the second madrigal. The solution adopted was to use the same openings for
three pieces, which results in these being different works: the following extract from a table
of contents will make this clear, indicating the folio and (in roman numerals) the stave on
which the pieces start in each book:

Piece	Cantus	Tenor	Altus	Bassus
24 *Liet'e seren'in vista*	D1ᵛ,i	d1ʳ,i	DD1ʳ,i	dd1ʳ,i
25 *Se la durezz' in voi fosse*	D1ᵛ,v	d1ᵛ,i	DD1ᵛ,i	dd1ᵛ,i
26 *Se tutto'l bel in questa sol*	D2ʳ,iii	d1ᵛ,iv	DD1ᵛ,v	dd1ᵛ,v
27 *Deh quanto fu pietoso*	D2ᵛ,i	d2ʳ,iii	DD2ʳ,iii	dd2ʳ,iii
28 *Madonna al volto mio pallido*	D3ʳ,i	d2ᵛ,i	DD2ᵛ,i	dd2ᵛ,i

This situation is most unusual, and would argue, at first sight, for the Cantus being part
of a separate edition, potentially earlier than the others, despite the comment on the title-
page that the pieces are 'corretti'. Perhaps supporting such a conclusion could be the
different wordings found on the title-pages:
RISM 1539²³ = A1374; New Vogel 156–7.
[Cantus:] IL TERZO LIBRO DE I MADRIGALI / NOVISSIMI DI
ARCHADELTH A QVATTRO VOCI, / Insieme con alchuni di Constantio Festa,
& altri dieci bellissimi a Voci mudate. / Novamente con ogni diligentia Stampati,
& corretti. / [flower] / LIBRO TERZO [Scotto's mark] A QVATTRO VOCI. /
VENETIIS / APVD HIERONYMVM SCOTVM. / [short rule] / 1539.
The other voices read:
DEL TERTIO LIBRO DE I MADRIGALI / DI ARCHADELT, ET DI ALTRI
ECCELLENTISSIMI / Authori. Con la gionta de alcuni Madrigali a Voci mutate
bellissimi / A QVATTRO VOCI. / T / LIBRO TERTIO
or, for the Altus and Bassus:
DEL TERZO LIBRO [...] A [B] / LIBRO TERZO
The presence of these differing title-pages is not a very strong argument for their belonging
to different editions, for a number of volumes printed by the Scottos at this period carry
different title-pages for the lower voices.
However, there are three other features, each of which specifically leads me to believe
that all four parts are probably of the same edition. One is the apparently random use of
the word *Tertio* as opposed to *Terzo*, and that of *Arcadelth* as opposed to *Archadelt*, in the
signature line for each gathering. *Tertio* is used only rarely, on fols. a1ʳ and 1ʳ and 2ʳ on
gatherings b and c, as well as in the title of the Tenor book: *Terzo* appears everywhere else.
Arcadelth is found more frequently: B1ʳ of the Cantus; b1ʳ, c2ʳ, d1ʳ, d2ʳ, e1ʳ, e2ʳ, f1ʳ and f2ʳ of
the Tenor; throughout the Altus; and on ffl ʳ of the Bassus book. (Note that the Venice copy
has the same pattern as that found in the Munich books.)
Second is the state of the initial letters used in these partbooks. Those in the first three
gatherings of the Tenor are marginally better than elsewhere. On the other hand, those in
the Cantus are neither better nor worse overall than in the other books, tending merely to
conform with the worst existing state elsewhere.
The sum of these two pieces of evidence argues that the first three gatherings of the
Tenor were the first to be prepared and printed. The rest of the Tenor then made one
complete process, with the Altus and the Bassus: the Cantus was either part of the same
process, or followed it immediately, without the intervention of any other printing.
But the decisive factor is that of the *TAVOLA*, appearing at the end of each book: this
shows quite clearly that all four copies were printed from the same setting of type, and that
the Cantus was printed last. There are idiosyncratic spacings and alignments repeated

116

Non-conflicting attributions and newly anonymous compositions

are some of the situations between this and the first and third editions of the book, and so interesting is the pattern that they suggest, that it is my suspicion that this was the point at which Gardane decided to sort out how to label compositions: certainly he found many difficult situations in working from the first, Scotto edition. Certainly, too, later volumes are much more systematic – even though they sometimes preserve wrong decisions, reached by working from the erroneous assumption that the earlier books were also systematic.[13]

I propose to leave aside three madrigals in this volume for which the first three editions all agree in their ascriptions (even within the constraints outlined above) against the new composer's name in RISM 1556[22], the fourth edition.[14] These are *Bramo morir*,[15] *Madonna al volto mio* and *Qual paura ho*, all of which are securely ascribed to Arcadelt in the earlier editions, and equally clearly to Festa in the fourth. All are accepted by Musch as being the work of Arcadelt,[16]

from book to book, as well as one or two places that have taken ink in identical manner. Apart from the normal and inevitable changes demonstrating that the Cantus was last in the sequence, there is a further detail: the tavola has, in addition to the normal two columns of contents, two additional columns flanking them, which contain the words *A voce pari.*, when needed. In the Cantus alone, the left column has slipped down half a line.

The apparent conclusion has to be that the Cantus was printed alone, and immediately after the other books, before the type for the tavola was dispersed. The probable reason for this is to be found in the presence of the dedicatory letter printed on fol. A1ᵛ. This letter, though signed *Geronimo Scotto*, draws attention to the desire of his brother, Ottaviano Scotto, to compliment the dedicatee, the Rev. Mons. Girolamo Verallo, then Papal Legate in Venice. Verallo was translated to the See of Bertinoro in February of 1539/40, which is sufficient to confirm that the date of 1539 on the title-page of the Cantus book is a genuine one, not falsified to conform with the other books. Gerolamo Scotto took over the printing shop from Ottaviano during 1539, and it is quite plausible that this dedication, with the consequent rearrangement of the Cantus book, represents one of his first publications as an independent printer.

13   For this reason, I should expect 1541[18] to have been prepared for the press rather later in the year than was the present volume. The arrangement of the composers' names is more in line with later practice, although not completely straightforward. However, it is worth bearing in mind Mary Lewis's remarks about the extent to which Gardane seems to have worked on several volumes simultaneously: see her 'Antonio Gardane and his Publications of Sacred Music, 1538–1555' (Ph.D. dissertation, Brandeis University, 1979), pp. 139–58.

14   This edition is not discussed in the present study. To demonstrate that the conventions outlined here continued in use for another fifteen years would require a considerable extension to this paper, an extension of no great relevance and, further, one which I am not yet in a position to offer.

15   Despite the suggestion, in *Arcadelt*, IV, p. xii, this is not strictly anonymous in 1543[20], for the same name, *Archadelt*, is found at the head of both relevant pages, xx and xxi. By 1543, Gardane was regularly implying that the composer of the piece straddling the opening was the name he printed at the head of the verso, unless otherwise indicated.

16   Musch, *Costanzo Festa*, pp. 158–67, and Fenlon and Haar, 'Fonti', pp. 237–8, both list the works, while Seay's edition of Arcadelt prints all three. It may be that all should be

and do not fit into the type of evidence being discussed here. *Si lieto alcun giammai*, apparently a similar case, will be discussed below.

One of the most interesting cases in Arcadelt's third book is that of *E morta la speranza*. In the first edition, 1539[23], it is to be found on fol. B2[v] of the Cantus and B2[r] of the other partbooks. There can be no doubt here that Scotto wished to assign the madrigal to Arcadelt: not only do all the folios say so, but the ascription in the Cantus is of a different setting of type from that found in the other three books. In 1541[11] and 1543[20], the madrigal appears split across an opening, at the foot of a verso and the top of the following recto (see Figure 2): in 1556[22], it is unequivocally ascribed to Costanzo Festa.

The pattern by which ownership of this madrigal was transferred from Arcadelt to Festa would seem to be fairly clear.[17] From occupying a page to itself in the first edition, it is reduced to fitting below other convenient pieces. In the edition of 1541, it happens to lie beneath a work surviving uniquely there (and therefore to be presumed to be by Arcadelt), and above *Se mort'in me potesse*.[18] If Gardane here were consistently following the pattern that he is apparently in the process of establishing (by which all pieces that begin on a page are by the composer whose name heads that page), he would be suggesting that *E morta la speranza* was still thought to be by Arcadelt.

However, the third edition, while retaining the madrigal at the foot of a page, happens to place it beneath a work securely by Festa.[19] (The need to place three pieces on some openings was a function of trying to control the total number of pages so that it might be divisible by eight, and thus use only whole sheets of paper: this in turn ensured that any pieces that were short enough to fit into a

---

reconsidered, in the light of the types of evidence to be offered in section III of this paper, below.

[17] Lest it be thought that the ascription in 1539[23] could be a simple error (as is, for example, that to *Madonna s'io credessi*; cf. J. Haar and L. Bernstein, eds., *Ihan Gero: Il primo libro de' madrigali italiani et canzoni francese a due voci*, Masters and Monuments of the Renaissance 1 (New York, 1980)), it is worth remarking that the pieces ascribed to Festa are all to be found on fols. B3[v]–C3[r], eight pages which form a discrete unit (and which, incidentally, may suggest something about how the music for this volume was collected). It should be added that both Musch and Seay (in his edition of Arcadelt) treat the ascriptions as if they were handled inconsistently by Gardane, in each case thereby supplying reinforcement of each author's position.

[18] For this madrigal, see below.

[19] In the first edition, this madrigal, *Lasso che pur hormai*, falls comfortably within the group of works assigned to Festa, while in the second there are no bibliographical grounds for rejecting the printed ascription to the same composer.

Non-conflicting attributions and newly anonymous compositions

1541[11]	B2[v]	B3[r]
	Archadelt. Benedetto sia'l di	Con. festa. E morta la speranza
	E morta la speranza	Se mort'in me potesse

1543[20]	C1[v]	C2[r]
	Con. festa. So che nissun mi crede	Archadelt. E morta la speranza
	E morta la speranza	Lasso che pur hormai

Figure 2

group of three would normally do so – and the nine such pieces in 1541[11] would provide only a limited range of options for the next edition, particularly since *Benedetto sia'l di*, the piece previously above *E morta la speranza*, was not retained to the third edition.) The result is that Gardane, when later preparing the fourth edition, assumed that the new systematic procedures were then in place, and that both the pieces on fol. C1[v] were by Festa: since the first of these was not included in the new edition, he would not have had its presence to remind him of the problem.

In this situation, then, my contention is that the change of ascription from Arcadelt to Festa is not the result of a conscious change in the printer's view of authorship; the change in ownership of *E morta la speranza* is simply an unforeseen result of a refinement of procedures in the printing shop. The new attribution to Festa is, at least bibliographically, of no value.

In the same book (1541[11]), there are only two other openings where this situation arises: one of these will be discussed below, and the other, involving pp. 20–1 (fols. C2[v]–3[r] of the Cantus), concerns *Se i sguardi di costei*. The opening contains *Se la durezz' in voi fosse*, with *Archadelt.* on the head-line; *Deh quanto fu pietoso* (starting on the fifth stave of the verso), with an attribution to *Archadelt.* above its first line in all partbooks; and *Se i sguardi di costei*, ascribed to *Con. festa*

119

immediately above its opening line (the third stave of the recto) in Cantus and Tenor, although anonymous in both Altus and Bassus. This last madrigal had been securely attributed to Festa in the edition of 1539[23], but it forms the last of a group of three on an opening in 1543[20], with head-lines on both pages giving the name Arcadelt. My belief is that the unexpected placing of the attribution in 1541[11] resulted in the typesetter of 1543 missing it completely – it appears in the space normally reserved for the text of the previous piece, while referring to a piece whose ascription would now normally be at the head of the page. He therefore saw the work as one within a volume of Arcadelt and without any other name attached to it.[20] As a result, he transferred the work to that composer. However, as I believe, it is actually by Festa, and the later ascription is a printing-house error, followed up in the edition of 1556[22].

The printer of 1541[11], or his typesetters, clearly attempted to clarify the ownership of individual pieces. The case discussed in the previous paragraph is one example, while another concerns *O felix color*. This starts on the third stave of p. 39 of the Cantus, and has the ascription to *Con. festa*. – confirmed by the first edition – placed above that stave. In this way, Gardane had in fact adopted the best possible way to display the authorship of each piece, with the ascription placed above its first notes. Unfortunately, this system was not always practicable, and his later system, while easier for the typesetter, did not necessarily follow up all the clues offered by this practice (especially if the earlier edition had long runs of text at the ends of pieces), and encouraged many slips. I believe that the process followed here in 1541[11] was an interim one, before the establishment of the later, more enduring one, first to be found in 1541[18].

Of the remaining cases of doubtful identity affected by this volume, 1541[11], all but one can be resolved using different classes of evidence, and will be discussed later in this paper.[21] The remaining dubious ascription can be clarified by means of the bibliographical analysis described here: it concerns *Se mort'in me potesse*, also found in

---

[20] The wording of this phrase is in accordance with a point which I shall be pursuing in section III of the present study, to the effect that apparent ascriptions are sometimes no more than the use of a name to act as a running head-line, that is, as an internal title.

[21] They are *Amor s'al primo sguardo* and *Si lieto alcun giammai*, both to be discussed in section II below, and *Divelt'el mio bel vivo*, *Languir non mi fa amore* and *Poi che'l fiero destin*, all of which will be covered in section III.

Non-conflicting attributions and newly anonymous compositions

1539[23] and 1543[20]. Musch suggests[22] that the piece is either anonymous or ascribed to Arcadelt in 1541[11]. Figure 2 (above) shows that it is probably not anonymous, but assigned to Festa, as beginning on a folio headed *Con. festa*, even though not starting at the head of that folio. There is no reason to doubt the ascription here, or its confirmation in 1539[23]. The pattern followed by Gardane confirms that there is in fact no conflicting attribution for this work.

The same can be said for *Apri'l mio dolce carcer*, found in the first two editions of Arcadelt's fourth book of madrigals (see Table 1).[23] In

[22] Musch, *Costanzo Festa*, p. 166.
[23] First edition: RISM 1539[24] = A1379; New Vogel 161.
IL QVARTO LIBRO DI MADRIGALI D'ARCHADELT A / QVATRO VOCI COMPOSTI VLTIMAMENTE INSIEME CON / ALCVNI MADRIGALI DE ALTRI AVTORI NOVAMENTE CON / OGNI DILIGENTIA STAMPATI ET CORRETTI. / CANTVS [mark] CANTVS. / CON GRATIA ET PRIVILEGIO.
The other voices carry the same title, with the part-name changed. The word *Tenor* is misspelled TENNR to the right of the mark.
All parts carry a colophon on the last verso:
IN VENETIA NELLA STAMPA D'ANTONIO GARDANE / Nellanno del Signore M.D. XXXIX. Nel mese di Setembre. / [mark] / CON GRATIA ET PRIVILEGIO.
Oblong quarto, 40 pages per part: A–E⁴; F–K⁴; L–P⁴; Q–V⁴.
Copy consulted: Munich, Bayerische Staatsbibliothek, 4⁰. Mus.pr. 95/3.

Second edition: RISM 1541[12] = A1380; New Vogel 162.
[flower] CANTVS [flower] / IL QVARTO LIBRO DI MADRIGALI D'ARCHA=/delt, a Qvattro Voci, Composti vltimamente insieme con alcvni Madrigali d'altri aut=/tori, Novamente con ogni diligentia ristampati, & corretti. / M. D. [Gardane's mark] XXXXI. / NON SINE PRIVILEGIO. / Excudebat Venetiis, apud Antonium Gardane.
The lower voices have the same title, with the change of the part-name and the addition of a signature line:
Quarto libro d'Archadelt. [plus signature letter]
Oblong quarto, 40 pages per part: A–E⁴; F–K⁴; L–P⁴; Q–V⁴.
Copy consulted: London, British Library, K.2.h.6.

Third edition: RISM 1545[18] = A1381; New Vogel 163.
[flower] ARCHADELT [flower] / QVARTO LIBRO / DI MADRIGALI A QVATRO VOCI D'ARCHADELT / Insieme alcuni di altri autori novamente ristampato et corretto / A QVATRO [Gardane's mark] VOCI / Venetijs Apud Antonium Gardane / [rule] / M. D. XXXXV. / CANTVS
The lower voices have the same title, with changed part-name.
Oblong quarto, 32 pages per part: A–D⁴; E–H⁴; I–M⁴; N–Q⁴. Paginated in roman numerals from the second recto, I–XXIX, [XXX].
Copy consulted: Bologna, Civico Museo Bibliografico Musicale, R 58.

New Vogel again makes a number of errors in ascriptions for these three editions: *Dal bel suave ragio* is not ascribed to Layolle in the first edition – the word *Archadelt.* appears at the head of the relevant page (see below); *Col pensier mai* is anonymous in the first edition, as (strictly) is *S'era forsi ripreso*, for the latter appears at the foot of a page headed with Arcadelt's name; *Pace non trovo* is only ascribed to *Yvo* in the second edition; finally, New Vogel fails to point out that eight pieces (nos. 10, 14, 18, 23, 24, 26, 27 and 29) are anonymous in the third edition.

VII

Table 1

RISM	Pages (folios)[a]	Verso (ascriptions and pieces)	Recto (ascriptions and pieces)
1539²⁴	IV–V (A2ᵛ–3ʳ)	Archadelt. / Si grand'e la pieta / Apri'l mio dolce carcer →	Archadelt. / Dal bel suave ragio
	VI–VII (A3ᵛ–4ʳ)	Archadelt. Petrus organista. (in margin) / Madonna per oltraggi / Calde lacrime mie sospir →	[anonymous] / Col pensier mai non maculai
1541¹²	21 (3ʳ)		Archadelt / Madonna per oltraggi
	30–1 (D3ᵛ–4ʳ)	Archadelt / Si grand'e la pieta / Apri'l mio dolce carcer →	Layole / Dal bel soave ragio
	35 (E2ʳ)		Archadelt / Col pensier mai non maculai
	37 (E3ʳ)		Petrus organista. / Calde lagrime mie sospir
1545¹⁸	I (A2ʳ)		Archadelt / Si grand'e la pieta
	XXVII (D3ʳ)		[anonymous] / Col pensier mai non maculai

[a] In this and subsequent tables, the folio numbers refer to the Cantus book.

122

Non-conflicting attributions and newly anonymous compositions

both editions, it occupies a position straddling an opening, from the foot of a verso to the top of the recto following, and is accompanied by the same two other pieces. In 1539[24], both pages (numbered IV–V) have the heading *Archadelt.*: in 1541[12], while the verso (p. 30) is headed *Archadelt*, the following recto reads *Layole.*. The implications of this for the third madrigal on the opening, *Dal bel soave ragio*, will be discussed below; however, there seems no reason to doubt that *Apri'l mio dolce carcer*, starting low on each verso, was assigned in Gardane's plan to Arcadelt. In support of this is the manner in which Gardane handles the appearance of *Calde lagrime mie sospir*, by Petrus organista, on fol. VI of the first edition, where it starts beneath a work by Arcadelt. In so far as the new piece is not by the composer named at the head of the page, Gardane prints the new name in the left margin, against the start of the madrigal. (In the second edition, this work has a page to itself.)

On the same opening, *Col pensier mai non maculai* is affected by this approach. Since there is no ascription at the head of p. VII, the madrigal must be deemed anonymous in the first edition. The evidence of house practice also argues that the absence of a name above the same piece in the third edition is deliberate,[24] while I shall be arguing below that the treatment of the caption *Archadelt* in the running head-line of 1541[12] is no real argument in favour of author-ship. My conclusion is that Gardane did not believe this piece to be

[24] There are two elements to this argument. First is the evidence that two typesetters were involved in setting the head-lines, and probably all the text. One man set the outer forme of the first gathering of each book (A, E, I and N), and the other did the inner. If we call these men X and Y, then X set 1ʳ, 2ᵛ, 3ʳ and 4ᵛ, while Y was responsible for 1ᵛ, 2ʳ, 3ᵛ and 4ʳ. The second gathering (B, F, K and O) has all the captions re-set: X worked on the inner forme and Y on the outer. In the third gathering (C, G, L and P), as many captions as possible were retained: it appears that Y set both formes. The fourth gathering (D, etc.) has new captions: it is likely that Y set both formes again, although only two pieces have composers' names attached to them. Neither of these can have been retained from the previous gatherings. *Col pensier*, on D3ʳ, in particular, does not retain the head-line *Archadelt*, found on C3ʳ.

Since there are no ascriptions on the outer forme of the last gathering (1ʳ, 2ᵛ, 3ʳ and 4ᵛ of D, H, M and Q – 4ᵛ contains the *TAVOLA Delli Madrigali*), one could suggest that all were omitted in error. However, the typesetter had another element to consider: five of the pieces in this gathering also have in the head-line the phrase *A voce Pari*. These five include two where the phrase does follow an ascription to *Archadelt*, and three (1ʳ, 1ᵛ and 4ʳ) where the work is anonymous. In these three cases, the phrase is placed in exactly the space that would otherwise have been occupied by a composer's name. It seems likely, therefore, that the typesetter did not simply forget to insert an ascription, but rather had to determine whether an ascription, or the new phrase, or both, were needed for each page in this gathering. As a result, it would seem that the omissions of composers' names were deliberate.

by Arcadelt, but did not know of any other name to put to it: it should stand as an anonymous work.

One other example may be taken from RISM 1545[19], a Verdelot anthology.[25] *Madonna io sol vorrei* is placed, as the second of three pieces, across pp. v–vi (fols. A3ᵛ–4ʳ in the Cantus). Fol. A3ᵛ is headed *Verdelot.*, and A4ʳ reads *Const. Festa*: the lower voices have the

---

[25]   RISM 1545[19] = V1231; New Vogel 2874.
      The first folio of the Cantus part is missing in the only surviving copy. The lower voices have identical titles, with the exception of the part-name:
      TENOR / VERDELOT TVTTI LI MADRIGALI DEL PRIMO / ET SECONDO LIBRO A QVATRO VOCI NVOVAMENTE RI=/STAMPATI, ET CON DILIGENTIA CORRETTI. / A QVATRO VOCI / VENETIIS M. D. XLV.
      Oblong quarto, 40 pages per part: A–F⁴; G–M⁴; N–S⁴; T–Z,+⁴.
      Copy consulted: Florence, Biblioteca Nazionale Centrale, Mus.ant. 129: lacks fol. A1.
      Mary Lewis discusses this and a number of other unsigned printed volumes of the period ('Antonio Gardane', pp. 314–29). She shows clearly that the typographical material for this volume was that normally used by Scotto, and assigns the book to him as publisher. However, the different treatment of certain details leads me to think that the book was edited (and possibly even set) by someone other than Scotto's normal house-men. Bridges, 'Publishing', pp. 119–29, reaches a similar conclusion, though for different reasons.
      It may be significant that two of Lewis's 'Group 2' (to which the present volume belongs) are probably among those volumes that, as Richard Agee has recently shown, were supported by privileges issued in Venice – see his 'The Venetian Privilege and Music-Printing in the Sixteenth Century', *Early Music History*, 3 (1983), pp. 1–42: on pp. [29–30] are references to privileges issued to Rore for motets (22 November 1544, and therefore plausibly to be sought in the publications of 1545) and to Cambio for madrigals of Petrarch (2 June 1545). Others of these unsigned volumes, those by Festa, by Vicentino and of *Madrigali de diversi autori* (RISM 1547[13]) claim the existence of privilege. It is notable that, in the same period, Gardane received a privilege for the works of Jacques da Ponte, while in September 1544 Scotto gained a privilege for several different volumes. None of these has survived among the unsigned volumes that Lewis discusses: but they do indicate that both Gardane and Scotto were able and willing to apply for privileges on their own behalf during this period. It is not an unreasonable assumption that neither was involved in the petitions for privileges for the unsigned volumes.
      However, both Rore and Cambio are among the musicians referred to by Andrea Calmo at just this period (1547) as being among the leaders of the period, alongside Arcadelt, Verdelot and Willaert. (The relevant extract from the later, 1580, edition of Calmo's letters is quoted and translated in Bridges, 'Publishing', pp. 57–8.) While neither Verdelot nor Arcadelt is known to have been in Venice at the time, all five composers are represented among the unsigned volumes discussed by Lewis, including Verdelot with the volume which stimulated this digression. It seems likely that a number of the unsigned volumes were published, or at least covered by privilege, by the composers concerned (as is suggested by the evidence of the privileges to Cambio and Rore), and merely printed by Scotto. This would certainly help to explain why no printer's name appears on the volumes, even after Scotto began inserting the salamander device on the title-pages. It would also raise interesting speculation as to where Verdelot was living during the 1530s and 1540s. If he was in Venice, this would to some extent help to remove the peculiar situation of a large number of volumes of music being published in Venice during the 1530s as the work of a non-resident. There is no parallel case during the period, if Arcadelt was resident, for he was not represented until the end of the decade (by which time the situation was changing rapidly): Festa had very few volumes to show, and, further, himself took out a privilege in 1538, as Agee shows (in 'Privilege', p. [29]). See Appendix, below.

same ascriptions, apparently re-set for the Tenor and Bassus. This madrigal survives in several other Verdelot anthologies, with the constant attribution to that composer. By the time of 1545, it had clearly been accepted as being by him. It would seem that the anonymous editor of 1545[19] also intended that ascription to be understood, rather than any possible suggestion that the work was by Festa. (The apparent reference to de Silva in the earliest editions will be discussed below, in section III).

The assumption in each of these cases has been that the composition beginning low on the verso, but ending on the recto, was thought of, by the Gardane of late 1541 and after (as well as by some other printers), as belonging to the composer cited on the verso. The evidence for this has been drawn not from the concordance pattern *per se*, but rather from the manner in which the printer himself interpreted the pattern when he came to prepare a later edition. For earlier volumes the procedure was clearly more fluid, and the transition from this to the more systematic has provided some of my evidence.

In the case of the Scottos working before 1541, the evidence is much less easy to interpret, because the family adopted different procedures for most of their editions from the 1530s. The following discussion of the situation in Scotto's 1540 edition of the combined contents of Verdelot's first two books,[26] while involving the same kinds of evidence, can therefore not produce the clear-cut pattern of

---

[26]   RISM 1540[20] = V1228; New Vogel 2871.
[flower] DI VERDELOTTO [flower] / TVTTI LI MADRIGALI DEL PRIMO, ET SECONDO / Libro a Qvatro Voci. Con la Gionta de i Madrigali del medesmo / Auttore, non piu stampati. / AGGIONTOVI ANCHORA ALTRI MADRIGALI / novamente Composti da Messer ADRIANO, & de altri Eccellentissimi / Musici, Come appare ne la sequente Tavola. / [flower] / [device] / Apud Hieronymum Scotum. / [rule] / 1540.
The lower voices have a different title, with the relevant part-name:
MADRIGALI DEL PRIMO, ET SECONDO LIBRO / di Verdelotto a Quatro Voci. Con la Gionta del medesmo Auttore, & de / altri Eccellentissimi Musici, novamente Stampati. / [flower] / TENOR
Oblong quarto, 60 pages per part: A–G⁴H²; a–g⁴h²; AA–GG⁴HH²; aa–gg⁴hh². Paginated from the second recto, I–LVIII.
Copy consulted: Wolfenbüttel, Herzog August Bibliothek, 2.13.14–2.13.17. Musica.
New Vogel does not correctly reflect the fact that eleven of the pieces lying across an opening are not specifically attributed, while the others are. Further, it suggests that the second setting of *Con lachrim'et sospir* (pp. XLIV–XLV, fols. F3ᵛ–4ʳ of each book) is by Verdelot: the names that appear at the heads of the relevant pages are *ARCHADELT* and *IACHET*, respectively. Finally, *Amor quanto piu lieto* (p. XLIII) is clearly ascribed to *VERDELOT* in all books. Both these pieces are discussed below.

typographical connections that makes the earlier argument so satisfying. In the eight gatherings of each partbook, there are eleven situations where an opening carries three madrigals. Eight of these are of no interest in the present connection, in so far as, in each, both pages carry the name *Verdelot*, and the three pieces involved are consistently attributed to him elsewhere. The other three cases can be tabulated as in Table 2.

Io son tal volta carries careful and deliberate ascriptions to Festa in all three of Scotto's early editions of Verdelot's second book.[27] When Gardane reprinted these volumes, in 1541[18] and 1544[18], he assigned the work to Willaert. He seems to have assumed that a piece occupying the position of this madrigal, even in an edition by Scotto, would be the work of the composer cited on the verso, in this case, Willaert; the evidence of Scotto's earlier editions suggests that he, on the other hand, thought it to be by the name cited on the recto following, that is, Festa. Scotto seems to have felt the same about *Madonna 'l bel desire*, which is specifically attributed to *Adrian* in the three earlier editions. I believe that, in both cases, the evidence offered here as to a bibliographical (or procedural) reason for the change of attribution argues strongly that there is support only for the earlier ascriptions, and that the later one has to be rejected.

(It might be thought that, if this were true, there should be some doubts as to whether the ascriptions on the rectos refer to two pieces (to the one across the opening as well as to that starting on the recto), or whether the second of these should not more properly be regarded as anonymous. However, the pattern seems to suggest that Scotto tried to arrange that the ascription could apply to both composers: the attribution of *Grat'e benigna donna* to Willaert and that of *D'amore le generose* to Festa are both securely supported by other sources. Further, that of *Vostre dolce parole* to *Iachet* is confirmed in Scotto's own earlier 1534[16].)

If this pattern holds, then questions need to be asked about the authorship of *Con lachrim'e sospir*. It would seem probable, working from the pattern proposed above, that Scotto believed this madrigal to be by *Iachet*. The fact that the work is assigned to Arcadelt in its only other source, Gardane's 1541[18], is of no value, for I have shown in more than one instance (including that of *Io son tal volta*) that

---

[27] Citations appear below, at note 45. For later sources, see the list in Musch, *Costanzo Festa*, p. 161, as supplemented by Fenlon and Haar, 'Fonti', p. 232.

Table 2

Pages (folios)	Verso (ascriptions and pieces)	Recto (ascriptions and pieces)
32–3 (E1ᵛ–2ʳ)	VERDELOT — Lasso che se creduto / Madonna'l bel desire ——→	ADRIAN Vuillaert. Grat'e benigna donna
36–7 (E3ᵛ–4ʳ)	ADRIAN Vuillaert. — Signora dolce, io te / Io son tal volta ——→	CON. FESTA. D'amore le generose
44–5 (F3ᵛ–4ʳ)	ARCHADELT — Ardea tutt'a voi / Con lachrim'e sospir ——→	IACHET Vostre dolce parole

Gardane, when he tried to make things more systematic, took such a piece as belonging to the composer cited on the verso; that is probably what happened here, which would serve to render his attribution derivative – although in an eccentric sense. It does seem clear, therefore, that the bibliographical case for Jachet as the author of this madrigal is actually stronger than that for Arcadelt.

II

The rapid streamlining of the processes of music printing during the early 1540s had other effects, one of which directly concerns the head-lines and signature lines, and therefore the ascriptions. It had been the practice of many printers to preserve as much as possible of this material from one sheet to the next, retaining it in a skeleton forme, rather than redistributing the type and then setting it up again for the next sheet. However, this did not mean that the same head-lines could appear in the same setting of type on every sheet, still less on each side of every sheet, for a printer normally used more than one forme for each book in progress. Two were regarded as a minimum – one for each side of the sheet of paper – and many books show evidence of having been prepared with three or four such formes. This would allow the typesetter to start preparing one sheet while a previous one was still going through the press.[28] The material retained in the skeleton forme regularly comprised a running head (to which page or folio numbers were added), a signature line (to which the gathering letter could be added), and necessarily some of the furniture – the uninked pieces of wood which kept the text and staves in place.[29] This material can provide evidence of the order of printing: since more than one skeleton forme was normally in use, and since the elements of each were liable to shift slightly or to deteriorate during use (apart from usually being set in slightly different relative alignments), they can sometimes also help to reveal a break in the sequence of work, or the presence of a cancel leaf. For

[28] For a discussion of this in the output of a major early Italian printer, see my 'Upon the Use of Running Titles in the Aldus House of 1518', *The Library*, 5th ser., 27 (1972), pp. 126–31. I use the same evidence to help in the analysis of Petrucci's printing methods, in the forthcoming paper, 'A Case of Half-sheet Imposition in the Early Sixteenth Century'.

[29] Lewis, 'Antonio Gardane', pp. 117–18, has suggested that Gardane may have employed distinctively shaped formes in order to keep the staves in the same relationships from page to page. Some such system would have been essential for Petrucci and other multiple-impression printers.

Non-conflicting attributions and newly anonymous compositions

the present discussion, the most useful element of the skeleton forme is the head-line, containing the name of the composer.

Most musical volumes, particularly anthologies, leave little scope for retaining a head-line, even though the signature line may stay the same. Scotto's early volumes occasionally use a consistent running head: *Verdelot* on every page of 1537[9], and also on all the versos but one of 1533[2]. In such cases, the presence of the caption at the head of any page is, of course, not an assertion that the pieces there belonged to that named composer – any more than the absence of any such captions in the first editions of Arcadelt's first book implies that all the pieces there are anonymous, or by Arcadelt.[30] However, the presence of some such patterns can yield bibliographical information, throwing light on the value (or otherwise) of the names that are printed, or of the blank space.

An innocuous example occurs in the book of Veggio madrigals printed in 1540 by Scotto.[31] Here, the formal pattern of the running head-lines was clearly systematised in the mind of the typesetter. The relevant part-name (*CANTVS*, etc.) appears on all rectos containing music. The composer's name (*CLAVDIVS Veggius.*) is to be found on all versos, except as mentioned below; in addition, it was to be set on the first recto of each gathering – where it would catch the binder's eye after he had folded the sheet, and confirm his choice. The book contains six madrigals by Arcadelt (according to the dedication, 'donated' by Scotto), on fols. C1[v], C2[r], D1[r], D1[v], D2[r] and D2[v] of each partbook. Each of these pages carries the word *ARCH-ADELT* in the running head, instead of Veggio's name, but, in the case of the three rectos, in addition to the part-name. In this volume the printer, faced with so simple a programme, was already keeping

[30] For more discussion of the implications of this procedure, see section III of the present paper, below.

[31] RISM 1540[19] = V1087; New Vogel 2844.
[flower] MADRIGALI [flower] / A QVATTRO VOCI / Di Messer CLAVDIO Veggio, con la Gionta di sei altri di Arcadelth della / misura a breve. Nuovamente con ogni diligentia stampati. / [device] / VENETIIS / Apud Hieronymum Scotum. / [rule] / 1540.
The lower voices have a different title-page:
MADRIGALI DI MESSER CLAVDIO / Veggio, a Quattro Voci. Nuovamente Stampati. / [flower] / TENOR / [etc.]
Oblong quarto, 40 pages per part: A–E[4]; a–e[4]; AA–EE[4]; aa–ee[4]. Paginated from the second recto, I–XXXVIII.
Copy consulted: Vienna, Österreichische Nationalbibliothek, SA.77.D.55.
J. Haar, 'The *Nota Nere* Madrigal', *Journal of the American Musicological Society*, 18 (1965), pp. 22–41, points out (on p. 25) that this is the first printed volume to refer to the new style.

as much material as possible in the head-line from one forme to the next: comparison of the same folio in different partbooks, or in consecutive gatherings of the same book, will rapidly confirm this. A natural, normal product of such a procedure is that the head-line would not always be checked for its accuracy: after all, the typesetter knew that it was normally retained, intact, from one gathering to the next. In this particular volume, there are two minor, though instructive anomalies. In gathering BB of the Altus, the formes were used in a different position from that found elsewhere: the forme that normally supplied the first recto of each gathering was here inverted. Therefore, the additional reference to the composer's name (which should have appeared on BB1^r) is found on BB3^r. The other head-lines in this forme confirm the nature of this slip as being purely procedural. In addition, the first recto of E in all partbooks lacks the additional reference to Veggio. Here, the probable explanation is rather different, for the typesetter had already had to take Veggio's name out of the skeleton forme for D1^r, when he inserted instead the name of Arcadelt. Apparently, when removing this latter name, ready for gathering E, he forgot to reinstate that of Veggio.

Clearly, there is no problem here over the ascription of the madrigal concerned, *Io son donna disposto di morire*. But, equally clearly, in books where the possibility of retaining a composer's name as part of the head-line exists, there also exists the possibility of making such an error where it becomes significant, omitting the name of a completely different composer, or alternatively forgetting to remove a now incorrect name. The obvious place to look for such possibilities is in those volumes largely devoted to the works of one composer – Arcadelt, Festa, Verdelot – rather than in a volume of *Madrigali diversi*, where the typesetter would expect to have to change the name in the head-line for each new page, and would therefore be less likely to forget about it.

Mary Lewis has drawn attention to a practice in Gardane's shop that, in fact, makes such errors even more likely: she has given the name of 'vertical setting' to a procedure whereby the second gathering, for instance, of every partbook was set in sequence, before work began on any of the third gatherings.[32] Clearly, this became a

[32] Lewis, 'Antonio Gardane', pp. 123–5. The evidence of the treatment of the head-lines in Veggio's book, which I have just outlined, argues that Scotto was following the same procedure.

Non-conflicting attributions and newly anonymous compositions

convenient procedure only after printers had begun to lay out all partbooks consistently, with the same pieces lying on the same folios in each: equally clearly, once that had happened, part of every running head-line, the composer's name, could be retained from one partbook to the next, for four sheets with four-voice madrigals, for five with five-part music, etc. (It should also be no surprise that, under such a pattern of work, the part-name appears less frequently on the inner pages of a sheet, and more frequently only on the first recto: this reduces even further the number of elements needing to be changed when moving from one voice to another.) As a result, the habit of automatically checking the composer's name at the head of each page must have slipped from memory even more often, and the prospect of finding erroneous names, held over from the last part-book of one gathering to the first of the next, increases correspondingly.

Some excellent examples of this type of evidence occur in RISM 1541[16], another Verdelot anthology.[33] A setting of *Deh perche non e in voi, tante pietade* appears on p. 22 of each book. In the Cantus book only (fol. C3[v]), it is ascribed to *Archadelt*, while in the other five books the madrigal is anonymous.[34] The immediate assumption that the entry in the Cantus might be an error, then corrected in the lower voices, is confirmed by a simple analytical observation: the type appearing on C3[v] of the Cantus is identical, both in exact alignment and in the condition of the letter *l*, with that found on the correspond-

---

[33] RISM 1541[16]; New Vogel 2890.
   VERDELOT / LA PIV DIVINA, ET PIV BELLA MVSICA, CHE SE / vdisse giamai delli presenti Madrigali, a Sei voci. Composti per lo Eccellentissi=/mi VERDELOT. Et altri Musici, non piu Stampati, & con / ogni diligentia corretti. Novamente posti in luce. / CANTVS / CON GRATIA ET PRIVILEGIO. / M.D.XLI. / VENETIIS APVD ANTONIVM GARDANE.
   The lower voices have different titles, with the appropriate part-name:
   TENOR / VERDELOT / M. D. [Gardane's mark] XXXXI. / Venetijs Apud Antonium Gardane. [plus signature line:] Madrigali primi, di Verdelot, a Sei [followed by the signature letter]
   Oblong quarto, 32 pages per part: A–D⁴; E–H⁴; I–M⁴; N–Q⁴; R–V⁴; X–Z, +⁴. Paginated from the first recto, [1], 2–31, [32] in all books.
   Copies consulted: Vienna, Österreichische Nationalbibliothek, SA.77.D.52; London, British Library, K.11.e.2(4) – Bassus only.
   Once again, there are serious problems with the list of ascriptions offered by the New Vogel: *Ultimi mei sospiri* is ascribed to Verdelot, as is *Ardenti miei sospiri*, while *In me cresce l'ardore* is anonymous. Four other pieces have ascriptions only in some of the partbooks, remaining anonymous in the others: all are discussed here.
[34] On the strength of this ascription, the work is edited in *Arcadelt*, VII, no. 27. The folios in the other partbooks of this edition correspond: G3[v], L3[v], P3[v], T3[v] and Z3[v].

VII

ing page of the previous gathering, p. 14 (fol. B3ᵛ of the Cantus, and corresponding folios in the other books). The error, then, was not even an active one on the part of the typesetter, that of deliberately inserting a composer's name – an act that would necessarily compel our attention. Rather, it was the passive error of leaving the name in place for one partbook too many.[35] The piece should not be regarded as by Arcadelt, but as anonymous, pending the discovery of further, independent sources.

There are three other pieces in this volume for which some of the partbooks lack an ascription, and which therefore might at first sight seem to fall into the same situation: for two of these, the presence of a name in some books has to be seen as an intentional entry on the part of the typesetter. *Cosi estrema de doglia* is ascribed to *Const. festa.* in all except the Tenor book, where there is no name.[36] This name does not appear anywhere else in the volume, so it can hardly have been retained in error. *Chi bussa*, fitted onto the lower staves of the last folio of music, has the name *Verdolot* [*sic*] above the stave on which it opens, only in the Cantus, Quintus and Sextus books. It is just possible to argue that the same ascription is lacking in the other three books only because of the presence of text from the end of the previous piece.[37] There is no reason to doubt the stated authorship of either piece.

More difficult is the case of *Madonna i prieghi mei*, on fol. A3ᵛ, ascribed to *Maistre Ihan*, only in the Cantus and Bassus books.[38] This madrigal has a heading which seems to me to be identical with that used for *Ditimi o diva mia* (the second setting, on p. 29, fol. 3ʳ of the last

[35] This must serve to underscore the extent to which we should adapt our view of 'errors', 'variants' and 'changes' in the surviving copies of early printed music – a view which is at present far from that of the contemporary purchaser of the volumes. For a printer to re-set a whole leaf or sheet, the errors had to be gross. For him to recall or correct pages that had slipped past him was virtually unknown. While Petrucci and other printers would regularly correct copies remaining unsold in their shop, supposing the errors to be serious musical ones, they felt almost no compulsion to correct non-musical mistakes. These were simply not deemed to be important enough, as is witnessed by the present erroneous ascription, which was merely 'corrected' for those partbooks which had not as yet gone through the press.

[36] Detailed analysis leads me to believe that the Tenor book was set first for the last gathering, which contains this madrigal: for earlier gatherings, the Cantus was certainly set first, perhaps followed by the Bassus.

[37] Despite the assertion of A.-M. Bragard, *Étude bio-bibliographique sur Philippe Verdelot, musicien français de la Renaissance*, Mémoires de la Classe des Beaux-Arts de l'Académie Royale de Belgique, 11 (1964), p. 58, this work is not to be found in later editions of Verdelot's six-voice madrigals. It is discussed and edited in D. Harrán, 'Chi bussa? or the Case of the Anti-madrigal', *Journal of the American Musicological Society*, 21 (1968), pp. 85–93.

[38] To be found on p. 6 – that is, fol. 3ᵛ of the first gathering – of each partbook.

Non-conflicting attributions and newly anonymous compositions

gathering). If that were true, it would require that the first gathering of all the partbooks should have been set after the rest of the book (a by no means unknown occurrence, although without any evident reason in the present case), and also that the caption should have been moved from a recto to a verso (p. 6) – a most unreasonable assumption.

Instead, I think that one has to suggest that the attribution to *Maistre Ihan* on p. 6 was newly set, and that the pattern of preparing the head-line for this page was influenced by what the typesetter had just finished on p. 5. Here, Berchem's *Madonna se volete* begins at the top corner of the page only in the Cantus and Bassus books, and on the third stave in all others. In the Cantus and Bassus, therefore, the ascription to *Iachet Berchem* appears in its customary place in the head-line to the page. In the other four books, it is fitted above the opening of the piece, in the space that would otherwise have contained the last words of the text of the previous madrigal. It seems at least possible that the typesetter (or his editor) merely left the head-line blank on p. 6 because, in the same partbooks, it was also blank on p. 5. If this is so, and I admit it to be rather far-fetched, the omission of the composer's name in these four partbooks was not the result of second thoughts on Gardane's part, and the ascription to Maistre Jhan can be assumed to have been acceptable to him.[39]

Maistre Jhan fares poorly in this volume: there are two settings of

[39] This assumes that each gathering was set entirely through in consecutive order. One of the merits of the procedure proposed by Lewis is that the typesetter could not merely set the same gathering for each partbook before proceeding to the next, but he could also do the same for smaller units, certainly separate formes, and even possibly individual pieces. This last would in practice seem to have been unlikely, for, in the instance of the present volume, the music would have had to have been set for nearly six whole gatherings (one for each voice-part) before any one forme would have been completed and ready to go to press – to be precise, for thirty-seven pages of standing type. It is more likely that the procedure involved setting 'vertically' the individual pieces that made up one forme for each sheet. Then nineteen pages would have been set by the time the first forme was ready for the press. While this may seem still to make great demands on the amount of type, the number of sorts in the case, it must be remembered that one more page set would release another forme for the press, as that for the second partbook was finished, and another page would release the third, by which time the first would be returning from the press, and the type could be redistributed. Since fifteen pages of standing type would be required even under straightforward setting procedures (when each gathering was set straight through in order), this alternative arrangement does seem to have been feasible: indeed, it has the great advantage that each sheet would have time to dry from the first impression before the forme for the other side was printed, considerably greater time than that allowed by normal linear setting. However, this alternative method of vertical setting does weaken my argument for the attribution of Maistre Jhan's *Madonna i prieghi mei*, unless I assume that the lapse lies with the house editor or a shop supervisor, rather than with the actual typesetter.

Ditimi o diva mia ascribed to him (pp. 23 and 29), of which the second is retained for the second edition[40] and there attributed to Verdelot (piece 23). There is no chance that the presence of the name *Verdelot* in the second edition can be a simple technical slip: it cannot have been retained from elsewhere, and so must have been a deliberate act on the part of the typesetter. However, the second attribution to *Maistre Ihan* in the first edition (on p. 29) could have been, and probably was, retained from the first (on p. 23). It seems plausible to suggest that the typesetter, seeing the same words for an incipit, assumed (without thought) that he was dealing with a work by Maistre Jhan, for he would not have had the first setting before him – the type would have been dispersed, leaving only the running head. My belief, therefore, is that the two settings of *Ditimi o diva mia* in 1541[16] are by different composers, the first by Maistre Jhan, and the second by Verdelot, as attested in the second edition.

There are also a couple of examples of the same technique, or lapse in technique, in RISM 1543[20] (the third edition of Arcadelt's third book).[41] *Amor s'al primo sguardo* is here attributed to *Archadelt.* on p. xvii (fols. C1r, H1r, N1r and S1r). But the heading which gives the composer's name had been retained from p. viiii (B1r in the Cantus), where it was used for all the partbooks, and was to be used further on p. xxv (fol. D1r of the Cantus), where it appears above *Qual paura ho.* In the other editions of this volume, *Amor s'al primo sguardo* is unequivocally ascribed to Festa.[42] In exactly the same manner, the heading on p. xviii (fol. C1v) of the third edition, an ascription to

40   RISM 1546[19]; New Vogel 2891.
        VERDELOT A SEI / MADRIGALI DI VERDELOT ET / DE ALTRI AVTORI A SEI VOCI / novamente con alcuni madrigali novi ristampati & corretto / A SEI [Gardane's mark] VOCI / In Venetia Apresso di / Antonio Gardane. / [rule] / M. D. XXXXVI. / CANTVS
     The other partbooks have the same title, with changed part-name.
     This volume has the same collation as that of the first edition (see note 33, above). Not paginated; the pieces are numbered, I–XXIX.
     Copy consulted: Munich, Bayerische Staatsbibliothek.
41   RISM 1543[20] = A1377; New Vogel 159.
        [flower] CANTVS [flower] / IL TERZO LIBRO D'I MADRIGALI D'ARCHADELT / A QVATRO VOCI INSIEME ALCUNI DI CONST. FESTA / & altri dieci a voci mudate novamente ristampato & corretto. / A QVATRO [Gardane's mark] VOCI / Venetijs Apud Antonium Gardane. / [rule] / M. D. XXXXIII.
     The lower voices carry the same title, with changed part-name.
     Oblong quarto, 40 pages per part: A–E⁴; F–K⁴; L–P⁴; Q–V⁴. Paginated from the first recto, [1], II–XXXIX, [40], in each partbook.
     Copy consulted: Glasgow, Euing Music Library, lacking the last folio of the Bassus.
42   These editions, 1539[23] and 1541[11], are detailed in note 12, above.

Non-conflicting attributions and newly anonymous compositions

Con. Festa., is retained for p. XXVI (D1ᵛ), where it changes the authorship of Arcadelt's *Si lieto alcun giamai*. In this case, it is little wonder that the next edition, 1556²², should retain Festa as the composer, for it displays a propensity for converting works to his property. However, the bibliographical evidence of the third edition shows that the changes of composer given there are not conscious decisions on the part of the printer, but merely technical slips. Both works should be regarded as belonging to their earlier authors – *Amor s'al primo sguardo* as the work of Festa, and *Si lieto alcun giamai* of Arcadelt.

Other cases can be found where an ascription is preserved from one folio to another, in all or some partbooks. Among them would be:

(1) the suggestion in the Bassus book of 1542¹⁶, *Madrigali de diversi autori libro primo*, that Alfonso de la Viola's *Ai pie d'un chiaro fonte* was by *Arnoldo*. This clearly erroneous ascription appears on fol. T4ᵛ as a relic from its correct use on T3ᵛ, which occupies a similar position in the arrangement of the inner forme for this sheet.⁴³

(2) the ascription to *Verdelot* of Festa's *D'amore le generose*, in the Verdelot anthology, 1541¹⁸, preserved in the Altus book.⁴⁴ This use, on fol. AA2ʳ, appears to be adapted from the same title employed on Z2ʳ and AA1ʳ. By contrast, the name of *Const. Festa.* is carefully applied to this work, not only in the other partbooks, but also in the Scotto edition 1540²⁰, in later anthologies, and in Ottaviano Scotto's earlier editions (1534, 1536 and 1537) of Verdelot's second book.⁴⁵

---

⁴³ This recurrence of identical captions on both formes of a single sheet tends to argue, as I discuss elsewhere in this paper, that some volumes were set more slowly, using only one or two formes for the work. This may be yet another reflection of Gardane's apparent habit of working on more than one title at a time.
⁴⁴ For this volume, see note 9, above. The Scotto edition, RISM 1540²⁰, is described in note 26.
⁴⁵ RISM 1534¹⁶ = V1220; New Vogel 2868.
The Bassus survives as
    Del Libro Secondo / B
with the colophon:
    Finisce il Secundo Libro de Madrigali di Verdelot, Nuovamente / Stampati, Et per Andrea Anticho intagliati, 7 con / summa diligentia corretti. / [Scotto's mark] / Venetijs Apud Octauianum Scotum / [rule] / M. D. XXXIII.
Oblong octavo, 32 pages: G–H⁸. Pieces numbered, 1–25. Tavola set in two columns, not headed. All but three composer ascriptions are set vertically in the left margin.
Copy consulted: Paris, Bibliothèque Nationale, Rés. Vmf. 40(2).
RISM 1536⁷ = V1221; New Vogel 2869.
    Il secondo Libro de Madrigali di Verdelot / insieme con alcuni altri bellissimi Madrigali di Adriano, 7 di / Constantino Festa, Nuouamente stampati, 7 con / summa diligentia corretti. / M. D. [large:]s XXXVI. / Con Gratia, 7 Privilegio.

VII

(3) the misascription of two pieces in the Cantus book of 1540[18], repeated exactly in 1541[17], both editions of Verdelot's five-voice madrigals.[46] In the earlier, Scotto, edition, Verdelot's *Quand'havran fin* is ascribed to *Archadelt* on fol. C1[v], while Arcadelt's *Se'l foco in cui sempr'ardo* is given to *Verdelot* on C2[r]. The clear implication is that these two head-lines, which lie close to each other in the forme, were exchanged in error, and were then corrected for the remaining voices. In the later edition, the two pieces appear on pp. 24 (fol. C4[v]) and 20 (C2[v]) respectively: the repetition here of the error found in 1540[18] is almost enough to determine that the later edition was copied directly from the earlier.

(4) the faulty ascription, on fol. cc3[r] of the Bassus of 1539[23], of

The lower voices have variants of a different title:
¶Del Libro Secondo di Verdelotto / T
Del Libro Secondo di Verdelot. / A
¶Del Libro Secondo di Verdelot. / B
On fol. H7[v]:
[Scotto's mark] / [short rule] / ¶Venetijs Apud Octauianum Scotum.
Oblong octavo, 32 pages per part: A–B[8]; C–D[8]; E–F[8]; G–H[8]. Pieces numbered, 1–25. *Tavola* in two columns, headed. Running head: part-name. Ascriptions at the head of the page in some instances.
Copy consulted: Bologna, Civico Museo Bibliografico Musicale, U 309.

RISM 1537[10] = V1222: New Vogel 1870.
Il secondo Libro de Madrigali di Verdelotto / insieme con alcuni altri bellissimi Madrigali di Adriano, 7 di / Constantio Festa: Nuouamente stampati, 7 con / somma diligentia corretti. / M D [large:]s XXXVII. / Con Gratia, 7 Privilegio.
The lower voices have a consistent title, with relevant part-letter:
¶Del Libro Secondo de Madrigali di Verdelotto. / [large:]T
On fol. H7[v]:
[Scotto's mark] / [short rule] / Venetijs Apud Octauianum Scotum.
Oblong octavo, 32 pages per part: A–B[8]; C–D[8]; E–F[8]; G–H[8]. Pieces numbered, 1–25. *Tavola* in one column, headed and with ascriptions. Running head-line: part-name, extended on the first recto of gatherings B, D, F and H.
Copies consulted: Munich, Bayerische Staatsbibliothek, 8[0]. Mus.pr. 40/2, lacks the last folio of the Bassus; Paris, Bibliothèque Nationale, Rés. Vmd. 23 (an Altus book); Bologna, Civico Museo Bibliografico Musicale, R 140/1 (a Bassus).
46   RISM 1540[18]; New Vogel 2884.
LE DOTTE ET ECCELLENTE COMPOSITIONI / DE I MADRIGALI A CINQVE VOCI DA DI/versi perfettissimi Musici fatte. Nouamente raccolte, / & con ogni diligentia Stampate. / AVTORI. / Di Adriano Vuillaert. & di / Leonardo Barri suo discipulo. / Di Verdelotto. / Di Constantio Festa. / Di Archadelt. / Di Corteggia. / Di Iachet Berchem. / De Ivo, & di Nolet, / Apud Hieronymum Scotum. / [rule] / 1540.
The lower voices have a consistent different title, with the appropriate part-names:
MADRIGALI A CINQVE VOCE DA PIV / Eccellentissimi Musici fatti. Nouamente raccolti, & / con somma diligentia corretti. / TENOR
Oblong quarto, 44 pages per part: A–E[4]F[2]; a–e[4]f[2]; Aa–Ee[4]Ff[2]; aa–ee[4]ff[2]; AA–EE[4]FF[2]. Paginated from the second recto, I–XLII.
Copy consulted: Munich, Bayerische Staatsbibliothek, 4[0]. Mus.pr. 52(7); Wolfenbüttel, Herzog August Bibliothek, 2.11.1–2.11.5 Musica.
For RISM 1541[17], see note 12, above.

136

Non-conflicting attributions and newly anonymous compositions

Festa's *Divelt'e'l mio bel vivo* to *Archadelt*. This is probably retained from fol. bb3ʳ and the corresponding pages in the other voice parts, although the evidence is rather indistinct.[47]

(5) the ascription to Arcadelt, in all books of 1541[12], of Verdelot's *Io son tal volta* (not to be confused with the Festa setting, discussed above). The ascription, *Archadelt.* (with the final point) on p. 19 of all partbooks, has been retained from p. 11, that is, from B2ʳ to C2ʳ of the Cantus (and corresponding folios in the other books). The piece is correctly ascribed to Verdelot in other editions.

III

It might seem that my procedure in the first and second sections of this paper has been to demonstrate that the earlier of two surviving ascriptions to a madrigal should be the preferred one. That is, of course, by no means always the case; but it is in the nature of the evidence I have been offering that it should suggest that some subsequent changes in ascription were the result, not of conscious thought, but of unconscious error or of technical change. If this has been adequately demonstrated, it has been capable of showing no more than that the later ascription has no evidence in its favour. It may be, in a few of these cases, that the later change was in fact deliberate; but one has no way of discovering such a possibility from the surviving evidence. All that can be shown is that it is more likely that the change was not deliberate.

On the other hand, there are several cases where no bibliographical or technical reason can be adduced for an erroneous change in ownership. In such cases, one has initially to admit that the two ascriptions remain in conflict, and look elsewhere for reasonable evidence: to the style of the music, to the relations between composer and publisher, to the known biographies of both, even to the concordance pattern. Occasionally, though rarely, there is bibliographical evidence suggesting that the later ascription is in fact the correct one. I propose in the paragraphs that follow to give a few examples of such instances.

I have already discussed one or two cases in Arcadelt's fourth book of madrigals, but I wish to turn to the volumes again, for the

---

47 For this volume, see note 12, above.

three editions[48] do not show the same basic approach to the provision of names at the heads of pages. In the first two, Gardane clearly wished to have a name at the head of every page: therefore, the word *Archadelt.* acted as a general running title and was retained on pages where no other entry could be made. Thus, in 1539[24], the setting of type for the head-line which appears on p. v (fol. A3ʳ) is to be found also on pp. XIII (B3ʳ) and XXI (C3ʳ), in each case with the corresponding folios in the other partbooks). This pattern can also be seen elsewhere in the volume. A few folios, A3ʳ, A4ʳ, E4ʳ and their corresponding pages in the other books (i.e. those numbered v, VII and XXXIX), carry the word *Residuum.* in the head-line. Other composers are only named at the heads of five pages (VIII, IX, XX, XXIII and XXXVII). In addition, no name at all is found on p. XXXVIII, for the start of the last piece of all, *Pace non trovo* (assigned to Yvo in the second edition).[49] This falls on the last opening of music in both editions, and it is plausible to assume (in the absence of any other evidence) that the name was merely forgotten in the first edition.

There are very few substantive changes made to the ascriptions for the second edition. As I have shown above, some apparent changes are the result either of trying to adapt practice when fitting three pieces to an opening, or of failing to change an obsolete ascription in the head-line: both are direct products of the printer's attempts at becoming more systematic. *Io son tal volta*, for example, is ascribed to Arcadelt only because the running head-line was not removed from the forme and changed: the same appears to be true of that composer's name as found above *Col pensier mai non maculai.*

This is hardly surprising: of thirty-eight captions, only seven are not to Arcadelt – only two of the first twenty-nine. One of these is the name *Layole.* on p. 31 (fol. D4ʳ of the Cantus). Well down on the page is the opening of *Dal bel soave ragio*, ascribed to Layolle in Moderne's editions of *Le parangon des chansons. Second livre . . .* (1538[16] and 1540[15]). Gardane's acceptance of Layolle as the composer in his edition of 1541 is but one more piece of evidence regarding his knowledge of Moderne's editions. However, the use of *Archadelt.* as a caption in the first edition (1539[24]) cannot be taken to imply that the printer originally thought the piece to be by that composer: it is probably no

[48] RISM 1539[24], 1541[12] and 1545[18], described in note 23, above.
[49] On this work, see J. Haar, '*Pace non trovo*: a Study in Literary and Musical Parody', *Musica Disciplina*, 19 (1965), pp. 95–149, especially pp. 110–19.

Non-conflicting attributions and newly anonymous compositions

more than a statement that he knew of no other name to put above the work, but that it was in an edition with Arcadelt's name on the title-page.

Indeed, in such cases throughout the first two editions, it seems that the name *Archadelt* functioned only as a standard running head-line, identifying the volume rather than the composer of any specific piece. If another composer's name was known to the printer, it could be used: otherwise, when nothing was known (or when Arcadelt was certainly known to be the composer) the running head could be left in place, and the word *Archadelt* would appear. In other words, this title was not intended as a statement of authorship so much as an identification of the volume. (The similar cases in early volumes devoted to Verdelot will be discussed below.)

By contrast, the third edition (1545[18]) follows an entirely different approach. This is highlighted by two features: one is the number of pieces without ascription – four that had appeared below the name of Arcadelt in the earlier editions, plus one, *Col pensier*, that had started well down a page, and another three not found in the first two editions. The second feature is an additional element in the head-lines, the phrase *A voce Pari*, accorded to nine madrigals. Where there is no ascription, for three of these works, this phrase occupies exactly the space reserved for the composer's name. This, by itself, is sufficient to support an assertion that these three pieces were not left anonymous by error – for the typesetter did have to give attention to the space in the head-line into which a name would have been fitted.[50] Therefore, the editor seems to have added to his responsibilities the additional decision of whether to leave a piece anonymous: in so doing, he had ceased to see the head-line merely as a running title. This is a most important change, for it gives a new range of significance to any composer's name appearing there.

Despite these points, there are, of course, occasions when the composer's name could legitimately be retained from one gathering to the next, and for some of these the same setting of type was retained in use. Those on pp. 9, 12 and 13 (fols. B2^r, B3^v and B4^r of the Cantus) are retained throughout all four partbooks and then re-used on pp. 17, 20 and 21 (C2^r, C3^v and C4^r), again for all four parts.

Such evidence might seem to weaken my case for precision on

---

[50] This point was used, above, in determining the printer's view of the authorship of *Col pensier mai non maculai*.

Gardane's part, but for the fact that he did not follow up several other opportunities to retain captions. It is further negated by two other occurrences: one is the reappearance of the name *Verdelot* against *Io son tal volta*, and the other is the use, for the first time, of an ascription to *Leonardus Barre.*, against *Tengan dunque ver me*. Neither of these names appears elsewhere in the volume: both have to have been deliberately inserted.

A few other compositions in this book need consideration at the present stage. Almost all appear in earlier editions ascribed to Arcadelt, and all, I believe, suffer from the use of that composer's name as a running head in the make-up of those editions (see Table 3). Seay accepts these works as being by Arcadelt, specifically so in the case of *Io son tal volta*, while according a 'probably' to *Tengan dunque ver me*.[51] I suspect that none of them is in fact by Arcadelt. In the case of *Tengan dunque ver me*, I have already hinted that the evidence is fairly strong against the ascription to Arcadelt. It is, in addition, likely that Barre was little known in Venice in 1539, so that Gardane could plausibly not have discovered his authorship until some years later. *Io son tal volta* has already been discussed. (The retention of Arcadelt's name from one forme to another in the second edition, affecting this piece, and discussed above at the end of the second section of the present study, is only a particular instance of the general case being stated here.) For similar reasons, I believe that the appearance of Arcadelt's name above the other five works carries much less weight than does its deliberate omission in the third edition: its use is no more than an admission on Gardane's part that he knew of no other composer to whom to give these pieces.

I fully recognise that a name in the hand is worth more than two – or none – in the murky undergrowth of bibliographical analysis. However, these names, and others, are hardly in the hand: they have to be taken as examples of decoys, names supplied to attract, if not other names (i.e. composers), then at least purchasers. They are statements that Gardane had no other name to offer. This may seem an unduly pessimistic position to adopt. On the other hand, to view these works as anonymous should allow us to examine more pre-

---

[51] *Arcadelt*, v, pp. xiii–xx. D. Hersh, 'Verdelot and the Early Madrigal' (Ph.D. dissertation, University of California at Berkeley, 1963), p. 289, suggests that *Io nol disse giamai* was composed by Verdelot. Bridges, 'Publishing', pp. 27–8, uses the fact that *Tronchi la parca* sets a poem of Lorenzo Strozzi to reinforce a suggested link between Arcadelt and the Strozzi family.

Table 3

Madrigal	1539²⁴ Page (folio)	1539²⁴ Ascription	1541¹² Page (folio)	1541¹² Ascription	1545¹⁸ Page (folio)	1545¹⁸ Ascription
Col pensier	vii (A4ʳ)	[anonymous]	35 (E2ʳ)	Archadelt	xxvii (D3ʳ)	[anonymous]
Dolcemente s'adira	xxiiii (C4ᵛ)	Archadelt.	16 (B4ᵛ)	Archadelt	xviii (C2ᵛ)	[anonymous]
Donna s'ogni beltade	xxxiiii (E1ᵛ)	Archadelt.	27 (D2ʳ)	Archadelt	xxiiii (D1ᵛ)	[anonymous]
Io nol disse giamai	xxi (C3ʳ)	Archadelt.	18 (C1ᵛ)	Archadelt	xiii (B4ᵛ)	[anonymous]
Io son tal volta	xiii (C4ʳ)	Verdelot.	19 (C2ᵛ)	Archadelt.	xv (C1ʳ)	Verdelot
Tengan dunque	xiii (B3ʳ)	Archadelt.	6 (A3ᵛ)	Archadelt	viii (B1ᵛ)	Leonardus Barre.
Tronchi la parca	xxxiii (E1ʳ)	Archadelt.	23 (C4ʳ)	Archadelt	xxiii (D1ʳ)	[anonymous]

cisely the style, not only of these specific pieces, but also of those that are securely attributable to Arcadelt.

For the same reasons, I believe that *Amor quanto piu lieto* was thought to be by Verdelot, rather than by Arcadelt. It is, to be sure, assigned to Arcadelt in the crucial third edition, 1545[18], on p. ix (fol. B2r): but this can be seen as an extension of the same attribution found in the first two editions (1539[24], p. xiii; 1541[12], p. 4). By contrast, the attributions to Verdelot are not found in those volumes where Scotto is using his name as a running head; rather, they are in 1540[20], as well as in the two earlier editions of *Libro primo de la serena*.[52] These two editions, where composer's names appear only in the *TABVLA*, are not identical in contents or in bibliographical detail. It is apparent that the ascriptions of the second edition are taken from those of the first. However, the statement of Verdelot's authorship found in 1540[20] is independent of both, and there seem to be no bibliographical grounds for rejecting it.

There is a similar range of cases in Arcadelt's third book,[53] where it is again evident that the first edition, 1539[23], used the word *ARCHADELT* as a running title. This may also be true of the second edition, 1541[11]: by the time of the third, 1543[20], however, Gardane had settled his procedure. A number of pieces gain new ascriptions in the progress through these editions. Some of these have already been discussed,[54] but two others remain:

[52]   RISM 1530[2].
Of this edition, only the Altus partbook survives, with (as title):
    A
Oblong quarto, 36 pages: J–L⁴M⁶. Presumably the Cantus and Tenor books also had four gatherings each.
Copy consulted: Seville, Biblioteca Colombina, 12–1–31(6) (Altus only).
    Chapman, 'Andrea Antico', no. 64, identifies this with a book cited in Colon's catalogue as printed in Rome in 1530. S. Cusick, 'Valerio Dorico, Music Printer in Sixteenth-century Rome' (Ph.D. dissertation, University of North Carolina, 1975), pp. 61 and 81, believes that the volume was printed by Pasoti and Dorico, and suggests there and in subsequent correspondence with the present writer that there was some connection with the Colonna family. See also K. Jeppesen, 'Die neuentdeckten Bücher der Lauden des Ottaviano dei Petrucci und andere musikwissenschaft Seltenheiten der Biblioteca Colombina zu Sevilla', *Zeitschrift für Musikwissenschaft*, 12 (1929–30), pp. 73–89.
[53]   For these editions, see above, note 12.
[54]   Despite Seay's assertion, in *Arcadelt*, iv, pp. xii–xiii, that these pieces are anonymous in 1543[20], both can be assigned to composers. The pieces are *Bramo morir* and *È morta la speranza*, and have been discussed above, in section i.
    I am not entirely satisfied that Gardane intended to regard the composer's name, *Archadelt*, as a free running-title in the second edition. As I am about to show, it was certainly retained from gathering to gathering, but this, of course, is not the same thing. However, the question does not affect the present issue.

Non-conflicting attributions and newly anonymous compositions

Poi che'l fiero destin is ascribed to Arcadelt in the first edition (p. XXXIX), but to *Iachet Berchem.* in the second and third (pp. 44 and XXXII, respectively): *Languir non mi fa amore*, also ascribed to Arcadelt in the first edition (p. XXXXI), is given to *Corteccia.* in the third (p. XXXIIII). In the second it carries the name *Archadelt.* in the Cantus but *Corteccia.* in all three other voices (p. 38). There is no other use of either name, Corteccia or Berchem, in the second or third edition, so that they cannot appear as the result of a lapse on the part of the typesetter, but have to reflect a conscious action. This cannot be said for the retention of the name Arcadelt in the first edition, or in the Cantus of the second (where its appearance on fol. E3^v (p. 38) is a relic from that on D3^v and corresponding places in the other partbooks). I am satisfied that neither of these madrigals was ever thought of, by the printer, as having been composed by Arcadelt.

Arcadelt's second book of madrigals does not present such problems. There are no ascriptions or running head-lines in the first two editions, and the ascriptions to other composers in the later editions are consistent. This may not mean that all the other works there are in fact by Arcadelt: but, if Gardane did not know of any other name to assign to them, he also left us with no bibliographical evidence to suggest any.

IV

The same pattern of using a composer's name as running head-line is found occasionally in the early editions of Verdelot. The first book of four-voice madrigals uses the rubric *Verdelot.*, or the part-name, or both.[55] However, the first book *à 5* has no composers' names, either in the head-line or in the tavola.[56] The second four-voice book is more interesting:[57] the first edition, 1534[16], has the composers' names in the left margin of the page, next to the start of the piece and set vertically (in an old-fashioned style that was soon abandoned by Scotto). The three exceptions are for pieces which open at the head of the page. In the third edition, 1537[10], the attributions have been transferred to the tavola, and the music pages carry only a part-name in the head-line. The second edition, 1536[7], is more complex in its treatment of the names, which are still on the music pages. Only

[55] For details of this title, see below, notes 60 and 61.
[56] See above, note 5.   [57] Details are above, note 45.

ten of the twenty-five pieces have names in all four partbooks: the Cantus has only fourteen composers' names, all but one at the head of the page, and the remaining one above the first stave of the piece. At the other extreme, the Altus labels twenty-three and the Bassus nineteen of the pieces, and the great majority of their composers' names are in the left margin. The evidence suggests that the typesetting was shared between two craftsmen, with a major point of division coming half-way through the Tenor book – although I do not believe that this represents any hiatus in the preparation of the edition. It does, however, help to explain two anomalies in the ascriptions preserved in this edition, both the result of this lack of a systematic approach:

On fol. D2^v (in the Tenor book) of 1536^7, the head-line *Adrian* appears above the second page of Verdelot's *Ne per gratia giamai*. There is no reason to believe that Scotto thought this work (much less a part of it) was by Willaert: the word *Adrian* was left in place from fol. C2^v, while Verdelot's name is entered at the start of the piece, on D2^r.

At the head of B5^r (Cantus) of the same edition, there is the caption *Andreas de Sylva*. Parts of two madrigals lie on this page: *Qual maraviglia o donna*, which had begun on the fifth stave of B4^v and is there ascribed to *Verdelot* (as it is in the tavola of 1537^{10}); and *D'amore le generose*, starting on the fourth stave, and ascribed to Festa (as it is almost everywhere else).[58] There is therefore no apparent reason for any reference to de Silva.

It is clear that a typesetter would not actively insert a new name, going through the process of selecting the type sorts and fitting them into the forme, without some reason. On the other hand, as I have shown, he might very easily leave one in place, if it were already in the forme and his attention were not specifically drawn to it. This suggests that one should look for the chance that this erroneous caption had been left over from an earlier forme, in use at the printing house immediately before gathering B of this edition was set up in type. Of course, gathering B is not the first in the book – but there is no reference to de Silva in the first gathering, A, of the Cantus, or indeed anywhere else in this title.

However, gathering A does have a different anomaly in the

---

[58] The single surviving partbook that names Verdelot as the composer has been discussed above, in section II.

running titles, and one that helps to explain the appearance of de Silva's name. All the partbooks carry the part-name at the head of the page. The first gathering of the Cantus has the word *Altus* appearing on the majority of pages of the outer forme. This argues for that forme, at least, having been used immediately before as part of an Altus book. While it is just possible that this could have been an Altus gathering of the present title, the type sorts suggest that to be unlikely. Coupled with the erroneous head-line in gathering B, the evidence suggests rather that Scotto was using at least four skeleton formes at this stage of his career, and that both errors are relics of the use of these two formes at the end of a previously printed volume.[59]

On the basis of this evidence alone, I began searching other editions of 1535 or 1536 for an attribution to Andreas de Silva, at the top of a page, on the correct page in the forme, and at the end of a volume, whence it could have passed to the present book. There is, in fact, no such case. But there is an important related instance: the first book of Verdelot's four-voice madrigals.[60] In the surviving Bassus of

---

[59] The incorrect use of the word *Altus* is on fols. A2^v, A3^r, A6^v, A7^r and A8^v. Of the other pages on this forme, the word is replaced on A4^v and A5^r by the word *Cantus*, and of course would not have been allowed to remain on A1^r, the title-page. The presence of this error, in gathering A of a book, suggests that this forme had been used for part of an Altus book of some previous publication. The additional presence of another error, the retention of the name of de Silva, in a different forme, suggests that both formes came from another volume, and that they represent only part of the total number of formes (probably four) currently in use by the printer – so that some formes might appear first in this volume in a correct state.

The argument that the reappearance of the word *Altus* might be from the Altus book of the present title is a weak one, for the following reason: it is probable that at least the inner forme used for gathering A (the first of the Cantus) would be preserved as far as possible, for the first gatherings of the other partbooks, for it contained the *Tavola*. Indeed, the tavola shows the same type and the same setting in all four partbooks, confirming that it was indeed retained for all. However, the setting of the word *Altus* in gathering A does not correspond to those in the Altus partbook. Further, the retention of the same formes throughout the first gathering of each partbook implies that not all four (or more, if the printer used more) would be needed for the first gathering: this helps to explain why the reference to de Silva need not have appeared until the second gathering of the Cantus, presumably being set up while the first gathering was going through the press.

As a result, the most simple explanation is that the forme preserving a different setting of the word *Altus*, together with another forme containing a reference to an irrelevant composer, represent elements of two gatherings at the end of work on some previous title, printed immediately before the present one.

[60] RISM 1533^2 = V1218; New Vogel 2866.

The surviving Bassus is headed with a capital *B* and has a colophon:
Finiscono li Madrigali de Verdelot. Stampati novamente / in Vinegia per Zovan Antonio 7 i Fratelli da Sa/bio: Ad instantia de li Scotti: 7 per An/drea Anticho da Montona inta/gliati: 7 con somma dili/gentia corretti. / Con Gratia 7 Privilegio. / [Scotto's mark] / M. D. XXXIII.
Oblong octavo, 32 pages, signed G–H^8. Pieces numbered, 1–28. The tavola is in two

VII

the first edition, 1533², a very careful ascription to *Andreas de Silva* is accorded the madrigal *Madonna io sol vorrei*, entered above the fourth stave on fol. H4ᵛ, with the piece continuing to H5ʳ. From the evidence of the edition of 1537⁹, the Cantus partbook would start this piece at the head of B5ʳ, and so would probably present the ascription as part of the head-line. I felt justified, as a result, in postulating an edition of the first book of Verdelot's four-voice madrigals that would be dated in late 1535 or early 1536, printed immediately before the second edition of the second book. The edition would probably have the name *Andreas de Sylva* at the top of B5ʳ, and perhaps of the other partbooks: this name would then have been left in place, along with the *Altus* headings and the correct running head of *Verdelot*, when work began on 1536⁷.

This analysis was completed, and the new/lost edition was postulated, while I was beginning to study all the surviving copies of the Antico–Scotto publications of the 1530s. Among them is a single partbook belonging, indubitably, to my conjectured edition. This is, unfortunately, not a Cantus, but a Bassus book, and is to be found in the Biblioteca Nazionale in Florence (Mus.ant. 229).⁶¹ My attention

columns with no head-line. A running head-line gives the part-name on the recto and the composer's name on the verso. There are errors on G3ʳ and H7ʳ⁻ᵛ.
Copy consulted: Paris, Bibliothèque Nationale, Rés. Vmf. 40(1).

RISM 1537⁹ = V1219; New Vogel 2867.
    Il primo libro de Madrigali di Verdelotto. / Novamente stampato, 7 con somma dili-/gentia corretto. / M D [large:]s xxxvii. / Con Gratia, 7 Privilegio.
The lower voices are differently titled, with their corresponding part-names:
    ꝗDel primo Libro de Madrigali di Verdelotto. / [large:]T
The last recto of the Bassus has a colophon:
    [mark of Scotto] / Venetijs Apud Octauianum Scotum. [with, in the only surviving copy, the manuscript addition of a date:] M D xxxvii
Oblong octavo, 32 pages per book: A–B⁸; C–D⁸; E–F⁸; G–H⁸. Pieces numbered, 1–28. *Tavola* in one column, and headed. Running head-line on all pages, of the part-name at the outer edge and the composer's name, centred: an extended form is used on the first recto of gatherings B, D, F and H.
Copies consulted: Paris, Bibliothèque Nationale, Rés. Vmd. 22 (Altus); London, British Library, k.8.b.11 (Altus); Oxford, Bodleian Library, Harding (vii) (imperfect Cantus); Bologna, Civico Museo Bibliografico Musicale, u 308.
    The table of contents offered by New Vogel for this edition seems to have been printed in error, for it bears no resemblance to the copies that I have seen.
⁶¹ [1536]. Cited in RISM at 1537⁹ = V1219, and in New Vogel at 2867.
The Bassus partbook is entitled:
    Del primo Libro de Madrigali di Verdelotto. / [large:]B
Oblong octavo, 32 pages: G–H⁸. Pieces numbered, 1–28. Tavola in two columns, no head-line. Running head-line on all folios from G2ʳ, as in the edition 1537⁹.
Copy at Florence, Biblioteca Nazionale Centrale, Mus.ant. 229. Bassus only, misbound, and lacking H8.

146

was first drawn to it because neither the title-page nor the tavola corresponds with those of either 1533[2] or 1537[9]. On inspection, it is clear that all the pages have been re-set, and that the music blocks show a level of damage lying between that of these two other editions; further, the font of the text type employed here was adopted by Scotto only after the first edition. Detailed analysis of the states of individual sorts and capitals reveals that this volume has to be dated either at the end of 1535 or early in the following year.[62] (If I incline to early 1536, it is only because the second edition of the second volume carries that date.) It is probable that a Cantus book, should it ever surface, would have de Silva's name on fol. B5[r].

All three editions set out to use the name of *Verdelot* as a running title, with the part-name. In the first edition, there are some minor anomalies, while the second and third both carry the two elements at the top of each page of music. However, both the first and the second edition take care to enter the name of de Silva at the start of *Madonna io sol vorrei*. While the second edition is clearly derivative of the first, there seems to have been no reason in the mind of Antico or Scotto

[62]   Unfortunately, the surviving Bassus book lacks the last folio, which would (if the normal procedure of Scotto and Antico was followed here) have carried at least Scotto's mark, and probably a colophon line, giving the date of printing. However, a few details of the analysis should suffice to demonstrate the dating of this volume – independently of its proposed close connection with 1536[7].

The state of the music blocks is already showing deterioration, though by no means as badly as in the 'second' (now known to be the third) edition of 1537[9]. An excellent example is at the end of the last stave in the book, on fol. H7[v]. But other obvious cases can be found on G2[v], G6[r], H1[r] or H4[v], to mention only one page in each forme of the book.

Several of the initial letters, showing progressive deterioration from 1533 to 1538, can be used to date this edition. Some are particularly vulnerable – and particularly valuable for analysis: the *J* that appears here on fol. G4[v] can be clearly seen to be in a worse condition than that displayed in 1534[16], 1535[8] or 1535[9], and in much the same state as that found in 1536[7]; the *M* on fol. G3[r] is also worse than in 1534[16] or 1535[8], though it is close to the example on H3[v] of 1535[8]; the *G* on H1[v] is again worse than in 1534[16], but it is marginally better than in 1536[7] and markedly better than in RISM V1224 (also dated 1536), while unfortunately not appearing in the other 1535 editions; of the different forms of the letter *L*, that found on H6[r] is very similar in state to its appearance in 1536[7], while that on H6[v] corresponds in condition to its state in V1223 (the first volume of Verdelot's madrigals *à5*); the letter *N* in the new edition is in fact a new letter, which is next to be found only in 1536[7] and later, while the *V* on H1[r] is in a state close to that of 1534[16] and 1535[8], markedly better than in 1536[7] and the succeeding V1224.

The sequence of printing that emerges from this is clear, and incidentally provides an admirable confirmation of the RISM date of [1535] for V1223: in 1535, RISM 1535[8] precedes 1535[9] and V1223, all to be followed by the new edition; then 1536[7] precedes V1224, and 1537[10] probably precedes 1537[9] and 1537[11]. It is therefore likely that the newly recovered edition of the first book of Verdelot madrigals should be dated [1536], pending the discovery of more parts, or of a Bassus part carrying a colophon.

for changing this name: my suspicion is that whichever of the two was responsible thought that the work was indeed by de Silva.

The minor anomalies of the first edition, 1533[2], seem, without the benefit of more than one surviving partbook, to be no more than inconsistencies. The intention seems to have been to put the part-name, *Bassus*, on the rectos, and the caption Verdelot on the versos. However, the part-name appears only on the first four rectos of each gathering (excluding the title-page, and including an *Altus* on G3[r]). Almost all other pages with music carry the composer's name as running head: the exception is the appearance of the name *Maistre Ian* on H7[r–v], above *Lasso che mal accorto*. It is virtually impossible to suggest that this entry arose as did the reference to de Silva in 1534[16]. Apart from the position of this ascription, well into the volume, there is no other plausible title from which such a head-line could have been retained. The only two candidates, books with any reference to Maistre Jhan, are the *Libro primo de la Serena* (1530[2]) and Verdelot's third book. Apart from the probability that the Antico–Scotto partnership had not been active before the surviving 1533[2], the first of these remote possibilities was put out by a different publisher (Dorico), while the second would presuppose three earlier lost editions, one of each of Verdelot's three books, simply so that one of the third book might have been lost.

It is much simpler, and much more plausible, to suggest that the typesetter of 1533[2] intended this ascription. Then it becomes comprehensible that the easy (or careless) retention of a running title in the second edition would lead to the suppression of any reference to Maistre Jhan in that (and therefore the third) edition.

I therefore believe not only that *Madonna io sol vorrei* is by Andrea de Silva, but also that *Lasso che mal accorto* was thought to be by Maistre Jhan. Certainly, the retention of the one ascription has to be seen as important, while the loss of the other is easier to explain than is its first appearance. (It is perhaps also significant that none of the other works in this volume have conflicting attributions elsewhere. While this does not confirm that they are all by Verdelot, it may help to reinforce the evidence that these two are not his work.) There is, in any case, no valid reason why de Silva should not have written a few madrigals, either for Rome (where he certainly would have come into contact with Verdelot's music) or perhaps as a result of his

Non-conflicting attributions and newly anonymous compositions

contact with the Duke of Mantua in 1522.[63] It is, after all, tempting to see some significance in the presence of only two extraneous works in a volume devoted to Verdelot, works possibly with connections to Mantua or Ferrara.

V

There are, of course, many muddled attributions which cannot be resolved by the methods developed here, either because the techniques are inapplicable or because, even though they may seem at first sight to be fruitful, they yield evidence which does not fully resolve the problem. Examples of the latter situation can be found in 1542[17], the first edition of Gardane's anthology, *Il primo libro di madrigali de diversi . . . a misura di breve.*[64]

A little can be inferred about how this volume was prepared, and that little does throw some light (though scarcely enough) on the question of the attributions in both this and subsequent editions. In gathering B of the Cantus, the second of the volume, five ascriptions are lacking – all present in the lower voices. Three of those missing are in the outer forme – on fols. 1ʳ (*Archadelt.* in the other partbooks), 2ᵛ (*Ferabosco.*) and 4ᵛ (*N. Vbert.*); the remaining page in this forme, 3ʳ, has an ascription to *Yvo* which lacks the otherwise ubiquitous final point, and which (I suspect) may have been added at the last moment. Logically, this forme would only be finished and then prepared for the press after the inner forme (for this volume was probably set up consecutively, page by page), and it is perhaps

---

[63] See A. Bertolotti, *Musici alla corte dei Gonzaga in Mantova . . .* (Milan, [1890], reprinted Geneva, 1978), p. 34.

[64] RISM 1542[17].
   [flower] D. AVTORI [flower] / IL PRIMO LIBRO D'I MADRIGALI DE DIVERSI ECCELLENTISSIMI AVTORI A MISVRA DI BREVE / NOVAMENTE CON GRANDE ARTIFFICIO / COMPOSTI ET CON OGNI DILIGENTIA / STAMPATI ET POSTI IN LVCE. / QVATVOR [Gardane's mark] VOCVM. / CON GRATIA ET PRIVILEGIO. / Venetijs Apud Antonium Gardane. / [rule] / M. D. XXXXII.
   The lower voices have a different title, each with its relevant part-name:
   TENOR / QVATVOR [Gardane's mark] VOCVM. / CON GRATIA ET PRIVILEGIO. / Venetijs Apud Antonium Gardane. / [rule] / M. D. XXXXII. [with the addition of a signature line:] Madrigali primi de diuersi autori a 4 [plus signature letter]
   Oblong quarto, 40 pages per part: A–E⁴; F–K⁴; L–P⁴; Q–V⁴. Paginated in roman numerals from the first recto of each voice-part: [I–II], III–XXXIX, [XL].
   Copy consulted: Verona, Società Accademia Filarmonica, Busta 208; gathering R is misbound.

149

VII

significant that the two missing head-line names in the inner forme
are for the last two pages – 3ᵛ and 4ʳ, both *N. Vbert.* in the other parts.
These names were added to the formes before the lower voices were
printed, and it is apparent that the caption *N. Vbert.* found on the
equivalent of B4ᵛ (p. xvi in all parts) uses the same setting of type to
be found on the equivalent page in the inner forme (B3ᵛ, p. xiv).

This suggests several interlocking elements of procedure in the
printing shop. One, implied by the pattern of omissions in the
Cantus alone, is that the typesetter was using a version of 'vertical
setting', working through the whole gathering in the Cantus, then
through the corresponding gatherings in the lower voices, before
going on to the next Cantus gathering. Secondly, he was probably
working with only one skeleton forme. (This is supported by the
evidence of skeleton formes being retained for all voices, as demonstrated by the retention of the names in the running head-lines, as
well as by the manner in which one setting of a composer's name can
appear on both sides of one sheet of paper.) Thirdly, it would appear
that the work was not progressing very fast. If the typesetter did have
access to only one skeleton forme, there would be occasions when
either he or the press-man was out of work, one waiting for the
other.[65]

The significance of this for the present context is that we can
possibly trace occasions when a head-line was left unchanged from
one forme to the next,[66] especially since the evidence of gathering B
points towards a certain carelessness on the part of the typesetter.
There are few occurrences which could be plausible – after all, an
anthology such as this will not often produce works by the same
composer in the same position in different formes, even when
allowing for the careless retention of a composer's name, itself less
likely in such a volume. However, all these possible cases do produce
situations in which the madrigal later through the press has an
ascription which Gardane rejected in subsequent editions – itself a

---

[65] Gardane's shop certainly had more skeleton formes available, and, in any case, would not
have wanted to have a press frequently standing idle. It may be that each typesetter could
be working with fewer formes than normal whenever the shop was printing more than one
title concurrently.
[66] The sequence of transfer from one forme to another would be as follows: inner forme of
gathering A (2ʳ, 1ᵛ, 4ʳ, 3ᵛ) to the corresponding outer forme (1ʳ, 2ᵛ, 3ʳ, 4ᵛ), and thence to
the inner forme of gathering B; as a result, improbable-looking sequences can occur, such
as B4ʳ to B3ʳ, or B1ʳ to C2ʳ.

suggestive factor. Table 4 shows these cases, where an ascription seems to have been retained from one forme to another.

Two of these are immediate candidates for correction: the erroneous retention (as I propose) of *N. Vbert.* from p. XIIII to p. XVI produces an ascription for *S'io credessi* which is corrected in all Gardane's next three editions to *Anselmo de Reulx*: the apparent error of leaving *Per Dio tu sei cortese* anonymous is also corrected in these later editions. For one work here, there is no further information, for it does not reappear elsewhere. For the remaining three, the situation is slightly more complicated, since the change in ownership does not occur until the third edition, 1546[15]. However, the probability seems strong that these, too, belong to the composer cited in the later editions, and were misattributed in the second merely because Gardane did not spot an error in the first.

If the evidence has perhaps solved two problems and made claim to solving three more, it can do no more than suggest solutions for others in the same book. It is tempting to claim, on the basis of the above analysis, that ascriptions in the third (1546[15]) and subsequent Gardane editions are to be preferred to those in the first two. Some support for this could be derived from the Scotto editions: the first, 1547[13], is without printer's name[67] and follows Gardane's first two editions for nearly all its ascriptions. However, later Scotto editions, from 1550[15], gradually accept more of the new attributions to be found in Gardane's 1546[15], suggesting that these were winning a general acceptance.

But I believe this to be one area where the bibliographical evidence cannot be of any assistance, especially in such cases as *Con lei fuss'io*: the ascriptions to Corteccia in 1542[17] and to Arcadelt in 1543[17] are both beyond question on purely bibliographical grounds; that to Arcadelt in Scotto's 1547[13] is derivative; but Gardane's 1546[15] and later editions propose the name of *Jaques de Ponte*, equally clearly a deliberate choice on the part of the typesetter. The argument that the more obscure the name, the more likely the correctness of the attribution may well be valid here: but it is not one that will find support from an analysis of printing procedure.

Nor is it possible to determine, on these grounds, the probable author of *Per alti monti*, ascribed in 1540[20] (Scotto) to *Con. Festa.*, and

---

[67] Lewis, 'Antonio Gardane', pp. 317–26, and Bernstein, 'Burning Salamander', p. 500.

Table 4

Page (folio)[a]	Contents	Ascription on both folios	Page (folio)	Contents	Ascription of second piece in later editions[b]
[II] (A1v)	[Dedication]	[anonymous]	IIII (A2v)	Per inhospiti boschi	2: [anonymous]
XIIII (B3v)	Ben che la donna mia	N Vbert. (T, A, B)	XVI (B4v)	S'io credessi	3, 5: Festa 2, 3, 5: Anselmo de Reulx
XIII (B3r)	Deh dolce pastorella	Yvo	XXIII (C4r)	Troppo scorsa madonna	2: Yvo 3, 5: Berchem
XVIII (C1v)	Tant'e l'ardor	N. Vbert.	XX (C2v)	Cesarea gentil	[not present in 2, 3, 5]
XVII (C1r)	Se la presenta vostra	[anonymous]	XXVII (D2r)	Per Dio tu se cortese	2, 3, 5: Naich
XXXI (D4r)	Perche la vita e breve	Corteccia.	XXIX (D3r)	Non ved'hoggi'l mio sole	2: Corteccia 3, 5: Pietro Brachario

a The folio numbers refer to the Cantus books and can be extended to the other parts.
b The later editions are: 2: 1543[17]; 3: 1546[15]; 5: 1548[6], all printed by Gardane. (The fourth edition, 1547[13], is one of the unsigned volumes, printed by Scotto.)

Non-conflicting attributions and newly anonymous compositions

in 1541[18] and subsequent Gardane editions to *Verdelot*. The piece also appears, as one of two anonyma, in 1534[16], 1536[7] and 1537[10], the three early Scotto editions of Verdelot's second book. There is no evidence in any of this as to who was the correct composer. In both 1540[20] and 1541[18], the ascriptions could possibly have been kept over from previous gatherings, although the evidence is not conclusive: for both, the evidence that I have presented earlier has almost no relevance. There is a slight suggestion that the two anonymous pieces in 1534[16] were not truly anonymous in Scotto's eyes: they appear on fol. G3[r] (*Con soave parlar*) and G3[v] (*Per alti monti*). These would correspond to fols. G1[r] (title-page) and G1[v] (tavola) in the immediately preceding formes – neither of which would have carried a head-line. It is possible, therefore, that the absence of an ascription for these two pieces was merely an oversight. But we cannot know which name would have been inserted for either of the two madrigals concerned; nor can we read anything further into the juxtaposition of the two pieces, even though *Con soave parlar* is elsewhere regularly ascribed to Verdelot.[68]

It will immediately be noted that there has been no discussion of the style of any of the pieces mentioned. That has been an inevitable, if unwelcome, constraint on the present paper. There is no doubt that some of the points made here would have been more easily accept-able if stylistic arguments had been summoned in their support. On the other hand, such evidence could as easily be misleading. For example, the madrigal *Ditimi o diva mia* that I believe to be by Maistre Jhan is a remarkably inept piece of work, going far beyond the bounds that we would normally accept for music that is 'stiff, almost awkward':[69] so much so, that I had hoped to be able to demonstrate that it had to be, not the work of Maistre Jhan at all, but rather consigned to the limbo of anonyma. There are similar problems among the pieces regularly ascribed to Arcadelt. For this reason, as for one other (to be mentioned), it has seemed preferable to restrict this essay to a study of the evidence presented by the sources.

[68]   The evidence that might seem to be offered by the Florentine manuscript, Florence, Biblioteca Nazionale Centrale, Magl. xix 122–5, is of little value if, indeed, the source is largely derived from printed editions.

[69]   G. Nugent and J. Haar, 'Maistre Jhan', *The New Grove Dictionary of Music and Musicians*, ed. S. Sadie, 20 vols. (London, 1980), xi, p. 541.

What these sources tell us, after bibliographical analysis, is who the printer thought was the composer of a particular piece. For this reason, the existence of conflicting attributions – even if one is merely the significant absence of any attribution – is of more use than a regular series of ascriptions to the same composer. Such variant attributions can be studied from the point of view of the provenance of the volumes concerned, giving weight to the different sources, in much the manner that stemmatics can be applied to the readings. But they have to be studied as bibliographical objects, as well.

In fact, in these books a statement of anonymity is often at least as deliberate an act as is the attribution to Verdelot or Arcadelt.[70] The printer is potentially saying that he knows the madrigal was not written by Verdelot – or by the name that appears elsewhere as a running title. By contrast, the preservation of that name in a head-line is likely to be, in the volumes principally discussed here, no more than a statement of ignorance on the part of the printer: 'The pieces in this book (or on this page) are associated with the name of Verdelot; some I know are by Festa, and I say so; some I know are not by Verdelot, and I can give no name to them at all; some I know are by him; for the rest, I know nothing. But I have to provide a running title, so I retain the name found on the title-page, Verdelot.' By implication, indeed demonstrably (as a result of my analysis), the name of Arcadelt or of Verdelot can therefore be found over a number of pieces for which the printer had no strong feelings as to authorship. It is only when volumes contain anonymous pieces that we can believe that the typesetter was being instructed *when* to use the name that appears on the title-page, and when to omit it. Without such evidence of care, we have to question every work in the earliest volumes of Arcadelt and Verdelot not attributed to anyone else.

Further, many of these pieces survive with the same name in every printed edition, some of which can be shown to have been copied from others. As a result, the presence of the same name, even in later, more carefully controlled editions, is still only evidence against any other name, evidence that the printer and typesetter knew of no reason for change. Therefore, a piece ascribed to Arcadelt in every

---

[70] An exception would be RISM [c1530][1], the *Libro primo de la fortuna*, where we cannot tell whether the attributions stop mid-way down the tavola because the printer left his anonyma to the end, or because he lost interest.

edition of one of his madrigal volumes is less necessarily his than a piece ascribed to Festa in the same books is Festa's. This may not be a major problem in the case of Arcadelt. Firstly, he may have been living in Venice during the period of the early editions of his madrigals, even though he was in Rome before the later ones.[71] Secondly, he does not appear in printed editions until the end of the decade, as a representative of the new generation, and when the evidence suggests that printers were spreading their nets more widely. However, it must be disturbing that madrigals printed in the first editions of all four books are later transferred to other composers; and one has to wonder how many of the others (especially among those deleted from later editions) have remained with Arcadelt's name to the present day solely because Gardane had no other information. The problem is even more extreme in the case of Verdelot, who is not known to have been in Venice, and perhaps was no longer alive, when the first Scotto editions appeared, but whose anthologies were reprinted for well over ten years. With the very limited pattern of manuscript transmission and circulation (and the absence of attributions in some of the more important manuscripts), the best authority for ascribing a work to Verdelot in any edition of the 1540s was likely to have been an earlier edition.

Here we have the second reason why it is unsafe to use the style of any piece discussed above as part of the evidence for authorship. Colin Slim can write:[72] 'The style of the madrigals [of Verdelot] varies from chordal, mostly syllabic settings for four voices to highly imitative ones; most of them, however, lie between the two extremes.' Despite the perceptive assessments of style by Slim and other writers (such as Haar), it is still difficult to characterise the personal style, particularly of those composers who have left a smaller corpus, or to pinpoint the stylistic features that distinguish a single work. For this reason it has seemed dangerous to attempt to analyse any one work, and thereby eliminate any one composer,

---

[71] Bridges, 'Publishing', p. 43, adduces some evidence for suggesting that Arcadelt may have been in Rome in 1538. Certainly, he argues well that Arcadelt was probably not still in Florence.

[72] H. C. Slim, 'Verdelot, Philippe', *The New Grove Dictionary*, XIX, p. 633. See also J. Haar, writing of Verdelot's influence on the development of the madrigal, and of the two extremes of style that had existed: 'he may be thought to have followed, and occasionally combined, both trends'. This appears in his 'The Early Madrigal: a Re-Appraisal of its Sources and its Character', *Music in Medieval and Early Modern Europe: Patronage, Sources and Texts*, ed. I. Fenlon (Cambridge, 1981), p. 78, fn.

when our perception of that composer's style is built up from pieces that may not be his, even allowing for the local knowledge of the printer.

I recognise that a similar position exists for almost all early music: we have to rely on what the scribe or printer thought, and we rarely have any other evidence – from theorists or from correspondence, for example. In this situation, we must necessarily take the copyist at his word, weigh it (if we can), and then decide – act upon it. My contention is that, once printing techniques for music became more systematic, negligence and the need for a consistent layout sometimes played as great a part as did conscious thought and action in producing the printed attribution. In such situations, many ascriptions lose their force.

By contrast, the majority of cases I have discussed here gain in strength, simply because they show evidence of this negligence or of a desire for consistency. In these cases, we can take a step beyond a pessimistic, passive acceptance of. rather weak bibliographical evidence for authorship, a step towards a surer awareness of those occasions when, as we can demonstrate, the printer, at least, believed in the name he was putting at the head of music.

APPENDIX

This appendix lists those cases, discussed in the preceding article, where the bibliographical evidence points strongly away from one ascription, and therefore towards another. (For comments on the extent to which this can confirm one ascription, see the article.) Only those sources relevant to the present argument are cited.

Madrigal	*Rejected ascription*	*Preferable ascription*
Ai pie d'un chiaro fonte	Arnoldo: 1542^{16} (B)	Alfonso de la Viola: 1542^{16}
Amor quanto piu lieto	Arcadelt: 1539^{24}, 1541^{12}, 1545^{18}	Verdelot: 1530^{2}, 1534^{15}, 1540^{20}
Amor s'al primo sguardo	Arcadelt: 1543^{20}	C. Festa: 1539^{23}, 1541^{11}
Apri'l mio dolce carcer	Layolle: 1541^{12}	Arcadelt: 1539^{24}, 1541^{12}
Chi bussa?	[anonymous]: 1541^{16} (T, A, B)	Verdelot: 1541^{16} (C, 5, 6)
Col pensier mai non maculai	Arcadelt: 1541^{12}	[anonymous]: 1539^{24}, 1545^{18}
Con lachrim'e sospir	Arcadelt: 1541^{18}	Jachet: 1540^{20} Verdelot: 1533^{2}, 1536^{8}, 1537^{9}
Cosi estrema di doglia	[anonymous]: 1541^{16} (T)	C. Festa: 1541^{16}
Dal bel suave ragio	Arcadelt: 1539^{24}	Layolle: 1538^{16}, 1540^{15}, 1541^{12}

Non-conflicting attributions and newly anonymous compositions

D'amore le generose	A. de Silva: 1536[7] (T) Verdelot: 1541[18] (A)	C. Festa: 1534[16], 1536[7], 1537[10], 1540[20], 1541[18]
Deh perche non e in voi	Arcadelt: 1541[16] (C)	[anonymous]: 1541[16]
Ditimi o diva mia	Maistre Jhan: 1541[16]	Verdelot: 1546[19]
Divelt'e'l mio bel vivo	Arcadelt: 1539[23] (B)	C. Festa: 1539[23]
Dolcemente s'adira	Arcadelt: 1539[24], 1541[12]	[anonymous]: 1545[18]
Donna s'ogni beltade	Arcadelt: 1539[24], 1541[12]	[anonymous]: 1545[18]
E morta la speranza	C. Festa: 1543[20], 1556[22]	Arcadelt: 1539[23], 1541[11]
Io nol disse giamai	Arcadelt: 1539[24], 1541[12]	[anonymous]: 1545[18]
Io son tal volta	Willaert: 1541[18]	C. Festa: 1534[16], 1536[7], 1537[10], 1540[20]
Io son tal volta	Arcadelt: 1541[12] Willaert: 1545[18] (T)	Verdelot: 1539[24], 1545[18]
Languir non mi fa amore	Arcadelt: 1539[23], 1541[11] (C)	Corteccia: 1541[11], 1543[20]
Lasso che mal accorto	Verdelot: [1536], 1537[9]	Maistre Jhan: 1533[2]
Madonna i prieghi mei	[anonymous]: 1541[16] (A, T, 5, 6)	Maistre Jhan: 1541[16] (C, B)
Madonna io sol vorrei	C. Festa: 1545[19] Verdelot: 1537[9], 1545[19]	de Silva: 1533[2], [1536]
Madonna'l bel desire	Verdelot: 1540[20]	Willaert: 1534[16], 1536[7], 1537[10], 1540[20]
Ne pergratia giammai	Willaert: 1536[7] (T)	Verdelot: 1534[16], 1536[7], 1537[10]
Non ved'oggi'l mio sole	Corteccia: 1542[17], 1543[17]	Brachario: 1546[15], 1548[6]
Pace non trovo	[anonymous]: 1539[24]	Yvo: 1541[12]
Per dio tu se cortese	[anonymous]: 1542[17]	Naich: 1543[17], 1546[15], 1548[6]
Per inhospiti boschi	[anonymous]: 1542[17], 1543[17]	C. Festa: 1546[15], 1548[6]
Poi che'l fiero destin	Arcadelt: 1539[23]	Berchem: 1541[11], 1543[20]
Qual maraviglia o donna	de Silva: 1536[7] (C)	Verdelot: 1534[16], 1536[7], 1537[10]
Quand'havran fin	Arcadelt: 1540[18] (C), 1541[17] (C)	Verdelot: 1540[18], 1541[17]
Se i sguardi di costei	Arcadelt: 1543[20]	C. Festa: 1539[23], 1541[11]
Se'l foco in cui sempr'ardo	Verdelot: 1540[18] (C), 1541[17] (C)	Arcadelt: 1540[18], 1541[17]
Se mort'in me potesse	Arcadelt: 1541[11]	C. Festa: 1539[23], 1541[11]
Si lieto alcun giammai	C. Festa: 1543[20]	Arcadelt: 1539[23], 1541[11]
S'io credessi	Naich: 1542[17] (T, A, B)	de Reulx: 1543[17], 1546[15], 1548[6]
Tengan dunque ver me	Arcadelt: 1539[24], 1541[12]	Barre: 1545[18]
Tronchi la parca	Arcadelt: 1539[24], 1541[12]	[anonymous]: 1545[18]
Troppo scorsa madonna	Yvo: 1542[17], 1543[17]	Berchem: 1546[15], 1548[6]

Addendum to note 25: J. Bernstein, 'The Burning Salamander: Assigning a Printer to some Sixteenth-century Music Prints', Notes, 42 (1985–6), pp. 483–501 (which appeared after this paper was completed), clarifies many points regarding these volumes. She leaves open the question why the interconnected group of printers and patrons should wish (most unusually among partnerships) to leave the volumes unassigned, as also any reason why these particular books should be involved. My discussion needs to be read in conjunction with her analysis, and with further detailed study of editorial practice.

VII

POSTSCRIPT

Much more information on the early volumes of madrigal settings can be found in Iain Fenlon and James Haar. *The Italian madrigal in the early sixteenth century: sources and interpretation* (Cambridge: Cambridge University Press, 1988). Note, however, that some of the conclusions proposed there for the evolution of the madrigal have recently been questioned, in Anthony M. Cummings, *The Maecenas and the Madrigalist: Patrons, Patronage, and the Origins of the Italian Madrigal* (Philadelphia: the American Philosophical Society, 2004); and many of the bibliographical details need correcting (see my "What bibliography can do: music printing and the early madrigal". *Music and Letters*, lxxii (1991), 236–58).

VIII

THE MUSIC PUBLISHER'S VIEW OF HIS PUBLIC'S ABILITIES AND TASTE

Venice and Antwerp

Publishers of music can be, indeed must be for this paper, divided into several specific types: and 16th-century music publishers in Antwerp and the surrounding areas happened to fit the patterns rather precisely.

First among them were those who specialised in what we first think of as Renaissance music - polyphony and multi-voiced music, lute and keyboard tabulatures, and so on. Pre-eminent in the Low Countries, of course, were the Phalèse family, who over a period of a century published more than 500 titles, almost all of sophisticated repertoires. But one would also include here Susato, and the Waelrant part of Laet's operations.[1]

My second group comprises those publishers who were primarily working in other fields, but who also published these ranges of music, though as a small part of their total output. Again the most important representative, Christophe Plantin, worked in Antwerp. His grandson, Balthasar Moretus, seems an even more obvious case, with a mere three polyphonic titles in 25 years, beginning in 1621. Another would be Laet, and a fourth Willem van Vissenaecken with his one volume of motets, and announcement of a second, in 1542.[2]

It is notable that, apart from Antwerp and Louvain, no centers were able to sup-

---

[1] Each of these printers has been the subject of extended study: catalogues exist for all three: H. VANHULST, *Catalogue des Éditions de musique publiées à Louvain par Pierre Phalèse et ses fils 1545-1578*, (*Mémoires de la Classe des Beaux-Arts de l'Académie royale de Belgique*, Collection in-8°, 2me Série, xvi/2), Bruxelles, 1990; U. MEISSNER, *Der Antwerpener Notendrucker Tylman Susato: eine bibliographische Studie zur niederländischen Chansonpublikationen in der ersten Hälfte des 16. Jahrhunderts*, (*Berliner Studien zur Musikwissenschaft*, xi), Berlin, 1967; K. FORNEY, *Tielman Susato, sixteenth-century music printer: an archival and typographical investigation*, Ph. D. diss., University of Kentucky, 1978; R.L. WEAVER, *A Descriptive bibliographical catalog of the music printed by Hubert Waelrant and Jan de Laet*, (*Detroit Studies in Music Bibliography*, lxxiii), Warren, 1994.

[2] For the Plantin music books, see J.A. STELLFELD, *Bibliographie des éditions musicales Plantiniennes*, (*Mémoires de la Classe des Beaux-arts, de l'Académie royale de Belgique*, Collection in-8o, v/3), Bruxelles, 1949. The central study of the Plantin house is L. VOET, *The Golden Compasses: a history and evaluation of the printing and publishing activities of the Officina Plantiniana at Antwerp*, Amsterdam, 1969-1972. The edition by van Vissenaecken is listed in *RISM* as 1542[7].

port music publishers of either of these sorts before the end of the century.[3] A third group is more curious, and more valuable from my point of view, for it comprises those many publishers who appear for one or two books of music, and then are lost to the bibliographical musicologist. One of the most obvious cases concerns De Opitiis' famous choirbook of 1515, cut in woodblock and published by Jan de Gheet; but there are others: Henry Loys and Jehan de Buys' edition of Appenzeller chansons in 1542; Nicolas Soolmans' edition, in 1582, of Desmasurier's four-voiced *Tragèdies sainctes*; and, again, several in the 17th century.[4] But, if there are only a few such cases during the 16th century, there are many more who publish one or two psalters or devotional books with music, often with the melody alone. These have to be considered a separate, fourth, group, coupled with those who published similar books of very simple secular music; and they are important for my argument.[5] A central tenet of most reformed churches, after all, was that the congregants should be involved in the music, both during the liturgy and at home. In particular, the singing of hymns and psalms was a means of including congregants in the service, and, perhaps more importantly, of using music at home for spiritual ends. The many surviving editions are the natural result of this approach: often very simple music, sometimes by known composers, with few note values and no rhythmic complications, usually tonally or modally simple, and in these ways parallelling the music that would otherwise have been sung at home. For the printers, too, the books were sometimes easy: they almost all used a very limited range of music type and required minimal musical knowledge. Further, they were normally printed in the format of small 'pocket'

---

[3] Perhaps the first, who printed very little music, was Cornelis Claesz., who printed in Amsterdam at the very end of the century: he would be followed by members of the Elzevier family, who (alongside their editions of treatises) did print a few books of polyphony. A small output of music, almost entirely the output of van den Hove, was printed by Salomon de Roy in Utrecht at the turn of the century. The first significant publishers of music outside these centres also worked in Amsterdam: these were Jan Janssens or Janssz (working between 1618 and 1653); Broer Jansz. (active from 1634 to at least 1646); Paul Matthysz., who printed or published at least 30 musical volumes between 1641 and 1684; and, of course, Estienne Roger. Late in the century, important music printers were again working in Antwerp: they were Lucas de Potter who, with his widow, produced some fifteen books of polyphony between 1676 and 1684; and Hendrick Aertssens [II], who from 1688 produced at least 21 books cited in *RISM*.

[4] These books are listed in *RISM* as O96 (1515), A1291 (1542) and D1779 (1582). Among later examples I would mention Jan vanden Kerchove, who published two volumes of two-voiced music by de Harduijn (*RISM* H2019 and H2020) in Ghent in 1620, and two members of the Streel family, working in Liège: these produced two editions of music by Hodemont (*RISM* H5670 and H5671) in 1630 and 1631, and, later (in 1668), an edition of Pietkin's motets (*RISM* P2343).

[5] We are fortunate to know as much about these editions as we do. Such repertoires have been more consistently catalogued for northern and protestant countries than they have for Catholic ones. For the Low Countries, and for much of the data that follow, I have relied on the invaluable work in C.A. HÖWELER and F.H. MATTER, *Fontes hymnodiae neerlandicae impressi 1539-1700: de melodieën van het Nederlandstalig Geestelijk Lied 1539-1700*, (*Bibliotheca Bibliographica Neerlandica*, xviii), Nieuwkoop, 1985.

books, rather than that of polyphonic part-books.
It is not surprising that in the Low Countries these books were printed more extensively than any other music before 1700, or that many printers exploring music at all offered them exclusively. Examples would include major printers of the time, such as Guillaume Sylvius in 1564-1565, Gilles van der Rade in 1575 and 1580, Rutgerus Velpius the younger in 1591, Hendrick Aertssens (from 1619), or Ian Cnobbaert (from 1631).[6] Other lesser printers seem only to have printed one or two music books, and they usually also kept to the reformed psalter: Claes van den Wouwere in 1564, Arnout s'Conincx in 1570-1583, Jaspar Troyens in 1578. The same holds true for other centres: Gisleyn Manilius in Ghent printed two music books in 1565 and 1574, both of *Liedekens*.
Even a printer of the musical stature of Jean de Laet relied on these books: once he had decided to prepare books without the name of Waelrant, he seems to have published only six musical books: : while two were by the sure seller, Lassus, and one by the local musician Séverin Cornet, three were of Souterliedekens. (For all the power of Waelrant's influence, musical knowledge and marketing skills, Laet does not seem to have been comfortable exploring the polyphonic or intabulated repertoires.) These books were apparently seen as relatively safe investments for the publisher. The standard bibliography by Höweler and Matter[7] lists nearly 150 editions between 1539 and 1600, from more than thirty publishers or printers. It is notable that few publishers put out more than one or two editions - in contrast to the pattern in the next century. It is also significant that the publishers were scattered all over present-day Belgium and the Netherlands. (Antwerp was, of course, the only important southern centre, a reflection of its strong trading position.) I assume, therefore, that print-runs were fairly large, and that circulation was fairly local for many of these books, and not only those that were dedicated to the rite of a specific town.
For us, the books are particularly important because they define the musical abilities of a large part of the Protestant population - or at least the level of musical ability that the publisher could assume. This has considerable bearing on my central issue, that of the musical ability and taste presumed by the published polyphonic books.
There are direct parallels between the pattern I have drawn and that of Venetian music publishing, although these lie only in the way we can divide up publishers into four similar groupings. There are real differences in the actual repertoires and in what they represent.
The first of my categories is similarly comprised of specialist music publishers.

[6] All of these but one worked in Antwerp: Velpius signed his books from Bruxelles. If the *Souterliedeken* repertoire be included in this group generically, then the important name of Symon Cock could be added to the list.
[7] See the work cited in note 5.

From 1538 to the 1670s, there were always at least two working at the same time in Venice. They had evidently the resources and the outlets to continue side by side, and they were astonishingly prolific. While the Phalèse family seems to have put out over 500 titles in a little over a century, the Gardano/ Magni family alone published at least twice as many: Vincenti and Amadino (together and separately), put out about 1500 editions in thirty years, or about one a week. The figures are staggering: and they imply what we know from other evidence, that each of these printers was known throughout Europe, and his editions sought out everywhere. The Venetian specialists, therefore, were able to publish music in all the forms, and in many (though not all) of the styles, current in any given year. The repertoire they printed should be wider ranging than that found in the work of Antwerp publishers – and to that we shall return.

My second category is of general publishers who also published a little music: the best parallel to Plantin is probably Rampazetto, an important publisher of humanistic and literary texts, who with his heirs published about forty musical books. Some seven other houses printed a little music.[8]

To them should be added the few others, publishers of a little music, and not known for much of anything else. The most important of these was the composer Merulo, with over thirty titles. In any city north of the Alps, he would have been a major figure: here, he belongs, as we will see, with one or two other minor names.[9]

Finally, there should be the Italian equivalent of my fourth group, the publishers of simple, devotional or secular music, usually homophonic or monophonic in character. Here, of course, is a second significant difference between the output of Venice and that of Antwerp. The liturgical requirements of the Catholic church were so different, and what we understand of the interests of musical amateurs also so different, that there is little common ground between the two.

The church's chant, unlike the music of the Protestant churches, required special performers - clerics and professional singers: further, the church actively discouraged singing even the psalter in the vernacular. Finally, the chant required a specific notation, a specific fount of type, and two-colour printing. For all these reasons, and particularly the last, there was little encouragement for music publishers to

---

8   In chronological order, these would be Francesco Marcolini, Plinio Pietrasanta, the heirs of Melchiorre Sessa, Giorgio Angelieri, Giovanni Bariletto, Francesco Ziletti and Andrea Muschio. A brief study of Rampazetto is in C.I. NIELSEN, *Francesco Rampazetto, Venetian printer: and a catalogue of his music editions*, M.A. thesis, Tufts University, 1987.

9   The significant members of this group are Gioseffo Guglielmo, Scipione Riccio and the Cenobio Santo Spirito, as well as the printer of the 1540 *Musica Nova*. For the last, see J.A. OWENS and R. AGEE, *La stampa della Musica nova' di Willaert*, in *Rivista italiana di musicologia*, xxiv (1989), 219-305.

   Merulo's career as musician and printer has recently been studied in detail: see R. EDWARDS, *Claudio Merulo: servant of the State and musical entrepreneur in later sixteenth-century Venice*, Ph.D. diss., Princeton University, 1990.

interest themselves in chant. Most of the books were commissioned; the outlets (specific dioceses or religious orders) were known and closer to those for theological and other books; and the techniques, after 1538 and the adoption of a single-impression process, alien to music publishers and printers. It is no wonder, then, that few music printers prepared much chant: among the exceptions was Angelo Gardano, a successor to the founder of the family business.[10]

The secular popular repertoire seems similarly to hold a place unlike that in the north, though for different reasons. Popular texted repertoires seem to have circulated in one of two ways: either in text-books, usually without music (though sometimes with the name of a melody), or in versions dressed up by a composer and treated like other light polyphonic genres. This is not to say that the repertoires did not exist as musical phenomena. Nino Pirrotta and James Haar have demonstrated convincingly that there was a large "underworld" of light entertaining music, often monophonic or with simple homophonic accompaniments.[11] However, it did not regularly reach print (or, often, manuscript). Frottole survive in many text sources, and, 'dressed up', in a number of editions and manuscripts, in simple 3- or 4-part guise.[12] This is even more true for the villanella and related genres. The inventories prepared by Galanti show the extent to which manuscripts carried large numbers of these texts without music, and to which the musical sources contain artificial compositions.[13] Even such a source as the so-called *Cancionero de Uppsala* with its Spanish elements, contains ensemble settings.[14]

This is even true for the one popular sacred repertoire from Italy that we know well.[15] Despite its manuscript tradition, the lauda again survives in a few edi-

---

[10] I am grateful to Richard Agee for pointing out the extent to which Angelo Gardano printed liturgical books.

[11] See, for example, the studies reprinted in N. PIRROTTA, *Music and Culture in Italy from the Middle Ages to the Baroque*, (*Studies in the History of Music*, i), Cambridge (MA), 1984, and J. HAAR, *Essays on Italian Poetry and Music in the Renaissance, 1350-1600*, Berkeley, 1986. See also F. LUISI, *Del cantar a libro ... o sulla viola: La musica vocale nel Rinascimento*, Torino, 1977.

[12] The standard catalogue of frottola sources remains the three volumes of K. JEPPESEN, *La Frottola*, in *Acta Jutlandica*, xl/2, xli/1 and xlii/1, Copenhagen, 1968-1970. Since then, the principle studies have been conducted by William Prizer and Francesco Luisi.

[13] B.M. GALANTI, *Le villanelle alla napolitana*, (*Biblioteca dell'"Archivum Romanicum"*, ser.1, xxxix), Florence, 1954, which lists a number of printed editions and manuscripts of villanella texts, with their contents. Her data on editions with music seem to be drawn largely from earlier sources.

[14] *RISM* 1556[30]. A facsimile of this edition from Scotto's house has been published (Peer, 1984).

[15] By using the word 'popular', I am not trying to suggest that laude were domestic music, or only sung by laymen. They often also remained the province of professionals and clerics, but were evidently aimed at a more popular audience, sung both for the members of *laudesi* groups, and for listeners to religious and moral plays, among other occasions. Studies of this repertoire in Italy have recently taken an upward turn, both in quantity and quality: see, for example, J. GLIXON, *Music at the Venetian Scuole Grandi, 1440-1540*, Ph.D. diss., Princeton University, 1979; B. WILSON, *Music and merchants: the laudesi companies of republican Florence*, Oxford, 1992; and F. LUISI, *Laudario Giustinianeo: edizione comparate con note critiche del ritrovato laudario Ms.40*, (*Edizioni Fondazione Levi*, IV.B.1), Venice, 1983.

VIII

tions as three- or four-part simple settings.[16] The principal exception is Razzi's book of *Laudi spirituali* of 1563, which contains both monophonic and very simple 2-part settings, alongside the more typical pieces.[17]
As a result, in Italy, the few publications of simple polyphonic versions are usually seen as the province of the music printer and publisher, rather than of the general publisher. As in the north, they are printed with normal music type: unlike in the north, they are presented in the same formats as music books, rather than in a different pocket format.
Thus, the picture is different from that found in the Low Countries, both in the numbers of volumes (and their presumed audience), and in the ranges of publishers responsible for them.

In this brief and superficial outline of the patterns in the two areas, I have attempted to highlight some obvious parallels, and some equally important differences. Implicit in all that I have said so far is the point that Venetian music publishers, unlike those in nearby Verona or Milan, were necessarily looking to an international market. By contrast, Antwerp music publishers, while certainly sending books to the Frankfurt book fairs, and selling via agents in France, England and northern Germany, did not have the same international scope, for their music books at least.[18]
But we can not dismiss the differences between Antwerp and Venice so easily: they were not merely a function of scale of production and diversity of outlets. Rather, they were a product of different views of how to take advantage of the available markets: and it is here that one can more easily compare the two.
The evidence lies in the pattern of choosing to publish local, regional, or internationally famous composers, or of covering or neglecting specific parts of the repertoire, or of styles of presentation. With that in hand, Venetian parallels to

16 There were two editions (one attributed to Innocentius Dammonis) put out by Petrucci in 1508, and three collections of Animuccia's settings, all published in Rome (in 1563, 1570 and 1577). In Rome there were a number of other later editions. On Dammonis' edition, see J. GLIXON, *The Polyphonic Laude of Innocentius Dammonis*, in *The Journal of Musicology*, viii (1990), 19-53.
17 *RISM* 1563[6]. The title-page of this volume states that it contains the music that was sung in Florence, in church after Vespers or Compline. Razzi's other collections tend to contain anthologies of texts to which some music has been added. It is significant that the majority of these volumes survive only in manuscript. Apart from the 1563 edition, only one (*RISM* 1609[8]) was certainly printed.
18 It is important to stress that I am here only referring to books of polyphonic music. The trade that Plantin carried on with Spain is well known, and M. ROOSER, *Christophe Plantin, imprimeur anversois*, Antwerp, 1882, pp. 168-176, discusses the extent of Plantin's trade in liturgical books with Spain, and his despatch of copies of a Hebrew Bible to an agent on the Barbary Coast. Both of these are also discussed in J. RAVEN, *Selling books across Europe, c.1450-1800: an overview*, in *Publishing History*, xxxiv (1993), p. 8. In addition, it is worth repeating that while Antwerp music publishers certainly sent music to the German Book Fairs and elsewhere, the repertoires that they printed suggest that their prime concern was in satisfying the local market of the Low Countries.

and contrasts with the output of the Antwerp and regional publishers come into focus.[19]

Market

The starting point for this lies in my discussion of the monophonic and simple repertoires. If, in Italy, music publishers largely left monophony and simple monophonic, two-part and chordal settings alone - unless there was a high literary content involved or the book was plausibly commissioned - then they were choosing to define their market as being almost exclusively the musically competent. The implication, to me, is that music publishers in Venice (and even more those in other Italian centres) saw their markets as essentially 'cultured', in the sense in which we think the Italian renaissance would understand the concept.[20] I have pointed out before that sets of part-books were not accessible to the casual book-shop browser, in the manner that books of verbal texts, or, for that matter, psalm-books were: by opening the *Superius* part-book, potential purchasers could form only a limited idea of unknown compositions in a new book of music.[21] The result is that Venetian printers made very explicit what was in a music book, and who had composed it. They knew that they were printing for purchasers of two basic types (whatever their professional situations): those who were adventurous and willing to try anything new; and those who were inclined to play safe. Both of these types might include professionals and their patrons, or amateurs. I suspect, however, that the *laudesi* and the amateur singers of villanellas tended to the conservative approach, and there is some slight reason for that. In those books, the text is highlighted: the nature of the text is evident from the titles, and its form and structure (with all the repeated verses, in Marenzio's case) are stressed. The simplicity of the music and of the text-setting is immediately apparent from the layout on the page. Finally, some of these books were printed in a smaller, pocket size, thereby announcing to everyone that they were suitable for *ad hoc* performance. In

---

[19] Those books, relatively few in number, which Venetians prepared specifically to contain music for Bavarian or other foreign patrons need not concern us here. They were the product of special commissions, or of agreements with composers trying to curry favour with a patron. While they do confirm how extensive was the reputation and the grasp of Venetian music publishers, they tell us nothing about how those publishers went about making their own decisions.

[20] Here, I would draw attention to the picture of Gardano's circle of acquaintance, drawn in M. LEWIS, *Antonio Gardano, Venetian music printer 1538-1569: a descriptive bibliography and historical study*, vol. i, pp. 25-27; and also M. FELDMAN, *City Culture and the madrigal at Venice*, Berkeley, 1995.

[21] S. BOORMAN, *Early music printing: working for a specialized market*, in G. TYSON and S. WAGONHEIM (ed.), *Print and culture in the Renaissance*, Newark, 1986, pp. 221-244.

other words, the music printers went out of their way to say something about the content of these books, something stronger than merely putting a suitable comment on the title-page. That 'something' was intended to attract amateurs, musicians of limited ability, or those with little taste for complex polyphony. This is the nearest we can get, in Italy, to books paralleling the northern psalm-books.

As I have remarked, in Antwerp and centres further north, there was one printer of polyphony who also published psalm books and similar volumes, that is, Laet. But the many others who published psalters and monophonic repertoire but no polyphony were saying something equally strong about their perception of the market. They were usually known, not for music of any sort, but for their books on other subjects, and many were actually book-sellers rather than printers or even regular publishers. The implication here is that the music books were sold through the same outlets as other texts, religious of course, but on other subjects as well. In fact, we can not accord to the publishers of these books the title of 'music publisher': rather they were dealers in general books who chose to include noted psalters in their stock. For them, the purchasers of music in this simple form were the same as the purchasers of current poetry, history or treatises on law, medicine and astronomy. The purchasers were not necessarily musicians at all: they need only to have been capable of singing the psalms and popular tunes, and *perhaps* of reading the simplified notation.[22]

Until we know more about the sizes of many editions for these books, it will be difficult to say how large this non-specialized market was. I don't think, though, that there is any great problem here. The evidence marshalled for the printing of the Calvinist psalter, or that of the myriad German settings of Luther's translations of the psalms, probably refers to situations very analogous to the Flemish one.[23] In other words, the market was extensive, and this is confirmed by the number of booksellers who were willing to exploit it.

At this level, at least, then, we can show, merely from the bibliographical

---

[22] By using the word 'perhaps', I am drawing attention to the manner in which church congregations can hold and appear to use hymn-books with musical notation, without actually being able to read music. The tunes used by most congregations form a limited repertoire, and one that is easily memorised. In many instances, this even applies to simple chordal settings, with tenors and altos creating and memorising their own counterpoints to the hymn tune. This end of the spectrum of users of notated books is not relevant for other parts of my argument, except insofar as it might bear on the size of printed editions of psalm- and hymn-books.

[23] For the former, see O. DOUEN, *Clément Marot et le psautier huguenot*, Paris, 1878, and the researches of Pierre Pidoux. For the latter, see the inventories of editions in the two volumes of *RISM* B/VIII, *Das Deutsche Kirchenlied*, edited K. AMELN, M. JENNY and W. LIPPHARDT, which also includes editions of versions of the psalms by Lobwasser and others. These were among versions set in editions printed in the Low Countries. Apart from Höweler and Matter's bibliography, cited above, see also H. SLENK, *The Huguenot Psalter in the Low Countries*, Ph.D. diss., Ohio State University, 1965.

record, that there was in the north a much larger cross-section of society involved in purchasing music. The existence of this market, and of the books, in
such numbers and with many reprints of the more popular anthologies, must
have affected Susato's or Phalèse's view of his potential market: the publisher
knew that there were many people out there who would purchase simple settings of music, not always monophonic, but essentially homophonic and syllabic. He knew further that a number of these potential purchasers were gathering together in Collegia Musica, to perform secular music, and therefore had
some interest in purchasing new material.[24] But both Susato and Phalèse will
also have been aware that the majority of purchasers of psalters was not interested in complex polyphony. The two markets were distinct enough to be kept
separate in almost all respects.

In this context, it is interesting that Claessen in Amsterdam had already
printed two editions of Dath's psalm translations before he ventured on his
edition of the famous *Livre Septieme* in 1608. It is perhaps equally important
that Jan Janssen, also of Amsterdam, withdrew slowly from printing polyphony, and turned to the psalter: after a false start in 1619, with three volumes of
Vallet's intabulations, he began again in 1632 with another edition of the *Livre
Septieme*: over the next twenty years he produced eight editions of psalm settings (including two of the Lobwasser German version) and only one further
edition of music, by Vallet.[25] Clearly, while Claessen was attempting to expand
the repertoire for a market that he had already exploited, Janssen found out
that the market was not as much larger as he had hoped, and returned to
psalm-books. The same may be true for Broer Jansson, working in the same
city at the same time.[26]

We do not have similar patterns of evidence for Italy: even while the Accade-

---

[24]   R. RASCH, *The Balletti of Giovanni Giacomo Gastoldi and the musical history of the Netherlands*,
       in *Tijdschrift van de Vereniging voor Nederlandse Muziekgeschiedenis*, xxiv (1974), pp. 112-145.
[25]   The editions by Claessen are listed in HÖWELER and MATTER on pp. 54, 59 and 62. The last is
       also cited at *RISM* 1608[11]. The four editions of Vallet's music by Janssen are found in the alphabe-
       tical series of *RISM*, and the edition of the *Livre Septieme* as 1632[5]. Six editions of psalters with
       music are listed in HÖWELER and MATTER, and two editions of Lobwasser's German texts are
       to be found in *RISM* B/VIII, *Das deutsche Kirchenlied*. In addition, Höweler and Matter list three
       editions, assigned to van Ravesteyn, and one assigned to Paul Matthysz., in which Claessen appears
       as a publisher or printer. One of these editions is dated 1625, though all the others come from 1632
       or later.
[26]   The musical output of Broer Jansz. seems to fall into three distinct sections. In 1634 he is named on
       one musical volume (*RISM* S4712). In 1640 he began a three-year spell of music books, with an
       edition of the *Livre Septieme* (*RISM* 1640[6]): this was followed by five books of music by Padbrué,
       virtually the whole of his output (and including a re-edition of a 1631 volume, printed in Haarlem).
       There follows a three-year hiatus, itself followed by the last edition of music by Padbrué, and two
       editions of settings of de Leeuw. Given the central role of Padbrué in this record, it seems plausible
       that he was responsible for the printing of polyphony - perhaps of any music at all - and that the
       two later editions represent a turning away from polyphonic music, while still employing the typo-
       graphical material.

mie were thriving, they evidently had a different musical focus, as well as involving a more limited cross-section of society. And, once we step outside the circles that behaved like Accademie, or the large and small courts, or the major religious institutions, we have no evidence for the mass purchase of music that is represented by German or Flemish psalm-books.[27]
From this, if not also from the scale of his output, it is obvious that a major Italian music publisher could not have been so prolific without an international network of distribution, and a reputation that encouraged Gdansk or Copenhagen or London to look to Venice for music: it seems probable that, without that international network, the Italian counterpart to Phalèse could not have published much more than did he.
The Venetian, therefore, was looking for several types of outlet: the artistic and cultural centres of northern Italy, the patrons and friends of a lesser composer, and a general diffuse international audience. He lacked that one specific outlet available to a Flemish publisher, that of the general bourgeoisie.
Having tried to define how I think they saw the shape, the demography, of the market, I want to discuss two other issues, which I see as being definers of the publishers' views. I shall start with the repertoire - the choice of music to publish - and the publicity given on the title-pages to the contents of music books, especially anthologies. I shall also touch on the question of the publisher's view of the competence of their purchasers.

Repertoire

As I have hinted, it is difficult to find repertorial patterns in the thinking of any of the Venetian music publishers, such as the Gardano or Scotto families, simply because they were so prolific and catered to so many centres of taste. There are certain obvious conclusions, but most of those are reflections of

---

[27] I should add at this point that I have grave doubts about extrapolating, from the few music collectors about whom we know, to an argument in favour of many cultivated amateurs as collectors of manuscripts and editions. The evidence of the Fuggers, the Knopfs, or the other collectors cited, for example, in Jane Bernstein's paper here, can not be extended to many other people. Nor do I think it should be. To cite only two examples of 'suitable' candidates: Johan van Hogelande, was Dean and Treasurer of S. Mary's, Utrecht, until his death in 1578. His collection of books, which included texts in French and Italian, seems to have contained no music at all, not even liturgical books. Even some-one interested in music, such as Luca Gaurico, formerly Bishop of Civitate (1545-1550), had very few music books: in his gift to his presumed birthplace, Gauro, near Giffoni to the northeast of Salerno, made in 1557, we read only of *Musica vulgaris nova* and *Musices libelli plurique*: whereas there are copies of treatises by Gafori, Fogliano and de Podio. See J. BURGERS, *The library of Johan van Hogelande*, in *Quaerendo*, xix (1989), pp. 48-82, and D. RHODES, *An unknown library in Southern Italy in 1557*, in his *Studies in Early European Printing*, London, 1983, pp. 221-231. After years of searching similar inventories for traces of music books, especially any printed by Petrucci, I am convinced that this is more nearly the normal situation.

general chronological change: the emergence of keyboard volumes, or the gradual appearance of collections of music for Vespers, for Compline, even for Tierce.[28] Each of these is a reflection, as far as we can tell, of a general shift in performing occasions or resources. The speed with which each was adopted, paralleled by the speed with which *basso seguente* or *basso continuo* parts appeared from diverse publishers,[29] is an indication of the diversified market, and the sure sense on the part of the leading music publishers in Venice that *someone* was bound to be interested. Certainly, we know that some of these and similar ventures were specially promoted. *Musica nova* is a special case, and I asssume that Razzi's *Laude* were sent from Florence because there was no Florentine music printer at the time. But publishers could afford to follow new trends quite quickly. The adventurousness of printing Viadana's vast collection of *Cento concerti ecclesiastici* in 1602 is a sign, like these other volumes, of the flexibility and omnipresent activity of Venetian music printing.

For comparison with much printing elsewhere, therefore, it is more useful to look at the second tier of Venetian printers, or at those who worked in Mantua, Verona or Ferrara. Perhaps the best example for our purposes lies in the career of Vincenzo Baldini in Ferrara. He succeeded the heirs of Francesco de'Rossi, who himself had printed two music books in 1571, a collection of Contino's Magnificats and one of Luzzaschi's madrigals. The whereabout of the former is not known in the early 1570s, although he had been in the area for many years: but Luzzaschi, of course, was a leading composer at the court Ferrara, the town where Rossi was printing.[30] Rossi was an active printer out-

---

28 The earliest printed setting of music for Compline known to me is attached to Willaert's 1555 setting of psalms (which went through two later Venetian editions). However, editions dedicated to Compline, often including a Litany, began to appear at the end of the century, beginning with Asola in 1573 (reprinted in 1576, 1583 and 1585), Asola (a different set), and Colombani in 1585 (printed in Brescia by Bozzola, another example of a printer in that city following the Milanese pattern), a third set by Asola printed in Milan (by the Tini) in 1586, Amadino's edition of Gastoldi in 1589, Vincenti's edition of Croce's setting in 1591, and following with Adorno (in Milan) and Colombani in 1593, Baccusi and Marino in 1596, Gastoldi and Viadana in 1597, Asola in 1598, de Lorenzi in 1599, Graziani in 1601. A set, by Montella, was published in Naples (by Sottile) in 1605. Printed settings of Terce were rarer, beginning again with Croce, in 1596. Early 17th-century editions include one by Lappi in 1607, and one by Bianco in 1621. One set was printed outside Venice, that composed by Levi (*RISM* L2306), which came from the press of Rolla, in Milan.

29 The earliest history of *basso continuo*, and of the documentation of its parallel practice, *basso seguente*, has been discussed often. Here, I merely wish to point out that, whatever composers felt about the idea, printers and publishers quickly decided that it was a viable method of producing music, and that the returns were worth the extra labour involved. After Marescotti, the Florentine publisher, produced Peri's and Caccini's works in 1600, Amadino immediately printed an edition by Fattorini (*RISM* F129), and his by-then-rival Vincenti followed suit the following year. Also in 1600, G.A. de Franceschi of Palermo, printed an edition of Raval (*RISM* R441) that required an organ book. By 1603, bass books were being published in Milan (by the Tini), in Parma (by Viotti) and in Rome (by Luigi Zannetti), and in 1605 the first such book appeared in Naples.

30 For the biographies of Contino and Luzzaschi, see the *New Grove*. The basic work on music at the court of Ferrara during these decades is A. NEWCOMBE, *The Madrigal at Ferrara, 1579-1597*, (*The Princeton Studies in Music*, vii), Princeton, 1980.

VIII

side music, mainly of local documents and poetry,[31] but died sometime
between 1572 and 1576: his heirs continued the business, with but one musical
book, by another court musician, Agostini. Baldini took over in the same year,
1582, and had published eighteen music books by the end of 1587. (This puts
him in the same league as Waelrant and Laet.) He started with five books that
betray a specifically local interest: *Il Lauro secco*, *Il Lauro verde*, and madrigals by Agostini, Girolamo Belli and Cortellini (the last active in Bologna,
where there was as yet no music publisher). Baldini continued in this pattern,
publishing almost entirely music by local composers, or by those favoured at
the Este court. He concentrated on madrigals, with at least twenty-four titles
and four more of canzonettes, to only eight of latin music and one of laude.
He was clearly catering to the market that he knew, and he continued to be
faithful to that market throughout seventeen years.[32]
The picture for publishers in Milan is very clear: in the 1550s and 1560s, the
Moschenio brothers still produced a light secular repertoire, seven books of
madrigals, two of canzonettas and one of capricci, to only one of motets, and
that by a local composer.[33] But, after the impact of the counter-Reformation,
the interest was all in the local sacred repertoire. Antonio Antoniano produced only two music books: one of masses for Milan, by Ruffo, and one of
Magnificats by the Novara composer Varotto: in the 1570s Paolo Pontio produced principally sacred works, attributable to single composers.[34] The Tini,
publishing well into the 17th century, continued to emphasise local and sacred
repertoires.[35] Of course, with the peculiar demands of the Milanese Ambrosian
liturgy, it is logical that they would do so: but it remains significant that they
saw virtually the whole of their business as wrapped up in this market.
In Brescia, Vincenzo Sabbio did the same at first, only beginng to publish a

[31] For bibliographical and biographical details, see F. ASCARELLI and M. MENATO, *La tipografia del '500 in Italia*, (*Biblioteca di bibliografia italiana*, cxvi), Florence, 1989.
[32] A. CAVICCHI makes the point that Baldini's editions "show a deeply cultivated and élitist tend-ency" (in D.W. KRUMMEL and S. SADIE (ed.), *Music Printing and Publishing*, London, 1990, p. 159), thereby confirming the view that he was catering almost exclusively to a local, largely courtly, market.
[33] The book of sacred music was by Werrecore (*RISM* M1407). The madrigal volumes included some that will have involved little commercial risk, books by Arcadelt, Caimo and Ruffo. The most use-ful guide to Milanese music publishing remains M. DONÀ, *La stampa musicale a Milano fino all'anno 1700*, (*Biblioteca di bibliografia italiana*), Florence, 1961.
[34] The two volumes printed by Antoniano appeared ten years apart. The music by Ruffo (published in 1570, *RISM* R3054) is designated as specifically for Milan. Varotto's Magnificats (*RISM* V988) were published in 1580. Six books signed by Paolo Gottardo Pontio appeared in the years 1570-1575: of these, two contained madrigals: none are anthologies.
[35] The Tini family, with their various connections to other printers and publishers, formed the main-stay of Milanese printing from 1572. With over 100 titles of liturgical or sacred music, the Tini printed about a third as many of madrigals, canzonettas and instrumental pieces. One catalogue of available editions survives from the Tini company, and can be dated late in the 16th century. See O. MISCHIATI, *Indici, cataloghi e avvisi degli editori e librai musicali italiani dal 1591 al 1798*, Florence, 1984.

selection of secular music in 1583.[36] Similarly, in Verona, the various members of the dalle Donne family, all active as publishers outside music, published one anthology of madrigals in 1579 and one of motets in 1585.[37] Neither can have sold well, for the family abandoned music until the mid-1590s. Then there followed a small run of music books: Francesco dalle Donne published three sacred volumes in 1594-1595, and with Vargnano a popular treatise of Scaletta and three secular books. Every one of the composers was a Veronese musician.[38] Outside Venice, therefore, music publishers saw their opportunities almost exclusively in terms of local markets. They published music by local composers, or music that (as in Milan) filled local and specific needs.

Even in Venice, this seems to have happened. Giovanni Bariletto, an active publisher, put out three music books in 1574: one was by an Ancona musician, Sitibundus, and dedicated to the local bishop; one was by an Aquileia musician, Mainerio, and dedicated to *his* bishop; and one was of *Canzoni napoletane*, by Primavera, who was probably living in Venice at the time. Each of these was apparently an extension of contacts the publisher had already made in his non-musical printing: and the first two were likely to have been subsidised by the composer or the dedicatee.[39]

Other similar publishers must surely have intended to start out in music by playing fairly safely: perhaps they published, very early on, a sure-fire seller: Arcadelt's first book of madrigals, or Lupacchino and Tasso's duos, for example. In Mantua, the otherwise active publisher Francesco Osanna, put out one music book towards the end of his career - a volume of Gastoldi's three-voiced canzonets. In the north, the books were again of Gastoldi, or the *Livre Sep-*

---

36 Of the roughly 16 editions with his name on them (three of which were prepared for the Tini firm in Milan), one is of canzone da sonare, two of madrigals (including the famous edition, *L'Amorosa Ero*, *RISM* 1588[17], available in a modern edition by H. LINCOLN [Albany, 1968]), and one is of madrigali spirituali. The rest contain liturgical settings, and one local setting of the *Turba* texts for a Passion.

37 Sebastiano and Giovanni A Donnis published a madrigal anthology (*RISM* 1579[4]), and Sebastian alone a collection of Bendinello's motets (*RISM* B1907) in 1585.

38 Of course, as I recognise, these details depend on the books which happen to have survived: we know of a considerable number of titles that seem to have disappeared. Further, losses are more likely for the output from small and local presses than they are from the big international distributors. However, the pattern of survival is remarkably consistent across a wide range of music publishers, and this tends to suggest that it will not change much under the impact of new discoveries.

39 The volumes are listed in *RISM* as S3550, M186 and P5453. The concept of the 'vanity press' does not seem to be a modern one. The very many *Libro primo* editions from relatively obscure or provincial composers can hardly have produced a profit for printers in any area other than their home cities: and even there it seems unlikely that many copies would have been bought of a set of five-voiced antiphons to the Magnificat (as published by Sitibundus). It seems very likely that printers such as Bariletto, scarcely active in music, will have demanded a subsidy, a guarantee of costs, perhaps the supply of paper (as happened in some surviving contracts), or even a straightforward fee, for publishing such a book. Indeed, Gardano or Scotto almost certainly did the same, for volumes of this type make up a significant percentage of their output in the second half of the century.

VIII

tieme, or a volume of Lassus (in the cases of Cornelius Phalèse and Pierre II Phalèse, starting up again in Louvain).[40] In centres selling to Protestant congregations, they may have started with one of the popular books of noted psalms, hymns, or the like.[41] Rather than being prompted by the presence of a local composer or collector, they were looking for an extension of their existing non-musical market.

For Venice, it makes sense to look for similar evidence in the work of the smaller printers of music, or those literary printers who dabbled with music. Here, the importance of a book like Arcadelt's first of madrigals is highlighted. Giorgio Angelieri published it as the second of his eight titles early in the 1570s: Gioseffo Guglielmo included it in his five published in 1575-1576: and it had been one of Plinio Pietrasanta's four music titles of 1557.[42] Pietrasanta was particularly cautious: his other three titles include the popular Verdelot anthology of Books 1 and 2, Rore's Book 3 (which had already had two other editions), and madrigals by the popular local composer Baldassare Donato.[43] Evidently, for Pietrasanta, these books were not commissions from wealthy patrons, but speculative ventures, of the safest kind. His view of the music-buying public was based entirely on what had worked well for other music publishers. While this case is extreme, others are similarly clear: Francesco Rampazetto's early editions, beginning in 1561, concentrate on Lassus and Morales: Claudio Merulo's, some five years later, include a heavy dose of Lassus and Palestrina, of Ruffo and Porta.

---

[40] The former printed *RISM* L872, listed in H. VANHULST, *Catalogue des Éditions de musique publiées à Louvain par Pierre Phalèse et ses fils 1545-1578*, (*Mémoires de la Classe des Beaux-Arts de l'Académie royale de Belgique*, Collection in-8o, 2me Série, xvi/2), Bruxelles, 1990, as no.172; the latter printed books by Lassus in 1577 and 1578, nos. 185-189 in Vanhulst, idem: the three extant editions are *RISM* L901, L907 and L908.

[41] Cornelis Claesz. of Amsterdam, already printing in 1582, attempted music for the first time in 1598: then and in 1606 he prepared editions of Dath's psalter, and only in 1608 did he print the *Livre Septieme*. A late example from Antwerp is in the output of Hendrick Aertssens II, who began printing music in 1688. The three books of that year include one of *Cantiones Natalitiæ* (HÖWELER & MATTER, *op. cit.*, p. 276, *RISM* B1985), one of motets (*RISM* M194), and the first of a long series of Italian instrumental works - Corelli's Op. 1 (*RISM* C3670). On the Cantiones Natalitiae, see R. RASCH, *De Cantiones Natalitiæ en het kerkelijke muziekleven in de Zuidelijke Nederlanden gedurende de zeventiende eeuw*, Utrecht, 1985 and *Spanish villancicos de Natividad and Flemish cantiones natalitiæ*, in P. BECQUART and H. VANHULST (ed.), *Musique des Pays-Bas anciens: musique espagnole ancienne (1450-1650)*, Leuven, 1988, pp. 177-191.

[42] Angelieri's edition was in 1572 (*RISM* A1334), following a single volume of music that had been edited by Claudio Merulo, the first of madrigals by Roccia. This was published in 1571, when Merulo had lost interest in his own publishing venture. R. EDWARDS, *Claudio Merulo: servant of the state and musical entrepreneur in later sixteenth-century Venice*, Ph.D. diss., Princeton University, 1990, pp. 199- 207, marshals the evidence for the relationship between Merulo and Angelieri. It is notable that Angelieri, with a long publishing career before him, abandoned music in 1575. Guglielmo's edition was in 1575 (*RISM* A1343 and 1575[13]): Pietrasanta's in 1557 (*RISM* A1329 and 1557[21]).

[43] *RISM* V1236 and 1557[26]; R2491; and D3412.

What these printers were doing was to introduce themselves to an already existing market, which had been buying from elsewhere: they were announcing
that they were willing to compete, and that their editions were as good (and as
cheap) as anyone else's. They were not like the provincial printers of Ferrara or
Verona. If they were succesful, they would have a broader-based market, and
the first volumes could be followed by less famous and ubiquitous material.
Rampazetto later produced books of motets and madrigals by less well-known
composers, always leavening them with a title by Morales or Willaert. He also
found it lucrative to produce two editions of Arcadelt's perennial favourite.[44]
For a few years, he was evidently successful: he was the printer sought out to
print Razzi's Florentine collection of Laude. But he was surely that successful
because he had built up a core market, that knew it could rely on his editions.
This is not so different from what Baldini was doing in Ferrara fifteen years later.
A similar thing happened with Ricciardo Amadino when he separated from
Giacomo Vincenti in 1586. Alongside the reliable sellers - reprints of Palestrina
and Marenzio, Gastoldi and Lupacchino - he published a number of volumes
of Asola's sacred works. Amadino was announcing to a public that had previously bought from the partnership, the monastic and religious cathedral
communities, that he was intending to continue supplying them.
Beth Miller has shown that both partners, Vincenti and Amadino, were succesful in seeking to make contacts with numbers of musicians outside the Veneto,
in specific parts of the Italian peninsula. While publishing popular music, they
were also trying to corner some of the local markets: buying the local talent
and selling back to them a wider repertoire as well. This was, as she says, probably
essential for printers who needed to break into a market dominated by the
Gardano and Scotto families.[45] (The reverse side of this coin is described in the
paper by Ciliberti, given at the present conference.)

These are the Venetians that can most successfully be compared with publishers in Antwerp. Not Gardano and Scotto with their international reputation and massive output: rather Vincenti and Amadino, trying to carve out
their own space in the market; and Rampazetto, Bariletto, Guglielmi, Merulo
and others, who explored the possibilities for music publishing. They all
belong in the first two of the four groups I delineated at the start of this paper.
The Antwerp publishers in the same leagues are obviously few: Susato, Laet
and Waelrant, Phalèse, and Plantin and Moretus. To this list I would add the

---

[44] The Arcadelt editions appeared in 1566 and 1568 (*RISM* A1333 = 1566[25] and A1341 = 1568[15]).
    After a chant treatise in 1571, Rampazetto printed music until 1568: he included Lassus in 1562,
    Lassus and Morales in 1563, Morales in 1564, Willaert in 1565 (his only extant book for that year),
    and Lassus in 1566 (his last productive year as a music publisher).
[45] This will be discussed in detail in her forthcoming dissertation on the history of the Vincenti and
    Amadino partnership.

collection of motets put out by van Vissenaecken in 1542, for three reasons: one that he planned to publish another music book, alongside his few non-musical volumes[46]; two, that his book immediately precedes the starting of Susato's firm (and has been associated with Susato)[47]; and three, because the list of composers is the first northern indication of a publisher trying to assess his market. The pieces are all for four voices, they are not in the simplest styles – for there are no works in the prevailing chordal French style – and they seem to have been collected from local manuscript sources. There is no connection with Moderne's editions, and practically none with those from Attaingnant. The composers themselves, when anything is known, are almost all local (like Barbe, working in Antwerp) or associated with the Empire (like Canis and perhaps Gallus) and therefore known to musical circles around the Regent, Mary of Hungary. The exceptions are Pieton (well-known throughout Europe) and Jacques du Pont, who also spent time in Italy. The latter's music, though, is more northern in style than Italianate, and it is interesting that his name has been struck through in the unique copy[48], to be replaced by that of Payen. It seems likely that this book was to some extent a commission, or at least tailored to the interests of the local religious and court clientele.

That it was not commercially successful has to be deduced from the pattern of the immediately following publications of Tylman Susato.[49] The *composers* were not the wrong ones - they were local celebrities, and seven of the eleven appear in Susato's first two years of chanson books. But, evidently the market for the motet was not quite large enough: or, perhaps, van Vissenaecken had not developed a satisfactory series of outlets for his books. The result is that Susato abandoned sacred music for a while: his first two years were devoted to seven books of chansons. Only in the third year do we see him begin to print sacred music, his first book of mass-settings, alongside another four of chansons. These secular volumes extend the list of composers published in the 1542 book, to include composers whom we now think of as the local leaders - Crecquillon, Gombert and Manchicourt among them - and to add a few imports: Sandrin's *Doulce memoire*, of course, and a few similar pieces, but also Willaert and Mouton, often hidden in the middle of the volumes. This implies that Susato had formed a market loyal to him and to his editions. But it also implies an adventurous mar-

---

[46] This is clearly stated in his letter to the readers, to *Divinae musices cultoribus*. He says that he plans to print more motets, *id genus alia, Quinque, Sex, Octo, pluriumve vocum, neque antea impressa.* For further discussion of this printer, see S. BAIN, *Music Printing in the Low Countries in the Sixteenth Century*, Ph.D. diss., Cambridge University, 1974, or her article in *Music Printing and Publishing*, p. 461.

[47] See the dissertation by Kristin Forney, cited in note 1.

[48] This copy is housed at GB-Lbl, as K.4.g.3. The manuscript change is not found in every part-book: it appears above the music except in the Bassus book, and in addition is entered on the *Table* of the Tenor book.

[49] See MEISSNER, *op. cit.*

ket, one to which he could introduce a wider range of music, even while he felt the need to do it cautiously. The next step, and a confirmation of his judgment, comprised a few chanson volumes devoted to single composers: Josquin, Jannequin's battle-piece, Manchicourt, and of course Susato himself. The extent to which this assessment of conservative adventurousness is accurate can be gauged in part by the continuation of Susato's output. When he tried to expand his range, to include books of masses and motets, during 1545-1547, he quickly learned that they were not selling as well as he had hoped. He had tried to interest his audience in them, by changing the presentation: unlike the majority of the chanson volumes, the mass books list the names of the composers on the covers, and the first carries an Imperial dedication. However, neither they nor the motet books, with a wider range of composers, seem to have been successful. In 1549, he returned to secular music for four more years.

The other evidence that Susato's secular books had been succesful comes from the pattern of early publications by Phalèse[50]: his concentration on tabulature volumes between 1546 and 1559 is matched by the emphasis in their contents on chansons. The composers are different, and this probably reflects both the publisher's contacts, and his desire to match Susato's success without merely copying his repertoire. The concentration on Parisian musicians - Févin and Mouton, Richafort, Sandrin and Sermisy - is quite distinctive. So, of course, is the balance of composers drawn on for the instrumental pieces - Pietro Paulo Borrono and Francesco da Milano from Italy, and Narváez from Spain, among others. For the Phalèse of these volumes, it is the local Flemings who are buried in the middles of volumes: Crequillon and Clemens non Papa make rare and discreet appearances before 1552.

Susato and Phalèse, therefore, seem to have come to the conclusion that the market for sacred polyphony was rather small, and better suited to manuscripts.[51] They also determined, and evidently correctly, that there was a large enough market for two repertoires of secular music, one based on works of local composers, and one reflecting the Parisians.

However, there is another significant feature of the editions, both of Susato and of the early years of Phalèse: this is the extent to which they were anthologies, and in particular, anthologies without any specific advertisement of the contents. Susato published some 41 editions of anthologies, often stating on the cover no more than *Ecclesiasticarum cantionum* or *Fleur des chansons*, as opposed to only 21 which advertised the names of the composers on the title-page. Phalèse started in the same manner: the balance is weighted even more heavily in favour

---

[50]   See VANHULST, *op. cit.*

[51]   This may not have been entirely a function of market size, but rather of a predilection on the part of a number of Imperial centres for keeping their church music to a small and restricted manuscript circulation. However, this does not affect the issue. Phalèse, in particular, could have printed parts of the already published Parisian latin repertoire if he had felt that there was a market for it.

of unspecific anthologies (in a practice which the firm continued until the 1630s when the great influx of Italian music caused a move towards many more one-composer volumes). Finally, Waelrant and Laet did the same. This pattern is not found with Italian music publishers. Of the lesser publishers I have mentioned above, very few printed any anthologies, and *they* almost always added a phrase to the title, defining the style of the contents, or praising them as court music from somewhere. The obvious case is again Baldini: his two anthologies, in an output of nearly forty musical volumes, are the famous books, *Il Lauro secco* and *Il lauro verde*.[52] In the terms in which I have been discussing northern printers, these hardly count as anthologies at all. The same figures apply to Merulo: here, one of his two anthologies had already been previously published in at least three editions, and was therefore well-known by its title, although the other does advertise itself in very neutral terms.[53] The family of Dalle Donne produce one anthology in total, and it, like the rest of their output, is of local Veronese music.[54]

If one turns to the major Venetian printers, the pattern is similar. True, in the early years, both Gardano and Scotto put out several anthologies in which the title is expressive rather than indicative: *Mottetti del frutto*, and so on. But, once Antonio Gardano had died, the percentage of anthologies dropped radically, to below one in ten titles,[55] and many of those anthologies are special in one way or another: the most obvious cases being the collections of villotte and villanelle, or the books of *madrigali a notte negre*.[56] In these cases, the title

52   It should be mentioned here that many editions listed in *RISM* Series B volume 1 (*Recueils imprimés, XVIe-XVIIe siècles: liste chronologique*) would not have seemed to the 16th-century purchaser to have been an anthology. That catalogue includes, for example, Baldini's 1585 edition of Arcangelo Gherardini's *Primo libro de'madrigali a cinque voci*, which contains only one work by a different composer, who is not cited on the title-page.

53   The well-known edition was of *Madrigali a tre voci de diversi eccellentissimi autori* (*RISM* 1569[23]), which had previously appeared in 1551, 1555 and 1561, all from the press of Gardano, which also issued an edition the same year. The other edition (*RISM* 1569[2]) was of *Motectarum divinitatus liber primus*, and contained a largely old-fashioned repertoire of Courtois, Mr. Jan, Penet, Phinot, Richafort and so on.

54   *RISM* 1579[4], entitled *Giardino de madregali a quattro voci de diversi eccellentissimi musici*.

55   The figures for the Scotto family are similarly instructive: Gerolamo printed about 55 anthology editions out of a total of nearly 400. His heirs, working from 1573 to 1613, published fewer than twenty editions of anthologies out of nearly 300 editions. It is true that Gerolamo published more anthologies in 1549, and again in the 1560s, but many of these fall into the categories about to be mentioned.

56   This is clearly true for the later years of Scotto. The early anthologies are often given non-specific titles, especially if they contain motets. Of the seven sacred anthologies he published in 1549, only one mentions a composer, Verdelot. The eighth anthology of that year (*RISM* 1549[30]) is of madrigals *a notte negre*. In the early 1560s, he again published a few books with generic titles, although the practice is very soon dropped. From 1567, of the 18 anthologies, only five do not have some distinctive characteristic listed on the title-page, ranging from *Corona della morte dell'illustre signore ... Anibal Caro* (*RISM* 1568[16]) or *Musica de'virtuosi della florida capella ... di baviera* (*RISM* 1569[19]) to *Il primo libro delle justiniane a tre voci* (*RISM* 1572[6]). For the heirs, the picture is equally clear, for they concentrated on editions of the *Spoglia amorosa* series, of of music advertised as by Roman composers.

carries so much a definition of style, that it acts much like the name of a composer. The purchaser could be as sure of what he was buying as he would be
with a volume bearing Arcadelt's or Rore's name.
As I say, this cannot be argued for purchasers of Susato's or Phalèse's books,
with their generally nondescript titles. Certainly, many purchasers had a
keener sense of the styles involved than we can ever hope to have, and, as a
result, a single part-book told them more than it would tell us. But, nonetheless, purchasing music by an unknown composer or in a miscellaneous
anthology must have been more speculative in the Low Countries than it was
for the average purchaser of Italian editions.
Thus, I see the purchaser of music from Susato or Phalèse as more adventurous
than the equivalent purchaser from Gardano, Merulo, or Vincenti and
Amadino. He was willing to do two things: to assume that the publisher exer-
cised good taste in making his selections; and to be encouraged to perform a
wider range of music and styles than he had met before. It is not surprising
that the northern printers, like all others, buried some composers in the middles of books. It is surprising, and a measure of their purchasers, that these
printers could do so in books that actually advertised no-one at all.
The publishers themselves therefore had this view of their purchasers: that they
were willing to buy in specific genres, and that they preferred specific groups of
composers, local or Parisian: but also that they were willing to buy without
knowing in detail the contents of the books, to take a risk, and therefore to
explore styles that were imported from elsewhere - if they were not too strange.
I add that last clause partly in deference to the pattern of a relatively conservative selection of Italian madrigals in northern editions late in the century. This
whole series of publications may represent a conservative view of Italian
music, as Mrs. Tsugami has said here, but it also confirms the picture I have
just drawn, of purchasers willing to try something new, thereby stretching
their musical experience while at the same time not straying too far.

Competence

A much more difficult problem is to determine what the publishers thought of
the musical skills of their purchasers, and how they took them into account.
One piece of evidence lies in the large numbers of books of three-part music,
published all over Europe. Such anthologies were widespread, and seem usually to have had the function of expanding the market for the printer. They are
frequently aimed at a taste for less complex music, or at groups with fewer
resources. In Italy, there is not much real evidence that they were intended to
make fewer demands on the musicians, that is, that they had a specifically
didactic function.[57] The books tend to have specific titles, or to relate to lighter
musical genres - canzone napoletani, villanelle and villotte, and also some can-

zone spirituale and laude[58] - for books of three-voiced motets are significantly absent before the last two decades of the century.[59] At the end of the 1580s, Asola seems to have undertaken an active role in composing simple, and particularly three-voiced, music for as much of the church's year as possible.[60] In Antwerp and Louvain, the pattern is a little different. Although the proportion of three-voiced music is probably about the same, there is a higher percentage of sacred music: of some twenty-seven different titles, six include a reference to motets on the title page, and another five include *Souterliedekens*.[61] The secular works are remarkable for the two books put out by Susato in 1544 and intended to be usable either by two or by three singers.[62] These draw attention to the later volumes, published in 1592, by Castro, who seems to have made a specialisation of writing for three voices. His activity, however, is quite distinct from that of Asola's: Castro ranges widely over the available genres, writing both for two and three parts. With his volumes containing a mixture of chansons, madrigals and motets, and declaring that they are arrangements of well-known works, he seems to be offering a range of music that will appeal to the 'upwardly-mobile' segments of his market.[63] The books seem to signal a need for music with a simpler scoring - not necessarily for

---

[57] While, it is evident that many books of duos were intended to be didactic, and many examples in treatises are duos, a similar argument can not be made for the vocal-trio texture.

[58] Apart from the many books devoted to a single composer, some 150 anthologies of three-voiced music were published in Italy during the 16th century, representing nearly 100 titles. There is a definite change around 1560 to publishing books containing these lighter genres, whereas earlier volumes had included madrigals by Arcadelt, Festa and Gardano, as well as three books of motets. In other respects, the Venetian output reflects the more general patterns I have mentioned above, with a decline in anthologies without specific titles (see *RISM* 1574[5], referring to the musicians of Bari).

[59] Only 24 books with 3-voiced sacred music seem to have been published in Italy before 1601, and in four of those (by Nanino in 1586, by Peetrinus in 1588 (reprinted the next year), by Clinio in 1595 and by Raval in 1600, printed in Rome), these pieces precede works for more voices. Apart from the popular volume put out by Gardano in 1543 (*RISM* 1543[6], reprinted in 1551, 1569 and 1589), and the two from Scotto's press in 1549, the first recorded edition is that of Lassus' three-voiced motets (printed by Gardano in 1579). This seems to have sparked an interest in the scoring: even so, many of the subsequent volumes imply special requirements - music for the Passions, for Lamentations, for a Requiem, or for Compline (by Falconio in 1580, and Asola and Clinio, both in 1595; by Asola in 1588 and Fonghetto in 1595; by Viadana in 1598; and by Asola in 1598). The Falconio edition is of the words of Christ for a Passion: in the same year, his setting of the Turba parts was published, for four voices.

[60] In 1588 he started an ambitious programme of publication, at the same time as he became almost a house-composer for Amadino. While he first appeared in print in the 1560s, from Rampazetto's press, and had been mildly active in editions printed by the Gardanos, his productivity really only took off after 1586.

[61] These comprise the book by de Lattre published in 1554, and four books of works by Clemens, published in 1556 and 1557.

[62] *RISM* S7238 and S7239. The first of these has been edited by Aimé Agnel (Paris, ca. 1970). Another book is presumably lost.

[63] I am grateful to Timothy McTaggart for his observations on this repertoire. The earliest of these books, *RISM* C1468 of 1569, is discussed on page 333 in the present volume, by Professor Bossuyt.

VIII

simpler music. I think the styles do argue for less-skilled performers: there are few long melismas, phrases continue to be largely syllabic, the points of imitation are often highly rhythmic (and therefore easy to correlate with each other) and pieces tend to stay modally secure. Taken with the announced associations to famous works by other composers, these features all suggest not only a specific musical taste and knowledge, but also a level of skill.

Given this apparent desire to encourage exploration and improved skills, it is strange that the publishers of the *Livre septieme* and other books kept inserting a single page of instruction in music. Certainly, the page did provide enough to allow any reader to cope with the notation in the following pieces, and the didactic argument seems to me to be the only possible solution - not least because the page is later translated into Dutch.[64]

There are, as far as I know, no such pages in Italian publications. Indeed, there are almost no tutors of this elementary sort throughout the 16th-century. One or two broadsheets do survive, although it is hard to date them. Significantly, however, there are many editions of very simple chant manuals, not only in Italy, which are aimed specifically at those in religious orders, and which attempt to do exactly what the single-pages do in these northern publications. This serves to highlight again the distinction in domestic and religious music-making, between Protestant and Catholic regions of Europe.

The northern tutorial pages, therefore, whether in Dutch or in French, served a purpose in expanding the numbers of musicians willing to move from simple psalters to four-voiced chansons, and thence perhaps even further. They act in much the manner that the lute, guitar and cittern instruction pages did. These latter[65] are full-blown instructions in how to read the tabulatures, how to play the instruments, and how to interpret. This again is almost unknown in Italy. The most famous lute instructions in a polyphonic book are those found in several of Petrucci's publications. But they differ from the present ones in a very significant manner: they are written to teach some-one, who can already play, how to interpret the notation, and how to play chordal progressions. They are, in other words, aimed at improvising lutenists, to encourage them to read composed intabulations.

Once again, the distinction between the northern instructions and those from Venice is a distinction between amateurs wishing to explore music and performance, and performers wishing to play what they already know about.

The distinction argues for a larger number of less competent singers and players in the Low Countries, but also for them being more adventurous in ex-

64 See the forthcoming dissertation on the *Livre Septieme*, and the discussion therein on its didactic function, by Anne Gross of New York University.
65 For an edition and discussion of these prefaces, see H. VANHULST, *Edition comparative des instructions pour le luth, le cistre et la guitarre publiées à Louvain par Pierre Phalèse*, in *Revue belge de musicologie*, xxxiv-xxxv (1980-1981), pp. 81-105.

ploring not only different composers, but also different styles. This is one of
the prime reasons, of course, for the emergance of Dutch translations of the
texts in the *Livre Septieme* or of Gastoldi's canzonettas.

These translations were not provided for motets or complex madrigals, nor
had there been a long tradition of Dutch or Flemish editions before this.
(Susato's series seems, as Timothy McTaggart has remarked here, to have been
another miscalculation.) While we can point to political reasons for the growth
in Dutch texts for music, we also need to emphasise the repertorial limits. It
appears to me that the translated pieces were intended for the less competent
musicians: not less exploratory, or less enthusiastic, but merely less competent.
There is a parallel in the rapid growth of settings of psalm-settings in Dutch.[66]

In this connection, I have wondered about the reasons for arranging the contents of music books in modal order. For collections of Magnificats or other
liturgical music, and for some other books, the reasons are clear.[67] But many
books ordered modally are not liturgical or illustrative of theory in their
intent, and indeed some contain exclusively secular music. It seems at least
plausible that the purpose of such an arrangement is then not at all to do with
modal orientation, but rather with the practice of solmisation. This would help
to explain some of the anomalies of arrangement, while at the same time
making the books more valuable for the less competent reader of music. By
knowing that several pieces in succession were to be solmised in a similar manner, the singer would be able to work at them as a group, and thus strengthen
sight-reading skills.

Finally, and in the same connection, I am intrigued by the contents of lute anthologies. Published lute books raise one very obvious question: whether they
preserve the detailed music and the virtuosity of the performer/arranger, or
whether they were adapted to the needs of a non-professional market. The
contents of several northern anthologies seem to me to be very much of the
latter type. The vocal models are often retrospective, they represent pieces also
found in the contemporaneous vocal anthologies (although often from different printers), they are intabulated fairly simply, and they re-appear (in different arrangements) from book to book. At the same time, the instrumental
forms in these books consist more of dances and short pieces than they do of
the complex fantasias and ricercars being produced in Germany, Italy or Spain.
While this is a dangerous generalisation, these anthologies do look as though
they were being prepared for, and sent to, the same purchasers that were
buying the chanson volumes, rather than to professional lutenists. Hence, also,
the extensive tutorial pages.

---

[66] For a discussion of the Gastoldi settings, see R. RASCH, *The Balletti of Giovanni Giacomo Gastoldi* (cited above).
[67] The literature on these books is fairly extensive: for the most recent contribution, see Isabelle His's study in the present volume.

I have argued for a publisher's view of the market in the Low Countries as being centered on three groups of musicians. One, by far the largest, contained those people who bought psalm-books and related volumes, and maybe went a little further. The second, and perhaps the most interesting, consisted of those amateurs who were willing to explore more widely - buying Susato's editions of the music of local masters, or Phalèse's of the French repertoire. They needed help, with instruction pages, with ordering of the pieces, and with additional assistance (as I believe) in careful underlay, additional indications of accidentals, and so on.[68] Finally, at the top stood the professional musicians and the sophisticated court amateurs. If I have hardly mentioned these musicians, it is because their needs were much the same all over Europe, and the manners in which publishers met those needs were similarly more consistent.

By contrast, the Venetian music publisher saw his musical market as having only two components - the full professional and sophisticated amateur, and the purchaser of villanelle and similar musics. Of course, the distinction between north and south, using these sets of categories, was not a rigid one. Musicians of more advanced skills certainly explored simpler repertoires, and lesser musicians probably also tried harder music. Similarly, Catholic musicians must have bought chant manuals and liturgical books in much the same manner, wherever they lived. Nor was the distinction valid for everything published in each area. On the one hand, as I have said, the Venetians were publishing for everybody. Yet it remains significant that they felt the need to label the contents of their books so precisely. On the other, Phalèse was certainly not restricted to the local market, as Henri Vanhulst has shown so clearly.[69] Nor was he limited to the adventurous amateurs that I have just been describing. For example, he can have had only one reason for publishing so much in choir-

---

[68] I have not taken the opportunity to discuss here the trend, found all over Europe, towards giving the performer less leeway in matters of underlay, *musica ficta*, or even details of ornamentation. I think that this stems in part from a move (early in the century) away from performing from memory, and towards performing while reading (even sight-reading). For this, see S. BOORMAN, *Two aspects of performance practice in the Sistine Chapel of the early sixteenth century*, in B. JANZ (ed.), *Collectanea II: Studien zur Geschichte der päpstlichen Kapelle: Tagungsbericht Heidelberg 1989*, (*Capellae Apostolicae Sixtinaeque Collectanea Acta Monumenta*, iv), Città del Vaticano, 1994, pp. 575-609. However, by this stage in the century, it has also become a reflection of the apparent problem of increasing numbers of amateurs performing music for which they have not necessarily had an adequate professional training. This must have led composers, editors and publishers to restrict the available options and to give the purchaser greater guidance. Whether it can really be taken, as has been asserted, to represent a narrower view, on the part of the composer, of what constituted acceptable detail, is far from evident. For an excellent discussion of the nature of the changes in presentation in the editions of Waelrant and Laet, see chapter 7, *House-Style and Editorial Concerns*, in R. WEAVER, *Waelrant and Laet: music publishers in Antwerp's Golden Age*, (*Detroit Monographs in Musicology/Studies in Music*, xv), Warren (MI), 1995.
[69] H. VANHULST, *La diffusion des éditions de musique polyphonique dans les anciens Pays-Bas à la fin du XVIe et au début du XVIIe siècle*, in H. VANHULST and M. HAINE (ed.), *Musique et societè: hommages à Robert Wangermée*, Bruxelles, 1988, pp. 27-51.

VIII

428

book format - the desire of professional choral institutions to purchase printed music. And Phalèse was not alone in this: his volumes, of music by Clemens non Papa, are paralleled by the early de Opitiis book and a number of titles from the Plantin/Moretus house, in the late 1570s and early 1580s (containing imperial repertoire), and again in the 17th century.[70] By contrast, there are almost no Venetian choirbooks - the Gardanos produced seven between 1562 and 1584 and the Cenobbio Santo Spirito put out three volumes of music by Lambardi in 1597-1601. From the rest of Italy, this format was used twice in Milan in 1600, and once in Bologna in 1587 (which is a special case).[71] There were, however, 24 uses of the format in Rome before 1600, including famous titles such as Antico's *Liber quindecim missarum*, and the editions of Palestrina and Morales.[72] These clearly carry implications of the most important Catholic chapels, including those in the Vatican. It seems reasonable to assume that Clemens and Phalèse were imitating them, rather than Venetian editions, and intending to make a similar statement about function and destination.[73]

Finally, of course, the pattern certainly changed with time: while I have tried to draw a general picture covering nearly a century of music, I am well aware that the power of the Venetian printer declined steadily from the end of the 16th century, at just the same time that printers in Antwerp and other centres began to assume the international roles that Venetian printers were neglecting.

However, I hope to have demonstrated that, in some very specific ways, the Antwerp and Louvain music publisher held a very different view of his market from that favoured by his counterpart in Venice or nearby cities. The Venetian publisher, a wide-ranging business man, catered to many sophisticated musi-

[70] Plantin printed several choirbooks: masses by La Hèle in 1578, du Gaucquier in 1581, Kerle in 1582, and de Monte in 1587; and a single mass by de Monte in 1579 (following the Phalèse model). Joannes Moretus produced a choirbook of Magnificats by Lobo in 1605: and Balthasar Moretus produced three such choirbooks: two of masses by Lobo (1621 and 1639), and one of Palestrina's hymns, in 1644.

[71] The Gardano books comprise music by Corteccia (two related volumes), Guerrero, Kerle, Ortiz, Costanzo Porta, Victoria. The two printed in Milan came from the press of the heirs of Tini and Besozzi, and contain music by Orfeo Vecchi. The one composition in this format printed in Bologna is a work by Trombetti in a festival volume.

[72] Domenico Basa seems only to have printed in this format: his seven volumes in the early 1580s comprise music by Guerrero and Victoria. The other comprise one book printed by Antico, one from the heirs of Blado, nine from the Doricos and their heirs, three from Francesco Coattino in the early 1590s, one from Alessandro Gardano in 1591, two from Muti (both of Palestrina, in 1599 and 1600).

[73] This carries important implications in two additional areas: one concerns performance practice, for it is hard to think that the institutional implications of using score rather than part-books were all social or concerned with status; the other concerns the thorny question of how institutional directors felt about the use of printed books rather than manuscripts, or even of printed books which imitated manuscripts. Much more research needs to be done in this area, but it is significant that the composers represented in printed choirbooks tend to be associated with institutions which themselves continued to use and commission manuscript choirbooks.

cians who needed to know exactly what they were buying: and, definitely as a secondary activity, to less experienced ones who bought by genre - villanella, lauda or dance music.

The northern music publisher apparently saw things differently: he saw, first of all, a vastly more varied market, reaching down to the many people able to read psalm-settings, and perhaps not much more. While at the top of the ladder of competence there were those highly professional musicians who were accustomed to singing from a choir-book, or lutenists who could play the complex works of Borrono, and while in the middle there were domestic singers of chansons and madrigals (in the original tongues), the printer also had to supply music for relative novices, singers and instrumentalists who did not even know the great names of music outside their own local circle. The northern publisher could continually stretch the repertoire a little, knowing that these purchasers were willing to explore what the publishers gave them. This could be in French, rarely in Dutch, and only gradually in Italian.

This is a picture that is much more exciting than the one we have to draw for the Venetian publisher, and its implications for musical practice much more interesting.

VIII

POSTSCRIPT

It is inevitable that recent research on musical styles in the Renaissance has tended to focus on innovations in style, and on the circles that supported and promoted them. Two recent and valuable examples are the book by Cummings cited at the end of Chapter VII and Martha Feldman's *City Culture and the madrigal at Venice* (Berkeley: University of California Press, 1995).

However, much of the music that was printed throughout Europe represented conservative styles, simpler music, or more popular genres. Obvious examples include the many volumes of villanelle or editions of Arcadelt published in Italy, and books of Protestant communal music in Germany or the Low Countries. The patterns of producing these books need to be considered as reflections of two features of the amateur and local market for music – the extent to which the musical taste of many people remained conservative, and the extent to which amateurs and marginally competent musicians sought to improve their skills, and explore new music. Patterns of publication throw some light on these issues.

IX

Notational Spelling and Scribal Habit

The proposition that forms the basis for this paper, that musical notation is both a product and an indicator of the provenance and the antecedents of sources, is not new. It has been used to some effect to study the origins of both works and sources for the Italian *Ars Nova*[1], and Italianate notational traits from this period have been detected in (and have affected our view of) sources as late as the 1430s[2]. More recently, a study and edition of anonymous English masses (found primarily in the Trent codices) has argued for a specifically English exemplar, on the basis of the notational pattern[3]. This, in common with certain manifestations of Professor Hamm's "English figure" or Tinctoris' *error anglorum*[4], hinges for its significance on the misunderstanding of one tradition of notation by the proponents of another: it involves one notational pattern, of one visual appearance, but with differing interpretations in the different traditions. The *Ars Nova* examples, on the other hand, stand at the opposite end of the spectrum, for (in many cases) different details of notation seem to yield the same rhythmic interpretation. Like the changes to be found in the notation of pieces in various 13th century sources[5], these seem to imply different patterns of notation with the same meaning. Both ends of the spectrum have, naturally, been taken by modern scholars as demonstrations of situations wherein the various scribes (perhaps merely as representatives of their locality and time) had distinct notational preferences[6].

There is a third position, perhaps lying between these two (although in some views it is seen as so irrelevant as to be far beyond the reach of either end of the spectrum that I have described): this is illustrated by those elements within a single notational tradition which appear to have identical meanings, and also to be freely available without obvious preference to the scribe. If, as has usually been assumed[7], the copyist selected equally freely from among his possibilities, then his decisions can have no real significance for the study of the provenance, or indeed of any other aspect, of the source or of its contents. I am, of course, referring here primarily to ligatures and, less obviously, to certain uses of coloration – and it is these that form the subject of this paper[8].

This sort of apparently random phenomenon has a peculiar, if morbid fascination for the scholar. It raises questions such as: why are some works of Josquin extant in many sources, while others (not musically inferior) are to be found in only one or two? or: what is it that makes some groups of sources survive merely in fragments, while others (representative of

66

different though similar institutions) are better preserved? and so on. Some of these phenomena have been studied with considerable success, and shown not to be random at all, but to have plausible, rational explanations in, for example, the subsequent history of institutions[9].

But other problems, so far having evaded analysis, are still being relegated to the realm of the fortuitous: papers of the last few years have begun to tackle some of these – in particular, work on stemmatics and source relationships has gone far towards explaining the patterns in which variants occur[10], and somewhat speculative papers have raised key questions regarding the occurrence of accidentals in 16th-century music, or the amount of text in chansonniers[11].

I believe that we are also at the stage of discovering the patterns behind the occurrence of ligatures and some other notational elements. In a paper at our previous meeting, Howard Brown drew attention to the patterns of ligatures in Florence 2442, offering sound reasons for the scribal decisions involved, and in my own paper at the same time I referred in passing to the extent to which the use of ligatures in some other sources was far from haphazard: indeed, both sets of evidence appeared to indicate a conscious series of decisions on the part of the scribe or type-setter – or perhaps of his editor[12]. I want now to return to the quesion of the motives for these decisions, and to suggest some of the reasons for the use or omission of ligatures and *minor color* in sources *circa* 1500.

*

We are accustomed to believing that the sources of polyphony prior to the later baroque give us little help on problems of performance practice. That this is indeed so is reinforced by the exceptional nature of what evidence there is in the sources – the indications of fauxbourdon or the use of the words *unus, duo* or *chorus* in some early 15th century sources; the marks indicating precise syllable placing in Oxford, Bodleian Library, Can. misc. 213, or the other evidence of careful text placement; the writing of complete texts below the lower voices of some chansons or the use of two colours for the text in a few English sources[13]. These have been used by scholars to erect edifices of varying degrees of stability, in the absence of more or better material. But, sadly, the three ranges of signs that occur most frequently – clefs for pitch, "key signatures" and added accidentals – have all turned out to be sign-posts, not to easier and surer performance realisations, but to thickets of uncomfortable speculation[14]. It may be that the same result will come from this paper, for it is in the nature of a preliminary statement of a solution to the problem.

We have accepted that ligatures have had, at various times, specific meaning for the performer. Their use in modal notation, most clearly in *cum littera* pieces, as an aid to text placement is documented by theorists and accepted by most modern editors[15]. Their appearance in chant seems to have had the same function, among others – and there is a significant number of polyphonic works in which a cantus firmus follows the ligature patterns of the chant sources[16].

At the end of the renaissance, *circa* 1600, the function of the ligature is again clear. It appears relatively seldom in most prints, (partly because much of the notation is in faster values), but has only two functions: either to restrict the text-setting absolutely, or to indicate a pattern that corresponds to that of the melody used as a basis for the composition[17]. There is, of course, no need to go so far to the end of the period to find evidence for the rôle of the ligature in text-placing, for it is discussed earlier by theorists[18]. These do not really cover the early years of the century, even though the paper by Howard Brown (already mentioned) convincingly shows that the newer styles of French chanson work well while conforming to the theoretical rules. Lowinsky has also demonstrated, with general success, that the same rules, alongside others for text placement, can be applied to the majority of pieces in the so-called Medici Codex[19], although he did admit that the more old-fashioned and melismatic works do not respond so easily to such treatment[20].

Yet it is precisely with these works and their predecessors, basically the fifteenth century, that ligature usage is most widespread, most variable between sources, and most important in the notation of slower-moving lower voices.

Are we still justified in using ligatures as indicators of underlay for works of this period? I believe so: indeed, I do not think that this is an interesting question, especially since they so often appear to be the only evidence that we can bring to bear on the problem[21]. The sole reason why it has ever been much in doubt must be the number of other ligatures in the sources – ones that can not, for whatever reason, be easily related to text placement. But, if some ligatures were, or could have been, used for guidance in text-setting, then we should not abandon the others on the assumption of haphazard behaviour: rather we should search for patterns of occurrence, and attempt to answer a two-fold question: why were ligatures kept so freely in use? and why do the patterns appear to differ so widely?

A simple answer to the first part of the question (and I assume that there is an answer) must be that they had some function. It can not be that they were used solely for the sake of visual attractiveness, for why then would scribes so carefully join in ligature some notes that had been copied separately (involving some sort of emendation)[22], and why would printers go to the trouble of having special sorts made for the ligature?[23] This function, I believe, has to be one that would not interest the theorists of the 15th century, with their concern for explaining the rhythm of notation, and has to have become unneccesary by the time those of the 16th begin to discuss underlay. If this is indeed the only possible answer, then the simple answer to the second part of the question (–why do the patterns of use differ so drastically?–) must be akin to that for patterns of use that we find in other areas of notation; that is, that the various patterns reflect different needs. This purely logical argument needs to be bolstered by evidence from actual patterns of ligatures, and by analogy from those other elements of notation (some of which I have already mentioned).

We are accustomed to notational elements having but one meaning each, and, even when we look at renaissance notation, we incline to think in the same manner, regarding imperfection and alteration as temporary changes for local reasons. This is not quite the manner in which renaissance theorists thought of note shapes and values[24], and there are other levels of notation which do have numbers of meanings, always subsumed under one general approach. Thus, accidentals always act as warnings about pitch relationships, although not necessarily as straightforward indicators[25]. In the same manner, the appearance of *color* always indicates some change in the rhythmic reading of the notation–even though it is only late in the 15th century that the number of possible changes is reduced to only a few and not until late in the 17th that the practice finally disappears[26]. And the point has been made earlier, but needs to be stressed, that different scribes had different approaches to both these features of notation, and that we can have no general set of expectations for numbers of sources.

I suggest that the various possible meanings for ligatures can also be drawn together, that they also indicate one single category of performance decisions, and that the nature of this category is suggested by the later rules on text-setting. In brief, I propose that the use of ligatures in late 15th and early 16th century sources is related directly to phrasing and to musical and textual articulation.

This can work in more than one way: the most obvious is also the one that is generally accepted–the restriction on syllable change. It is so widely followed by modern scholars that I see no need to provide illustration of it in this paper. It must have been generally understood, and appears in many sources throughout the 15th and 16th centuries–not entirely consistently, but frequently enough to argue that all scribes and type-setters recognised the ligature as a method of indicating text placement. As such, of course, it also had an effect on phrase structure and on articulation.

This perhaps was the stimulus to the use of the ligature in other situations in which a guide to phrasing or articulation was needed. Indeed, I can see no other explanation for the continued importance of the ligature in the notation of lower, untexted voices throughout the century.

These other situations have been deduced by observing the patterns of appearance in many sources and situations. Ligatures tend to recur

IX

frequently in certain specific contexts, such as for the penultimate two notes of a phrase in a French chanson, which I take to be related to the presence of feminine endings in the text. Many of the other contexts seem to have attracted ligatures less regularly. This is only to be expected: for one thing, phrasing is one of the most idiosyncratic aspects of performance, varying from performer to performer and from place to place, even today: for another, most churches and professionals will often not have needed such indications, for their habitual responses to musical clichés and formulaic patterns would have included both phrasing and articulation. It is therefore not surprising that these other uses for ligatures are both more random in appearance and, at the same time, most frequent at just those places which could be expected to require solutions running counter to the first reactions of the performer reading from his own part.

The most important of these involves the cadential formula which does not occur at a cadence. Every singer, of whatever range, must have come to recognise those formulae in his line that normally implied the presence of a cadence in the whole texture. Examples 1–3 illustrate these situations, and (in each case) the figure does not actually correspond to a cadence in the other voice parts[27]. The most common variety is that where the ligature merely indicates that the phrase continues for only one or two more notes (Examples 1a and 1b), but this can be extended to the point where the cadential formula lies in the middle of the whole phrase, as in example 1d or 3. If the ligature customarily had the meaning (in conjunction with that of retaining the sung syllable) of joining together notes as part of a continuous line, then this is the meaning that can be ascribed to the present situations also: as a result, in examples 1–3, the singer would avoid articulating the phrase as if a cadence were present.

The opposite situation can also exist – that in which there is really a cadence in all voices, but the composer or scribe wishes the performer to continue his own line through the cadence: examples 4–6 illustrate these situations with the formulae appropriate to each voice. Here the singer would hear the cadence in the other voices, even if his own were not strongly cadential in appearance (as in example 6c), but the ligature would act as an injunction on the treatment of his own line. Thus, while the compositional intention in examples 4–6 is quite different from that in examples 1–3, the practical effect is identical – that the performer, faced with an apparently cadential figure, is enjoined by means of the ligature to ignore its effect on the articulation of the phrase of music.

Ligatures with these functions often appear closely together, or in conjunction with those for other purposes – such as text placement (example 7).

These are by the far the most frequent of the additional uses of the ligature. That this is so, and that (alongside the ligature used specifically for underlay) they are the most commonly preserved from source to source, is an indication of the power of the standard cadential formulare in the singer's approach to the music. The second group of situations (example 6 a, in particular) is fairly common among chanson settings of earlier generations.

Another group of appearances of ligatures concerns the confirmation of triple-metre patterns in works with a duple-metre mensuration sign, and *vice versa*. Among the best-known examples of the former will be Josquin's settings of *"Ave Maria . . . Virgo serena"* and *"Christum ducem"* (examples 8 a and 8 b). It is notable that Regis' setting of the former text has the same pattern: while one could argue that the ligatures are present to reflect the chant and demonstrate the correct underlay, the presence of such an underlay merely confirms this rhythmic pattern for the work. as indicated by the ligatures. Josquin introduces the same rhythmic groupings later in the second work in a complex pattern of overlapping rhythms and imitations (example 8 d). The same effect can be achieved at a faster speed by using dotted semibreves, and it may not be an accident that those in example 9 are also in ligature.

These patterns remind one of those frottole in imperfect tempus and minor prolation which are built on tunes in triple metre[28], and, taken with them, suggest that mensuration signs had already acquired a significant implication of tempo. This has direct bearing on the use of C and ₵ during Josquin's lifetime; but, in the present context, it is sufficient to note that the ligatures are used for metric stress and for grouping together certain notes in cases where the mensuration sign does not provide enough guidance.

While the detection of triple-metre groupings within a duple mensuration is not difficult (particularly when ligatures are present), the opposite is less certain – and less easy to demonstrate convincingly. In particular, there seems to be no work where a duple interpretation is intended throughout, despite perfect tempus. Instead, we are faced with many situations such as those of example 10; in each of these, I believe that a temporary hemiola pattern was intended by the scribe, and that the intention was made clear by the use of ligatures. The last two of these examples have more than one ligature each, at the critical point: in such instance, there is little problem in asserting that a hemiola pattern is needed.

There are, however, many situations where only one ligature is present, but which can be interpreted in the same manner (example 11). An element of speculation enters the argument here, for, despite the patterns implied by the harmonic movement or the use of coloration, there is not really enough evidence.

There is perhaps a little support for this interpretation, however, in the existence of ligature patterns which deliberately confirm the standard triple groupings (example 12). Neither of these cases uses the ligature to restrict text placing (beyond a general level), and both have to be seen as indicating a ban on hemiola groups. If this needed to be indicated, then at least the possibility of a duple-metre interpretation must have been in the mind of the scribes: it further implies that such an interpretation could also be indicated, if wanted.

These are indications of contradiction (examples 8–11) or of agreement (example 12) between mensuration sign and musical rhythm, specifically made clear through the use of a ligature. They are parallel to some other, more subtle types of cross-rhythm, which certainly could have been indicated by ligature, and which, I believe, occasionally were. One instance is the manner in which ligatures are used within triple-metre works to indicate changes in the pattern of accentuation, for example, from iambic to trochaic (example 13). These changes are closely akin to those involving hemiola patterns, and it is not surprising that the two should be shown by the same method.

This argument can be carried, of course, to a logical extreme that is far less satisfactory. It would be possible to suggest that all otherwise inexplicable appearances of ligatures relate to changes in accentuation. This has led to editions in which notes are grouped in complex sequences of 3, 4, 5 and more minims or semibreves, according to what I believe is an entirely arbitrary view of the structure of the music[29]. We do not have anything like enough evidence to justify such an approach. But the patterns indicated by ligatures and, as we shall see, by *minor color* do argue that, sometimes at least, the composer or the scribe thought in this way, and that (on these occasions) he wished to communicate the idea to the reader.

It was possible, though, to use ligatures to indicate an unusual relationship between parts, without them implying anything about the grouping of notes within a single voice. The most frequently-met example of this notational pattern is shown in example 14 (see also example 4 c). The use of a ligature to indicate to the singer that his part continues to move when the others are still, or even have finished, is really little different from its employment to cover a cadential formula; and it seems that, in the present context, the significant feature is indeed the relationship between the parts, for the lines are not cadential.

In the same manner, a ligature often appears at a point where a rhythmic pattern or a cross-rhythm in one voice might, at first sight and working from a single voice-part, have looked or sounded incorrect. A simple case is that of example 15 a, where the ligature serves to confirm that the syncopation has finished. In cases such as that or example 15 b, the ligature serves a cautionary function within the single line, indicating that there is in fact no error in the notation. In 15 c and 15 d, the ligature works in the same manner, but here the context is not that of the tactus within the line, but rather that of the other voices. I believe that these occurrences can be distinguished from those hypothetical groupings of notes that I have criticised above, insofar as they do correspond to an identifiable situation, in which the musical problem is real and not merely the product of a modern interpretation.

The complex of uses for ligatures that I have described is significant for an understanding of how a symbol – be it a point, an accidental or a ligature – can attain a range of meanings. In each of these cases, the symbol started its history having a specific meaning (the point as a marker of division, the accidental as a sign for a change of pitch, the ligature as a guide to metre) and then asquired a position as a more general cautionary sign, covering a diverse range of situations. However, while points and accidentals have discussions of interpretation in theoretical writings, comment on ligatures is restricted, until the 16th century, to explanations of their rhythmic values. This is hardly surprising, for the functions that I have suggested for them did not lie within the interests of earlier theorists, but rather within the field of interpretation, one apparently left to the choirmaster.

Virtually all the functions of ligatures that I have been able to discern, therefore, concern one of two things: either, on one hand, rhythmic groupings and cross-rhythms, or, on the other, text groupings (which can also be equated with rhythmic patterns). The last use of ligatures that I can define brings the two together: it concerns the deliberate placing of a ligature to draw attention to the possibility of text repetition (example 16, where the repeated text in the superius confirms this interpretation) or to prevent such repetition (example 17). These last are most interesting in those cases (such as 17a or 17e) where the repetition of a musical pattern might otherwise suggest a textual repeat.

There are, unfortunately, still too many ligatures which do not fall into any of these categories. Many of these are in contratenor parts, especially in parts notated in values of a breve or above and in which there are often no real guides, except perhaps ligatures, to rhythmic or any other structural features. It may be that greater study of the functions of ligatures will illumine our view of the performance of these parts, for it is clear that they were used until the early 16th century as guides in interpretation. This function declines rapidly during the first half of that century, but this is less because of a change of attitude than because of the change in note-values.

*

It is this change, the gradual speeding up of notation that can be traced all through the fifteenth and sixteenth centuries, that produced the need for *minor color*, as it has been called[30]. Indeed, Zacconi asserts that the need for color in imperfect tempus and minor prolation arose from the need to put into ligature notes that were shorter than a semibreve[31]. He specifically mentions that the notes have to be in ligature to indicate the text setting: in this case the *minor color* would seem to be a result of the need for the ligature, rather than functional in its own right. However, the presence of these groups involving half-colored ligatures can be traced well back into the fifteenth century, and they appear to have existed nearly as long as has the *minor color* pattern.

Although coloration as a general phenomenon is older, it appears that the pattern of *minor color* (as I propose to continue calling it) emerged at the end of the 14th century[32]. I suspect that it is a result of new approaches to cross-rhythms (after the extremes of the *ars subtilior*), approaches that begin for the first time to suggest what we understand by the term syncopation. At the same time, the notation of superius parts was becoming less and less susceptible to the use of ligatures – too many of the notes were below the semibreve level.

The result is that *minor color*, as Zacconi implied later, assumed very similar functions to those I have postulated for ligatures. They have at least to be of a similar nature, for only then can we explain the frequency with which *minor color* appears and disappears in the sources, or the many situations in which it replaces what are otherwise equal notes in some sources. It must, then, have a range of meanings that are solely concerned with interpretation or underlay.

The first of these, as in my discussion of ligatures, will be the impact of *minor color* on text placing. There is a surprising number of situations such as those in example 18, where the use of *minor color* seems to allow an immediately following change of syllable. This runs counter to one of the underlay rules of the 16th century[33], and I believe that to be the reason for the presence of coloration in such cases.

This is analogous to the pattern of ligatures when used for text placement. Some of these ligatures restrict the choice absolutely: others leave some options open to the singer. The same is true of some examples of *minor color*: each of those in example 19 seems to require a syllable change on the first note after the coloration. In each case, the other syllables can be placed in more than one way – but this does not invalidate the function of the *minor color*: indeed, in a few instances, this interpretation of the presence of the color supports a text placing that we might otherwise be reluctant to accept (example 20).

The uses of *minor color* at real or deceptive cadences must be more limited than those of ligatures, if onlv because many cadences do not use figures moving at the right speed. However, the need to keep one voice moving, to bridge the join at a cadence while allowing the others to hold their notes, made the falling *minor color* figure very suitable. both melodically and rhythmically. Thus, it is to be found at just such points, when the singer seems to have to regard it as another indication of continuity in the face of the evidence of his ears (example 21).

Like ligatures, too, *minor color* sometimes appears to have the function of signalling movement in one part while the others are still: example 22 a is representative of a number of cases in which one voice moves earlier than the others, and is accordingly warned, by the use of the coloration, to be on the alert.

However, by far the greater number of uses of *minor color* act as warnings of rhythmic complexity. Perhaps the most common of these is the case where one voice follows another in a dotted rhythm, one of them off the beat (example 23). In cases like this, it seems that the coloration serves to give both voices warning that there is a rhythmic confusion implicit in the writing. In many examples, only one of the voices is colored, usually the syncopated one (example 24).

But this is only one specific (albeit easily identified) situation in which cross-rhythms lead directly to the use of *minor color*. In many other cases, one voice has a cross-rhythm, superimposed on other voices which follow the normal metre of the piece. In such situations, many scribes seem to have opted to add coloration to the cross-rhythm, again as a warning sign. Example 25 shows three typical situations which attract this notation, while example 26 shows the mirror image, in which the syncopated pattern does not allow for the use of *minor color*.

More complex situations also acquire this notation, apparently as a warning that there is some rhythmic complexity between the voices, one which might at first performance throw the singer (examples 27). It is notable that some of these use the half-colored ligature, apparently to reinforce the signal–although the manuscript involved in both examples 27 b and 27 c, Pepys 1760, is one that shows little *minor color* unless it is associated with a *c. o. p.* ligature.

Sometimes this use of coloration can be explained merely by reference to the structure of the one line in which it occurs. Example 28a starts normally with the accent of the music falling with the tactus. At the first use of *minor color*, however, an extended section begins in which the accent is shifted. This is terminated at the end of the example, and another colored section serves to warn the singer, for the section had been long enough for the new metrical structure to have become stabilised in his mind. Example 28b shows another similar case.

In constructing a series of possible functions for *minor color*, we raise the question of whether the singer needed to be able to distinguish between its different meanings. I believe that was not necessary–or, rather, that the specific function did not, in most cases, need to be further spelled out. The same is true here as with the presence of accidentals or ligatures, that the general warning was (apparently) normally sufficient for the experienced

IX

performer. The only interpretation that stands slightly outside the range of the others is that concerning the change of syllable. In most cases, this is evident from the context, and there can have been very little doubt in the mind of the singer that a syllable change was intended. All the other possible contexts merely required of the singer that he believe what he saw in front of him and sang it as written, even when the rhythm seemed at cross-purposes with that of the other voices. In other words, this form of warning sign, like many of the occurrences of ligatures, merely required a passive response.

If this is so, it should be possible to look at a section of music with several appearances of *minor color* and make some reasoned guess as to why each example is there. To some extent this is still not possible, for there are as many cases of *minor color* as of ligatures that have as yet eluded interpretation. However, there are many places where each appearance of coloration makes excellent sense: such is example 29. The coloration in the two upper voices apparently serves to indicate the cross-rhythms and the irregular rhythmic structure of the *altus*: the first in the *bassus* both signals the cross-rhythm and, probably, implies a change of syllable, while the second is clearly for textual reasons.

Much the same can sometimes be done for appearances of ligatures. Here, as I have said, it is rather harder, but example 30 shows the only ligatures appearing in a hymn setting in Montecassino 871N. The first is apparently to indicate an irregular rhythm, and the second acts as a bridge over a cadence. The third perhaps functions to ensure that the text setting is as I have it here. Certainly, all three act to prevent syllable change.

*

Part of the reason, I believe, why many occurrences of ligatures and coloration are still hard to interpret is that few of the uses were universally understood or thought necessary; therefore few were regularly applied to the music when it was copied into the source. Each individual scribe, whether or not he was working to the commission of a specific institution, had his own patterns of notation, in these as in other matters or of text spelling. However, it is apparent that every scribe knew that ligatures, at least, did have some meaning. This explains the extent to which they were retained in use, and also the extent to which many sources follow each other's ligature patterns. But it would be too facile to postulate a not-very-literate scribe choosing to copy the ligature patterns in the exemplar before him, for literate scribes who worked in the same milieu tended to follow similar patterns: secondly, some scribes who occasionally copied exactly could also adopt a different pattern of copying at will. Finally, it is notable that Glareanus, in some cases, duplicated the ligature patterns of his exemplars[34], and charges of not comprehending the notation can hardly be laid at his door. However, if the theorist realised (as I suggest he did) that ligature practice represented something in the way of an explanation of aspects of the work, it makes sense that he, who was not publishing his transcriptions for any single performing institution, would not choose to change any consistent pattern of the details of notation that he found.

We do have to admit (merely on the basis of the available evidence) that many scribes and type-setters did feel free to change ligatures, perhaps only retaining those that suited their own inclinations.

The wide range of variation to be found among sources is even greater in the case of *minor color*. I have already mentioned one source, Pepys 1760, in which virtually all the coloration is in conjunction with ligatures. This must represent some sort of deliberate decision on the part of the scribe: indeed, it is tempting to suggest that he saw little use for *minor color*, while understanding the function of ligatures, and hence retained only those uses of color. Other sources show similar patterns: there is no *minor color* in *Motetti A*, although this can perhaps be put down to merely technical problems. However, there is relatively little in London, Roy. 8. G. VII, and some of the Modena Duomo sources also seem to suggest that the scribe had limited uses for this notation. If the same is true, as I think it is, for Padua A17, this may be another aspect of a source which appears to me (in its text treatment and its readings) to be edited for readers who had some difficulty with the more complex aspects of the repertoire.

On the other hand, there are sources which use much more coloration: London Add. 35087 is one such, a source which can also be characterised by a relative shortage of ligatures. I believe, in fact, that part of the difficulty in understanding ligatures and, in particular, *minor color* lies in the extent to which some scribes saw them as decorative additions to the source, ornamenting the page with graceful curves and elegant black notation.

This apart, however, and once allowance is made for a certain amount of direct copying, we should expect to find two features in the surviving patterns of both elements of notation. One is that most sources should show some sort of underlying consistency in the manner in which they carry ligatures and *minor color*, and in the meanings that they appear to ascribe to each; the other is that specific pieces should show diverse patterns in the different sources, simply because these are the work of different scribes all faced with their own specific situations.

The second point hardly needs comment: it arises whenever we meet the problem of deciding whether or not to list variants of these notational features in the commentary to an edition. But it is worth adding that the patterns of ligatures and coloration should reflect the suggestions that I have made above, and should also respond to the understanding that we acquire of the nature of each source in which the work survives. Any ligatures or coloration that survive in all or most sources for a work should presumably be those with the most clear-cut and the most necessary function (as I have outlined them above), while those with no apparent function other than decoration should only appear in those sources that are extravagant in such visual uses of the notation.

These demands are indeed met in many works, among them Josquin's *"Missus est Gabriel"*. Thus, the only ligatures to be found in all sources are the four that open the motet, one in each voice, and one near the end, which represents a clear injunction to avoid the implications of a cadential figure. In this particular case (example 31), the injunction concerns both phrase structure and text setting: but the implication is clear that both are conditioned by the melodic contour of the voices, and that it is the latter that creates the need for the ligature.

In this motet, there are four other points where a clearly cadential line ends with a ligature, surely for the same reason: one of these, in the bass voice (example 32) is present in all but two sources, one of which, Ulm 237a–d, seems idiosyncratic in other ways. Indeed, it is the only source carrying the ligature bridging a cadence at m. 78 of the tenor, a ligature that seems to me to be unnecessary, in view of the treatment accorded the motive in other voices (example 33). Neither of the other two cadential ligatures even appears in a majority of sources, though both (examples 34 and 35) do survive in sources from more than one family. Each does also, perhaps not surprisingly, survive in more sources than the remaining ligatures – with one exception.

Between them, the collection of ligatures in the tenor voice, mm. 46–48 (example 36) appear in all but one of the surviving sources. It seems to me that the diversity in detail, despite the preponderance of the final syllable-controlling three-note ligature, argues for a general concern that the melodic line be seen as continuous, rather than for specific meaning for each variant. If this is so, then the ligature variants make good sense as being no more than local modifications of a general position.

As would be expected, none of the other ligatures fulfill explicit needs such as those of a cadential figure: it is, I believe, as a result of this that they appear in fewer and more peripheral sources. It is possible that the pair of ligatures in the bass, mm. 45 and 47 (example 37) has something to do with preventing a text repetition, or even something to do with signalling the end of a section that could be sung in groups of three minims: but this is largely speculation. The evidence that I advanced earlier does show that ligatures had both these functions: but this case is merely one of many in which the evidence is not clear enough for the modern commentator to be sure that he is fitting the ligature into the right category.

Perhaps surprisingly, some of the patterns of use of *minor color* are much clearer: in particular, the distinctive manner in which two scribes were interested in, respectively, the drive through cadences and coloration as a guide to underlay is highlighted by the transmission of the present piece. Of the forty appearances of *minor color* in the various sources, only five can be attributed to the need to indicate a drive through the cadence (example 38). None of these is very widely disseminated among the sources, so that it is significant that four of them appear in Brussels 9126. Even more relevant is the fact that Sistine 63, the source whose scribe was most attracted to color, is the only source that consistently carries that notational variant at points where it could act as a guide to underlay (example 39).

Both of these small strands of evidence confirm the need to look at even such habits of notational spelling as being reflections of the practice of the individual scribe, and perhaps through him, as some reflection of the needs of the institution concerned. The same conclusion has to be reached when notice is taken of the pattern of coloration in those sources that use it sparingly. *Minor color* appears in only four places altogether in the four sources Florence 164–7, London Roy. 8. G. VII, Uppsala 76 C and the Cortona-Paris part-books (example 40): it is remarkable that all these involve either a half-colored *c.o.p.* ligature or coloration at the breve-semibreve level. Further, at one of the only two other places with coloration at this higher level (m. 83 in the tenor), a different reading in two of the sources, Florence 164–7 and Cortona-Paris, prevents the use of coloration. While this type of evidence can never be conclusive for any argument, yet its presence (and its recurrence in other works in these sources) suggests that even scribes who normally avoided using the *minor color* notation felt that it had some function in certain contexts.

Almost all the other uses of color in this motet can be ascribed to an apparent need to indicate cross-rhythms or rhythmic complexity. The few that can not easily be explained in this manner tend to appear only in those sources that are prolific in their use of black notes, pre-eminent among them Sistine 63.

This liking for the appearance of a page with coloration on it is surely one of the reasons why the patterns of its use are so confusing to the modern scholar: and the same is true for those many fifteenth-century sources in which the scribe seems to have enjoyed gracing the page with long, artfully-curved ligatures. Neither should surprise us any more than it would to learn that certain singers were more inclined to ornament their cadential approaches than were others: or, indeed, that certain institutions and choir-masters were more tolerant of this ornamentation than were others.

This is the other key to the apparently confusing pattern of the uses of ligatures and coloration. Since the symbol's function for the reader was largely in the realm of interpretation and performance, it is not surprising that the patterns of their appearance vary so much from institution to institution and from one type of manuscript to another, for it is merely a reflection of the demands that the scribe knew were likely to be made on the source.

The balance between decoration and function does, of course, have to be determined for each source studied. In some cases, this is easy. *Minor color* is not used at all in a number of the early Petrucci prints, and can be assumed to be functional in any source in which it is used sparingly. On the other hand, Sistine 63 is far from being the only source in which it has clearly also served a decorative function. In such cases, it will often be impossible to analyse even a majority of the occurrences of *minor color*. However, once the basic distinction is made, between those sources where color (or the ligature) serves a decorative purpose and those wherein it is functional, it becomes increasingly difficult to believe in the view that the appearance of such notational spelling is merely haphazard.

*

This does, of course, raise some very interesting questions. The point that I have been stressing is that the signs, especially *minor color*, acted as indications of the presence of something that might on first sight or hearing have looked or sounded strange. If this is so, does it tell us anything about how manuscripts and prints were used by performing institutions?

Indirectly, I suspect, it does. My argument is based on the following additional points: firstly, that the uses of both ligatures and *minor color* settle down, as it were, and become more easily definable once part-books come into circulation – or perhaps slightly earlier in the case of sacred music. Secondly, that the worst sources for this analysis have been the large and beautifully-prepared chansonniers of the later 15th century, apparently not compiled for much more than their own sake as beautiful objects or as gifts. Thirdly, that we do have to continue to make some allowance, during the 16th century, for the scribal liking for *minor color* as ornament to a number of sources. Fourth, the later Petrucci volumes seem to be more consistent (at least for each craftsman) than do the earlier – all of a piece with a belief that I have that the printer, as he developed, worked with a better understanding of his performing or institutional market. Fifth, there is the point that I have mentioned before, that we can see attempts at making the notation easier, or the underlay more clear, as merely other aspects of the same sources, those which were certainly prepared for a specific institution, and very probably for use there [35].

All this suggests to me that the pattern of *active* use of sources changed – that, in fact, they were less and less being used to learn from or to refresh the memory of the choirmaster, but were rather being used more and more to sing from. If this is so, it explains why the singers would need some aid at critical points, and also why the most common functions of these notations, apart from that of assisting in underlay, are of ligatures for avoiding cadential patterns, and of *minor color* to point to some sort of syncopation or cross-rhythm.

Professor Hamm argued yesterday that some sources appear to have been prepared for reading, at least in rehearsal. These sources are those that tend to be more consistent in their patterns of notational spelling, in the same way that they tend to be those that are more helpful or more consistent in their text placing. There might still be little need to make corrections to errors of pitch or rhythm, if the sources were used primarily for rehearsal, although we are continually discovering careful erasure and correction in many sources.

The other sources, those that are not consistent in these patterns, tend to be ones that we assert were not intended for use. They include the chansonniers I have mentioned, presentation volumes or the private collection of Glareanus. These are the sources, of course, which will tend to reflect more closely any patterns of notation that existed in their exemplars, since the scribe could have no reason for editing them. In many of the early chansonniers, for example, there is no strong musical (as opposed to aesthetic) reason for the copyist to follow *or* edit the ligature and coloration of his exemplars. The result is that these sources do not have any consistent pattern that could be ascribed to the taste of the scribe or of his institution, but rather a series of small-scale patterns and haphazard arrangements. These, I believe, tell us something about the number and type of the exemplars from which the scribe worked, and the extent of his use of each.

I am in practice suggesting a modified version of Hamm's demonstration of the presence of fascicles of English pieces in earlier continental sources[36]. The analogy is fairly close, for I suggest that the variants of ligatures and coloration did have some meaning for some scribes (for those that deliberately made changes for any reason other than the purely aesthetic one), and that it is likely to be in the later copies where they mean little or nothing. This is to some extent a side-issue in the present paper. However, it is worth remarking that some evidence of this sort can be found in the work of the first scribe of the chansonnier now divided between Seville and Paris. He seems to have little idea of the function of either element of notation: the result is that adjacent groups of pieces survive laden with both, or perhaps nearly devoid of them, or else using them intelligently (that is, according to the interpretations that I have suggested). The implication that the scribe here reveals the different exemplars from which he worked is almost too easy and too tempting; although no other plausible explanation has emerged, the details of this analysis would have to be modified to take account of various styles of chanson, the different text forms, and so on.

It is the internal consistency of the patterns of both ligatures and coloration that is crucial to understanding their possible values to the scribe. An analysis of their occurrences will probably reveal much about the structure and nature of the sources under study, as well as something about how they were intended to be used. But the situations in which these two notations recur in the sources are even more significant: it may be that they are the best evidence we have for understanding how to phrase and articulate renaissance polyphony.

Notes

1 See, for example, Kurt von Fischer: Studien zur italienischen Musik des Trecento und frühen Quatrocento, Bern 1956 (Publikationen der Schweizerischen Musikforschenden Gesellschaft, II, 5), pp. 111–122, and the discussion thereof in Les Colloques de Wégimont, II (1955), L'Ars Nova: recueil d'études sur la musique du XIVe siècle, Paris 1959, pp. 27–34.

2 There are, for example, semibreves with caudas in BU (f. 1v–a Kyrie by A. de Lantins; 17v–18r–a Patrem ascribed elsewhere to the same composer; 49r–the anonymus *Fugir non posso*; etc) and semiminims with dragmas on f. 37v. In BL (which I have argued elsewhere has close contacts with both Padua and Vicenza) one opening involves the use of six-line staves (on which see the discussion in Les Colloques de Wégimont [s. note 1 above], pp. 27–28).

3 Fifteenth-century liturgical music II: four anonymous masses (edited Margaret Bent), London 1979 (Early English Church Music, xxii), p.x.

4 Charles Hamm: A Chronology of the works of Guillaume Dufay based on a study of mensural practice, Princeton 1964, pp. 52–54: this figure is not necessarily colored, though when it is, it does seem to raise problems.

5 Rebecca Baltzer: Notation, rhythm and style in the two-voiced Notre Dame clausula, dissertation, Boston University 1974, argues from the premise that the different notations are to be equated with different rhythmic interpretation. Edward Roesner has suggested that both possibilities may have been present in the transmission of notation of organa dupla – that is, that scribes may have used alternative, locally-preferred ligature designs for the same rhythm, or that local traditions of performance may have resulted in certain ligature patterns being read in different, even contradictory manners: see his The Problem of chronology in the transmission of Organum Duplum, in: Music in Medieval and Early Modern Europe, ed. by I. Fenlon, Cambridge 1981, pp. 365–399.

6 Specifically making this point, Edward Roesner: The manuscript Wolfenbüttel, Herzog-August-Bibliothek, 628 Helmstadiensis: a study of its origins and of its eleventh fascicle, dissertation, New York University 1974, p. 279, refers to the presence of rhombs in early sources, saying that it "is frequently taken as an indication of insular provenance". Discussing English notation of the 13th century, Ernest Sanders: Duple rhythm and alternate third mode in the 13th century, in: Journal of the American Musicological Society 10 (1962), pp. 272–8, maintains that it would be "needlessly inconsistent" to suppose that such

notations would have been read in the same manner as their Continental counterparts. He goes even further in doubting that Continental mensural notation preserved in English sources was intended to be read in the manner taught by the Continental theorists.

7 Hamm (s. note 4, above), p. 53, points to a situation in which this assumption can not be made, when he draws attention to the extent to which flagged (rather than colored) semiminims represent part of an English tradition, although elsewhere (p. 26) he remarks the presence of the two forms in different sources of the same Dufay chanson. The later reference to the two forms by Tinctoris suggests a clear understanding of different patterns of use: see Albert Seay, The *Proportional Musices* of Johannes Tinctoris, in: Journal of Music Theory 1 (1957), p. 30.

8 I have touched on both these questions in my dissertation: Petrucci at Fossombrone: a study of early music printing with special reference to the Motetti de la Corona (1514–1519), London University 1976, chapter 9. I suspect that the diverse patterns of the use of mensuration and proportion signs will reveal much the same levels of local and scribal interpretation that I am about to argue existed for both the present levels of notation.

9 Winfried Kirsch touches on the first problem, in his: Josquin's motets in the German tradition, in: Josquin des Prez, ed. by Edward Lowinsky, London 1976, pp. 265–6, when he says that "the number of sources for individual works does not seem to be related to the number of non-German sources. On the other hand, in many cases the German tradition of a single work may be traced to the special character of the first source, from which later copies were made." On this point, see also Lewis Lockwood's comment on the "continued Ferrarese awareness of the French court chapel as a source of new polyphony", in his: Jean Mouton and Jean Michel: new evidence on French music and musicians in Italy, 1505–1520, in: Journal of the American Musicological Society 22 (1979), p. 208.

10 Such work can not normally offer any explanations for individual variants, most of which will continue to come from detailed palaeographical and codicological studies. For a discussion of this point, as well as a bibliography of works on stemmatics of use to musicologists, see my Limitations and extensions of filiation technique, in: Music in Medieval and Early Modern Europe (s. note 5, above), pp. 319–346.

11 Don Harrán: New evidence for *musica ficta*: the cautionary sign, in: Journal of the American Musicological Society 29 (1976), pp. 77–98, with comment on it by Irving Godt and Harrán, ibid., 31 (1978), 385–395, and the latter's "More evidence for cautionary signs", ibid., 31 (1978), 490–494. Louise Litterick: Performance of Franco-Netherlandish secular music in the late 15th century, a paper read at the 42nd meeting of the American Musicological Society, Washington, D.C., 6 November, 1976.

12 Howard Brown: Words and music in early 16th-century chansons: text underlay in Florence, Biblioteca del Conservatorio, Ms. Basevi 2442, in: Quellenstudien zur Musik der Renaissance I. Formen und Probleme der Überlieferung mehrstimmiger Musik im Zeitalter Josquins Desprez, ed. by Ludwig Finscher, München 1981 (Wolfenbütteler Forschungen, vol. 6), pp. 97–141; Stanley

Boorman: Petrucci's type-setters and the process of stemmatics, in: ibid., pp. 245–280.

13 For comments on each of these, see Heinrich Besseler: Bourdon und Fauxbourdon, 2nd edition, Leipzig 1974, pp. 11–14; Manfred Bukofzer: The beginnings of choral polyphony, in: Studies in Medieval and Renaissance Music, New York 1950, pp. 176–189; Hans Schoop: Entstehung und Verwendung der Handschrift Oxford, Bodleian Library, Canonici misc. 213, Bern 1971 (Publikationen der Schweizerischen Musikforschenden Gesellschaft, II, 24), pp. 61–63; Howard Brown (s. note 12, above) and Louise Cuyler: Georg Rhaw's *Opus decem Missarum*, 1541: some aspects of the Franco-Flemish Mass in Germany, in: Renaissance-Muziek, 1400–1600: donum natalicum Rene Bernard Lenaerts, Louvain 1969, p. 73; Frank Harrison: Music in Medieval Britain, London 1958, fn. to p. 232.

14 See, for example, the comment by Arthur Mendel in: Pitch in western music since 1500 – a re-examination, in: Acta musicologica 50 (1978), p. 59, regarding the interpretation of *chiavette*. Since this paper was written, an admirable article has appeared by Roger Bowers: The performing ensemble for English church polyphony, *c*. 1320 – *c*. 1390, in: Studies in the performance of late mediaeval music, ed. by Stanley Boorman, Cambridge 1983, pp. 161–192. This with other Studies by Brown, Fallows and Planchart in the same volume, goes a long way toward establishing useful criteria for studying patterns of clef usage.

15 See the comments by Edward Roesner (s. note 6, above), fn. to p. 165, on the theories of Theodore Karp, whose subsequent work does not seem to me to have answered Roesner's objection.

16 But, as Jacquelyn Mattfeld remarked twenty years ago (in: Some relationships between texts and cantus firmi in the liturgical motets of Josquin des Prez, in: Journal of the American Musicological Society 14 (1961), p. 178), Josquin "evidently understood the selection of a liturgical text to imply that a whole cantus in the sense of a union of words and melody was 'the given'." See also Ludwig Finscher: Zur Cantus-Firmus-Behandlung in der Psalm-Motette der Josquin-Zeit, in: Hans Albrecht in memoriam. Gedenkschrift mit Beiträgen von Freunden und Schülern, Kassel 1962, pp. 55–62 and Willem Elders: Plainchant in the motets, hymns and magnificats of Josquin des Prez, in: Josquin des Prez (s. note 9, above), pp. 523–542.

17 This seems to be particularly true of those German prints that contain latin texts, especially when written in the polychoral style. See for example Samuel Scheidt's *Cantiones sacrae octo vocum*, Hamburg 1620.

18 Apart from the prescriptions of Zarlino (translated in Oliver Strunk: Source Readings in Music History, Norton 1950, pp. 260–1), guidance is offered by del Lago (see Don Harrán: The theorist Giovanni del Lago: a new view of the man and his writings, in: Musica Disciplina 27 (1973), pp. 114–121), by Lanfranco (Don Harrán: New light on the question of text underlay prior to Zarlino, in: Acta Musicologica 45 (1973), pp. 24–56), by Stocker (Edward Lowinsky: A treatise on text underlay by a German disciple of Francesco de Salinas, in: Festschrift Heinrich Besseler zum sechzigsten Geburtstag, Leipzig 1961, pp. 231–252) and by Vicentino (Henry Kaufman: The Life and works of Nicola Vicentino, p. 158).

19 Edward Lowinsky: The Medici Codex of 1518, Monuments of Renaissance Music, iii–v, Chicago 1968, vol. iii, pp. 90–107.

20 S. note 19, above, p. 91, in reference to Le Santier's *Alma redemptoris mater*, and elsewhere.

21 There is the earlier evidence of the anonymous scribe of Venice, Biblioteca Marciana, Ms. Lat. 336, coll. 1581, folio 1, discussed in Don Harrán: In pursuit of origins: the earliest writing on text underlay (c. 1440), in: Acta Musicologica 50 (1978), pp. 217–240, which provides a convenient point of reference from before the period under discussion here. In this case, the point is stressed by the manner in which the scribe seems to refer to a ligature, no matter how long it be, as a single note. There is no reason to believe, as Harrán suggests, that the phrase "coluy che la a notare" must refer to a composer, and not to a scribe.

22 This is common throughout the fifteenth century in many sources, at least as far back as Padua, Biblioteca della Universita, 684.

23 The number needed increased dramatically with the introduction of single impression type. Oblique ligatures were then quickly abandoned, while others (principally the *c. o. p.* ligature) were usually made by butting together separate breves and longs. This careful joining together of sorts, lasting well into the seventeenth century, confirms the understanding that must have existed of a need for ligatures in the notation of the music.

24 It would seem, for example, that the idea of the major semibreve as a distinct note, not to be identified with the minor semibreve, survives well into the Renaissance. This is implicit in the remark of Vanneus: *Recanetum de Musica Aurea*, Rome 1533, Book 2, chapter X, that nothing is changed in the shape of a note, not even though it is major.

25 While it is difficult to accept many of Don Harrán's arguments (s. note 11, above), especially in the light of James Haar: False relations and chromaticism in sixteenth-century music, Journal of the American Musicological Society 30 (1977), pp. 391–418, yet the evidence presented by Frank d'Accone (in: Matteo Rampollini and his Petrarchan canzoni cycles, in: Musica Disciplina 27 (1973), pp. 65–106, and building on the work of Theodor Kroyer) does suggest that the complexities of accidentals and their usage were beyond some readers in the sixteenth century, and were in need of some codification during a period of stylistic flux.

26 The uses of coloration in the later 16th century seem to be fairly limited – principally restricted to the treatment of hemiola patterns and of the occasional acknowledgement of the old *similis ante similem* rule: examples of both can be found in the sources of Monteverdi or Praetorius or Scheidt. English use was still more diverse, as witness the Fitzwilliam Virginal Book. During the early 17th century, as proportion signs and coloration acquire separate existences, the latter is retained for some complete pieces in triple metre.

27 Throughout the music examples, the use of diamond-shaped notes indicates the original notation, while the modern equivalent is given in reduced note-values and modern note-forms. Details of all the examples and the sources used are given at the end of the paper.

In examples 1, 2 and 3 the formulaic cadence patterns are arranged, respectively, in the order *superius, tenor* and *contratenor* even though the music

is not necessarily from the corresponding voice-part of the work illustrated.
28 See, for example, Cara's *Amero non amero*, as printed in Petrucci's eleventh book of frottole.
29 While there may be some justification for performing the music in this manner, I can see little for producing editions that preserve such performance decisions without any support. Perhaps an extreme case is the Œuvres complètes de Philippe(?) Caron, edited by James Thomson, New York 1971–1976, where the intellectual stimulus of considering the editor's decisions is matched by the challenge of attempting to perform from his edition. Many of the $^6/_8$–$^3/_4$ patterns are much less suspect, if only because one can postulate that the decline of the major prolation signatures was partly a result of the ability to indicate $^6/_8$ patterns in minor prolation.
30 As far as I can tell, this is purely a modern term.
31 Lodovico Zacconi: *Prattica di Musica*, Venice 1596, Book I, chapters 43 and 45. See the discussion in Michael Collins: The Performance of Coloration, Sesquialtera and Hemiolia (1450–1750), dissertation, Stanford University 1963, pp. 15–18. Collins includes in his Appendix 3 a list of the 16th century theoretical references to the notational convention.
32 It is certainly present as soon as void notation is adopted, and Charles Hamm has drawn my attention to the use of void notation and *minor color* in different sources of Power's *Anima mea liquefacta est*. Before that time, it is difficult to be certain wheter a triplet interpretation is or is not intended.
33 See Zarlino's rule 4 (as translated by Strunk [s. note 18, above], p. 260): "It is not usual to place a syllable below a semiminim, or below those figures that are smaller than the semiminim, or below the figure immediately following." I can see no reason to assert that the suspension of this rule in *minor color* is based on the fact that the second colored note is no longer a semiminim but a colored minim.
34 See Martin Staehelin's paper at the present conference, to which I would add the example of Glareanus' version of *Tulerunt Dominum meum* (ascribed to Isaac on p. 314 of *Dodecachordon*), apparently copied exactly from Petrucci's *Motetti de la Corona*, volume III.
35 The obvious examples from this period include the Sistine Chapel manuscripts, Padua A17, and those prepared for Casale Monferrato, Bergamo, Milan and other cathedrals.
36 Charles Hamm: Manuscript structure in the Dufay era, in: Acta Musicologica 34 (1962), pp. 166–184, and: A catalogue of anonymous English music in fifteenth-century continental manuscripts, in: Musica Disciplina 22 (1968), pp. 47–76.

86

MUSIC EXAMPLES

Only those sources that have been checked in the preparation of this paper are included in the references.

1a Carpentras: *Bonitatem fecisti.* Superius, mm.
 RISM 1514[1], No. 3.
1b Josquin: *Memor esto verbi tui.* Altus, mm. 90–96.
 RISM 1514[1], No. 2.
 I-Rvat, Sist. 16, ff. 165v–169r.
1c Craen: *Ave Maria.* Altus and tenor, mm. 63–67.
 RISM 1502[1], No. 20.
1d Févin: *Sancta Trinitas.* Superius, mm. 1–10.
 GB-Lbl, Roy.8.G.VII, ff. 12v–14r.
2a anonymous: *Sancta Maria / O werder mundt.* Bassus, mm. 51–56.
 GB-Lbl, Roy.8.G.VII, ff. 21v–22r.
2b Brumel: *Sub tuum presidium.* Bassus, mm. 30–36.
 GB-Lcm, 1070, ff. 35v–36r.
 GB-Cmc, Pepys 1760, ff. 17v–18r.
2c Févin: *Gaude francorum regia.* Bassus, mm.
 RISM 1514[1], No. 15.
3 Eustache de Monte Regali: *Magnificat VIII.* Bassus, mm. 59–63.
 I-MOd, III, ff. 102v–108r.
4a anonymous: *In illo tempore Maria Magdalene.* Superius, mm. 150–155.
 GB-Lcm, 1070, ff. 55v–57r.
4b Févin: *Nobilis progenie.* Tenor, mm. 32–38.
 GB-Cmc, Pepys 1760, ff. 21v–23r.
4c Josquin: *Officium de passione,* iv. Superius, mm. 6–9.
 RISM 1503[1], ff. 5v–6r.
5a anonymous: *Haec est illa.* Altus, mm. 29–35.
 RISM 1503[1], No. 29.
5b anonymous: *Ave vera caro Christi.* Tenor, mm. 6–10.
 RISM 1502[1], No. 27.
 RISM 1502[1], No. 27.
6a Busnois: *Est-il mercy.* Tenor and Contratenor, mm. 18–20.
 F-Dm, 517, ff. 59v–60r.
6b anonymous: *Congratulamini mihi.* Bassus, mm. 70–74.
 GB-Lbl, Roy.8.G.VII, ff. 42v–44r.
6c anonymous: *Profitentes unitatem.* Bassus, mm. 94–99.
 GB-Lcm, 1070, 80v–83r.
7a Mouton: *Dulces exuviae.* Superius and altus, mm. 13–19.
 GB-Lbl, Roy.8.G.VII, ff. 54v–55r.
 RISM 1559[4] (lacks altus ligature).
7b anonymous: *Peccantem me quotidie.* mm. 9–22.
 GB-Lbl, Add. 35087, ff. 17v–19r.
8a Josquin: *Ave Maria... virgo serena.* Superius, start.
 GB-Lcm, 1070, ff. 31v–33r.

8b Josquin: *Christum ducem.* Superius, start.
  RISM 1503[1], ff.12v–13r.
  RISM 1514[1], No. 25.
8c Josquin: *Mittit ad virginem.* Bassus, start of 2da pars.
  I-Rvat, Sist. 46, 129v–133r.
  GB-Lcm, 1070, 82v–87r.
8d Josquin: *Christum ducem.* All voices, mm. 32–40.
  RISM 1503[1], ff.12v–13r.
  RISM 1514[1], No. 25.
9 anonymous: *Vivo ego dicit Dominus.* All voices, mm. 10–16.
  GB-Lbl, Add. 35087, ff.75v–76r.
10a Lafage: *Elizabeth Zacharie.* Superius, ending.
  I-Fl, Acq. e doni, 666, ff.41v–44r.
  RISM 1519[1], No. 24.
10b Brumel: *Lauda Sion salvatorem,* v. 23. Superius, mm.8–13.
  RISM 1503[1], No. 16.
10c Martini: *Ave decus virginale.* Tenor and bassus, last bars.
  RISM 1503[1], No. 28.
11 Mouton: *Nos qui vivimus.* Tenor, mm.
  RISM 1514[1], No. 5.
12a Vaqueras: *Domine non secundum.* Part 3 – Adiuva nos, ending.
  I-Rvat, Sist. 35, ff.2–5r.
  RISM 1503[1], No. 9.
12b Josquin: *Preter rerum seriem.* Bassus secundus, mm.65–77.
  I-Rvat, Sist. 16, 160v–164r.
  GB-Lcm, 1070, ff.63v–68r.
13a anonymous: *Palas actea.* mm. 40–45.
  GB-Lcm, 1070, ff.3v–5r.
13b Molinet: *Tart ara.* Superius, opening.
  F-Pn, n.a.fr. 4379, ff.e8v–e9r.
14 Brumel: *Lauda Sion salvatorem,* v. 11. Final measures.
  RISM 1503[1], No. 16.
15a Févin: *Benedictus Dominus Deus.* Tenor, final measures.
  I-Rvat, Sist. 26, ff.152v–156r.
  RISM 1514[1], No. 10.
15b anonymous: *Stella celi.* Superius, mm. 13–18.
  I-Fn, Panc. 27, ff.69v–70r.
  RISM 1502[1], No. 25.
15c anonymous: *Palas actea.* Tenor, mm. 18–26.
  GB-Lcm, 1070, ff.3v–5r.
15d Compère: *Crux triumphans.* Tenor, mm. 14–21.
  I-VEcap, DCCVIII, ff.20v–21r.
  F-Pn, f.fr. 1597, ff.61v–62r (lacks first ligature, because it would cross
    a line-end).
  RISM 1502[1], No. 6.
16 de Silva: *Puer natus est.* Opening of 2da pars.
  I-Fl, acq. e doni, 666, ff.127v–132r (with text repeated).
  I-Rvat, Sist. 46, ff.23v–28r.

88

17a anonymous: *Descendi in hortum meum.* Bassus, mm. 80–88.
     I-Rvat, Pal.lat. 1976–9, ff. 85r–86v.
     GB-Lbl, Roy.8.G.VII, ff. 10v–12r.
17b Brumel: *Regina coeli.* Altus and superius, opening section.
     I-Rvat, Sist. 42, ff. 123v–125r.
     RISM 1502[1], No. 13.
     I-VEcap. DCCVIII, ff. 13v–15r (very few ligatures).
     I-Fn, Panc. 27, ff. 61v–63r (no ligatures).
17c anonymous: *Alma redemptoris mater.* Tenor, mm. 40–48.
     GB-Lbl, Roy.8.G.VII, ff. 48v–50r.
17d anonymous: *Nesciens mater.* Tenor, mm. 35–45.
     GB-Lbl, Roy.8.G.VII, ff. 6v–8r.
17e Mouton: *In omni tribulatione.* Superius, mm. 31–37.
     I-Fl, acq. e doni, 666, ff. 79v–80r.
18a Mouton: *Laudate Deum in sanctis.* Tenor, mm. 53–57.
     GB-Lcm, 1070, ff. 15v–17r.
18b anonymous: *Forte si dulci.* Bass, opening measures.
     GB-Lcm, 1070, ff. 1v–5r.
18c de Silva: *Laetatus sum.* Superius, 2da pars, mm. 36–39.
     RISM 1514[1], No. 4.
     I-Rvat, Sist. 46, 69v–72r (no color).
18d Compère: *Plaine d'ennuy.* Tenor, opening measures.
     GB-Lbl, Add. 35087, 86v–87r.
18e Brumel: *Laudate Dominum.* Altus, 2da pars, mm. 24–27.
     RISM 1514[1], No. 26.
     I-Rvat, Sist. 42, ff. 1v–8r (no color).
19a anonymous: *Sancta Maria / O werder mundt.* Bassus, mm. 64–69.
     GB-Lbl, Roy.8.G.VII, 21v–22r.
19b Mouton: *Dulces exuvie.* Bassus, mm. 15–19.
     GB-Lbl, Roy.8.G.VII, ff. 54v–55r.
19c Gascongne: *Nigra sum.* Superius, mm. 52–58.
     GB-Cmc, Pepys 1760, 43v–46r.
20a Josquin: *Ave Maria . . . virgo serena.* mm. 35–39.
     GB-Lcm, 1070, ff. 31v–33r.
     I-Rvat, Sist. 42, ff. 22v–24r (no color in top voice).
     E-Bc, 454, ff. 124v–25r (no color or ornamental note in top voice).
     I-MOd, IX, ff. 24v–26r (no color or ligature).
20b anonymous: *O beatissime Domine Jesu Christum.* Altus, mm. 33–39.
     I-Rvat, Pal.lat. 1976–9, ff. 60v–62r.
     GB-Lbl, Roy.8.G.VII, ff. 34v–36r.
21a Josquin: *Liber generationis.* Bassus, mm. 182–186.
     GB-Lcm, 1070, ff. 96v–102r.
     I-Rvat, Sist. 42, ff. 42v–50r.
21b anonymous: *Sancta Maria piarum piissima.* Tenor, mm. 97–101.
     GB-Lbl, Add. 35087, ff. 76v–78r.
21c Agricola: *Da pacem, Domine.* Bassus, mm. 23–28.
     GB-Lbl, Add. 35087, ff. 39v–40r.

22a Fogliano: Magnificat VIII. Start of v. 10.
   I-MOd, IV, ff. 50v–54r.
22b Mouton: *Tota pulchra es.* Opening.
   GB-Lcm, 1070, ff. 34v–35r.
23a Fogliano: Magnificat VIII. Verse 4, mm. 3–5.
   I-MOd, IV, ff. 50v–54r.
23b anonymous: *Erubescat Judeua.* mm. 15–18.
   GB-Lbl, Add. 35087, ff. 2v–3r.
24a Mouton: *Laudate Deum in sanctis.* mm. 12–16.
   RISM 1514[1], No. 7.
   GB-Lcm, 1070, f. 15v (no color).
24b anonymous: *Popule meus.* mm. 23–25.
   GB-Lcm, 1070, ff. 117v–121r.
25a anonymous: *Tristis est anima mea.* mm. 41–44.
   GB-Lbl, Add. 35087, ff. 10v–11r.
25b anonymous: *Popule meus.* mm. 113–116.
   GB-Lcm, 1070, ff. 117v–121r.
25c Josquin: *Liber generationis.* 3a pars, mm. 121–123.
   GB-Lcm, 1070, ff. 96v–102r.
   I-Rvat, Sist. 42, ff. 41v–50r (no color).
26 anonymous: *Jesu autem transiens.* mm. 45–48.
   GB-Lbl, Roy.8.G.VII, ff. 58v–59r.
27a Richafort: *Sufficiebat nobis.* mm. 22–24.
   GB-Cmc, Pepys 1760, ff. 36v–37r.
   I-Bc, Q19, ff. 82v–83r (no ligature or color).
27b Gascongne: *Nigra sum.* mm. 5–8.
   GB-Cmc, Pepys 1760, ff. 43v–46r.
27c Gascongne: *Dulcis mater.* mm. 25–30.
   GB-Cmc, Pepys 1760, ff. 39v–41r.
28a La Rue: *Salve Regina.* Superius, mm.
   B-Br, 9126, ff.
28b Josquin: *Stabat mater.* Contra altus, mm. 113–120.
   GB-Lcm, 1070, 23v–27r.
29 Compère/Richafort: *O genitrix gloriosa.* mm. 13–19.
   GB-Lcm, 1070, ff. 83v–85r.
   I-Fr. 2794, ff. 9v–10r.
   I-Rvat, Sist. 46, ff. 98v–99r.
30 anonymous: *Conditor alme siderum.* mm. 1–3, 7–10 and 14–16.
   I-MC, 871N, pp. 292–3.
31 Josquin: *Missus est Gabriel.* Superius, mm. 76–79.
   GB-Lbl, Roy.8.G.VII, ff. 23v–25r.
   All other sources also have the superius ligature.
32 *idem.* Bassus, mm. 68–70.
   All sources except D-Usch, 237a–d and I-Rvat, Sist. 63.
33 *idem.* Tenor, mm. 72–81.
   D-Usch, 237a–d.
   Ligature is missing in all other sources.

34 *idem.* Tenor, mm. 57–62.
    GB-Lbl, Roy.8.G.VII, ff.23v–25r.
    Ligature also present in D-As, 142a, *I*-Rvat, Sist. 63,
    D-Usch, 237a–d, S-Uu, 76c.
35 *idem.* Altus, mm. 74–78.
    I-Fn, II.I.232, ff.94v–95r.
    Also present in D-Usch, 237a–d, I-CT, 96, I-Fn, XIX. 164–7,
    S-Uu, 76c.
36 *idem.* Tenor, mm. 42–48.
    All sources, except I-Fn, XIX, 164–7.
37 *idem.* Bassus, mm. 42–48.
    GB-Lbl, Roy.8.G.VII.
    Both ligatures also in D-Usch, 237a–d, I-Fn, II.I.232.
    Second also in B-Br, 9126, S-Uu, 76c.
38a *idem.* Tenor, mm. 11–14.
    B-Br, 9126 and D-Usch, 237a–d.
38b *idem.* Tenor, mm. 57–59.
    D-As, 142a and D-Usch, 237a–d.
38c *idem.* Altus, mm. 60–61.
    B-Br, 9126 and I-Fn, II.I.232.
38d *idem.* Altus, mm. 62–63.
    B-Br, 9126 and D-As, 142a.
38e *idem.* Bassus, mm. 65–66.
    B-Br, 9126.
39a *idem.* Altus, mm. 27–32.
    B-Br, 9126, D-As, 142a, D-Usch, 237a–d, I-Rvat, Sist. 63.
39b *idem.* Altus, mm. 39–43.
    I-Rvat, Sist. 63.
39c *idem.* Superius, mm. 60–64.
    B-Br, 9126, I-Fn, II.I.232, I-Rvat, Sist. 63.
39d *idem.* Superius, mm. 70–75.
    I-Rvat, Sist. 63.
39e *idem.* Superius, mm. 76–81.
    D-Usch, 237a–d, I-Rvat, Sist. 63.
39f *idem.* Bassus, mm. 80–85.
    I-Rvat, Sist. 63.
40a *idem.* Superius, mm. 14–16.
    B-Br, 9126, D-As, 142a, GB-Lbl, Roy.8.G.VII, I-Fn, II.I.232,
    S-Uu, 76c.
40b *idem.* Altus, mm. 18–19.
    B-Br, 9126, D-As, 142a, I-CT, 95–96, S-Uu, 76c.
40c *idem.* Superius, mm. 41–43.
    B-Br, 9126, D-As, 142a, GB-Lbl, Roy.8.G.VII, I-Fn, II.I.232,
    I-Fn, XIX.164–7.
40d *idem.* Altus, mm. 75–77.
    D-Usch, 237a–d, I-CT, 95–6, I-Fn, II.I.232, I-Fn, XIX.164–7,
    S-Uu, 76c.

1d)

Sancta trinitas unus deus

2a)

2b)

deprecationes

Ne despicias

2c)

recte   petisti

3)

Et sanctum nomen

4a)

incredulus   Alleluya   alla.

4b)

fuit pastor noster   remigius

4c)

pastor bo   ne iustos 9serva

Pas - tor   bo -   ne   jus - tos

5a)

hoc ēveregrati   o   sa   sup

est ve - | re gra - | ti - o - - - sa   su - per

5b)

q̄ in cru   ce pepēdisti

6a)

6b)

8a)

Ave maria

8b)

Christum ducem   redemit nos   ab hostibus   laudet cetus

8c)

virgo susci pias dei de posi tū In   quo perfi   cias

8d) Pena fortis tuae mortis

9) dicit dominus

10a)

Sancte ioannes   ora   pro nobis

12b)

que dis - po - nit om - ni - a tam su - a - ve

tam su - a - [ve tam su - a -] ve.

13a)

paradi-so Nos u - bi cri - stum

13b)

Tart ara mon cuer Sa plaisance

14)

15a)

Adversarios meos adver sarios meos.

ad - ver - sa - ri - os me - os ad -

- ver - sa - ri - os me - os.

15b)

que lactavit   q̄ lactavit   dn̄m

15c)

Samos ē t'buta

Sa - mos et tri - bu - ta   [et tri - bu - ta]

15d)

crux a xp̱o   sanc ta   et amabilis

16)

parvulus   filius   parvulus   filius

parvulus   filius

parvulus   parvulus   filius.

17a)

te   alleluya   alleluy   a

17b)

Alleluya

Alleluya   alleluya

17c)

et   stel -   la ma -   ris
[et   stel -la   ma - ris, stel-la   ma - ris]

17d)

sal -   va - to - rem se -   cu -
[sal -   va - to - rem se - cu - lo -

lo -   rem
rem,   se - cu - lo - rem]

17e)

Maria   Maria

Maria

IX

104

25b)

qua - dra -gin - ta   an -   tis

genuit iesse

25c)

26)

illorum

27a)   com -pu -ta - ren -   tur, ut di - vi - tis

com - pu -ta - ren -   tur

fuis -   set   pe -   cu -   nia

ut di - vi -

27b)   sed   for - mo -   sa

sed   for -   mo -   sa.

IX

30)

Con - di - tor al - me si - de - rum

Con -di - tor al - mi si - de - rum

lux cre - den - ti - um Chri - ste re - demptor

lux cre - den - ti-um Chri - ste re-demptor

au - di pre - ces sup - plicum

au - di pre - ces sup - plicum

31)

Alle luya Alleluya

32)

IX

108

IX

39f)   Sist. 63

al - le - lu - ya, al - le - lu - ya

40a) Augsburg, Brussels, London
Florence II.I.232, Uppsala.

40b) Augsburg, Cortona,
Brussels, Uppsala

40c) Augsburg, Brussels, London,
Florence II.I.232, Florence XIX.164-7

40d) Sist. 63

Cortona, Florence II.I.232,
Florence XIX.164-7, Ulm, Uppsala

X

False Relations and the Cadence

The present essay puts forward a hypothesis for which there is no theoretical support, but which depends on a series of interlocking patterns of evidence—of the notation in the sources, of formal awareness on the part of composers, and of questions of performance practice. Since there is theoretical evidence which seems to argue against my case, it may be thought that what follows is no more than a house of cards, ready to collapse on the removal of any single paragraph.

The proposition to be placed atop this apparently fragile structure is that certain composers of the early sixteenth century expected theoretically forbidden false relations to occur in performance, that they apparently liked the sound, and that (as a result) they composed in such a way that these harmonically rich sonorities would be included in performance. They seem to have been aware of the impact of certain 'dissonances' and to have chosen where in a composition they should be heard, and then to have composed so that singers would be drawn towards, or away from, applying specific *ficta* accidentals. There are cases where individual lines are awkward or apparently unstylistic, deliberately (insofar as we can tell) to avoid the possibility of a false relation—and other cases where the voices are drawn towards the same false relation, at strategic points in the composition.

* * * * *

I

The musical situation which stimulated this study involves the presence of 'leading notes' in more than one voice at the approach to a cadence. Normally, one of the 'leading notes' will rise to the 'tonic', and will be treated as a 'subsemitone' (except in the case of a Phrygian cadence). The other 'leading note' must then move in another direction, almost always falling. Example 1 shows the most simple version of this pattern, in which the falling seventh merely leaps down to the fifth of the final chord, and stays there. Examples 2(a) and 2(b) show cases which are more interesting in the present context, those in which the two 'leading notes' either overlap momentarily or else are attacked simultaneously.[1]

If one were to assume that the solution to the problem of the 'subsemitone' in Example 1 would be to provide *ficta* accidentals as I suggest, the result merely conforms to a reasonable (and often essential) presumption that 'leading notes' were usually not sharpened until the last possible moment. In this case, the effect would be of a chromatic alteration of the F. Compositionally, the voice-leading produces the effect of sounding the suspension (G) against its resolution (F), resulting in the so-called *Satzfehler* discussed by Osthoff and Sparks for the music of Josquin.[2]

Examples 2(a) and 2(b) provide apparently harder cases when considering *musica ficta*. Example 2(a) is little more than a modified version of Example 1, in which the first sounding of the resolution pitch (again an F) is held, and therefore overlaps the true resolution (in the *superius*). Example 2(b) pushes the problem even further. There is every reason to believe that, at first sight at least, the *tenor* would expect to sing an F natural and the *quintus* an F sharp. If the two were to sing the same version of F in performance, one or the other would have to suspend his normal approach to *musica ficta*. The alternative is a simultaneous sounding of *mi* and *fa*.

Two of the principal avenues of investigation which should help us decide what singers might have done—rather than what the theorists wished to have happened—have been addressed by scholars already. One concerns the simultaneous sounding of suspension and resolution, relevant here when they could be *mi* and *fa*; the other is the extent to which sources do already indicate chromatic alteration of pitches.

Osthoff's discussion of his *Satzfehler* in Josquin's music[3] refers to it in cadential situations. The effect is indeed most common when approaching a cadence, and in works for five or six voices. The reasons for this are fairly obvious: in a basically four-voice style, with a significant V–I cadence (and especially where no voice introduces a new phrase before the resolution of the cadence, to provide an overlapping texture), there are only three usable pitches, two of which can normally be duplicated. If, for any reason, the fifth of the V chord is not doubled, or when writing for six or more voices, the most likely result will be the sounding of both the fourth and the third of the V chord, usually in some version of the patterns found in Examples 1 and 2.

Example 1. Arcadelt: *Missa de beata virgine;* Credo, bars 77–9

Example 2(a). ?Josquin: 'Basiez-moy', final cadence

Example 2(b). Arcadelt: 'Io che di viver', final cadence

And yet, many composers went to considerable lengths to avoid the resulting effect. The sounding of suspension against resolution seems to have been an irregular occurrence in the late fifteenth century. There is an instance in Ockeghem's *Missa 'Au travail suis'* (Example 3), and Sparks refers to two occurrences in the five-voice *Missa sine nomine*;[4] in addition, there is a clear case in 'J'en ay dueil', corresponding to Example 4(c), below. While Sparks reports one instance in the music of Isaac, he finds none in compositions by Compère, Regis or Obrecht. There are also no examples, as far as I can see, in the music of Ghiselin, Prioris, Barbireau or Barbingnant. None of the instances of cross-relations in Obrecht's Masses, recently discussed by Noblitt,[5] falls into this category; they will be addressed below. However, there are several occurrences in the music of Josquin, even if the examples cited by Osthoff and discussed by Sparks are ignored.[6] Several are shown in Examples 4 (six-voice works) and 5 (five-voice works).

The impact of the simultaneous suspension and resolution varies considerably from case to case. It could be argued, in the cases of Examples 4(a) and 5(a), that the impact is considerably lessened by the way in which the lower voice moves away before the upper resolves—even if allowing for the ornamented resolution found in Example 4(a). Perhaps Example 4(b) is only a slight extension of the same situation. Examples 4(c) and 5(b), however, have a different impact, depending on the delayed movement of the lower voice to heighten the effect (although this does depend on how *legato* a style was employed by the singers); the actual part-writing is otherwise identical. In each case, the 'seventh' in the lower of the two voices falls to the fifth of the final chord, as it did in Examples 4(a) and 5(a). The only distinctive case in this group of examples is that of 4(d)—which is closely related to the so-called 'English cadence' (of which examples appear below, for example, at 9(a)). Here, the 'seventh' falls through the fifth in stepwise motion, to settle on the third of the final chord—in this case, perhaps a minor third.

The motet 'Regina celi letare' for six voices, which Jeremy Noble has plausibly added to the Josquin canon,[7] also shows versions of the *Satzfehler* figure, once in an internal cadence (at the end of the word 'letare' and before 'alleluya'), and again in the final cadence (see Example 6).

Once we begin to look at works once attributed to Josquin but now either rejected or put among the *opera dubia*, there are more, and perhaps more significant, cases. Among these are the motets 'Cantate Domino' (questioned by Finscher),[8] 'Lectio actuum apostolorum' (safely attributed, by Sherr, to Viardot, as 'Dum complerentur'),[9] 'Missus est Gabriel' (where Lowinsky convincingly demonstrated Mouton's authorship),[10] and three of Sparks' group of rejected works—'In illo tempore stetit', 'Nesciens mater' and 'Victime paschali laudes' (the last presumably the work of Brunet). Among secular works

Example 3. Ockeghem: *Missa 'Au travail suis';* Credo, bars 169–72

Example 4(a). Josquin: 'Benedicta es celorum regina', bars 63–5

Example 4(b). Josquin: 'O virgo prudentissima', bars 103–6

Example 4(c). Josquin: 'Ave nobilissima creatura', bars 46–9

Example 4(d). Josquin: 'Preter rerum seriem', bars 81–3

Example 5(a). Josquin: *Missa de beata virgine;* Credo, bars 156–9

Example 5(b). Josquin: 'Je ne me puis tenir', bars 72–5

Example 6. ?Josquin: 'Regina celi letare', final cadence

are the chansons 'Faulte d'argent' (6vv.), 'Mi lares vous' (5vv.) (both questioned by van Benthem)[11] and 'Basiez-moy' (6vv.) (rejected by Hewitt and Lowinsky).[12] The majority of these produces examples similar to those already presented from Josquin's works. The pattern found in 'Basiez-moy' (see Example 2(a)) also appears in 'Cantate Domino'. The styles of Examples 4(a) and 5(a), if unornamented, can also be found in 'Dum complerentur' (see Example 7(a)). That of Example 4(c) appears also in 'Cantate Domino', 'In illo tempore' and 'Mi lares vous'; heavily reinforced by repeated notes, it is also to be found in 'Nesciens mater'. An interesting modified version, in which the 'resolution' pitch itself resolves upward, appears a couple of times in 'Cantate Domino' (see Example 7(b)). A final pattern, shown here as Example 7(c) from Brunet's 'Victime paschali', also was used by the composer of 'Faulte d'argent'.

These illustrations show, even more clearly than he can have hoped, the strength of Sparks' point that the presence of the *Satzfehler* is irrelevant in any discussion of Josquin's authorship of specific works. Not only do compositions

Example 7(a). Viardot: 'Dum complerentur' (Josquin: 'Lectio actuum'), bars 103–7

Example 7(b). ?Josquin: 'Cantate Domino', bars 114–16

Example 7(c). Brunet (Josquin): 'Victime paschali laudes', bars 111–13

convincingly by Josquin have the figure, but it is also evident that his contemporaries believed him capable of using it—or at least that scribes working at the end of his life or soon after were willing to write it into his works. They were by no means always correct in their attributions, but in this case their sense of style appears to have been reliable.

The 'suspension-and-resolution' figure is even more common in works from composers of the next generation. In one form or another, versions of Examples 2(a), 4(c) or 7(a) can be found, though only rarely, in works of Brumel, Festa, Févin and Mouton.[13]

As Sparks has pointed out the figure becomes much more frequent in the work of Lhéritier.[14] Indeed, I find one or more examples in at least ten of his works, and also in 11 composed by Arcadelt, all for five or six voices. The evidence seems to be that Lhéritier, at least, regarded the device as part of his normal polyphonic repertoire; the ten works here come from a total of only 14 for five or six voices.

Other composers of this generation who also used the figure include Charles d'Argentil (*Missa de beata virgine*, Credo and Agnus; 'Moneta signor mio' (5vv.)), Beausseron (*Missa de beata virgine* (4vv.), the Credo and Agnus (both 5vv.); *Missa de feria*, Agnus; *Missa de beata virgine* composed with Dor, Credo), Brunet ('Veni sancte spiritus' as well as the 'Victime paschali laudes' already mentioned), Carpentras (*Missa 'A l'ombre d'ung buisonnet'*, Agnus; and *Missa 'Le coeur fut mien'*, Credo and Agnus, (both 4vv.)) and Misonne (*Missa 'Que n'ay-je Marion'*, Osanna; and *Missa de beata virgine*, Gloria (4vv.)). It is interesting that a few of these examples appear when only four voices are involved.[15]

The significant aspect of this list is that almost all the music was composed for, or at least copied at, the Vatican. While little or nothing is known of some of the composers, Charles d'Argentil was a member of the papal chapel from 1528, Beausseron served there from 1514 until his death in 1542, Lhéritier was in Rome from at least 1521, and Misonne was there in 1515 and again in the mid-1520s. The works by Brunet and Viardot are also to be found in Vatican manuscripts.[16]

Arcadelt was the exception, not appearing in Roman circles until 1540. It may be significant that the majority of his secular works with the *Satzfehler* appeared first in RISM 1540[18]; they comprise five of the seven works by Arcadelt in that volume, published in Venice, by Scotto.[17] It is tempting to suggest that all these works were composed before Arcadelt left Florence in 1537, though not very likely. But there is an attractive association between a Roman taste for the *Satzfehler* (or rather for its probable manner of performance), and a similar taste surfacing in Florence while a Medici, Clement VII, was occupying the papal throne, especially since a few examples survive in Roman manuscripts of Verdelot's music.

After this generation of composers, interest in the figure seems to decline in Italy. (No doubt, this is the result of changes of style spilling over from French secular styles, but also because composers had other means of achieving the same effect.) The principal proponents became northerners—Gombert, in particular, but also Crecquillon, Lupus Hellinck and some of the composers working in the Empire.

But our present concern is not over the compositional use of these patterns, but rather with their performance. In cases such as all the above, should the 'subsemitone' be sharpened? Some of the examples seem to be written as if to provide simple answers to this question. In Example 1, for instance, Arcadelt moved the fourth voice from F as if to avoid any possible conflict with the same pitch in the *cantus*; the latter can therefore be sharpened normally. Indeed, it is hard to see how any singer would have failed to do just that. (The group of questions surrounding rehearsal and performance, memory and annotation, collaboration and mutual alertness are all involved here. Insofar as we seldom have good answers for any of these questions, tending to credit singers with good or bad or phenomenal memories according to our temporary scholarly needs, it is hard to see how far they affect solutions to the present problem. It seems safer to work from the evidence that exists, particularly from the presence or (more significantly in this context) absence of accidentals in the sources. Certainly, it should be clear that the references to disputes about accidentals imply that not everything was resolved in rehearsal, and that the choirmaster did not always have autocratic authority.) Maybe the same holds true for Examples 4(a), 5(a) (in both of which the only overlap is purely decorative), 6 and 7(a). In other cases, it seems that the composer arranged the voice-leading so that the 'leading note' could *not* be sharpened; certainly this looks more likely, at the moment, for Examples 4(c) and 5(b). Either solution may as easily be true of those cases where the 'resolution' (the third of the chord) moves, but a little too late; see Examples 2(a) and 4(b).

And yet, these cases do raise nagging doubts. The top voice in the figure is very clearly cadential—the end of a major section of the work. We need to know at what point the pattern of Example 1, with sharpened 'leading note', gives way to that of a flattened 'leading note'. Is it at the situation of Example 2(a) or 4(b)? Or is it when we have a decorative camouflaging of the dissonance, as in Example 4(a)?

My concern here is reinforced by the presence of rather awkward writing in some of the examples. It appears, on occasion, as if the composer felt that he had to force the singer's hand, requiring him to sing a sharp or flat seventh. The most frequent of such cases can be illustrated by Examples 4(b) and 7(a). In both, the voice providing the lower of the dissonant notes (*sextus* in 4(b), *tenor I* in 7(a)) must sing it in its flat form as *mi*. In both, the note is an F, approached by leap from a C (temporarily placed beneath the *bassus*) so that the F must be natural. (In the case of Example 7(a), this produces a peculiarly ungainly line, although one that is found elsewhere.) While the F natural is evidently essential in both cases, it is not clear whether an F sharp in the other voice is equally required. The different rhythmic treatments of the two voices taken together raise questions to which I will return. But, following on from this, an example such as 6 or 7(c), where the part-writing avoids all pretence of simultaneity for the two 'leading notes', should reasonably raise the same doubts. Why should not chromatic alteration be acceptable here—from F natural (*altus II*) to F sharp (*cantus*) in Example 7(c), from G natural (*tenor*) to G sharp (*cantus*) in Example 6, especially since the latter occurs at the end of the work?

It is significant that two of these examples concern the written pitch G and cadences on A, in a work without a flat signature (Examples 5(b) and 6). All the other cases presented so far have involved cadences on G, whether a signature was employed or not, so that all revolve around questions of *musica recta* and *musica ficta*—albeit on the pitch F, for which it might be possible to argue an expanded tolerance on the part of musicians and composers. In fact, the great majority of cases of the cadential *Satzfehler* that I have found so far do cadence on G.

With the work of Lhéritier, there is an increasing number of dissonant approaches to cadences on D, while examples on other pitches, particularly on C, seem popular with the minor Vatican composers. The series of Examples 8(a)–8(c) shows some of these, each clearly marking a major cadence point in the work. Cadences on A with a one-flat signature occasionally appear, but they do not present the problems found in Example 8(a), involving the *tenor* and *cantus* pitches G. The remaining examples are all analogous to earlier cases, while having the great benefit for the rest of this study, of extending the range of pitches to be considered.

The musical question therefore remains: did composers, no doubt hearing false relations and chromatic alteration (in rehearsal at least), develop ways of utilizing the effect, enjoying its sound on occasion, sometimes writing virtually to impose it on the singers, while at others encouraging its avoidance? This is coupled with the question of how far singers were able to recognize formulae. I am satisfied that any competent singer, seeing the figure found in the *quintus* at the end of 'Basiez-moy' (Example 2(a)) and noting that it came at the end of a work, knew where it stood *vis-à-vis* the *finalis* of the piece, and could have sharpened the upper note—unless the composer had prevented that possibility. By this, I am implying that such a singer could have provided an F sharp for the final cadence of the *altus* of Example 5(a) (if that were part of the convention), but could not have done so for the *quintus* of Example 2(a). Nor could the *tenor* of Example 8(a) have sung a G sharp. There is no evidence in the sources to indicate how the *cantus* would have inflected his corresponding pitch in each case; indeed there is no evidence to suggest that the singer of the lower part would have inflected his pitch either. But, it would take very little experience for a singer to recognize the figure—little more than it would take a *cantus* singer

Example 8(a). Misonne: *Missa 'Que n'ay-je Marion'*; Osanna, final cadence

Example 8(b). d' Argentil: *Missa de beata virgine;* Credo, bars 155–8

Example 8(c). Arcadelt: 'Crudel acerba', bars 15–17

to recognize the 'subsemitone'—and thus we have to allow for the possibility of homogenized sharpening of the two 'leading notes', at least in some performing traditions.

This reinforces the point: we cannot know, merely from the notation, which version of the 'leading note' was preferred by either voice, nor whether the two were expected to agree under certain circumstances.

* * * * *

II

The second part of this essay, therefore, takes note of how far scribes and composers of the period appear to have expected or allowed for false relations or chromatic alteration from the singers reading their music. Fortunately, a number of recent studies have opened up the field. First among them is an article in which James Haar[18] argues for an awareness, on the part of sixteenth-century composers, of the usefulness of the false relation. Almost without exception, his examples come from secular works, principally madrigals that appeared between 1538 and 1560. The earlier pieces include a few which show a chromatic inflection of pitch between phrases—which, as Haar himself points out, is 'a point at which many of the rules for correct counterpoint seem to have been suspended'.[19] One of the reasons for this, of course, is the practice of raising thirds at the ends of more important sections, though it is by no means the only one.

The other characteristic situation involves momentary or short-term harmonic movement by a third. (This can also include movements over the joins of phrases, which may be combined with a sharpened third at the end of the earlier of the two phrases.) Haar presents a number of examples, both between and within phrases, and the strength of his argument lies in the presence of *notated* accidentals. In a number of the early cases, there is no alternative but to believe that a sequential chromatic alteration was intended by composer or printer.

The practice of bass movement by thirds, which Haar discusses in some detail, is also an important feature of the approach to many cadences in the repertoire I am discussing here. Often the harmonic skeleton involves a rising major or minor third in the bass, with an intervening chord a pitch below the first of the pair ('VI–V–I'). I have already shown two cases of this progression, in Examples 5(b) and 7(c). In Example 5(b), in fact, the chord built on the sixth degree is a first inversion, and it could be argued that the same sonority is implicit in Example 7(c). This is the more common version of the progression (perhaps because in many cases the chord on the sixth degree is itself approached from a chord on the fifth). In Example 9(a), the chord (at the beginning of the second bar) passes through an inversion with *altus II* and *tenor*, and at the same time controls the solmization of the second F in *altus II* and *bassus II*. In Example 9(b), the chord is an inversion from the beginning, as is made clear in the movement of *tenor I*.[20]

More frequently, the secondary chord on 'IV' is introduced later, and its root is sung momentarily in the lowest sounding voice. Three cases are shown at Example 10. The advantages of inserting the chord, either momentarily (as in Examples 10(a) and 10(b)) or with some importance attached (as in Example 10(c)) is that it helps the part-writing from the 'flat 6th' chord to the 'dominant'. (Example 10(b) is in fact only a slightly more active form of Example 9(b), perhaps because it marks the final cadence in the same composition.) There would otherwise be considerable risk of parallel motion between some voices. There are many examples of the pattern shown in Example 10(c), in the works of Arcadelt and Lhéritier in particular, where, as I have said, it almost becomes a formulaic manner of approaching the cadence when writing in five voices. But it is far from uncommon, and we have already seen earlier examples.

Example 9(a). Brunet: 'Victime paschali laudes', bars 163–5

Example 9(b). Lhéritier: 'Nigra sum', bars 27–9

Example 10(a). ?Josquin: 'Mi lares vous tousjours languir', bars 19–21

Example 10(b). Brunet: 'Victime paschali laudes', final cadence

Example 10(c). Arcadelt: 'Donna per amarvi', bars 28–30

While the cases shown in Examples 9 and 10 above (and in many others) do not necessarily conform to the situations described in Haar's discussion of false relations (only Example 10(c) has a notated sharp third in the resolution chord), they raise another thorny problem of cross-relations. All four, and indeed most such cases, are further illustrations of the practice of sounding the suspension against its own resolution—the *Satzfehler* which opened this argument. Indeed, the use of the chord on the sixth degree, whether or not a chord on the fourth intervenes, seems to lead very frequently to this dissonant situation—but with an added complication. Almost without exception, the pre-sounded resolution has to be solmized as *fa*, as in the second bar of Examples 9(a), 9(b) and 10(a) where it has been approached by a leap of a fourth. Although this is the most usual approach, the composer did have other means of ensuring the pitch would be sounded as *fa*. In Example 10(c) (second bar), the *tenor* has to sing C natural, coming from a B flat; in Example 10(b), the second *altus* will sing F natural, whether or not it has sung E flat on the previous note. The same restraint holds for the *quintus* in Example 2(a), the *sextus* in Example 4(b), for *tenor II* in Example 4(d), *tenor I* in Example 7(a), etc.

In other words, there is a significant number of cases where the composer forced one of the voices involved to sing a flat 'leading note'. It should be evident by now that, in some of these situations, such as Example 7(a), the other voice could reasonably sharpen the note. The extent to which this also applies to other situations depends on how far we believe composers were aware of the situation when they constructed their part-writing, and how far we think that they carefully engineered one of a number of very subtly controlled and lightly varied versions. Thus, it is intriguing for scholars who accept the practice of sharpened 'leading notes' as being almost an over-riding rule, to see the extent to which the potentially chromatic effect appears at very important cadences. Examples 2(a), 2(b), 4(b), 6, 8(a) and 10(b) all represent major divisions in, or the final cadences of, compositions. They are all places where the natural inclination to apply a 'subsemitone' to the 'leading note' would be strongest. And yet the situation posited at the end of the first part of this essay, whereby a competent singer of another part might recognize his own ending and sharpen his 'leading note' 'in sympathy' with the impending 'subsemitone', cannot be made to apply to all these cases. In Example 2(a), although the *quintus* singer might well recognize the final formula, he could not sharpen the C in the second measure; nor presumably could he sing an interval of a tritone. The same holds for Examples 4(b) and 8(a).

In these situations, I do not believe it is sufficient to say that both singers must sing *fa*. The evidence advanced by James Haar shows that composers were well aware of the fact of chromatic alteration. The only question is whether it can be applied to the situations presented here, that is, to slightly earlier music,

X

False Relations and the Cadence 237

to instances with a marginal or 'decorative' overlap, and to cases where alterations are not indicated in the manuscript or printed sources. A recent study by Thomas Noblitt[21] of false relations from the years around 1500 shows examples where one accidental is notated in the source. Noblitt's illustrations are all drawn from Mass movements attributed to Obrecht, and consist largely of cases where the two versions of B (or of E in a one-flat signature) appear to be required in close succession. In such cases, a flat before only one B does not, of course, mean that the other, unsigned B was to be sung 'natural', as *mi*, for both versions of B were available as *recta* notes. For that reason, one or two of Noblitt's cases seem less than convincing. In the majority of these instances, however, there seems little reason to doubt his contention that the two forms of B (or of E with a one-flat signature) *were* meant to be sung in close conjunction. Certainly, in a few cases, this is the most satisfactory, perhaps the only way, of escaping from the whirlpool of continually added accidentals. Some more interesting cases must be seen as standing on their own, as special effects, for they do not seem to raise the spectre of further later implications. Example 11(a), taken from Noblitt's article, shows a situation in which the notated accidental seems to have, as its principal function, the avoidance of a melodic tritone in the *altus*; but, more immediately for the listener, it creates a powerful shift from the necessary E natural of the *superius* to the E flat of the *altus*.[22] In this case, it would appear that either Obrecht or the scribe of the unique source (the Segovia manuscript) felt that there was a good reason, musical or otherwise, to notate the false relation. It is possible, in this one case, that the fear of a linear tritone was great enough to cause the scribe to enter the flat in the *altus*. But it is unlikely that the same implication can be read into Example 11(b), even though the unexpected B natural prevents a potential leap of a tritone. This can be said with some confidence, for the B natural is here a note in *musica ficta*, and there is no reason why the interval should not have been B flat to E flat, with both notes within the range of *recta* notes.

Noblitt states that 'Perhaps the most surprising result of the study of cross-relations in these Masses of Obrecht is the fact that virtually all can be understood as resulting from the addition of accidentals according to one or more generally accepted rules of *musica ficta* or of hexachord theory'.[23] However, I think this should not be very surprising, even for the notated accidentals. Both composers and scribes worked within the traditions of hexachord theory, and the principles of modality and *musica ficta*. Composers would normally have followed these rules, and would have made quite clear, by one means or another, those few occasions when they chose to create progressions raising problems with the rules. Scribes followed the norms, too, but a version that they would also have employed when singing, notating additional accidentals when their understanding of the rules made such editing seem to be of value. Thus, we should expect many signs to reflect the scribe's view, and to conform to his 'rules'. This is

Example 11(a). Obrecht: *Missa 'Libenter gloriabor';* Gloria (from Noblitt)

Example 11(b). Obrecht: *Missa 'Je ne demande';* Agnus II (from Noblitt)

wherein Noblitt's examples, and the other similar accidentals in late fifteenth-century music, stand in a position quite different from that adopted for Haar's examples. These latter, while often also producing chromatic semitones in the content of adjacent or nearby sonorities, do not have to follow the traditional solmization or hexachord practice—especially when the semitonal change occurs within one voice part or at a constant notated pitch. Thus, while Noblitt's examples stay within the general modal and hexachordal range of the composition, Haar's introduce a much wider range of pitches.

The examples which I have raised so far in this essay tend to fall between these two situations. Melodically, each voice behaves as if staying within conventional practice of the late fifteenth century. Even the potential for sharpening the 'leading note', producing the *subsemitonium*, does not stray beyond the normal practices of the singer. Yet this sharpened 'leading note', if applied, will produce exactly the use of the chromatic inflection discussed by Haar.[24] This conflict between following the rules and the resulting anomalous results, while producing a few notated accidentals (such as those discussed by Noblitt), should normally not result in any additional guidance in the source. The only cases where accidentals needed to be added were those where the scribe or composer wished to insist on his own version—and these would normally only involve the second accidental of the pair (again, as in Noblitt's examples).

The implication of this argument is that a *regular* pattern of false relations resulting from the consistent application of linear rules for alteration would no more be evident in the sources than would be a pattern of homogenization. If there were to be any way of indicating to the performer which solution were to be adopted in such a situation, it could only have survived in the part-writing. This is, therefore, the starting point of the third section of this essay.

But, first, there is one more range of notated accidentals which has to be brought to bear on the issue: those found in tablatures, for plucked strings or for keyboard, where the accidentals are specifically notated. (In keyboard tablature, this can only apply, if at all, in the lettered section of German notation; lute tablatures are necessarily more specific.) One of the strongest pleas for the position that accidentals in intabulations do correspond in general with those used in vocal practice was that made by Howard Mayer Brown, at the Josquin conference of 1971.[25] There is little reason to reject his arguments, especially since the various patterns of added accidentals seem to represent different but explicable positions on the part of different intabulators—towards or away from specific patterns of *musica ficta*. As Brown says, the intabulators appear to extend *musica ficta* 'in the direction of a more colourful harmonic palette'.[26] Yet we cannot know that they do not give a fair picture of a similar vocal tendency, once the special nature of the instruments concerned is taken into account.

It is clear that Francesco da Milano inclined to think, when adding accidentals to his intabulations, in small units. The fast notes between each chord change tend to be coloured towards the harmonic or melodic implications associated with the following chord, and not with the one from which they start. It is for this reason that he seems to add a good many 'subsemitone' inflections, for he was thinking of the ensuing chord as a controlling centre, in the way that singers thought of the ends of phrases.

There are many cases where Francesco gives a rapid shift between the two forms of a pitch—B natural to B flat, E flat to E natural, etc. Some of these show a supple and sophisticated awareness of the voice-leading of his model.[27] Example 12(a) is a good case: the use of C sharp in the inner voice shows Francesco reacting to the progression from the second to the third bar; its transformation to C natural in the next bar is looking forward from the chord on D to that on G two bars later. Example 12(b) is even more interesting: the F sharp in the upper voice of bar 189 is a 'subsemitone' to the following G (unless it is to be seen as a major tenth before the minor tenth of the next bar). The F natural, part of the vocal model, is also to be seen as influenced by the general descending line.

There are occasional examples of the two versions of a pitch overlapping—or being so close that they would seem to the listener to overlap. Example

X

240

12(b) may be one such. So are the cases in Example 13, both of which demonstrate a concern for individual voice-leading not necessary for a lutenist, and perhaps all the more clearly reflecting vocal practice. Even stronger is Example 14: while we might expect Francesco to introduce the *superius* on F sharp (as leading to G), yet, by bringing it in a beat earlier than does the vocal model, he highlights the dissonant transition from the previous F natural. One would be tempted to regard this as an error in the edition, were it not for the similar manner in which he elsewhere treats chromatic alteration; and, of course, even with the entry delayed by a beat, the effect is still present.

Other intabulators follow similar procedures—not only for lute, but also for keyboard, where we should presume the effect to be audibly more evident. Example 15 shows how two very different intabulators treat a *Satzfehler* situation in Josquin's 'Adieu mes amours'. Both men, Francesco Spinacino (in 1507) and Johann Weck (in c.1515), gave clear indications for a chromatic false relation.[28] Kotter's manuscript shows the same figuration in one other piece, Moulu's 'Sicut malus', and gives simultaneous C natural and C sharp in Isaac's 'Gracieuse plaisante' (see Example 16).[29]

These cases are significant. Chromatic alteration in quick succession seems to have existed in a number of different situations, with different repertoires coming from different parts of Europe, and reflecting different performing traditions. How far should such chromatic colouring be taken in the situations with which we began? Does the evidence suggest that composers saw

Example 12(a). Josquin: 'Pater noster', bars 31–2 on top, and Francesco da Milano: 'Pater noster', bars 61–4 below

Example 12(b). Josquin: 'Pater noster', bars 96–7 on top, and Francesco da Milano: 'Pater noster', bars 188–91 below

Example 13(a). Josquin: 'Ave Maria', bars 15–17 on top, and Francesco da Milano: 'Ave Maria', bars 30–3 below

Example 13(b). Francesco da Milano: 'Que voulez-vous dire', bars 22–5

Example 14. Févin: 'Fors seulement' (transposed), bars 26–8 on top, and Francesco da Milano: 'Fors seulement', bars 52–7 below

Example 15. System 1 Josquin: 'Adieu mes amours', bars 8–10
System 2 Spinacino: 'Adieu mes amours', bars 8–10
System 3 Weck (Kotter): 'Adieu mes amours' attrib. Isaac, bars 8–10

Example 16. Kotter: 'Gracieuse plaisante' attrib. Isaac, bars 22–4

three options, and not the two that we have assumed? When we recognize that a composer could impose or avoid sharpened 'leading notes', by arranging the voice-leading, should we also recognize that he could equally impose a combination of sharp and flat 'leading notes' by the same means?

If this option were available, it would rarely show in the accidentals added to the choirbooks and partbooks preserving vocal versions. The more clearly an option was understood by performers, the more clearly would they have expected the voice-leading to tell them what to do. In this sense, we are only proposing a situation slightly more sophisticated than that involving recognition of the 'subsemitone' 'leading note'. Analysis of the composers' patterns (always accepting that what we actually see are the scribes' patterns) may show how far the third situation, of chromatic inflection within a few notes, really existed. The patterns in tablatures may show us where to start.

* * * * *

III

The pattern of Example 15 is not only to be found in the work of the intabulators. It exists here in the vocal model, and is also found in vocal versions of other works of the time: Examples 7(c) and 8(c) have already been presented (and Examples 9(a) and 10(b) come from one of those two works). The same pattern also appears in Josquin's 'Faulte d'argent', Brumel's *Missa 'Et ecce terrae motus'* (Kyrie) and Verdelot's 'Deus in nomine tuo', in exactly the form presented here, in all cases cadencing on G. It is also found, modified lightly, in Arcadelt's 'Estote fortes' and 'Istorum est enim regnum', and in Beausseron's *Missa de feria* (Agnus (5vv.)) (see Example 17). Both the Arcadelt examples show the treatment of the descending line that is to be found in Brunet's 'Victime paschali' (see Example 7(c)) or Arcadelt's 'Crudel acerba' (see Example 8(c)). In both, the first following note is omitted, because the rest of the descending scale is delayed. This delay is a product, rather than a cause, of the longer pause on the resolution of the cadence, effectively two *tactus* in each case. In the first, in particular, this comes at an important point in the structure of the work, at the end of the first, emphatic phrase of text. In both the Arcadelt examples, the music actually moves on with a new point, but, in each, this is embedded within the texture, not to appear in the upper voices for another beat. Beausseron's cadence is even more clearly a hiatus in the onward flow of the piece. Perhaps related to this formal effect, it also allows for a momentary simultaneity, the pitch G, in two voices; we will return to this situation.

The other cases (Examples 7(d), 8(c), 9(a), 10(b), 15 and 17(a)) seem to present no problem. In each, the 'lower' voice (in fact, the upper in Arcadelt's

Example 17(a). Arcadelt: 'Estote fortes', bars 16–19

Example 17(b). Arcadelt: 'Istorum est enim', bars 51–4

Example 17(c). Beausseron: *Missa de feria*; Agnus, bars 62–4

'Crudel acerba', Example 8(d), and Josquin's 'Adieu mes amours', Example 15) must sing the highest pitch in its phrase as *fa*. In each, the 'upper' voice would tend to sing the same written pitch as *mi*, F sharp as opposed to F natural (or C sharp opposed to C natural, B natural following B flat). If the Arcadelt examples, by their voice-leading, tend to reinforce this inclination on the part of the singer, it is quite significant that the composer placed these cadences at points where they would have particular impact. The surest way to make such an impact more strongly felt would be to encourage the singers to introduce a false relation.

Examples of the *Satzfehler*, or other cases with potential false relations, tend to fall into a number of distinct types. At one end is a group which includes the examples just discussed, and at the other are the (apparently) most thorny problems. They all can be grouped as follows:

(1) In which the two versions of the 'leading note' are sounded sequentially, without overlap. This group would include the cases discussed in the preceding paragraphs, as well as those in Arcadelt's 'Donna per amarvi' (see Example 10(c)), Lhéritier's 'Nigra sum' (see Example 9(b)), Misonne's *Missa 'Que n' ay- je Marion'* (see Example 8(a)) and Viardot's 'Dum complerentur' (see Example 7(a)). Similar situations can be found in Brumel's 'Nato canunt omnia' (only surviving in Vatican City, Biblioteca Apostolica Vaticana, Cappella Sistina, Cod. 46) and his eight-voice Gloria to the *Magnificat 8° toni*, in Josquin's 'Faulte d'argent', in Arcadelt's 'Se'l foco in cui' and his *Missa de beata virgine* (4vv.–5vv.) (at the end of the first major section of the Credo), and in Verdelot's 'Pater noster'.

(2) In which the two voices do overlap, although the 'lower' moves away before the upper resolves. The instance from Beausseron's *Missa de feria* in Example 17(c) makes a good demonstration. In practice, this group has to be further subdivided according to whether or not the composer or scribe stressed the overlap, thereby making it a significant part of the sequence of sonorities:

(a)   Includes a few cases where the overlap is purely a result of a decorative figuration on the 'upper' 'leading note', the 'subsemitone'. For this, see Examples 4(b) (Josquin's 'Benedicta es celorum regina'), 5(a) (from the same composer's *Missa de beata virgine*) or 8(b) (d'Argentil, *Missa de beata virgine*). The same situation occurs in Josquin's 'Miserere', a case to which I shall return. Each of these should be seen as directly comparable with the situation of the examples in group (1), not least because we cannot know in such cases how far the decoration is the result of scribal initiative.

(b)   Comprises those cases where the 'lower' voice slides away from its version of the 'leading note' soon after the 'upper' has sounded its version.

Example 4(b) (from Josquin's 'O virgo prudentissima') illustrates how the overlap is apparently not meant to be more than the slightest effect. Example 10(b), from the end of Brunet's 'Victime paschali', shows the composer combining this delicate overlap with the pattern found in my group (1). (The same composer has similar effects in his 'Veni sancte spiritus'.)[30] Further cases appear in Lhéritier's 'Surrexit pastor bonus' and the 'Cantate Domino' attributed to Josquin (see Example 18), the latter interesting for the manner in which the 'lower' voice rises to the cadence.

(c) Includes a few situations where the composer seems to have wanted the overlap of the two notes to be more noticeable. This is usually a function of the rate of movement of the music, especially of harmonic movement, whereby the 'subsemitone' is itself sounded for longer, as in Example 2(a), the six-voice 'Basiez-moy' attributed to Josquin. This effect is also found in the work of Lhéritier (see Example 19).

Example 18(a). Lhéritier: 'Surrexit pastor bonus', bars 39–42

Example 18(b). ?Josquin: 'Cantate Domino', bars 94–6

Example 19(a). Lhéritier: 'Sub tuum presidium', bars 30–3

Example 19(b). Lhéritier: 'Miserere mei', bars 21–6

(3) This is really related to group (2), for here both soundings of the 'leading note' last until the resolution of the chord. A few such cases have already been shown: Josquin's 'Ave nobilissima creatura' (see Example 4(c)), his 'Je ne me puis tenir' (see Example 5(b)) and Arcadelt's 'Istorum est enim' (see Example 17(b), *superius* and *tenor*). Some of these situations will be so constructed as to require *fa* from the lower voice; three such appear as Example 20. In Example 20(a), the *contratenor* has to sing a C natural because of the placing of its next note—I suspect that the decoration of the final F in this voice allows for an eventual major third.[31] In Example 20(b), the same holds true for *tenor I*, although with a much less angular line, and again the composer allows for a later sharpening of the third of the final chord. In Example 20(c), the first *tenor* sings G natural, having come from the D a fourth below. But in all three, the composer ensures that the two soundings of the 'leading note' will be clearly audible.

The same pattern exists in other works: many by Arcadelt (*Missa 'Ave Regina'*, 'Non mai sempre', 'O pucherrima mulierum') and Lhéritier ('Deus in nomine tuo', 'Nigra sum', 'Petrus apostolus', 'Sub tuum presidium'), as well as others, by Beausseron (frequently in the *Missa de beata virgine*), d'Argentil

Example 20(a). ?Josquin: 'Vous ne l'aurez pas', final cadence

Example 20(b). Lhéritier: 'Salve Regina', final cadence

Example 20(c). Lhéritier: 'Repleatur os meum', final cadence

(*Missa de beata virgine*), Festa (*Missa de Domina nostra*), Févin (*Missa 'O quam glorifica'*), Mouton (*Missa 'Lo serai-je dire'* and 'Missus est Gabriel') and Verdelot ('Non turbetur cor vestrum'), as well as in works of Gombert.

(4)   The most curious group, involves those cases where the two 'leading note' pitches begin simultaneously, as in Example 2(b), Arcadelt's 'Io che di viver'. Clearer instances are shown in Example 21; in all, the potential clash is clearly a hazard to be faced by singers. It is possible in both Examples 21(a) and 21(b) to suggest that the singer of the falling 'leading note' might have recognized his figure, and sharpened the note 'in sympathy' with the 'subsemitone' in the other voice (as I suggested at the end of part I of this essay), especially in the case of Example 21(b), with its anticipation in the *superius*.[32] However, this is clearly not possible in Example 21(c).

Exactly the same effect occurs in Arcadelt's *Missa de beata virgine* and 'Qual'hor m'assal'amore', Févin's *Missa pro fidelibus defunctis* (at the end of the Benedictus), Gombert's *Missa 'Media vita'*, Josquin's 'Petite camusette', La Rue's 'Cent mille regretz' (also ascribed to Josquin), Misonne's *Missa 'Gracieuse plaisant'*, Senfl's 'Ave Maria' (6vv.), Viardot's 'Dum complerentur', and two anonymous works in the Sistine Chapel manuscripts in Vatican City, Biblioteca Apostolica Vaticana ('Domine non secundum', in Cappella Sistina, Cod. 55, and 'Gloria de beata virgine' in Cappella Sistina, Cod. 51). I have only found one instance in the works of Lhéritier, in his 'Sub tuum presidium'. This pattern might be taken as further evidence of the ways in which individual composers took some care over handling the potential false relation.

(5)   This is an interesting group, for the composer here organizes the vocal lines so that both singers should sing the 'leading note' as *fa*. Of the fair number of such situations in the repertoire, I have chosen three (see Example 22) from works already illustrated for different patterns of figuration. The lines in the *superius* and *tenor* of Example 22(a) both need C naturals, for both require B flats. In the same way, the canonic voice of Example 22(b) must sing C natural. It seems probable here, too, that the *superius* would sing C natural; he has probably just sung E flat, both because the line has just risen from the F below, and because it has done so directly from B flat. (There is an analogous situation, with the E flat notated, in Example 10(c).) Example 22(c) is a little less obvious: there is no doubt that the *quintus* would sing F natural leaping as it does from C. The *cantus* would probably have come to its F from an A flat, modified to accord with the E flats in both *altus* and *bassus*.

The interest in cases like these lies in the manner in which the composer has imposed his will on the singers. In Example 22(a), the evidence lies in *tenor I*, for the *cantus* is not cadential, although the *tenor* part appears to be. The treatment of the *tenor* is sufficiently different from that of the *superius* of

Example 21(a). Brumel: *Missa 'Et ecce terrae motus'*; Gloria, bars 27–8

Example 21(b). Forestier (Josquin): 'Veni sancte spiritus', final cadence

Example 21(c). Arcadelt: 'Io che di viver', bars 37–40

X

252

Example 22(a). Lhéritier: 'Nigra sum', bars 77–9

Example 22(b). Lhéritier: 'Salve Regina', bars 41–3

Example 22(c). Arcadelt: 'Io che di viver', bars 9–11

Example 9(b) to suggest that Lhéritier felt more strongly about a flat 'leading note'. The same is seen to be true when comparing the *superius* of Example 22(b) (C natural) with that of Example 20(b), where a flat 'leading note' is not imposed on the singer by the character of the single line. And, finally, the *tenor* line of Example 2(b), identical with the *quintus* of Example 21(c), would not produce an A flat in the way that seems to be required in Example 22(c).

So far, I have shown no case where a true 'subsemitone' is sounded before the 'lower' seventh. That is hardly surprising, for the nature of the suspension would tend to argue for the reverse order. Yet, a few such cases do exist: one by Lhéritier appears as Example 23. Here, I suspect that both *superius II* and *tenor II* should sing B natural in bars 59 and 60. The pattern is different from any other I have shown so far, indeed, is hardly to be paralleled in the repertoire. Related to it, though, is Example 24, where Arcadelt or his editors felt the need to indicate sharpened 'leading notes' in both voices. (In fact, the sharp in the upper voice is only to be found in RISM A 1384; the scribe of Vatican City, Biblioteca Apostolica Vaticana, Cappella Sistina, Cod. 155, apparently felt it to be unnecessary.)

Examples 22, 23 and 24 show, as we ought to expect, that composers had in their armoury enough weapons to let them indicate to the singer what they wanted him to do. While we are justified in assuming that they did not always mind which inflection he chose (especially in the early years of the century), yet the evidence shows that sometimes they felt strongly enough to try to control him.

There are three points that flow from this: one is the obvious one, that the voice-leading does sometimes tell us what the composer wanted. This is true not only of Example 22, but also of those examples where the two performances of the 'leading note' are carefully arranged not to overlap. Thus, I believe, my category (1) above (when put against the other examples) shows composers carefully structuring the part-writing to allow for, and virtually to encourage, the false relation.

The second point is that composers do seem to have had a subtle awareness of vocal sonority and of the effects of tension and relaxation that can flow from dissonance and chromatic alteration. Haar's examples, to which I have referred, seem to speak clearly to that point, as does the presence of the *Satzfehler* itself, however it was sung. Noblitt's examples, as well as those from tablature, show that musicians could always indicate quick chromatic inflection when they thought such guidance to be necessary.

Thirdly (and this is not a very subtle point), the presence of dissonance, including suspensions, at the approach to many cadences, like the frequent increase in rate of movement, acted as a dramatic formal device. In such an environment, we are justified in asking how far the subtle and carefully varied

Example 23. Lhéritier: 'Sub tuum presidium', bars 58–61

Example 24. Arcadelt: *Missa de beata virgine*; Credo, bars 94–6

treatments of any single figure may represent more than just a desire for variety, but also an indication of different designs on the part of composer or scribe.

It might be thought that the presence of the sharp in the lower voice of Example 24 is an argument against my suggestion that tenors could often recognize the composer's intention and themselves sharpen such a note. (If so, it is also an argument in favour of the false relation.) However, a valid case in favour of tenors being able to identify and sharpen notes in such positions lies in the number of cases when composers deliberately prevented the possibility, by approaching the note with a leap of a fourth, or from a tone below the written pitch, and so on. The treatments of Example 25 illustrate this point. (Here I give only the two lowest voices; each instance is the approach to a cadence on G, and (in each) one of the upper voices has a leading-note approach to G.) It is hard to believe that the differences between Examples 25(a) and 25(b), or between Examples 25(c) and 25(d), are merely the result of a desire for linear variety, for

Example 25. Brunet: 'Victime paschali laudes'; respectively bars 149–51; 180–2; 189–91; 175–7; 163–5

the amount of change is slight. Yet, if the difference in line also alters the total sonority—as it would if the upper voice saw the line as cadential and sharpened the F when he could (in Examples 25(b) and 25(d))—then we have ample justification for such slight changes.

The implication of this is fairly straightforward: it is that some cases exist, including many of the cases cited in my groups (2) and (3) above, where both voices would sharpen the 'leading note', singing *mi*, even though the 'lower' vocal line then fell. These would include those situations where three conditions were met: that the two notes overlap, that the 'lower' voice had no linear reason not to sharpen the note, and that both singers would know they were arriving at a significant cadence. Examples 4(b) and 18(a) show this, for in each the lower voice could easily recognize the situation.[33]

There are also cases from my group (4) which can be resolved in the same manner: in both Examples 21(b) and 21(c), the lower voice should be able to respond to the clear linear pattern. Indeed, this presumption of an elementary level of stylistic awareness on the part of tenors (or other singers of lower parts) helps to resolve what has been seen by scholars and performers as a peculiarly thorny situation.[34]

So far, therefore, I have attempted to define those cases where the composer wanted to have sequential *fa* and *mi*, in different voices, as well as those in which alert singers would either flatten or sharpen both notes. If the first group depends on linear considerations of *musica ficta*, the second depends entirely on the suggestion that composers carefully indicated what they wanted from their singers, and that singers were well experienced in handling the standard situations.

The remaining cases depend just as critically on the same considerations. When the composer wrote, as in Examples 25(a) and 25(c), so that the 'lower' voice could not sharpen the seventh (F), could not sing *mi*, that still tells us nothing about what he expected of the upper voice. In practice, the cadential nature of this 'upper' voice figuration is often reinforced in one of very few ways. Either it marks the end of a major section of the composition (see Examples 2(a), 2(b), 4(b), 4(d), 10(b) and 20(a), 20(b), and 20(c)); or it is composed with a long note at the end, with a following rest, or with a deliberate change of texture (see Examples 5(b), 9(a), 17(c) or 18(b)); or it is strengthened in the singer's mind by having some light decoration added (see Examples 4(a,) 4(c), 8(b) or 23). Some cases, of course, use more than one of these effects, especially at the end of a work (see Example 21(b)); but all seem constructed to ensure that the singer saw his line as invoking a 'subsemitone'.

The result is a series of situations in which the composer appears to have tried to coerce his two singers into singing different versions of the 'leading note', even though they overlap. I can see no other satisfactory solution for a number of the examples I have presented, especially those that meet two specific, simple criteria: (1) that they have survived in Roman sources and versions from the second quarter of the sixteenth century; and (2) that the composer seems to have used his awareness, not only of the rules of *musica ficta*, but also of the singers' expertise at recognizing figuration, to create expectations in their minds.

Thus, I would propose that the second bar of Example 20(b) (Lhéritier's 'Salve Regina') would have an F sharp in the *superius* and an F natural in the first *tenor*. I believe the same effect should occur in the second bar of Example 21(c). On the other hand, the two 'leading notes' in Examples 21(a) and 21(b) should both be sharpened. The example from Arcadelt's *Missa de beata virgine* with which I opened this essay, therefore, would probably not be sung, at least by experienced Roman singers, in the manner which I suggested there, but rather with two sharpened versions of F.

These suggestions and solutions help directly in explaining a number of apparently problematical situations, in ways which have not been available to us before. The most interesting, and often the easiest to solve in the terms proposed here, are those where there are several 'leading notes'—more than just each of versions that we have discussed. Example 26 shows a few such cases, with my proposed solutions. Example 26(a), from the 12-voice Brumel Mass, employs both sequential and simultaneous F 'leading notes', but they present no problem if the sixth voice recognizes its figure as a cadential cliché.[35] In Example 26(b), the only question is one of how late a singer would wait before sharpening the 'leading note'. The *superius* might sharpen only the last F, or might add the

Example 26(a). Brumel: *Missa 'Et ecce terrae motus'*; Kyrie I, final cadence

Example 26(b). ?Josquin: 'Vous l'aurez s'il vous plait', bars 43–6

Example 26(c). Févin: *Missa pro fidelibus defunctis*; Benedictus, final cadence

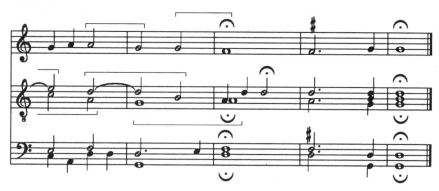

previous one, as being in the same figure (as shown in parentheses); the *contratenor* might then see its second F as cadential (in the terms I have discussed here) or not, and the two could still agree. My inclination in most such cases (as in Josquin's 'Petite camusette') is to delay the sharpening of the 'leading note' until as late as possible. (Here, this solution would traditionally be required in response to the movement of the *quintus*.[36]) Certainly such a procedure is acceptable for Example 26(c), where the pause acts as a phrase end, and allows for any necessary chromatic change for the final cadence.

The extent to which the false relation may have been a local idea is highlighted by the manner in which Bidon added his sixth voice to Josquin's 'Miserere mei'.[37] In at least one place (shown in Example 27), Bidon seems to have heard a potential sequential false relation as homogeneous, and consistently to be sung as *fa*. This appears to be the implication of his entry, leaping from C to F over a cadence on D.

It seems reasonable to suggest that the occurrences of both the *Satzfehler* and potential false relations in the works of Févin and Mouton are mostly to be seen as not real false relations, and that the appearances of these phenomena in the works of other composers of the earlier generations, including Brumel and perhaps Josquin (bearing in mind that many of 'his' examples are probably the product of later writers and 'revisers'), represent occasional events or the results of the early transmission.[38] These works contain very few overlapping 'leading notes', concentrating on their sequential occurrence. Perhaps it was these effects that appealed to Roman musicians, for we find an enormous growth in the simultaneous use of 'leading notes' in more than one voice, and of the subtlety and skill with which they were handled, in composers working in Rome, and in pieces transmitted in Roman sources.

Example 27. Josquin: 'Miserere mei', bars 42–5

As a result, the proposal central to this essay is that, at least in Rome in the
second quarter of the sixteenth century, all three possibilities of treating doubled
'leading notes' at cadences were equally available to composers, and thus to
singers: they could choose between sharpening both as *mi* (or the 'subsemitone'), flattening both as *fa*, or singing both versions of the note.   This
proposition does not depend on theoretical evidence or on our (artificially
imposed) modern concept of homogeneity. Nor does it need to reflect our views
of whatever concept of rehearsal the Renaissance musician may have had, that
is his view of 'learning' the music.

        Yet we should, perhaps, not be surprised that the clearest evidence for this
false relation as encouraged by composers should come from Roman sources
and musicians. The evidence that the musicians of the papal chapel sang without
rehearsal (except for once a year, to prepare for Tenebrae), that they could
change the selection of music even during the performance, and also that the
singers for solo sections seem not always to have been selected in advance may
come from the seventeenth century,[39] but there is no reason to believe that the
tradition was different in the previous century, and some evidence to suggest that
it was the same.[40] If singers effectively sang at sight during the service, it would
certainly encourage composers (or scribes) to make explicit their own preferences, by the details of the way they constructed their melodic lines. These
wishes appear to have included the false relation, perhaps because singers,
performing without rehearsal, had accustomed composers and patrons to hearing, and even enjoying, the sonority.

        Thus the present argument does not depend on the absence of accidentals
in the sources (as an excuse for the false relation), although it does explain why

so few of these situations actually needed them to be added. Instead, it rests on the extent to which composers allowed, invited or required different solutions in different contexts, and on the extent to which our perception is subtle enough to see the care with which they did this.[41]

NOTES

1. Throughout this essay, I use terminology which I know to be anachronistic. The object of the essay is not to discuss the theorists' view of the situation: that has been the subject of other essays. Instead, I am seeking to understand what happened in performance, and what, if anything, the composers wanted to happen. All the analytical terms should be seen as no more than a convenient and comprehensible modern shorthand describing a situation or identifying a pitch in an example.
2. Helmuth Osthoff, *Josquin Desprez* (Tutzing, 1962–5), i, 19; and Edgar H. Sparks, 'Problems of Authenticity in Josquin's Motets', *Josquin des Prez*, ed. Edward E. Lowinsky with Bonnie J. Blackburn (London, 1976), 344–59.
3. See the references in n. 2.
4. Sparks, 'Problems', 353.
5. Thomas Noblitt, 'Chromatic Cross-Relations and Editorial *musica ficta* in Masses of Obrecht', *Tijdschrift van de Vereniging voor Nederlandse Muziekgeschiedenis*, 32/1–2 (1982), 30–44.
6. These are 'Ave verum corpus' (5vv.), 'In illo tempore stetit Jesus' (6vv.), 'Inter natos mulierum' (6vv.), 'Nesciens mater' (5vv.), 'Responsum acceperat Simeon' (6vv.) and 'Victime paschali laudes' (6vv.). The last is almost certainly by Brunet (to whom it is attributed in Vatican City, Biblioteca Apostolica Vaticana, Cappella Sistina, Cod. 42). Like the others, it appears only in sources dating from after Josquin's death.
7. Jeremy Noble, 'A New Motet by Josquin?', *The Musical Times*, 102 (1971), 749–53. An edition was issued by Messrs Novello in conjunction with this issue of the journal.
8. Ludwig Finscher, 'The Present State of Josquin Research', *Report of the Eighth Congress, New York, 1961* (Kassel, 1962), ii, 64; this refers to a congress of the International Musicological Society.
9. Richard Sherr, 'Notes on Two Roman Manuscripts of the Early Sixteenth Century', *The Musical Quarterly*, 63 (1977), 48–73.
10. Edward E. Lowinsky, *The Medici Codex of 1518 . . . Historical Introduction and Commentary*, Monuments of Renaissance Music, iii (Chicago, 1968), 222–4.
11. Jaap van Benthem, 'Zur Struktur und Authentizität der Chansons à 5 & 6 von Josquin des Prez', *Tijdschrift van de Vereniging voor Nederlandse Muziekgeschie-*

denis, 21/3 (1970), 170–88.

12. *Ottaviano Petrucci: Canti B numero cinquanta, Venice 1502*, ed. Helen Hewitt, Monuments of Renaissance Music, ii (Chicago, 1967), pp. ix–x and 71–2.

13. Brumel: in 'Nato canunt omnia' (5vv), the 'Sicut erat' of his *Magnificat 8° toni*, and in the *Missa 'Et ecce terrae motus'* (12vv.); Févin: *Missa 'O quam glorifica'*, in the Agnus (6vv.); Festa: *Missa de Dominica nostra*, again in the Agnus (5vv.); Mouton: *Missa 'Lo serai-je dire'*, Agnus (6vv.). There are also two cases in an anonymous 'Celebremus conversionem' found in Padua, Biblioteca Capitolare, MS A17; see John Constant, 'Renaissance Manuscripts of Polyphony at the Cathedral of Padua' (Ph. D. dissertation, University of Michigan, 1975), 270–82, bars 41 and 126. The pattern of occurrence suggests that the effect was not so much consciously sought, but a product of five- or six-part writing. This explains its appearance in final Agnus sections.

14. Sparks, 'Problems', 353.

15. Some four-voice examples of this figure do occur in Josquin's music; see, for example, his *Missa 'Una musque de Buscaya'* and 'In exitu Israel', illustrated in Jaap van Benthem, 'Fortuna in Focus: Concerning Conflicting Progressions in Josquin's *Fortuna dun gran tempo*', *Tijdschrift van de Vereniging voor Nederlandse Muziekgeschiedenis*, 30/1 (1980), 1–50 (see pp. 14–15 and 19).

16. Biographical information is taken from *The New Grove Dictionary of Music and Musicians* (London, 1980).

17. The five are 'Crudel acerba', 'Donna per amarvi', 'Io che di viver', 'Non mai sempre fortuna' and 'Se'l foco in cui'. I have shown elsewhere that the reference to Verdelot at the head of 'Se'l foco in cui' is no more than a printer's error; see Stanley Boorman, 'Some Non-Conflicting Attributions, and Some Newly Anonymous Compositions, from the Early Sixteenth Century', *Early Music History*, 6 (1986), 109–57, esp. 136. In the same article, pp. 131–2, I suggest that the only other secular piece attributed to Arcadelt, and containing a *Satzfehler* situation, may not be by him; that is 'Deh per che non e in voi', found in RISM 1541[16]. RISM also makes reference to an apparently earlier volume, with basically the same collection of music as that found in RISM 1540[18], that is RISM [c.1538][20]; one scholar has shown that this volume was actually printed in 1554: see Mary S. Lewis, 'Antonio Gardane and His Publications of Sacred Music, 1538–1555' (Ph. D. dissertation, Brandeis University, 1979), i, 272–4. The other relevant works by Arcadelt are the *Missa 'Ave Regina'* (Gloria), *Missa de beata virgine* (Credo), 'Estote fortes', 'Istorum est enim regnum' and 'O pucherrima mulierum'. Of these, the last appeared in 1539, apparently composed before Arcadelt's arrival in Rome.

18. James Haar, 'False Relations and Chromaticisim in Sixteenth-Century Music', *Journal of the American Musicological Society*, 30 (1977), 391–418. As will appear, I follow Haar in believing to be unlikely the situation proposed in Don Harrán, 'New Evidence for Musica Ficta: The Cautionary Sign', *Journal of the American Musicological Society*, 29 (1976), 77–98; and *idem*, 'More Evidence for Cautionary Signs', *Journal of the American Musicological Society*, 31 (1978), 490–4.

19. Haar, 'False relations', 396. His examples for which this is true include Fogliano's 'Tua volsi esser sempre mai' (published in 1515) and the anonymous setting 'Ben che la facia' *per sonetti* (1506).

20. The basic progression I am discussing here is involved in the short section of music that caused an argument in Rome; see Lewis Lockwood, 'A Dispute on Accidentals in Sixteenth-Century Rome', *Analecta musicologica*, 2 (1965), 24–40. It is also at the centre of Lewis Lockwood's study, 'A Sample Problem of *musica ficta*: Willaert's *Pater noster*', *Studies in Music History: Essays for Oliver Strunk*, ed. Harold S. Powers (Princeton, N.J., 1968), 161–182. The Willaert composition, as presented by Lockwood, only comprises the first two bass notes of the progression, E flat to D. Of the nine occurrences that he cites in the 'Pater noster', only two eventually go on to chords on G, both at major structural points.

21. Thomas Noblitt, 'Chromatic Cross-Relations'.

22. The Kyrie of the same Mass presents an interesting problem in the application of accidentals, which has been addressed in the literature. See Marcus van Crevel, 'Verwandte Sequensmodulatie bij Obrecht, Josquin en Coclico', *Tijdschrift van de Vereniging voor Nederlandse Muziekgeschiedenis*, 16 (1941), 19–21; and Margaret Bent, 'Diatonic *ficta*', *Early Music History*, 4 (1984), 34–40.

23. Noblitt, 'Chromatic Cross-Relations', 37–8.

24. It is interesting, in this context, that one or two of Haar's examples (in his article cited in n. 18) seem to be much more conservative in their approach. His Example 11(d), from Gero's duo 'Dolcemente s'adirà' (p. 400) produces a transition from E flat to E natural, exactly analogous to the Example 11(b) above, taken from Noblitt. Interestingly, both use diminished fifths in their melodic outline, thereby avoiding entering the cycle of continuously added accidentals. (The restrictions on tritones do not apply, of course, to diminished fifths.) Haar's Example 10(a), from Mouton's 'Benedicam Dominum' (p. 399), also produces a chromatic alteration, but again as a direct result of avoiding melodic tritones in the voices concerned.

25. Howard Mayer Brown, 'Accidentals and Ornamentation in Sixteenth-Century Intabulations of Josquin's Motets', *Josquin des Prez*, ed. Edward E. Lowinsky with Bonnie J. Blackburn (London, 1976), 475–522.

26. *Ibid.*, 522.

27. The examples from the works of Francesco da Milano have been drawn from *The Lute Music of Francesco Canova da Milano (1497–1543)*, ed. Arthur J. Ness, Harvard Publications in Music, iii–iv (Cambridge, Mass., 1970).

28. Weck's intabulation, with an attribution to Isaac, is found in the Kotter tablature. A facsimile of part of the intabulation appears in *Tabulaturen des XVI. Jahrhunderts, i: Die Tabulaturen aus dem Besitz des Basler Humanisten Bonifacius Amerbach*, ed. Hans Joachim Marx, Schweizerisches Musikdenkmäler, vi (Basel, 1967), p. x. The layer of the manuscript which contains 'Adieu mes amours' was written by Johann Weck in 1515 or soon after: see John Kmetz, *Die Handschriften der Universitätsbibliothek Basel, iv: Katalog der Musikhandschriften des 16. Jahrhunderts. Quellenkritische und historische Untersuchung* (Basel), in the press.

29. *Tabulaturen*, ed. Marx, 72 and 78; Kmetz, *Handschriften*, dates this layer at no later

than 1523. Brown, 'Accidentals', 479, shows an example of simultaneous E flat and E natural in an intabulation of Josquin made by Hans Gerle, and on the following two pages compliments Francesco da Milano for following Josquin's intent. Willi Apel has twice addressed the presence of chromatic alterations and false relations in tablatures. His *Accidentien und Tonalität in der Musikdenkmälern des 15. und 16. Jahrhunderts* (Strasbourg 1936; reprinted Baden-Baden, 1972), 35, gives a short list of examples from the sixteenth century. The only one early enough for consideration in the present context occurs in an intabulation published by Attaingnant. In a more recent article, '*Punto intenso contra remisso*', *Music East and West: Essays in Honor of Walter Kaufmann*, ed. Thomas Noblitt (New York, 1981), 175–82, Apel adds to the earlier list. Among his examples are one each from tablatures of Kotter and Kleber, as well as late intabulations of works by Josquin, Gombert and Urreda, and a keyboard work of Tallis. Given the existence of simultaneous *mi* and *fa* in works of Tallis and in many compositions of his successor Byrd, it is tempting to ask whether the English tradition was older than we now know, and whether Arcadelt and Lhéritier and other French composers first met the tradition early in the sixteenth century.

30. Sparks, 'Problems', 349.
31. Osthoff has questioned the authenticity of this work, in *Josquin Desprez*, ii, 223. See also van Benthem, 'Struktur'.
32. Jeremy Noble, in *The New Grove*, ix, 731, has suggested that this work is by Forestier, referring to the observation of Bonnie J. Blackburn, in 'Josquin's Chansons: Ignored and Lost Sources', *Journal of the American Musicological Society*, 29 (1976), 30–76, esp. 52, n. 60.
33. Even with the assumption that both notes are sharpened (or in those cases where both were to be flattened) we cannot assume that they actually sounded the same pitch. Theoretical descriptions of major and minor semitones, as well as of smaller intervals, strongly suggest that the two pitches would not have been thought of, or performed, in the same manner. The general implication seems to be that, if both were sharpened, they might well have sounded more dissonant than if the false relation were allowed to stand.
34. I do not think that we can assume that this was a generally applicable solution. So many of my examples come from music as preserved in very few centres that we cannot say what would happen if a Roman work were sung in, say, Munich. However, we can safely invoke here the accepted view that the application of *musica ficta* did differ from centre to centre. What would have been done in Munich might be evident from a study of how resident composers wrote their own solutions, or more clearly in the adaptations of other works to Munich conventions.
35. If this solution were to be rejected, we would have the curious situation, in this Mass (and in many of the other works cited here), in which the principal cadences in the piece were exactly those where the upper voice sang the 'leading note' to the cadence in its flat form.
36. Jaap van Bentham, in 'Struktur', follows Osthoff (in *Josquin Desprez*, i, 223–6) in doubting the authenticity of this work. It is not surprising that here, as in two other

X

264

questioned chansons of Josquin used in this essay—'Mi larez vous' (Example 10(a)) and 'Vous ne l'aurez' (Example 20(a))—the problems of *musica ficta* disappear if the work is reduced to a presumed original three-voice composition.

37. This version survives in Switzerland, St Gall, Stiftsbibliothek, MS 463.

38. Most of the music examples cited in this essay can be found in modern editions within the series *Corpus mensurabilis musicae*. This applies to the works of Arcadelt, Brumel, Carpentras, Festa, Gombert, Lhéritier, Mouton and Verdelot. Compositions by d'Argentil, Beausseron and Misonne have been edited by Nors Josephson in *Early Sixteenth-Century Sacred Music from the Papal Chapel*, Corpus mensurabilis musicae, 95 (American Institute of Musicology, 1982), 2 vols. The works of Josquin, as well as those for which the attribution is doubtful, appear in the edition of Albert Smijers, *Josquin Desprez: Werken* (Amsterdam, 1921–69). Citations have already been given for the intabulations; the Obrecht examples are taken from Noblitt, 'Chromatic Cross-Relations'.

39. Jean Lionnet, 'Performance Practice in the Papal Chapel during the 17th Century', *Early Music*, 15 (1987), 4–15. There is an interesting record from the early sixteenth century, reported by Richard Sherr, in 'The Singers of the Papal Chapel and Liturgical Ceremonies in the Early Sixteenth Century: Some Documentary Evidence', *Rome in the Renaissance: The City and the Myth*, ed. P.A. Ramsey, Medieval and Renaissance Texts and Studies, 18 (Binghampton, New York, 1982), 249–64. In n. 33 on page 262, Sherr cites a document in connection with the adoption of *falso bordone* in the chapel: '... cantores nescientes regulas ceremoniarum prepararunt cantum per falsum Bordonum ...'. As Sherr says, the Latin is obscure, but it seems to refer to the use of rehearsal for the new style. Whether this represents an exceptional case, we cannot know.

40. The disagreement over accidentals documented by Lockwood (see n. 20 above) would seem to be a straw in the wind here.

41. It is a curious phenomenon that so many of the later examples in this essay come from Marian Masses or motets. Lhéritier, it is true, does seem to have used the effect regardless of the content of the text, and no special pattern emerges in the work of Verdelot, either. Arcadelt is one of the few composers to use the *Satzfehler* pattern in secular Italian works, although he also included it in two Marian Masses. (It may be significant that neither Lhéritier nor Verdelot was employed in the Sistine Chapel, and that Arcadelt had already written many of his madrigals by the time he took up residence there.) But, among the other works by Vatican composers, there is a preponderance of Masses *de beata virgine, de Domine nostra* and 'Ave Regina'. This would seem to be a reflection of the relative importance of Marian feasts in Vatican usage. Certainly, if there were an interest in the sonority of the false relation, it seems to have been reserved for specific occasions, rather than for specific moments or emotions in the text. Lhéritier and Verdelot, as outsiders, would then be responding in a general way to a taste which, in the Vatican, had a specific application. (I would like to express my thanks to graduate students at New York University—Edward Jarvis, Karl Kügle and Beth Lee Miller—for their help in uncovering many of these examples, and in checking their readings.)

POSTSCRIPT

Peter Urquhart has explored a number of similar issues, studying the evidence for false relations and other effects in manipulating sonority: he uses some of the same examples. A central problem in this sort of study is the difficulty in asserting the origin of the patterns. If we can show that the figuration is in some way abnormal, is preserved in more than one source, and yet produces unusual (even "forbidden") sonorities, we are justified in claiming that the results were something that was specifically sought: once that figuration appears in the work of specific composers and not in others found in the same sources, we can argue that it may represent a compositional (and not a copying) decision.

XI

Two Aspects of Performance Practice in the Sistine Chapel of the Early Sixteenth Century

The two aspects of performance practice which I want to address today are very different in character. The first concerns the relationship between performer and manuscript, and hence that between performer and scribe; it also asks what we can learn about performers' expectations and performance behaviour. The second, in presenting evidence for a particular performing convention, throws light on the relationship between performer and composer. I recognise that my case is not complete. However, I believe that it presents an essential way of looking at some interesting evidence.

We have known many of the broader patterns of early sixteenth-century performing practice for some time: these would include the extent of use (or rather, in this instance, non-use) of instruments, an outline of the changing place of polyphony in religious feasts, or the manner in which works with religious texts were apparently sung at what we might call the "wrong" feasts, and indeed elsewehere. We also think we understand the general manner of treatment of text and added accidentals, and perhaps also of pitch.[1] But these are only the large-scale decisions. For the small-scale, we can often know almost nothing when using traditional forms of evidence. The archives will not tell us how fast the choir sang—unless in the form of a vague criticism, or complaint about the singers taking too long over one piece:[2] we certainly have no precise evidence about the style of singing, the timbre adopted, the treatment of absolute pitch, or the manner in which a manuscript was actually used. Even the evidence that survives of contemporary controversies about *musica ficta* does no more than tell us that such controversies existed. It

---

1 See the discussions of these and many other issues of performance practice in PERFOR-MANCE 1989.
2 But see the paper by Richard Sherr, presented at this conference.

does not say anything about the performing decisions that were regularly adopted.

But once these questions of detail are addressed, they draw the scholar into looking at the surviving evidence, especially that of the sources, in new ways. There have been many recent (and contradictory) studies of the surviving theoretical evidence, whether on *musica ficta* or embellishment, on modal theory or the mensural system, on text setting or compositional practice (so-called), which lay claim to explaining exactly how the performer of the day responded to various musical situations. Yet it is virtually a truism that the theorists of the early sixteenth century were often more concerned with the integrity of their own constructs than with actual compositional or performing practice. The only evidence that must refer to the practice of specific composers, scribes and performers lies in their musical sources — in the details of compositional style, of performing indications, and of variations in the transmission.

I am not going to talk here about transmission, variant readings, or stemmatics. This evidence, and the methodological processes which support it, may tell us a great deal about the provenance of readings, about the (presumed) authenticity of specific variants, and so on: but it can act only as a preliminary guide to the questions I will discuss today. The source, of course, does provide an amalgam of the readings of its exemplars and the wishes of its scribe or destination institution, and we ignore the balance of that amalgam at our peril. But today I want to leave aside the question of the provenance of individual readings, and instead use the source to examine the habits of the performers who used it.

Can we use the Sistine manuscripts to answer questions about the singers' preferences in the application of accidentals; about their concern over text-placing, in general or in detail; about their level of knowledge, for liturgical texts and for musical practice; or even about their degree of competence, or (which may not be distinguishable for us today) the extent to which they prepared music before the mass or office began? In many respects, these questions do not involve looking at the manuscripts in very new ways: they do, however, require an awareness of the manners in which detail on the page would relate to the performing context.

My wish to apply these questions to the members of the Sistine choir stems from a number of pieces of recently presented information. Perhaps the first to worry me was the evidence, advanced by M. Lionnet, of the normal lack of rehearsal for Sistine liturgical performances. It is true that his references were drawn from material of the seventeenth century. But we cannot ignore the possibility, and indeed some slight evidence, that the same situation may have prevailed during the previous century. M. Lionnet also demonstrated that solo sections were not necessarily rehearsed by the singers, but that individuals could stand up to sing, on the spur of the moment, as it were.[3] Equally important was a piece of evidence brought forward by Richard Sherr, which refers to performance by Vatican singers as just the time which concerns us here. He cited a document which reads in part that the *"cantores nescientes regulas ceremoniarum prepararunt cantum per falsum Bordonum"* (24. VI. 1513).[4] As Sherr says, the meaning of *"prepararunt cantum"* is not clear: and yet it is not stretching the Latin to suggest that the text is a reference to rehearsal, and apparently to the unusualness of rehearsal.

A third, more general point, concerns the make-up of the Chapel, or rather the extent to which its members had experience in many other places: there can have been few of the leading singers of any other chapel in Franco-Flemish or Italian Christendom who had not sung with colleagues who became members of the Chapel, and probably few scribes who did not know several members personally. This works in two ways: it means that scribes or institutions sending music to the Sistine Chapel already knew individual members of the Chapel and their musical inclinations; it also means that the Chapel itself and its scribes continually faced a need to integrate new singers (with their own performing conventions) into its practices. We can not believe that each Chapel in Christendom sang in the same way—with the same patterns of text treatment, of *musica ficta* and other accidentals, of tempo, or phrasing and articulation, and so on. In one respect, that of the use of instruments, we are fortunate in having references to specific differences in various institutions. In this, as in other ways, the new member of the Sistine Chapel, therefore, had quickly to assimilate his practices to those of the institution. If there were indeed few rehearsals, then the musical

3   Lionnet 1987.
4   Sherr 1982a.

XI

578

source became an increasingly important means of helping him do this.

A paper by Howard Mayer Brown alerted me to the possibility that scribes bore this in mind when preparing manuscripts, or when sending them to other centres. His study of the transmission of a La Rue mass in four Alamire workshop manuscripts drew attention to the extent to which incidental information—text placing, ligatures, and so on—differed from source to source.[5] His evidence happens to show that much more care was taken over these details in the manuscripts to be sent away to Rome or to Saxony than in the manuscript retained at home. It is not unreasonable to see this as something other than the merely fortuitous handling of variant notational elements that is proposed by Brown.

We also have to face the increasing evidence that singers performed polyphony from the book.[6] I do not mean that books were not used in performance before this time. They must have been, unless we believe that all polyphony was sung from memory, which is unlikely, if only because singers were expected to be able to read notation. However, it seems that there was an intrinsic change in the way books of polyphony were used. Before this change, the books were needed for rehearsal, for the director to learn the music, and for the singers to learn it also. In the liturgical service, they probably acted more as an *aide-memoire*, and less as a direct source for the music as sung. After this proposed transition, however, these books become more essential during the performance, and both size and format, on the one hand, and the details of notation and text presentation, on the other, reflect this. After the transition, such books would be used for something much closer to sight-reading.

---

5   BROWN 1983.
6   There are, of course, many illustrations from the fifteenth century which show a group of singers gathered around a music book: but, before the end of the century, almost none of these can be securely shown to indicate ensemble singing of polyphony, rather than of chant. Among early examples which do would be an illumination in a gradual for Matthias Corvinus I, painted in northern France, probably in the 1480s. Another set of well-known early examples comprises the paintings showing Walter Frye's *Ave Regina*, although it is difficult to assert that these represent contemporary performance practice. However, by 1500, the practice of singing polyphony from the book is apparently becoming more widely recognised, if the evidence of painting, as much as that of manuscript structure, is any guide.

The evidence that follows, then, is drawn from manuscripts prepared for use at the Sistine Chapel, and almost entirely from the work attributed to Claudius Gellandi during the second decade of the sixteenth century. It falls into two large groups: the first is of evidence for patterns of normal usage, but evidence which seems to be either a reinforcement of normal patterns or a clarification of the layout of the music, making the task of performing easier for the reader: this is the section which relates performers to scribes. The second group presents some evidence of a specific performance pattern, apparently practiced at the Vatican, and one which can be related to a stylistic feature of Roman compositions of this and subsequent decades.[7]

The first group comprises a series of observations on the organisation of the music within manuscripts, and on the sorts of clues given to performers via that organisation, as well as some comments on notated accidentals. The topics to be mentioned are the arrangement of page-turns, the treatment of pauses and of *duo* indications, the presence of virtually redundant accidentals, and the patterns of text treatment: all these, it will be obvious, are, to a greater or lesser degree, the province of the scribe, and it is from the perspective of his contribution that I wish to discuss them.

Two small features are surprising, even though at first sight insignificant. First is the manner in which the scribe chooses the exact place for a page-turn. A competent scribe working in choirbook format had of necessity to select a suitable point for the turn, one which would be both convenient for the singers and comfortable for himself. In examining his practice, we can ignore the turns which fall at the ends of major movements or *partes*, as well as those which immediately precede a new mensuration or proportion sign: but, in all other cases, the scribe either must have decided in advance where he would place the turn, or else must have decided while copy-

---

7 I owe a great debt here to those scholars who have worked in detail on the Sistine manuscripts of the first half of the sixteenth century: Mitchell Brauner, Jeffrey Dean, Adalbert Roth, Joshua Rifkin and Richard Sherr. Without their careful distinctions between scribes and layers, the appearance of many of these details would be as a confused muddle. With these scholars' conclusions in hand, however, several different layers of performance guidance can be discerned, correlating with stages of activity on the part of the scribes.

XI

580

ing the first part—normally the *cantus*. This process required some familiarity with the music, for the cases in which one of the voices had a note which should have been tied across the page-turn are relatively rare.

Many scribes seem to have chosen the page-turn more or less at random, with the only restraints being the amount of music in the parts, and the need to avoid breaking tied notes. A number of Vatican manuscripts, on the other hand, show a consistent pattern, in which the last note of a cadential formula—the 'arrival' note—appears at the start of a new opening. Examples 1 and 2, drawn from different manuscripts, show the manner in which this works.[8] The pattern is evidently one which runs counter to normal thinking, in which it was more customary to end a section before the page turn.

The advantages of this pattern in performance, however, are obvious. The singers could approach the cadence via one of the large number of available formulaic melodic contours (one or other of which is normally to be found at most cadences in this repertoire), and would be able to guess the arrival pitch, the resolution of the pattern without seeing it. Thus the moment of turning the page is one in which they least needed to see the next note (especially since it was shown by the *custos*). Arriving on the new page, they would see rests or a new point of imitation. This is clearly easier than the more traditional pattern in which the role of the first note over the page-turn was unknown until the page was actually turned.

This new pattern is unusual in manuscripts of the papacy of Julius II, such as CS 41 or CS 42, while it is remarkably prevalent in manuscripts copied during Leo X's pontificate. The work of all the scribes involved in CS 46 follows it without exception, sometimes producing very empty or very cramped pages as a result. Indeed, the idea was strongly enough in the mind of the scribes that, in one case in CS 16, the last note of a cadence marking a major division of a piece is copied twice, once on each opening. In Gellandi's copy of Pipelare's *Missa Fors seulement*, shown in example 3, the first opening concludes with a strong cadence, in which all voices end with a longa. The next opening begins with the same note (with the ex-

---

8 These examples use original note-values. They also indicate line-ends and page-turns by small checks placed within boxes.

ception of the tenor, where a wrong pitch was corrected on the first opening), followed by the start of the new section. The scribe clearly had confused one habit, that of ending major sections before turning the page, with another, that of putting cadence conclusions on the next page.

It is presumably a similar desire to help the reader that leads the scribe to other most unusual practices. In his copy of Willaert's *Enixa est puerpera* (CS 46, on ff. 44^v – 45^r), he conventionally arranges the page-turn so that the introduction of a *tripla* proportion starts a new opening. However, he additionally enters the new sign, "3", at the end of the previous opening, in each part. The same happens in the anonymous *Ave Regina* copied on folios 140^v – 141^r. This was no mere miscalculation, but an intentional notation, to help the singers.

In the same manner, though to an even more extreme extent, the scribe of Josquin's *Mittit ad virginem*, CS 46, puts not merely the new mensuration sign but also the first one or two *tactus*-worth of music from the next page, after the *custos* at the end of the first opening. I show this as example 4. This practice does occur in some volumes printed by Petrucci in his earlier years, and it may well be that the Roman scribe was here copying the pattern from his exemplar. However, this occurrence, like the extra reference to a new mensuration sign, is one more indication of the scribe's desire to help the unprepared singer.

It is similarly apparent that this scribe is more-than-usually generous with pauses. At many occasions he will add pause signs in all (or most) voices when concordant sources omit them, and he rarely omits pauses that are found elsewhere. This sign – the *corona* – is obviously not a performance indication *per se*. Nobody believes (I hope) that it represents an instruction to hold a note beyond its normal value. Instead, the corona was used to indicate a point in the piece at which any one singer would not hear movement from the other voices, even though he and they were to continue in tempo. Such pauses serve a valuable function when a choir is performing from separate parts, but their value is obviously enhanced when new music is involved: the singer is immediately made aware both that he will have to keep his own tempo, and also that there will be no part-movement in the other voices to help him in pitching the next notes in the line. Gellandi is particularly generous with these signs, and I will mention only two unusual cases. In Josquin's *Ru-*

bum quem viderat, when three voices end the movement in the middle of a line, but the last notes of *Altus* are squeezed into the end of a stave, the altus part is accorded a pause over the last note. In Festa's *In illo tempore*, a pause is placed over a rest in the cantus firmus.

At the start of sections in reduced scoring, too, Gellandi goes further than previous Vatican scribes. Like most contemporaries, he marks both *Tacet* in the relevant voices and *Duo* in those singing: even though the parts are adjacent to each other, he does so in large and florid display scripts. The scribes of earlier Sistine manuscripts occasionally do this, occasionally omit all indication of the reduced scoring, and occasionally include one element.

Each of these points may seem trivial to the reluctant listener: yet, taken together, they present a picture of a scribe who takes care to make the layout as helpful as possible to a singer/reader not fluently familiar with the composition concerned.

There is one other, and perhaps more obvious, manner in which this scribe was more conscientious than most in supplying details to help the singer – and this involves the notation of accidentals. There is a surprising number of redundant accidentals, supported by many others which would seem unnecessary after the shortest moment of reflection, or on hearing other voices more than once. I would have liked to call these accidentals, almost always flats, 'cautionary' accidentals, were it not for the recent writings of Don Harràn, who has pre-empted that term for his own ends.[9] Nor can I call these signs 'redundant' accidentals, for the scribe clearly felt them to be useful to the singer. Perhaps, for the sake of this paper, I can call them 'advisory'.

In a very few cases, these advisory accidentals duplicate an accidental indicated at the beginning of each line of the part – as a 'signature'. (Examples of this practice can be found in the work of d'Argentil and Beausseron, as copied into CS 13.) More often, they act as confirmation of the choice to be made between the two available *recta* forms of a pitch – of *b* when there is no signature, or of *e* with a signature of one flat. For a majority of these instances, we

<hr>

9   See his articles in *JAMS* for 1976 and 1978, with the correspondence in the Journal for 1978 and 1979.

would see little problem in reaching the right solution. But we, of course, can see a score, and can take our time over the decision. It is probable that the original Sistine singers would also have had no problem if they had had ample rehearsal time. But, again in the majority of cases, the signed accidental saves even a moment's hesitation.

A good example comes at the end of the *Agnus Dei* of Misonne's *Missa Gracieuse plaisant*, Gellandi's copying of CS 26, ff. 61^v–62^r, shown as example 5. Neither the *e flat* in the *Secundus Discantus* (m. 3) nor that in the *Bassus* (m. 2) is strictly necessary, for each line reaches *e* by direct movement from a *b flat*. Perhaps the flat sign in the *Tenor* (m. 4) was necessary, although I would expect that a sense of the directional movement of the cadence, coupled with only a moderately sensitive ear, would have suggested a flat to any singer. (I will return to the notated *b* natural later.) Much the same limited, 'advisory' role of a notated accidental can be seen in the *Pleni* of the same mass (example 6), in the final bars of the *Altus* of the *Credo* of Gascongne's *Missa L'autre jour* (same scribe, ff. 110^v–111^r) (example 7) or in Festa's *Missa de Domina nostra* (same source and scribe). Example 8 is taken from the opening *Kyrie*. I recognise that, here, an accidental is virtually essential in the *Bassus*, for the low *A flat* is a note in the realms of *musica ficta*. But this is not true for the notated accidental in the *Altus*. The same scribe provides similar guidance in CS 55 (Beausseron), CS 46 (various works) and CS 16 (Févin's *Missa Mente tota*), among other cases: but he is not alone in doing this. The practice continues for several decades, and can be found in CS 13 (Beausseron and d'Argentil), 19 and 38 (Jaquet and Festa). (There is actually a slight question about the *A flat* in the *Bassus*. In Escribano's *Paradisi porta* (the work of a different scribe, but of the same period), there are four different sharps before low *B*, all in cadential progressions from the *B* to an *A*, and thus preventing Phrygian cadences. Maybe the Bass singers were more prone to add *ficta* than were the others. This would certainly make sense of example 7.)

Occasionally, there are two such cautionary flats together: in a line with a one-flat signature, and a leap from *b* to *e*, both pitches will sometimes be qualified with flats. This occurs in the copy of Josquin's *Qui habitat in adiutorio* found in CS 38. Again, it prevents the possibility of a momentary hesitation on the part of the performer.

The frequent occurrence of these advisory accidentals must engender speculation as to the level of consistency and homogeneity reached by the singers of the Chapel on those occasions when such help was not present. There must have been many occasions when false relations resulted, or when time was not available to learn a satisfactory solution—for if such problems did not arise, there would have been no need to write accidentals into the sources. Intriguingly, these advisory accidentals are more common in the Bass part than in the others, especially in CS 16. Some of this pattern is admittedly due to the need to indicate low *b flat* or *a flat* when they are to be sung; but this does not by any means account for all the difference. It is as if the Bass singers were more in need of guidance—or perhaps of restraining measures. I suspect, as we shall see, that they were more prone to sing on the sharp side.

The use of sharps for the same purpose is rarer, though it can be found. There are instances, again in Misonne's *Missa Gracieuse plaisante* and in his *Salve Regina*, as well as in de Silva's *Puer natus est* (examples 9, 10 and 11). The second of these is interesting to the extent that it requires a linear diminished fifth in the *Altus* part. But that interval, of course, unlike the augmented fourth, was not strictly forbidden.

The third instance is also interesting. A considerable number of cadences in this repertoire are approached by a chord involving the flat sixth of the scale, either as root or (more usually) as third of a chord, progressing to a chord on the fifth and then to the resolution: an occurrence can be seen in measures 2–3 of example 5 above. It is evident that the present example 11 uses the sharp sign deliberately to avoid that effect.

This is one respect in which we may be able to deduce something rather more specific about performance practice. It seems to me probable that this repertoire encouraged the use of the flat sixth in these positions, to the extent that a sharp sixth had to be specially indicated. It is certainly true that the generation of composers working in Rome during the 1520s and 1530s regularly approach a cadence via a chord on the sixth, and include flat sixth chords among them. It may be therefore that this was already true in performance, so that the contrary effect did indeed need to be notated.

Other accidentals, of course, are more necessary, such as those in the *altus* of example 12, from Févin's *Missa Mente tota* or examples 13 and 14 from the later *Missa de beata virgine* of Charles d'Argentil (CS 13). In all these cases, the accidental serves more than a merely advisory function. The examples do not need further comment, for they fall into the more normal conspectus of notated accidentals, giving apparently essential information.

If the treatment of accidentals shows extra care on the part of the scribe, care which is analogous to that which he took over layout, the treatment of the texts often shows a very different attitude. But it is an attitude which in fact fits our general view of the scribe's sense of his responsibilities. When the details of text setting in the manuscripts seem to be casual, as they often do, we should not take that as a contradiction of my previous position. After all, the great majority of these texts will have been very well-known to every singer, however new he was to the Sistine Chapel.

It is not surprising, therefore, that many settings of the Ordinary of the Mass or of other popular texts show only a mild modification of the traditional approach to text placement. In most cases, as it appears, the text was entered after the music, and it was inscribed a phrase or a group of words at a time. Word division, and phrase division in fairly syllabic sections, are becoming much more common, if not yet the general rule. The principal exception concerns those divisions of words occurring across the ends of staves. This pattern is prevalent in almost all copies of works by Josquin, Mouton or Festa, as well as those from earlier composers, such as Ockeghem, Prioris or Busnois. It is particularly common in settings of the Ordinary, whose text was perhaps the best known of all. The pattern represents in this respect a major aspect of traditional text presentation, although it is fair to say that many more phrases are broken up into separate words than in manuscripts of the previous decade, and that word division at the ends of lines has become a much more normal feature of 'modern' compositions.

The scribe was also quite capable of omitting a phrase of text, or of ignoring the need to repeat words: these *lacunae* are apparently more common in Tenor and Bass parts, but can be found in all voice parts at various times. They occur most frequently either when there is no choice over syllable placement (as in a syllabic section) or when there is no need to restrict choice (as in a long melismatic section). Good examples can be found in Pipelare's *Missa Fors seulement* or l'Héritier's *Alma redemptoris mater* and *Sancta Maria*, all in CS 26, or in Mouton's *Noe noe*, in CS 46.

It does not follow, however, that the scribe did not care how the text was placed, nor that he could not give guidance when he felt it necessary. For those many musical phrases which pass from one stave to the next, Sistine scribes of the 1510s and 1520s carefully indicate which syllables belong to each stave. See examples 1 and 2 again: further, if there are only a few notes on the first stave, the right number of syllables is always present (see examples 21, 22 and 23): if the majority of the musical phrase is on the first stave, and a melisma follows on the second, the last syllable of text is always reserved to the new line.

Secondly, when the text is particularly cramped, so that the start of a text phrase does not align with the start of its corresponding musical phrase, there is usually a line connecting the two. I can not tell, of course, whether this line was always drawn at the time the text was entered — in some cases it does appear to have been a later addition. But that merely transfers to a later stage the same fulfillment of a need which I am suggesting the original scribe tried to meet.

Neither of these features tells us anything new. They are part of the common practice of many scribes of the period, working as much as fifty years earlier or later. But they do set the stage for a few, more interesting features.

Gellandi, when copying Brumel's *Missa de nostra domina*, now in CS 16, tended to follow a traditional pattern, grouping the text into sets of words copied together. However, in the *Gloria* sections setting the less familiar text of the trope *Spiritus et alme*, he carefully placed every word, even on occasion splitting up words to show the exact alignment of note and syllable. Here, again, more words are split in the *Cantus* and *Altus* parts than are so treated in the *Tenor* and *Bassus*.

In CS 46, the scribes were often careful with the underlay. In Carpentras' *Conserva me Domine*, he has to squeeze words in, and to place words above or below the line, so that all could be roughly aligned. And yet, when he comes to the *Amen*, he apparently forgot to enter the capital letter *A* in the *Altus*, the only voice which does not have a short motto phrase to sing to the word *Amen*. The missing letter *A* is added later. It appears at least possible that the scribe, who carefully placed the syllables in the other three voices, in order to make them correspond with the musical structure, was at first unsure as to where the letter *A* of *Amen* should be placed in the *Altus*. These manuscripts also show additions to the text, in a different hand. Examples would include the copy of Mouton's *Quaeramus cum pastoribus* in CS 46, among others. This phenomenon is not uncommon in the early sixteenth century. It can be found, for example, in copies of printed editions prepared by Petrucci and Antico, as well as in a number of other manuscripts. But it is less commonly found in sources from the mid-fifteenth century, and may be another reflection of the changing use of sources in performance.

This pattern of text treatment is elusive. The trends that I describe are just that, trends which I believe I have detected in a large cross-section of the pages copied during the second decade of the sixteenth century. They argue for a consistent set of criteria on the part of the scribes, one of casualness when nothing more was needed, and of care when care would help a singer. In that respect, the pattern does fit those others which I have presented so far — that is, one of attempting to give to the singer any help which would save him from possible confusion. It is obvious that, rehearsal or no rehearsal, the Sistine singers would tend to have their own patterns of text treatment, and these patterns would have to be quickly learned by newcomers. It seems that the places where the scribes took care over text placing are precisely those where a new singer would be most at doubt. It is also interesting that the Bass (and to a lesser extent the Tenor), who was sometimes given more guidance over accidentals, was frequently given less over text placement. It is tempting to see in this some evidence for the issues which interested the singers of the lower parts.

The first (and by far the longer) part of this paper has attempted to draw together all the evidence which might reflect on the extent of rehearsal or performance preparation in the Sistine choir. Each of the pieces of evidence has been to some extent nebulous. Yet, taken together, as a whole, the evidence is rather more effective. When a scribe takes care over page-turns, over pause marks, over signalling some features more boldly than might be necessary, over giving warnings about accidentals and text placing, it seems clear that he is responding to a perceived need. Most of the information over which the scribes spent a little extra time or effort is information which would be readily absorbed in rehearsal, or which would not be needed with singers who had sung the same work together for a long period of time.

While the evidence does not prove that rehearsals were either completely avoided or unusual in the Sistine Chapel of the second decade of the century, it does point rather strongly in that direction. I can think of no other explanation for why so much care should be taken, care which is not easily paralleled in other manuscripts of the time. (Parenthetically, the only manuscripts I know of which take so much trouble, albeit not always over the same things, are those of Casale Monferrato. Here, the chapel was a completely new institution, and the choirmaster was responsible for training the musicians, and clearly took extra pains, in his own copying of the music, to ease his burden.)

* * *

From the work I have done so far, none of the evidence offered by patterns of text placing tells us anything new about how texts were sung. This is unfortunate, for it would be useful to have concrete evidence of at least one institution's approach to text-setting.

However, there is strong evidence which points to one group of performing decisions for which the Sistine Chapel did have a definite preference.

One of these I have already mentioned — the tendency to flatten the sixth degree when approaching a cadence. It would appear that this was fairly normal practice, both from the occasions on which a flattening accidental is notated and also from those where the opposite is specifically demanded.

Another concerns the practice of sharpening the third at major cadences. We know that a number of writers in the sixteenth century regarded the *tierce de Picardie* to be almost obligatory. Yet we have little evidence in the sources for this practice of raising the third.

The Vatican manuscripts present an abundance of evidence, which is only slightly ambiguous. I want to present three different features.

First is the relative rarity of cadences with a third which would
normally be flat, *fa* as opposed to *mi*. The presence of the third in
cadences at the end of sections or of whole works increases rapidly
throughout the early years of the century, becoming almost normal
by the 1530s. Yet, for the second decade, many sections of masses
and ends of *partes* in settings of other texts still do not contain the
third. This is particularly true if the third might have been flat.
Thus, Festa's *Missa de domina nostra* (CS 26), which has a two-flat signature for the *Kyrie* and *Credo*, one flat for the *Gloria*, and no flats
for the *Sanctus* and *Agnus*, has only two cadences with a third in
them, one in the *Christe*, and one at the end of the *Agnus*, both on
C. His Mass *sine nomine* in the same manuscript, with no signature
and in an *A* mode, has only one cadence with a third in it, in the
Credo. Pipelare's *Missa Fors seulement* cadences fairly frequently on
d, but most of these cadences lack the third. Many more examples
could be cited. There seems to be a tendency to avoid what we
would call the 'minor' third in cadential chords, even in those situations where it could easily have been inflected sharp. The picture is
as if composers were coming to terms with the question of sharpening thirds on last chords, and yet had not resolved the issue. Hence, the ready omission of thirds in 'minor' modal situations, and the
rather more frequent acceptance of them when the chord would necessarily be major. However, there are cases where the potentially
minor third does appear, particularly at the end of the *Christe*, or at
one of a small number of internal cadences in the *Credo*.

A number of these cadences are copied with accidentals to show
quite specifically which version of the pitch was chosen. Examples 15 and 16 from the ends of *Christe* movements show the sharpened third, in each case an *f*, entered quite clearly. In both cases,
as in the final sharp of Escribano's *Paradisi porta*, the accidental is
placed before the note, and the spacing shows that it was part of the
original copying process. The same is true for the final *b sharp* in example 5. Perhaps significantly, each of these compositions is the
work of a composer closely associated with the Sistine choir: the
same can also be said of those examples of sharps which I have already presented—the work of d'Argentil, Misonne or de Silva. It
seems possible, at this stage of my argument, that there was an increasing use of sharps, both as advisory signs and as inflections in

their own right, in the Sistine repertoire of the second and third decades of the century.

There is a fair number of other similar terminal accidentals, however, which were inserted later, for they lie above or below the note, and the spacing of the notes implies that they were not planned. Examples of this situation appear in Brumel's *Missa de Beata Virgine*, Misonne's *Salve Regina* and Carpentras' *Deus in nomine tuo* (examples 17−20).[10] These works do not come from the same manuscript, nor do they all represent compositions which might have been newly composed for the Sistine Choir. Taken with the earlier group of accidentals, however, they seem to confirm an increasing interest in sharp inflections, particularly at the more important cadences. Indeed, from the work which I have done so far on the earlier sources (those from the previous decade), I suspect that this change in taste is more or less contemporaneous with the appearance in the repertoire of works by Misonne and Carpentras, and continues in effect for at least 15 years.

However, such sharps are by no means reserved only for cadence points. They are used, as are flats, to make imitative points into what we would now call 'real' rather than 'tonal' answers. Among cases involving flats, I could cite the opening of the *Christe* of Beausseron's *Missa de Beata Virgine*, in CS 19, or the troped section, *Primogenitus Mariae*, of the *Gloria* and the first *Agnus* of d'Argentil's *Missa de Beata Virgine*, found in CS 13. Cases with sharps are, of course, much rarer, and are, in any case, not always so consistent. Example 21, from the anonymous *Cantate Domino* at the opening of CS 46 makes my point. Note how, in the lower of my two systems, the tenor entry apparently uses an *f sharp* to create a whole-tone step at the beginning of the point of imitation, even though the progression of chords is towards *c*. Notice, too, that this sharp, like the earlier one in the *cantus*, is before the note, as part of the original copying layer, rather than added later. The *cantus* sharp has the same effect, and is additionally interesting in that there is no sharp present in the *Bassus* of the previous measure. With every other sta-

---

10 This last is, incidentally, another work by Carpentras which shows considerable re-writing in the sources, although, in this case, the changes do not seem obviously to improve the style or texture.

tement of this point opening with a whole-step, and the already-noted pattern of different scribal treatment for the *Bassus* part, I would expect to sing an *f sharp* here, in the bassus as well. The next example, example 22, is drawn from the same work. It shows what appears to have been an additional regular use of the sharp, as acting to widen a sixth before the octave: notice the third bar of the upper system, or the second bar of the lower. This corresponds to some extent with the notated sharp in the fourth bar of the *cantus* of example 21. It also parallels the appearance of the flat in example 22, tenor, measure 6, which narrows the gap to the following fifth. Both these practices are, of course, well known from theoretical writings: but it is valuable to see them being applied in practice, and thus to be able to define the contexts in which they were actually regarded as precepts.

It is probably with this in mind that we should regard the sharps present in examples 23 and 24, both drawn again from Carpentras' *Deus in nomine tuo*. The first of these shows a sharp added later, and one which exactly creates a major sixth heading towards an octave. As with other occurrences, especially of sharps added later, the 'leading note' (as I will lazily call it) is not actually to the tonic of the whole phrase, but merely to a temporary octave or unison. The same is true of the later sharp in example 21. Example 24 shows a similar type of sharp, though one which was here part of the original line. Apart from its effect on the *c*, it has the added advantage of virtually precluding *b flats* in the following notes.

Such sharps, whether inserted from the beginning or added later, form an integral part of the performing style represented by these pieces. Indeed, so strong is the inclination towards the 'major' sonority, that sharps are added even in places which we could hardly anticipate. I draw your attention back to example 19 where the sharps in the first two bars definitely colour the whole sonority. Neither is without parallel examples however. The more surprising of the two is the *c sharp* in the altus, the one producing the greater harmonic dislocation (in our eyes at least); but this is matched by the effect of the tenor in example 21. It seems to me, in fact, that this is only surprising because it involves a sharp, *mi*. If the same effect had occurred with a flat, *fa*, we would accept it, as we do many Phrygian cadences. The implication is that, for a while at least, the Sistine singers and their patron favoured the sharp effect. They seem to have been enough attracted to it to have effects such as that of the tenor at the start of example 19, or the altus at the opening of the third *pars* of the anonymous *Cantate Domino* which I have already cited (example 25). The second pars closes on a cadence on *A* without a third, while this pars opens with a clearly indicated *A major* chord.

This desire for a strong and immediate major statement, both at the beginning and within works, seems to run parallel with a willingness to accept immediate changes in inflection of individual notes. Within two measures the *c sharp* of example 25 has become a *c natural* acting as the root of a chord. Exactly the same effect is achieved in example 19, where *g sharp* changes to *g natural*. Other similar rapid inflections abound: in example 23, the *f sharp* of the cantus is presumably replaced two measures later by an *f natural*. In example 22, the *f sharp* of the cantus is itself a replacement for the lower form of the pitch; and one of the most attractive examples is that of example 15, where the sharp final cadence produces an immediate false relation.

There seems to be no doubt that some composers and singers of the Sistine choir of these decades liked, even exploited, these accidentals and the momentary effects which they produced. This is both a compositional and a performance tool: although the accidentals are rarer in works from composers not then working in Rome, they are not unknown, nor does their absence mean that they were not included in performance. After all, the major works of Josquin, for example, were probably well-known to almost any singer coming to the Vatican from elsewhere, and yet a cadential *B sharp* is added to a principal cadence on *G* in his *O virgo virginum*, as copied in CS 46.

But the works of Misonne or d'Argentil, or even Carpentras, would not so probably be in the repertoire of new arrivals, and the scribe would need to supply more of this extra information. Thus the fact that this performing convention is found most freely in the works of the lesser, local composers does not mean that it was restricted to their work: it merely confirms that the scribes took extra care over performing conventions and assistance when works were less well-known.

From the evidence which I have gathered so far, this phenomenon of exploiting the major chord, and of producing rapid shifts of inflection seems to be new during the second decade. It seems to represent a taste which emerged and which must, I assume, have been applied to other music as well. The question, of course, arises as to whether these accidentals represent a norm, or indicate exceptional situations: we also need to know how long the taste lasted, and whether it influenced composers of the next generation. Can it still be seen in the manuscripts, or do we have to determine whether it became so general that there was no need to notate it? Should it be applied as late as Palestrina? I would like very briefly to address these points, and thus introduce another way of looking at the confluence of compositional and performing styles.

* * *

At the start of this paper, I listed some of the pieces of evidence which led me to the present, incomplete enquiry. Here, I should draw attention to one more. In studying the repertoire of the next generation, Festa, l'Héritier and Arcadelt among others, I was much struck by the frequency of a particular stylistic quirk — the sounding of a suspension against, or in quick juxtaposition with, its own resolution. This figure, which tended to happen with great frequency at the approaches to cadences, seemed to be a product of deliberate choice on the part of the composer. Thus lines would occasionally take angular or unusual shapes apparently solely to produce, or equally to avoid, the effect of suspension and resolution. A couple of simple examples of the effect, taken from different generations, appear as examples 26 and 27, voices 1 and 4. In each, you will notice, the two versions of the leading note avoid overlapping. Many other cases exist, from composers of the same circles, in which the two versions of the leading note do overlap, or are even struck simultaneously. In a recent study, I came to the conclusion that this phenomenon was also peculiar to the Roman circle (although certainly not unknown elsewhere, indeed, to be found in works securely ascribed to Josquin).[11] Composers wrote the device in a number of different ways, designed to create a number of possibilities, ranging from sharpening both notes to flattening both, with every

---

11 A full presentation of this argument is in BOORMAN 1990.

possible intermediate permutation available. Example 28 is typical of some of the more extreme cases, where the voice leading would surely cause problems if performed without adequate rehearsal.

Yet it is notable that accidentals are not normally written into the Sistine manuscripts at such places. Occasionally, an accidental will be inserted, apparently suggesting that it represents an unusual solution. Example 29 shows the accidentals which appear at one cadence in the *Credo* of Arcadelt's *Missa de Beata Virgine*, as presented both in CS 155 and in *RISM* A 1384 (the 1557 Le Roy and Ballard edition of masses by Arcadelt: the additional sharp in their edition merely confirms that they had a musical editor, and that they were aware of the problems raised by part-books.)

It can hardly be a coincidence that the performing practice of added sharps and of consequent false relations developed in the same years that saw this treatment of suspension and resolution. My belief is that this performing practice was new in the 1510s, that it was liked and exploited, and that it led composers towards a certain freedom in using it. They therefore wrote lines which produced false relations. These could involve lines like the so-called English cadence (example 30, where I have suggested performing accidentals), and also more straightforward juxtapositions (example 31), and even simultaneous clashes. It should not be surprising that the accidentals are rarely marked in the sources. With the exception of those cases which are themselves exceptions (such as the example 29), there are very few indications: presumably the sonority rapidly became a normal resource. It will be remembered that it was apparently on its way to being normal at the time when Misonne's and Carpentras' works were being copied.

However, the evidence suggests that it was a short-lived phenomenon. By the end of the 1540s (at the latest), musical style, performing and notational, had changed. There is no evidence of these accidentals, not even through their absence, for the compositional style had abandoned the situations in which the false relation is likely. The other scribal practices which I have outlined here have disappeared even earlier. The treatment of text becomes more conservative, the handling of page-turns and similar details is more conventional, although scribes continue to insert 'advisory' accidentals. In general, scribes are behaving as if they need to give less help to the performer. Most convincingly, the works of these composers are not being re-copied. There is no evidence of any interest in Brunet or Misonne after the end of the pontificate of Paul III in 1549; the works of d'Argentil or Beausseron are soon forgotten; even much of Carpentras is apparently abandoned soon after his departure from Rome; and l'Héritier is also not copied. All this at a time when Festa's music was being freely re-copied, when the more straightforward works of Morales remained in the repertoire, although not those of Arcadelt, and at a time when Josquin, Mouton and other composers from outside the narrow circle of 'sharp-sophisticates' were still cornerstones of the Sistine repertoire.

I use the word 'sophisticates' advisedly. I want it to be taken as a deliberate reflection on the narrowness of the circle which explored the possibilities of accidentals in their performing and compositional style. The patterns of scribal behaviour show us a circle in which a wider range of particular effects were being sought, while at the same time it was one where more and more information had to be put on the page—whether because of lack of rehearsal or because of the incompetence of new members of the choir we cannot now tell.[12] What we can certainly see, however, is that this short-lived phase did involve the exploitation of particular sonorities, and that they were a part of performing convention, as well as of compositional practice.

12 I had written this paper before hearing Richard Sherr's proposal that much of the Marian music in the Sistine manuscripts might be related to the Feast of the Assumption, when one of the singers could celebrate mass. The great majority of Vatican occurrences of the effects I have described are to be found in settings of Marian texts, and it might be that we are dealing with a performers' preference, adopted by composers for their 'own' feast.

Literature

BOORMAN 1990   Boorman, Stanley, *False Relations and the Cadence*. In: *Altro Polo X: Essays on Italian Music in the Cinquecento*. Ed. Richard Charteris. Sydney 1990, p. 221−264.

BROWN 1983   Brown, Howard Mayer, *In Alamire's Workshop: Notes on Scribal Practice in the Early Sixteenth Century*. In: QUELLENSTUDIEN II, p. 15−63.

JOSEPHSON 1982   *Early Sixteenth-Century Sacred Music from the Papal Chapel*. Ed. Nors S. Josephson. Neuhausen-Stuttgart 1982 (CMM 95).

LIONNET 1987   Lionnet, Jean, *Performance practice in the Papal Chapel during the 17th century*. In: *Early Music* 15, 1987, p. 3−15.

PERFORMANCE 1989   *Performance Practice: Music Before 1600*. Ed. Howard Mayer Brown and Stanley Sadie. London 1989 (*The New Grove Handbooks in Music*. First American edition: New York 1990).

QUELLENSTUDIEN II   *Quellenstudien zur Musik der Renaissance*. Vol. II. *Datierung und Filiation von Musikhandschriften der Josquin-Zeit*. Ed. Ludwig Finscher. Wiesbaden 1983 (*Wolfenbütteler Forschungen* 26).

SHERR 1982A   Sherr, Richard, *The Singers of the Papal Chapel and Liturgical Ceremonies in the Early Sixteenth Century: Some Documentary Evidence*. In: *Rome in the Renaissance. The City and the Myth. Papers of the Thirteenth Annual Conference of the Center for Medieval & Early Renaissance Studies*. Ed. Paul A. Ramsey. Binghamton, NY 1982. p. 249−264.

Example 1: Mouton, *Illuminare*; CS 46, f. 55^V – 57^r.

Example 2: Févin, *M. Dictes moy*; CS 16, f. 105^V – 107^r.

Example 3: Pipelare, *M. Fors seulement*; CS 16, f. 25^V – 27^r.

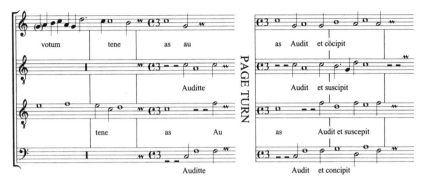

Example 4: Josquin, *Mittit ad virginem*; CS 46, f. 131$^\text{v}$ –133$^\text{r}$.

Example 5: Misonne, *M. Gracieuse plaisant*, end of *Agnus Dei*; CS 26.

Example 6: Ibid., *Pleni*; m. 6 – 10.

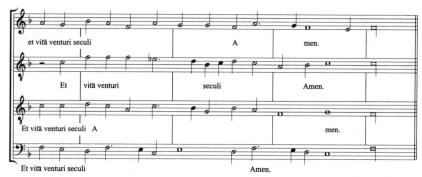

Example 7: Gascongne, M. *L'autre jour*, end of *Credo*; CS 26, f. 110^V–111^r.

Example 8: Festa: M. *de Domina nostra*, *Kyrie*, m. 8 – 15; CS 26, f. 3^V – 4^r.

Example 9: Misonne, M. *Gracieuse plaisant*, *Gloria*, m. 10 – 12; CS 26.

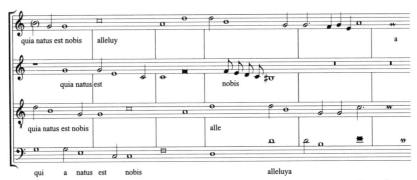

Example 10: de Silva, *Puer natus est*, m. 67 – 71 (c.f. *tacet*); CS 46, f. 24^V – 25^r.

Example 11: Misonne, *Salve Regina*,
m. 34 – 36; CS 26, f. 130^V – 131^r.

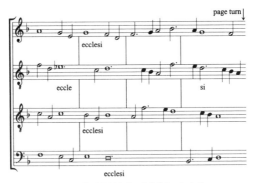

Example 12: Févin, M. *Mente tota*,
Credo; CS 16, f. 54^V – 5^r.

Example 13: d'Argentil, *M. de Beata Virgine, Gloria*, m. 59–63; CS 13.

Example 14: Ibid., *Agnus Dei*, m. 1–5.

Example 15: Misonne, *M. Gracieuse plaisant*,
end of *Christe*; CS 26.

Example 16: d'Argentil, *M. de Beata Virgine*,
end of *Christe*; CS 13 (after JOSEPHSON 1982).

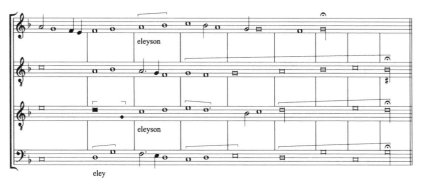

Example 17: Brumel, *M. de Beata Virgine*, end of *Christe*; CS 16, f. $2^v - 3^r$.

Example 18: Misonne, *Salve Regina*,
final cadence; CS 26, f. $130^r - 131^v$.

Example 19: Carpentras, *Deus in nomine tuo*, start; CS 46, f. 20^v −21^r.

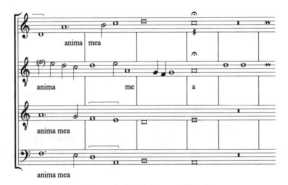

Example 20: Ibid., m. 78 − 82.

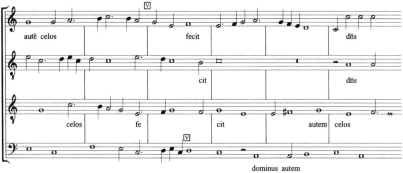

Example 21: Anon., *Cantate Domino*, part 1, m. 80 – 93; CS 46, f. 3^V – 4^r.

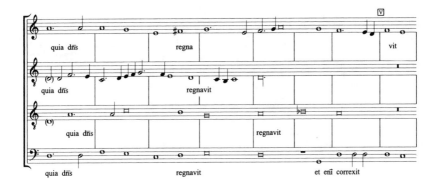

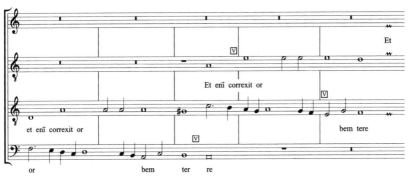

Example 22: Ibid., part 3, m. 17–29; CS 46, f. 5^v–6^r.

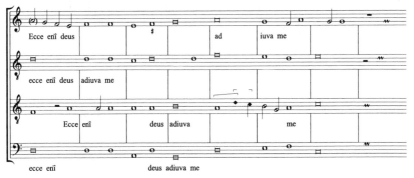

Example 23: Carpentras, *Deus in nomine tuo*, m. 65–71; CS 46.

Example 24: Ibid., m. 94 – 99.

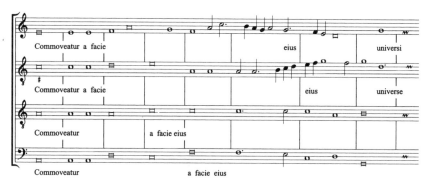

Example 25: Anon., *Cantate Domino*, start of part 3; CS 46.

Example 26: Arcadelt, *M. de Beata Virgine*,
Credo, m. 77 – 79; CS 155.

Example 27: Viardot, *Dum complerentur*,
m. 104–107; CS 42.

Example 28: Brunet (Josquin), *Victimae paschali laudes*,
m. 77–79; CS 24.

Example 29: Arcadelt, *M. de Beata Virgine*,
m. 94–96 ("Homo factus est"); CS 155, RISM A 1384.

Example 30: Brunet, *Victimae paschali laudes*,
m. 189–191 (modern notation).

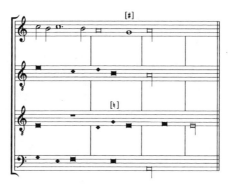

Example 31: Misonne, *M. Que n'ay-je Marion*,
end of *Osanna*; CS 26.

POSTSCRIPT

This paper leads to a conclusion opposite to that of Chapter X. Here the evidence points directly to the conclusion that the changes represent something sought in a specific institution, and reflecting the performing interests of the institution, or needs of individual singers. It is plausible to argue that singers moving from one institution to another would have to learn a new performing practice: the evidence that I present does suggest that cues for the new practice could be entered on a manuscript.

INDEX

Cantate Domino: X 224, 227–8,
247
Faulte d'argent: X 227, 244, 246
In illo tempore stetit: X 224, 227
Mi lares vous: X 227, 235
Nesciens mater: X 224, 227
Vous l'aurez s'il vous plait:
X 257
Vous ne l'aurez pas: X 249

Kellman, Herbert: II 246, 248
Kirsch, Winfried: II 246, 253
Kotter, Hans: X 240, 243
Krummel, Donald: VI 228

La Rue, Pierre de: XI 578
Cent mille regretz: X 250
Laet, Jean de: VIII 405, 407, 411,
416, 419, 422
Lassus, Orlando: VIII 407
lauda: VIII 409–11, 424
Layolle, Francisco de: VII 122–3
Dal bel soave ragio: VII 122–3,
138, 156
Lewis, Mary S.: IV 2596, 2602;
VI 226, 235–6; VII 130
Lhéritier, Jean: X 229, 231, 234;
XI 593
works:
Alma redemptoris mater: XI 586
Deus in nomine tuo: X 248
Miserere mei: X 248
Nigra sum: X 234, 246, 248, 252
Petrus apostolus: X 248
Repleatur os meum: X 249
Salve regina: X 249, 252, 256
Sancta Maria: XI 586
Sub tuum presidium: X 248, 250,
254
Surrexit pastor bonus: X 247
Liechtenstein, Peter: V 235fn, 242–4
ligatures, musical: I 197; II 249–52,
258–9; IX 66–73, 76–9;
XI 578
Lionnet, Jean: XI 577
liturgical editions: V passim; VI 230;
VIII 408–9
Livre septième de chansons: VIII 413,
418, 425–6
Louvain: VIII 405, 424
Lowinsky, Edward E.: II 255; IX 67
Loys, Henry, & Jehan de Buys:
VIII 406
Lupacchino, Bernardino:
VIII 417
Lupus Hellinck: X 230

Lurano, Philippus: IV 2588–9
Luzzaschi, Luzzasco: VIII 415

Maio, I.T. de: IV 2596–7
Manilius, Gisleyn: VIII 407
Marenzio, Luca: VI 225; VIII 411
market for music:
characteristics of: VI 229;
VIII 406, 411–14
publishers' view of: VIII 414–29
size of: VI 229, 234; VIII 413–14;
see also purchasers of music
Martin, Saint: II 258
McKerrow, R.B.: III 301
McTaggart, Timothy: VIII 426
Medici, family: II 246, 255
mensuration: II 248, 250, 252
Merulo, Claudio: VIII 408, 418, 419,
422
Milanese, Ludovico: IV 2597
minor color: I 205; II 248, 250, 251,
252, 255, 258; IX 71, 73–80
Misonne, Vincent: X 229; XI 589,
590, 592, 594–5
Missa Gracieuse plaisant: X 250;
XI 583–4
Missa que n'ay-je Marion: X 232,
246
Salve regina: XI 584, 590
Moderne, Pierre: VI 233; VIII 420
Monteverdi, Claudio: VI 229
Morales, Cristobal de: VI 235; XI 595
Moretus, Balthasar: VIII 405, 419,
428
Moschenio family: VIII 416
Moulu, Pierre:
Sicut malus: X 240
Mouton, Jean: VIII 420; XI 585, 595
works:
Ecce genuit nobis: II 260,
268–70
Gaude Barbara beata: II 255–8
Missa Lo serai-je dire: X 250
Missus est Gabriel: X 224, 250
Noe noe: XI 586
Queramus cum pastoribus:
XI 587
Vulnerasti cor meum (?Rein):
II 254
Musch, Hans: VII 109
musica ficta: X 221–2, 230; XI 577,
583

Naich, Hubert:
Per Dio tu sei cortese: VII 151–2,
157

INDEX OF EDITIONS

INDEX OF MANUSCRIPTS